Clioh's Workshop

II

THE PARTICIPANTS:

Karl-Franzens-Universität Graz (Austria)
Universiteit Gent (Belgium)
Sofiyski Universitet Sveti Kliment Ohridski (Bulgaria)
Masarykova Univerzita (Czech Republic)
Roskilde Universitetscenter (Denmark)
Tartu Ülikool (Estonia)
Helsingin Yliopisto (Finland)
Université Pierre Mendès-France Grenoble (France)
Université de Poitiers (France)
Université de Rouen (France)
Universität Bielefeld (Germany)
Universität Hannover (Germany)
Universität Leipzig (Germany)
Eberhard-Karls-Universität Tübingen (Germany)
University of Edinburgh (Great Britain)
University of Sussex (Great Britain)
Ethniko kai Kapodistriako Panepistimio Athinon (Greece)
Debreceni Egyetem (Hungary)
Háskóli Íslands (Iceland)
National University of Ireland, Cork (Ireland)
National University of Ireland, Maynooth (Ireland)
Università di Bologna (Italy)
Università di Pisa (Italy)
Latvijas Universitáte, Riga (Latvia)
Vilniaus Universitetas (Lithuania)
Rijksuniversiteit Groningen (Netherlands)
Universitetet i Bergen (Norway)
Uniwersytet Jagiellonski, Krakow (Poland)
Universidade de Coimbra (Portugal)
Universitatea Babes Bolyai din Cluj-Napoca (Romania)
Univerzita Komenského v Bratislave (Slovakia)
Univerza v Mariboru (Slovenia)
Universidad de Alcalá de Henares (Spain)
Universidad de Deusto (Spain)
Universidad Autónoma de Madrid (Spain)
Universidad de Salamanca (Spain)
Uppsala Universitet (Sweden)
Universität Basel (Switzerland)

Political systems and definitions of gender roles

edited by

Ann Katherine Isaacs

EDIZIONI PLUS
Università di Pisa

With the support
of the Culture 2000 programme
of the European Union

Education and Culture

Manager
Claudia Napolitano

Editing
Francesca Petrucci

Informatic assistance
Michele Gasparello

© Copyright 2001 by Edizioni Plus – Università di Pisa
Lungarno Pacinotti, 43
56126 Pisa
Tel. 050 970934 – Tel. e fax 050 970927

www.edizioniplus.it - Section "Biblioteca"

ISBN 88-8492-072-8

Cover: Anton van Dyck, *Nicolò and Giovanni Francesco Lomellini with Barbara Spinola Lomellini and the children Vittoria and Agostino* (detail), Edinburgh, National Gallery of Scotland, by kind permission.

Contents

CONDUCT

MODELS

FAMILIES AND SEXUALITY

Preface

"POLITICAL SYSTEMS AND DEFINITIONS OF GENDER ROLES": CLIOH'S SECOND NOTEBOOK

Extremes in the way gender roles are defined and codified under different political regimes have recently been set before the eyes of the world. Today there is a broad consensus that human rights and nearly universally recognised values have been violated in Afghanistan. Women have been excluded entirely from public life; female children have been forbidden instruction. The gynaephobic policies of the Taliban government have become part of the general political discourse although only now, in a context of open, armed conflict. Until now the question was kept alive, in a limited way, by humanitarian and women's groups: indignation coexisted with a systematic, anti-ethnocentric doubt as to whether or not each people has the right to decide such things for itself, however barbarous certain practices may appear to others.

A few timid voices have suggested that if the *burqa* symbolises slavery and obscurantism for Afghan women, the anorexic and nearly nude fashion model with whom European women are invited everyday to identify themselves symbolises another kind of undesired servitude. Resolving such questions is certainly not the task of the present volume. Nonetheless it would be difficult to imagine a more dramatic scenario in which to present a text which aims at illuminating, in a pan-European context, the importance of connections between changing political systems and ways of imagining, representing, encouraging or imposing particular gender models.

This volume is the second in a series with which we wish to contribute to bringing a new historical awareness to students, teachers and citizens in general. The Culture 2000 Programme of the Directorate-General for Education and Culture of the European Commission, with its approval and financial support, has made "Clioh's Workshop" possible. The University of Pisa's new publishing house, Edizioni Plus (*Pisana Libraria Universitatis Studiorum*) is carrying out the project on behalf of 38 Universities in 27 European countries operating under the name of CLIOH. The "Workshop" is co-organised and co-financed by four of the partner institutions, the University of Pisa, the University of Alcalá de Henares, Ghent University and the University of Iceland, Reykjavik.

The 38 participating Institutions will be the first to use and test the volumes, the 'Notebooks' produced by "Clioh's Workshop", and to evaluate and disseminate the results. The acronym CLIOH alludes, of course, to the Muse of History, Clio, but with a distinguishing feature: Clioh, Clio with an H, stands for "Refounding Europe: Creating Links, Insights and Overviews for a new History agenda". The name underlines the group's heuristic and methodological approach, based on comparison and connection of diverse historical traditions. The group has now been joined by 14 more Universities, bringing the total number of Institutions to 52 in 31 countries. Together we form the new Socrates Thematic Network for History and the Humanities entitled CLIOHNET, our name again underlining the comparative method which inspires our activities.

Europe is diversity. European history is not one history but many, each of which can illuminate the others. In our experience, when national historiographies and historical realities are directly compared immediate and powerful insights arise about the ways in which such histories are created. Through observing the differences between the national narrations, students and teachers become aware of how (and when and why) their own historiography, and even the general public's view of historical facts has formed. An optimal way of gaining new insights into existing curricula and designing new teaching materials is to bring students and professors from many countries together in a real teaching-learning situation. In the past years we have been able to do this in a series of Socrates Intensive Programmes held with the support of the European Commission and the partner Universities, and thanks to the personal abilities and energies of the coordinators, the teachers and the students.

The challenge is to make the insights gained more widely available. This is the motivation for "Clioh's Notebooks". The "Notebooks" are not intended to be systematic comprehensive textbooks: each country already has its own, and an international version would risk being, today, a homogenised version of texts which are often judged unsatisfactory by students and teachers alike. Rather, the 'Notebooks' attempt to bring the cutting edge of comparison and confrontation, as experienced in an international context, into printed form.

"Clioh's Notebooks" have been developed by students and professors together. Each volume deals with a broad, significant issue in European history. Each 'chapter' is written by a teacher, taking into account the interaction with the students. Furthermore, thanks to the Culture 2000 project, students and professors from all the countries represented in the group have been able to discuss the format of the volumes in Pisa, in May 2001. The publisher and the editorial board have taking into account their suggestions and hope to have interpreted them successfully, producing attractive, reader-friendly texts.

"Political Systems and Definitions of Gender Roles" is the second of the Notebooks to be published. It provides a new starting point for observing similarities and differences, links and contrasts in the history of gender roles in Europe. The present volume shares some characteristics with the one already published ("The Sea in European History") and with those which will be made available in the future. First, the general theme is treated in a broad chronological framework. Second, the geographical context is today's larger Europe. Although limited to this continent, the volume includes and allows direct comparison and connection of the histories, recent and remote, of Eastern and Central Europe as well as the more widely known histories of the so-called Western European countries.

The volume is divided into five parts or thematic strands. The order in which they are printed suggests a way, not the only way, of reading them. All themes are connected, all chapters contribute to the others. The first part is entitled "Politics and Power". There the problem of gender and access to the political arena and institutions is examined directly. In the first chapter Jean-Luc Lamboley shows the way that the ancient Greeks recognised the power of women, as priestesses of important cults, as representations of victory and love, and indeed, in the words of Aristotle, as one half of the free citizenry, not withstanding their exclusion from the public magistratures. Raphaela Averkorn sees the power of queens and princesses in the Middle Ages as important: women interested in politics could be quite active thanks to a power structure dependent on the court as a 'house', in which the queen's court had political functions – although it tended to lose them as the feudal structure was progressively substituted by the modern state structure. The codification of gender roles in 19th Germany provides a particularly significant case study of the link between gender roles and nationalism: Sybille Küster makes clear how the development of a warlike male role and a sweet supportive female role were entwined with the rise of nationalism, and drew on visions of German-ness going back to Tacitus. Iceland, at the time of the first introduction of local voting rights, shows its specificity. Guðmundur Hálfdanarson points out that well-off farm widows were easily granted political rights corresponding to the existing local evaluation of their social importance, although the Danish political superstructure proved unable to accept such gender equality. Of course, the vote itself does not solve all problems magically: Pat Thane's discussion of the consequences of women's suffrage for 20th century Britain show them to be gradual but substantial. Roumen Genov's chapter illustrates the development of women's rights and gender relations in Bulgaria from earliest times to the present.

The second part of the volume is dedicated to "Writing and Culture" in a gender perspective. Examining signatures on wills in early modern Lisbon, Ana Cristina Araujo measures the extension of the practice of writing in different social strata, divided as to sex. This procedure has the merit of distinguishing changing relationships with the practice of writing abilities according to chronological phases and social groups, showing that change is not linear, and is markedly different in different milieus whatever the social level. Women's contribution to writing the national history of Italy in the time of the country's unification allows us to investigate critically the idea that women – except in recent times – occupy the private sphere but are excluded from the public sphere. Instead Ilaria Porciani shows how 19th century women were pioneers in certain kinds of public political writing, although the consolidation of an academic interest in the subject later tended to push them back into the role of amateurs. Women's cultural associations in 19th and early 20th century Germany are at the centre of Ines Katenhusen's chapter: an analysis of the changing relations of gender with artistic instruction and the structure of the art market shows how widespread ideas about gender made it difficult for women to pursue careers in the arts. Ausma Cimdiņa introduces the theme of Latvian feminist literature before and after the Soviet period.

The third part is devoted to "Conduct", that is, prescribed or recommended behaviour according to social milieu and epoch. Lisa Saracco reads for us Baldassarre Castiglione's influential 16th century description of the ideal court. This shows us the elaboration of a kind of elite in which gentlewomen and gentlemen were given explicitly intertwining roles in permitting social exchange to take place in a peaceful and elevated setting. The other side of the coin is the working woman in Italy in the early modern period described by Daniela Lombardi. Here we can see a theme which recurs in numerous chapters, that of the role of women's work, considered marginal respect to that of men, but actually very significant in quantity, quality and flexibility – as well as offering an explanation of some aspects of women's exclusion from political and guild power. Marja van Tilburg examines the conduct books written for young people in the 19th century in the Netherlands; young men and women are advised about such matters as the use of time and the place sexual attraction should have in the choice of a spouse. Vinzia Fiorino shows, using Roman clinical records, how late 19th-century society, as the state became more powerful and demanding, increasingly imposed uniform models of behaviour, interning in asylums those judged to be mad.

The fourth part is entitled simply "Models": it includes chapters devoted to long-lasting generalised models or stereotypes and their relationship to changing reality. Francesca Cenerini shows us the model of the Roman matron – silent, *domiseda*, *lanifica* – a model that persists for many centuries, even though reality is far different. Anne Lemonde examines the political functions of female sovereigns in a scenario of images which evoke protection, order and peace. Henrik Jensen interprets changing societal values in the last two centuries, dominated first by hierarchical patriarchal relations; then by brotherly relations and most recently by a 'motherly' state; Fabio Dei shows the contradictions into which cultural anthropology may fall in its attempts to analyse the variants and constants of gender roles.

The concluding part illustrates in three specific contexts (Austria, Romania and the Czech Republic) the ways in which state policies towards families, role division, sexual practices and gender identities interact with the lives of men, women and children. Karin Schmidlechner's study of Austrian politics in the post-war period shows changes in different directions in the area of family, services, access to the workplace and gender mentality; Maria Habernig asks Austrian women of different ages to comment on their professional and personal lives; Vasile Vese delineates the effects, at times dramatic, of Romanian government policy on gender roles and division of burdens between men and women; Věra Sokolová investigates the changes – and the lack of change – in attitudes and legislation regarding homosexuality, male and female, and transgender in the Czech Republic in the last decade.

The chronological and the geographical context is broad, ranging from earliest times to the 20th century. Whenever possible documents or extracts from relevant documents have been supplied, both in the original language and in translation. Men and women in their daily lives, in their complex and contradictory interactions with institutions, laws, culture, art and with other men and women, are always present. They, and their heirs, the young people and children of today and of tomorrow, constitute the real reason for embarking on the project of bringing historical perspective to bear on gender roles.

Particular thanks are due to many: first, as explained above, to the European Commission in its two guises, through its Culture 2000 programme and its Socrates programme; and then to the authors who contributed the texts and the students who collaborated in discussing them and in developing the publishing format. Their expertise and the support of their universities have been essential for the success of the project. The Faculty of Letters and Philosophy of the University of Pisa and its Dean, Prof. Gianfranco Fioravanti, have given special support, facilitating the project and making possible the collaboration of Dr. Elisa Mattiello and Dr. Laura Nelli. The Department of Modern and Contemporary History hosted the Intensive Programme in its structures. The University of Pisa has financed our valiant student collaborators – Mattia Bellomi, Benedetta Pinzuti, Costantino Efisio, Jessica Zamagni, Laura Mori – in organisational duties, proof-reading, missions to libraries, and pony express. Prof. Teresa Caruso of the Department of Historical Sciences of the Ancient World has contributed time, work and resources far beyond the call of duty. The Pisa Chamber of Commerce, the Opera Primaziale del Duomo, the Guarnacci Museum of Volterra have helped in significant ways. The National Gallery of Scotland, Edinburgh, has kindly granted permission to reproduce on the cover of this volume a detail of its splendid Van Dyck portrait of a great merchant and banking family belonging to the Genoese nobility, the Lomellini. To all, we express our gratitude.

We hope that showing a variety of ways of approaching this theme can lead students and teachers in each country to take a new look at their own history and that of their neighbours – to look at the world afresh in a gender perspective.

Ann Katherine Isaacs
University of Pisa

Ann Katherine Isaacs was born in Astoria, Oregon, in 1943. She studied at the University of California, Berkeley, and the University of Milan where she received her Laurea degree in Modern History in 1967. She has taught Renaissance History at the University of Pisa since 1975. Her research has concentrated on various themes of social and political history, particulary cities, state formation and justice. She is active in experimentation and innovation in European higher education; she coordinates the Thematic Network for History and the Humanities, CLIOHNET.

Introduction

HISTORY, HERSTORY, OURSTORY

When the ECTS Pilot Project was completed, the Universities which had worked together in the field of History to implement the project decided to continue their collaboration in order to preserve and build on the expertise they had gained in the preceding years. Our new activities first found support in the framework of a Socrates curriculum development programme, entitled "The idea and reality of Europe", coordinated by the University of Groningen. We hoped to be able to give a valid contribution to finding new ways of teaching and learning about European history. The project was articulated along several major themes; two of the partner institutions assumed the responsibility for coordinating the interested institutions in gathering knowledge about and developing innovative teaching approaches to each theme. The University of Iceland, Reykjavik, and the University of Pisa coordinated a large theme group on "European Empires, States and Regions, Nations and Nationalities, Political Colonisation and Decolonisation, Frontiers" – basically, on the political aspects of European History.

As the activities of the group developed, we found that one of the most fruitful ways to gain insight into contents and methods was in the multinational, multilingual real-life teaching-learning situation that could be created in Intensive Programmes. We decided that each year two partner institutions would present a proposal for an Intensive Programme in one of the thematic areas. In 1998 and in 2000, we were able to hold Socrates Intensive Programmes on two related themes ("Empires, States and regions in a European Perspective" and "Nations and Nationalities"). The partner institutions in the project – besides Pisa and Reykjavik – were the Universities of Uppsala, Helsinki, Roskilde, Groningen, Edinburgh, Sussex, Maynooth, Cork, Hannover, Bielefeld, Tübingen, Basel, Graz, Grenoble, Poitiers, Rouen, Madrid Autónoma, Deusto, Alcalá de Henares, Salamanca, Minho, Bologna and Athens. Subsequently it seemed important to consider the same themes in a gender perspective. Representing the University of Pisa, I applied in fall 1999 for support for an Intensive Programme on "Political Systems and Definitions of Gender Roles". This represented a development in the on-going work on political systems. In 2000 the proposal was accepted by the European Commission and it was possible to hold the Programme in Pisa from 15 May to 24 May 2001, now involving all the CLIOH partners, 38 in number, including members from the Eastern and Central European countries that have now joined our Network.

In designing and carrying out the project we were fortunate to be able to rely on the expertise and willingness to collaborate of colleagues from all the partner institutions, on the centres for gender studies of the University of Hannover, the University of Latvia, the

University of Salamanca, the Charles University of Prague, on GOLD (the women's workgroup of the University of Pisa), on the conference of delegates for gender studies, culture of differences and equal opportunities issues in teaching and research of the Rectors of Italian Universities.

As a result it was possible to bring together teachers and students from a wide variety of countries to present, discuss and compare their knowledge and insights. Twenty students were from Pisa and 40 from the partner Universities of all parts of Europe. Teachers had complete academic freedom, but the intersecting themes and general discussion necessarily produced an interdisciplinary and comparative approach. Interactive courses were organised in the morning; intensive workshops in the afternoon. The activities were completed a study visit to Volterra, where in the Guarnacci museum important testimony of gender roles in ancient Etruscan society could be observed.

Thanks to the Culture 2000 programme of the European Commission it has been possible to draw on the materials and insights generated and to produce this volume. Twenty-two teachers have prepared new texts, based on their formal presentations and on the informal, but equally important, discussions and workshops held with the students in May 2001. Their contributions have been grouped into five sections: power and politics, writing and culture, conduct and context, models, and families, sexuality and gender policy.

The single chapters have been completed with illustrations, photographs, bibliographies and a selection of original documents. Each contribution is preceded by a short biographical note about the author and by a summary of the text in his or her native language. Some of the texts and other materials are available in other languages as well on the "Clioh's Workshop" site (www.edizioniplus.it/) and on the Clioh site (www.stm.unipi.it/Clioh). The book is accompanied by video materials. The sites give full information on the project and how to receive the volumes and the videos for use and testing in universities and schools.

We hope that this volume will bring new knowledge and a new, pan-European gender perspective into the teaching/learning of history.

Ann Katherine Isaacs
University of Pisa

Women in Ancient Greece: a Political and Artistic Approach

Jean-Luc Lamboley
Université de Grenoble II

D'un point de vue strictement institutionnel et politique les femmes n'ont pas grande place dans le fonctionnement de la démocratie athénienne, souvent définie comme un "club d'hommes", et l'on a tendance à réduire leur rôle de citoyenne à la reproduction des citoyens. Toutefois, par le biais de la religion dont on connaît l'importance dans toutes les activités de la cité, les femmes occupent une place qui est loin d'être négligeable. L'étude par exemple des fondations coloniales montre que les femmes, quand elles sont prêtresses d'un culte poliade, sont indispensables à la fondation de la colonie. C'est le cas d'Aristarchè d'Ephèse pour Marseille, ou de Kleoboia pour Thasos. De façon encore plus nette, les artistes grecs, dans ce que la tradition a reconnu comme des chefs d'œuvre, expriment une très haute idée de la femme. C'est le cas pour les Ergastines de la frise ionique du Parthénon, oeuvre de Phidias; ces vierges, issues de la plus haute aristocratie de la cité, conduisent la procession jusqu'à l'Assemblée des dieux et apparaissent ainsi comme des figures médiatrices entre l'humain et le divin. La Victoire de Samothrace, derrière la simple allégorie d'une victoire navale, exprime elle la force vitale conduisant l'humanité, image du progrès des peuples; c'est le même type que l'on retrouve dans le fameux tableau de Delacroix, La Liberté guidant le peuple. Enfin la fameuse Vénus de Milo, avec son buste de femme émergeant de la matière qui prend forme, incarne la sensualité féminine et l'amour comme source de toute vie et de toute création. Ce sont donc trois aspects de la femme qui vont bien au delà d'un simple rôle politique; les Grecs ont su montrer qu'elle incarne l'humanité dans ses dimensions les plus universelles.

Jean-Luc Lamboley was born in 1953 in Toulouse, France. He was a student of the École Normale Supérieure and of the École française de Rome. He is now Professor of History and Archaeology of the Ancient Worlds at the Université de Grenoble II. His special interests are the contacts between the Greeks and the native populations in the colonial world and problems of acculturation. His works include *Lexique d'histoire et de civilisation romaine*, Paris 1994; *Les Grecs d'Occident (la période archaïque)*, Paris 1996; and *Recherches sur les Messapiens*, Rome 1996.

If we consider the Greek civilisation from a strictly political angle, that is to say, looking at civil rights, or public activities inside well-established institutions, it is clear that the definition of women's roles is very poor, even non-existent. Citizenship is conceded to women insofar as they give birth to children, and this way, allow to perpetuate a City always controlled by men only. At this point, I could end my speech or take the risk of being outlawed as regards the topic. But if we admit that our modern societies are still based on solid elements coming from classical antiquity – the very notion of citizenship, democracy, civil and human rights and so on –, if we admit that Greek philosophy has conceived universal values, it is not possible to imagine that this civilisation has cancelled womanhood. So my challenge is to show you that the Greeks were able to give us a very high idea of womanhood, but, as is suggested by the title of my text, it will be necessary to move from the political to the religious and artistic field.

First, we can note that the law established by Pericles around 451 B.C. is important because it proves that the legal notion of citizenship is pertinent for women who are not completely excluded from the civic community. Let me recall that according to this law a young Athenian could be a citizen only if his father and his mother were citizens in their own right. We may also recall Aristotle's statement that the education of women is bound to be important, since they make up a half of the free population (*Politics*, I, 1260b). [*See Source 1*]

Secondly, the overriding importance of religion in Greek communities in general leads to consider another path to integration in the civic community: I mean priesthood. Indeed, the role of women appears very clearly when we consider the religious life of Greek cities, especially in the archaic period – when private and public activities were not as separate as in the classical period – and in a particular situation: when a colony, that is to say, a new Greek community, was founded. It seems that a foundation could not be done without the presence of women who brought with them the cults from the mother country, because it was standard practice for the colonists to establish in their new cities the cults that were maintained in their mother cities. So it is impossible to imagine the performance of the rituals of Greek women's cults by a population of largely native women and the idea of Greek men setting out alone to establish a new Greek community without any Greek women is absurd [1].

For instance Herodotus (I, 146) [*See Source 2*] states that when they founded Miletus in Ionia, the Athenian colonists took no women with them and took their wives amidst the local population. The indication of such an attitude from the colonists is the mark of uncommon behaviour, and implies that in Herodotus' opinion it was normal for colonists to take women with them.

In a more positive way, the presence of women in the colonial expedition is attested by several examples. There is one case where we are expressly told that women and children took part as well as men. This is the Phocean expedition which shared briefly the settlement at Alalia in Corsica (565 B.C.), and later established itself permanently at Elea. However, since this was intended as a complete evacuation of the mother city after the Persian conquest, it is obviously an exception in the history of Greek colonisation. In the case of the foundation of Thurioi by Athenians in 444-443 B.C. in order to reinforce the Sybarites who had failed in their attempt to re-establish their destroyed city, we are told that disputes arose between the original Sybarites and the newcomers. One of the causes of friction was that the Sybarites thought their wives should have preference over the wives of the new colonists when making sacrifices to the gods. So the Athenian colonists of Thurioi brought wives with them. Lastly we have positive evidence for the presence of two Greek women whose name is preserved by the literary sources: Kleoboia at Thasos, and Aristarchè of Ephesus at Massalia. It is interesting to observe what they did and what they were. Kleoboia was the first to bring the rites of Demeter from Paros to Thasos. A painting by

Polygnotos at Delphi depicted her as having on her knees a chest of the kind that was usually made for Demeter. She is very likely to be considered as the first priestess of Demeter in Thasos. Aristarchè of Massalia was an aristocrat from Ephesus who was instructed in a dream by the goddess Artemis to accompany the Phocean expedition and establish in Massalia a new branch of the cult of Ephesian Artemis. So she took with her the means for such a transfer of a cult, and when the colony was established, the new sanctuary was duly built. Aristarchè was given the outstanding honour of being appointed priestess. These last two examples draw our attention to the role of women in the religion of the *polis* (Greek city).

Indeed, intermarriage between Greek and native populations in colonial areas was very common, but such intermarriage is to be distinguished from the practices regarding Greek women during the foundation of a colony. In the case of intermarriage, the question is to favour demography; in the case of the Greek women, the question is to settle the religious basis of the new community. Which is the more political role? In so far as it was common in Greece for female deities to be served by female ministrants – and there were many female deities – the role of female priestesses was unavoidable. This is already clear from the famous passage in the *Iliad* (VI, 297) where Theano, the wife of Antenor, who has been chosen priestess of Athena by the people, is requested to open the doors of the temple to worship the goddess. We also know of the very important role performed by the wife of the Archon Basileus at Athens; she had to lead the celebration of the secret rites of Dionysos at the Anthesteria, and make sacrifices that could not be named. There were many cults and festivals in Greece which belonged to women or offered women a special role; it is not possible here to give a list of them, but the fulfilment of this task is often used as proof of a woman's citizenship and legal marriage. [*See Source 3*]

So the Greek communities, as early as the most archaic period, gave women a very important role through the religious activities which were essential components of private and public life. And now let us study the second approach, the artistic one. What image of womanhood have Greek artists left us? I shall focus on sculpture, choosing only three masterpieces that everyone knows, and I shall try to show that these are masterpieces just because they give us the noblest idea of womanhood.

The first one is the slab of the Ergastines, carved in high relief, from the Parthenon east frieze, the work of Phidias the sculptor, the artistic adviser to Pericles for the project (Fig. 1). The frieze, 160 m long, ran around the outside of the central block of the temple, at the top of the wall just inside the outer colonnade. According to the common interpretation, it shows the Panathenaic procession, during the great festival in Athens; all the civic community is represented on the frieze, and the Ergastines are heading the procession (at the end of the frieze just before the Olympian Assembly). These maidens, who belonged to the highest aristocratic families of the City, had to weave for a year a sacred veil for Athena, and during the Panathenaic procession they brought this veil to the Temple of the goddess on the Acropolis. But on the frieze, they do not carry the veil and their duty is different. They march in step very slowly and demurely, under the control of some masters of ceremony, towards the Assembly of the Olympian Gods waiting for their arrival. So we can say that they introduce and enthrone the human city in the divine House. These young priestesses appear as the mediators between men and gods and give manhood its highest dignity.

Fig. 1
East frieze of the Parthenon showing the Ergastines in procession.

In Sophocle's tragedy *Antigone* – Sophocles lived at the same time as Pericles and Phidias – we can read (verse 332): "the marvels of nature are many, but among all these marvels the most beautiful is man". This is the message Phidias wanted to carve for eternity in the marble of the frieze, and he used the cortege of the wise maidens leading the people to the majesty of the Olympian Assembly. [*See Source 4*]

You can observe that the artistic language is very classical: the intensity of this sacred moment is expressed with very few effects; no agitation, no pompous staging, no dramatic composition as is the case at the beginning of the frieze where the young Athenian cavaliers are parading. The figures are less expressive and emotional than others of the same period, but more deliberately seeking to express an ideal and generalised view of the human subject.

You can see the repetition with some variations of the same figures: maidens who are marching two abreast (the first two on the left are very close; in the second group they are further apart, and in the last group on the right, the two girls are completely separated). They seem motionless, static, because they are suffused with the majesty of the gods, but the idea of the slow procession is given by the position of the men who stand still, looking in the opposite direction: the solemn movement is given by the variation between these two attitudes. There is also another movement, very tenuous and subtle: the dropping folds of the *peplos*. It looks like a shimmer or a trickling, but the best metaphor is a musical one: the folds are at the same time theme and variations, and play as a trill or a tremolo. The trill is a sort of dynamic pause: it varies the note but gives the fullness to the sound; it reconciles the tempo necessary for the succession of the sounds and the pause necessary for enjoying the plenitude of the emotion. But in this case, what is the meaning of this sculptural trill? It is the expression of the sacred shiver caused by the proximity of the gods; it is the way for the artist to immobilise the tempo of the procession before crossing the threshold of transcendence, and the key of this transcendence is woman, and more exactly the maiden.

We can now understand why this frieze was relatively inconspicuous and only to be glanced at between the *peristasis* and intermittently from a very steep point of view. The message was too hard to be accepted in the middle of the 5th century when the official dogma was that human and divine condition were radically different and without any possibility of intercession. Remember that some friends of Phidias and Pericles had already been condemned for impiety.

Now let us have a look to the second masterpiece, the Nikè (the goddess Victory) from Samothrace (Fig. 2). The statue no doubt commemorated a great naval victory of an Hellenistic king. The island of Samothrace was a favoured sanctuary for royal dedications.

Fig. 2
The Nikè (Victory) of Samotrace.

One of the great Antigonid sea victories of the mid-3rd century (for example the battle of Cos in the 250 B.C.) is the most likely context, although a later date, for a Rhodian victory in 190 B.C., has also been favoured. The goddess, with mighty wings outstretched, lands in a rush of fine drapery on the prow of a warship. The statue was framed in its own exedra on a hill above the sanctuary. The ship's prow was set obliquely in the exedra so that the statue presented a left three-quarter view, the view for which it was clearly designed. The twisting axes of hips and shoulders and the contours of wings and flying drapery are most telling from this viewpoint.

According to the common interpretation, the goddess in landing on the ship wants to be victorious, but I think that the main effect is another one; it gives a leading or pulling effect. The massive and ruffled wind-blown folds, flattened against the body, have a very powerful effect; the goddess is fighting against the natural elements, the wind and the spray or spindrift, and she is irresistibly leading to the Victory. The most striking effect in this statue is its vigour and immediacy. Under the wet clothes, we can observe a very feminine anatomy, for instance the abdomen, the navel, the very graceful left leg ; but in the same time this femininity shows great strength because of a well-built frame with the different anatomic volumes perfectly distributed; they seem animated by a powerful energy expressed by the contrast between the baroque swirl of the folds and the classical solidity and stability of the body; nothing and no one could tear the goddess away from the ship, and nothing and no one could stop the ship from sailing to victory.

We can observe the two main lines that structure this work: the first one is the long oblique line constructed with the forward thrust of the breast, and the inclination of the trunk and the left leg like a long spindle; the second one, upright, is the movement of the wings spread backwards. The left wing forms a perfect right angle with the left leg – which is very visible because the head is missing; then this right angle itself emphasises the obliquity of the big diagonal designed by the rest of the body. So these two main lines which express at the same time heroic stability and irresistible momentum are the key to understanding the meaning of this statue. The Allegory of Victory does not symbolise simply military power but something more essential: the life forces that generate the progress of peoples and History. Woman is here a "capo popolo", the embodiment of such a force. The goddess is not a superwoman in the sense of a super soldier. She is the basic energy able to pull humanity forward in spite of all the obstacles. Along the same line, you may recall the famous painting by Delacroix "Liberty leading the people": the artist has put the French flag in place of the wings of the statue, but the figure is the same, the inspiration is the same, the message is the same.

Last, but not least, let us observe the famous Aphrodite from Melos found in 1820, and bought for the Louvre as the work of a classical master; in fact, it is an Hellenistic statue dated from the 2nd century B.C. (Fig. 3). The very impersonal expression of the face indicates clearly that it is not a portrait but an ideal and abstract view of woman. The visual approach must be frontal; the slightly raised left foot generates a general waving movement expressed by the long sinusoidal line which frames the general structure of the body, and suggests the apotheosis of woman.

We can also notice a strong contrast between the upper and the lower part of the statue emphasised by two parallel lines, the line of the shoulders and the line of the edge of the

Fig. 3
The Aphrodite from Melos.

cloth: while the naked upper body is worked with great sensitivity expressing the great sensuality of feminine flesh, the heavy folds of the drapery, carved in a rather rough manner give a massive form which is masking the nudity only suggested by the outline of the left leg and the toes of the right foot. It has been said that this Aphrodite, originally the goddess of Love, represents profane or secular carnal life. But there are two approaches to this work: we can favour the drop of the drapery revealing the complete female nudity, and so we turn our attention to the erotic power of a voluptuous form. But we can also favour the opposite movement, that is to say the blooming of a female body which is coming to light, emerging from the shapeless matter under the invisible chisel of the sculptor, like a cocoon from the chrysalis. In this case, we witness the birth of Eve and the mystery of creation. What is the message here? Woman is the source of life and love, she comes out from the chaos of the shapeless matter to which she gives form and sense.

It is time now to conclude by summing up the main roles that the Greek artists – not Greek politicians – have defined for women:

- Woman as a link between humanity and divinity

- Woman as embodiment of the irresistible life force of History

- Woman as source of any life or archetype of any creation.

You can see the artistic language is very far from the political speeches, but I think it is stronger and able to suggest fundamental mysteries such as "Humanity thy name is woman». The Greek artists told it, and I just wanted to be their spokesman because at the beginning of this new millennium it is important to rekindle the fire of classical antiquity. Do not forget: this light will be new only if it is yours.

 NOTES

[1] Cf. Graham A.J., *Religion, women and Greek colonization*, in *Religione e città nel mondo antico*, Atti, Centro di ricerche e documentazione sull'antichità classica, 11, Roma 1981-2 (1984), p. 293-314.

 SELECTED BIBLIOGRAPHY

Histoire des femmes en Occident. 1. L'antiquité, sous la direction de P. Schmitt-Pantel, Plon 1991.

Graham A.J., *Religion, women end Greek colonization*, in *Religione e città nel mondo antico*, Atti, Centro di ricerche e documentazione sull'antichità classica, 11, Roma 1981-2 (1984), p. 293-314.

 SOURCES

1. Aristotle, Politics, I, 1260b, from Aristotle in 23 volumes, vol. 21, translated by H. Rackham, Cambridge Mass.

> Ἀλλὰ περὶ μὲν τούτων διωρίσθω τὸν τρόπον
> τοῦτον· περὶ δὲ ἀνδρὸς καὶ γυναικὸς καὶ τέκνων
> 10 καὶ πατρός, τῆς τε περὶ ἕκαστον αὐτῶν ἀρετῆς,
> καὶ τῆς πρὸς σφᾶς αὐτοὺς ὁμιλίας, τί τὸ καλῶς
> καὶ μὴ καλῶς ἐστι καὶ πῶς δεῖ τὸ μὲν εὖ διώκειν
> τὸ δὲ κακῶς φεύγειν, ἐν τοῖς περὶ τὰς πολιτείας
> ἀναγκαῖον ἐπελθεῖν, ἐπεὶ γὰρ οἰκία μὲν πᾶσα μέρος 12
> πόλεως, ταῦτα δ' οἰκίας, τὴν δὲ τοῦ μέρους πρὸς
> 15 τὴν τοῦ ὅλου δεῖ βλέπειν ἀρετήν, ἀναγκαῖον πρὸς
> τὴν πολιτείαν βλέποντας παιδεύειν καὶ τοὺς παῖδας
> καὶ τὰς γυναῖκας, εἴπερ τι διαφέρει πρὸς τὸ τὴν
> πόλιν εἶναι σπουδαίαν καὶ τοὺς παῖδας εἶναι
> σπουδαίους καὶ τὰς γυναῖκας σπουδαίας. ἀναγ-
> καῖον δὲ διαφέρειν· αἱ μὲν γὰρ γυναῖκες ἥμισυ
> 20 μέρος τῶν ἐλευθέρων, ἐκ δὲ τῶν παίδων οἱ κοινωνοὶ[1]
> γίνονται τῆς πολιτείας. ὥστ' ἐπεὶ περὶ μὲν τούτων
> διώρισται, περὶ δὲ τῶν λοιπῶν ἐν ἄλλοις λεκτέον,
> ἀφέντες ὡς τέλος ἔχοντας τοὺς νῦν λόγους, ἄλλην
> ἀρχὴν ποιησάμενοι λέγωμεν, καὶ πρῶτον ἐπισκεψώ-
> μεθα περὶ τῶν ἀποφηναμένων περὶ τῆς πολιτείας
> τῆς ἀρίστης.

But on these subjects let us conclude our decisions in this manner: while the question of virtue severally belonging to man and woman and children and father, and of the right and wrong mode of conducting their mutual intercourse and the proper way of pursuing the good mode and avoiding the bad one, are matters that it will be necessary to follow up in the part of our treatise dealing with the various forms of constitution. For since every household is part of a state, and these relationships are part of the household, and the excellence of the part must have regard to that of the whole, it is necessary that the education both of the children and of the women should be carried on with a regard to the form of constitution, if it makes any difference as regards the goodness of the state for the children and the women to be good. And it must necessarily make a difference; for the women are a half of the free population, and the children grow up to be the partners in the government of the state. So that as these questions have been decided, and those that remain must be discussed elsewhere, let us relinquish the present subjects as completed, and make a fresh start in our discourse, and first let us consider those thinkers who have advanced views about the ideal State.

2. Herodotus, *Histories*, I, 146, from *Herodotus with an English translation* by A. D. Godley, Cambridge Mass. 1920.

146, 1. ταῦτα δυώδεκα μέρεα νῦν 'Αχαιῶν ἐστι καὶ τότε γε
'Ιώνων ἦν.   τούτων δὴ εἵνεκα καὶ οἱ "Ιωνες δυώδεκα πόλιας
ἐποιήσαντο, ἐπεὶ ὥς γέ τι μᾶλλον οὗτοι "Ιωνές εἰσι τῶν ἄλλων
'Ιώνων ἢ κάλλιόν τι γεγόνασι, μωρίη πολλὴ λέγειν, τῶν
5 "Αβαντες μὲν ἐξ Εὐβοίης εἰσὶ οὐκ ἐλαχίστη μοῖρα, τοῖσι 'Ιωνίης
μέτα οὐδὲ τοῦ οὐνόματος οὐδέν, Μινύαι δὲ 'Ορχομένιοί σφι
ἀναμεμίχαται καὶ Καδμεῖοι καὶ Δρύοπες καὶ Φωκέες ἀποδά-
σμιοι καὶ Μολοσσοὶ καὶ 'Αρκάδες Πελασγοὶ καὶ Δωριέες 'Επι-
δαύριοι, ἄλλα τε ἔθνεα πολλὰ ἀναμεμίχαται·   2. οἱ δὲ αὐτέων
10 ἀπὸ τοῦ πρυτανηίου τοῦ 'Αθηναίων ὁρμηθέντες καὶ νομίζοντες
γενναιότατοι εἶναι 'Ιώνων, οὗτοι δὲ οὐ γυναῖκας ἠγάγοντο ἐς
τὴν ἀποικίην ἀλλὰ Καείρας ἔσχον, τῶν ἐφόνευσαν τοὺς
γονέας.   3. διὰ τοῦτον δὲ τὸν φόνον αἱ γυναῖκες αὗται νόμον
θέμεναι σφίσι αὐτῆσι ὅρκους ἐπήλασαν καὶ παρέδοσαν τῆσι θυ-
15 γατράσι μή κοτε ὁμοσιτῆσαι τοῖσι ἀνδράσι μηδὲ ὀνόματι βῶσαι
τὸν ἑωυτῆς ἄνδρα, τοῦδε εἵνεκα ὅτι ἐφόνευσαν σφέων τοὺς πατέ-
ρας καὶ ἄνδρας καὶ παῖδας καὶ ἐπείτε ταῦτα ποιήσαντες αὐτῆσι
συνοίκεον.   ταῦτα δὲ ἦν γινόμενα ἐν Μιλήτῳ.

For this reason and for no other, the Ionians too made twelve cities; for it would be foolishness to say that these are more truly Ionian or better born than the other Ionians; since not the least part of them are Abantes from Euboea, who are not Ionians even in name, and there are mingled with them Minyans of Orchomenus, Cadmeans, Dryopians, Phocian renegades from their nation, Molossians, Pelasgian Arcadians, Dorians of Epidaurus and many other tribes; and as for those who came from the very town-hall of Athens and think they are the best born of the Ionians, these did not bring wives with them to their settlements, but married Carian women whose parents they had put to death. For this slaughter, these women made a custom and bound themselves by oath (and enjoined it on their daughters) that no one would sit at table with her husband or call him by his name, because the men had married them after slaying their fathers and husbands and sons. This happened at Miletus.

3. Homer, *Iliad*, Book VI, line 297, from Homer, *Homeri Opera in five volumes*, Monro D.B., Allen T. W. (eds), Oxford 1920

Αἱ δ' ὅτε νηὸν ἵκανον 'Αθήνης ἐν πόλει ἄκρῃ,
τῇσι θύρας ὤϊξε Θεανὼ καλλιπάρῃος,
Κισσηΐς, ἄλοχος 'Αντήνορος ἱπποδάμοιο·
300 τὴν γὰρ Τρῶες ἔθηκαν 'Αθηναίης ἱέρειαν.
αἱ δ' ὀλολυγῇ πᾶσαι 'Αθήνῃ χεῖρας ἀνέσχον·
ἡ δ' ἄρα πέπλον ἑλοῦσα Θεανὼ καλλιπάρῃος
θῆκεν 'Αθηναίης ἐπὶ γούνασιν ἠϋκόμοιο,
εὐχομένη δ' ἠρᾶτο Διὸς κούρῃ μεγάλοιο·

When they reached the temple of Athena, lovely Theano, daughter of Kisseus and wife of Antenor, opened the doors, for the Trojans had made her priestess of Athena. The women lifted up their hands to the goddess with a loud cry, and Theano took the robe to lay it on the knees of Athena, praying the while to the daughter of the great Zeus.

4. Sophocles, *Antigone*, 332-341, from Sophocles, *The Antigone of Sophocles*, Jebb R. (ed.), Cambridge, 1891

ΧΟΡΟΣ
Πολλὰ τὰ δεινὰ κοὐδὲν ἀν-
θρώπου δεινότερον πέλει·
τοῦτο καὶ πολιοῦ πέραν
335 πόντου χειμερίῳ νότῳ
χωρεῖ, περιβρυχίοισιν
περῶν ὑπ' οἴδμασιν, θεῶν
τε τὰν ὑπερτάταν, Γᾶν
ἄφθιτον, ἀκαμάταν, ἀποτρύεται,
340 ἰλλομένων ἀρότρων ἔτος εἰς ἔτος,
ἱππείῳ γένει πολεύων.

Chorus

Wonders are many, and none is more wonderful than man. This power spans the sea, even when it surges white before the gales of the south-wind, and makes a path under swells that threaten to engulf him. Earth, too, the eldest of the gods, the immortal, the unwearied, he wears away to his own ends, turning the soil with the offspring of horses as the plows weave to and fro year after year.

Women and power in the Middle Ages: political aspects of medieval queenship

Raphaela Averkorn

Universiteit Hannover

In diesem Paper stellt sich die Frage nach der Rolle und den Aufgaben der mittelalterlichen Königin in West- und Südeuropa. In den letzten Jahren sind zahlreiche Studien zu diesen Aspekten erschienen, jedoch sind noch weitere Forschungen notwendig, um Klarheit über die Bedeutung der mittelalterlichen Kaiserin und Königin zu gewinnen. An dieser Stelle soll lediglich eine Einführung in einige Fragestellungen gegeben und anhand von ausgewählten Beispielen erläutert werden. Die mittelalterliche Königin hatte nicht nur Aufgaben im eigenen Haushalt wahrzunehmen, sondern konnte ebenfalls in der Rechtsprechung, in der Verwaltung, in auswärtigen Beziehungen, als Mäzenin und caritative Wohltäterin etc. tätig werden. Welcher Spielraum ihr eingeräumt wurde, hing von den jeweiligen Umständen und Epochen ab.

Es gibt unterschiedliche Typen mittelalterlicher Königinnen. Zunächst einmal finden wir Königinnen, die den Thron ererbt hatten, weil ein männlicher Erbe fehlte. Die größte Gruppe jedoch wirkte als Ehefrauen von Königen, als Witwen von Königen, als Mütter und Regentinnen von Königen. Regentinnen konnten eine beträchtliche Machtfülle erlangen. Im folgenden werden einzelne Beispiele angeführt, um zu zeigen inwieweit mittelalterliche Königinnen eine aktive politische Karriere verfolgen konnten bzw. auch, wie einige von ihnen durch widrige Umstände bestimmt, scheiterten. Die ausgewählten Beispiele beziehen sich auf einen Zeitraum vom Früh- bis zum Spätmittelalter und umfassen einen geographischen Bereich, der von Deutschland über England und Frankreich bis auf die Iberische Halbinsel reicht.

Born in Münster, Germany, Priv. Doz. Dr. Raphaela Averkorn completed her studies at the Universities of Bordeaux and Münster. She received her Ph.D. in Medieval History from the University of Münster and completed her "Habilitation" at the University of Hannover (Germany). She now teaches European Medieval History at the Department of History at the University of Hannover.. She is particularly interested in Medieval and Renaissance history and has written books about "The county of Armagnac in the 11th and 12th centuries" and about "The writing of history in the kingdoms of Aragon and Castile in the late middle ages" and has published various contributions concerning French, Spanish and German political, social, religious, cultural and gender history. She has been a Visiting Professor in several countries, is involved in different European projects and also works as an ECTS Counsellor.

1. INTRODUCTION

"Women and power in the Middle Ages" is a very broad field of research and often a quite complicated one, because we are not too well informed about medieval women [1]. Some general works and several case studies have been published during the last decades, but nevertheless a lot of research work is still to be done [2].

In this text we shall focus on queens because if we were to discuss the political participation of all noblewomen, like duchesses, countesses and princesses, the topic would become much too broad. Sometimes those women had even more possibilities to participate actively in politics than queens and empresses.

First of all, we must examine the possible sources. Do they really inform us about the activities of medieval queens? If we take a closer look at chronicles (one of the most frequently used kinds of medieval sources), we notice that they are mainly written by men and they do not often mention women. Chronicles written by women are very rare. Very often queens are only mentioned in some of the so-called decisive moments of their lives or the life of their husband, the king. Chroniclers mention the royal wedding, the birth of the royal children (the names of the daughters are even often omitted), the death of the queen (quite often after giving birth to a child), the new marriage of the king and so on. Medieval noble women often appear to be reduced to performing one task alone: they had to produce children and naturally give birth to a male heir.

But was this indeed the daily life of a queen? If we have a closer look at other sources such as private letters, household books and personal testaments, we can see, in many cases, that these women were quite often directly involved in politics in the different fields mentioned above. Therefore a serious research work should include an analysis of different types of sources – not only official ones like royal chronicles, because in these chronicles the role, position and importance of the king is specially emphasized. He is depicted as the active person and the leading character. But if we observe private correspondence, household books and testaments and so forth we will see that very often the queen too was actively involved in political life. Such sources show us, for example, that queens had their own household, their own responsibilities and that they also made charitable donations with their own money.

In general queens had to assume different tasks. First of all the queen was responsible for her own household. It was separate from that of her husband and sometimes even in a different palace, especially in the Later Middle Ages. The queen's name is more or less often mentioned in royal documents of all kinds. The royal household could be compared to a kind of company with many employees. But the queen had to assume tasks not only within the palace but in the kingdom itself as well. Some queens took part in the practice of law, acting as judges and issuing legal documents.

We must take into consideration the fact that the queen normally was not a poor woman; she had her own possessions and lands and she was a feudal seigneur having her own subjects and her own income. She gave fiefs to her vassals and controlled them; therefore she was the head of an administration. And in many cases the queen helped her husband govern the kingdom. In quite a few documents her name was mentioned as being associated with that of the king, as participating in power, as being present in assemblies and so forth. Many times the queen had her own opinion if the king wanted to appoint administrators. But the tasks of queens were not limited to the territory of their own kingdom. Many queens participated actively in the field of international relations, especially when they were strangers themselves in their kingdom and acted as ambassadors for their home-country. Sometimes, queens were even sent abroad or to a part of the kingdom which was far away from the centre, the capital. There they acted as lieutenants on behalf of the king and were provided with special administrative and governmental power.

Like the king, the queen was also a patron of culture. Often she used her own money for her projects. She ordered civil and religious buildings to be built and decorated by the most fashionable artists. Queens often founded monasteries and chapels and contributed therefore to the establishment of dynastic memory. Many works of charity were not made only on the basis of pious considerations and for the relief of the poor; they were closely linked to the memory of the donor's own family and its members and the alms were directed to specific scopes.

We may distinguish between different types of queens. First of all, we can find reigning queens who received this right by heritage. They inherited the kingdom because their father did not leave a male heir. Some of these medieval queens are quite well known. By analysing this list we can see that there were no reigning queens in France because of the Salic law, which excluded women from the 14th century on. There were no empresses ruling in their own right, because emperors were always elected and it was not foreseen that a woman could be elected. But nevertheless some empresses were involved in politics. Secondly, we can find queens who received their title and power because they were married to a king. This was the normal and most frequent case. Thirdly, we have to mention the widowed queen or the dowager-queen. She acted as a regent during the minority of her son. Legally a widow had many more rights than a married woman who was under the "tutorship" of her husband.

Before presenting some examples, let us mention that not all medieval queens were really interested in politics; some really did not want to participate actively. But many queens were well educated and even learned persons and often had more intellectual interests than their husbands. Many of these women really had to struggle within the royal family to be allowed to participate in politics. But when successful what were they allowed to do? Were there special fields of activities entrusted to royal women? Or did they act like their male colleagues? We will examine some specific cases relating to the Empire, the kingdoms of England and France and the Iberian kingdoms of Aragon and Castile in order to have an overview.

2. QUEENS AND EMPRESSES

First, we will consider briefly some examples concerning the Empire. Already in the times of the Merovingians and the Carolingians we see that queens participated actively in politics and power [3]. Bertrada (†783), the wife of king Pepin III, took part in government, for example while her husband was leading a military campaign in Italy against the Langobardian kingdom. Bertrada represented him at home and negotiated in critical situations between both kingdoms by travelling to different regions in Europe such as Bavaria and Italy. Her successors as well were very often directly involved in politics, but they also had other tasks. The Carolingian queen was the head of the royal household. In some texts the queen is expressly considered as an assistant for all matters concerning the government of the kingdom and the administration of the palace. The king and the queen formed a team.

The empresses during the Ottonian and the Salian periods often occupied a central position in the government. Their tasks were not officially defined or written down but nobody argued against their active participation. We may mention the case of Queen Maud (†968), the wife of king Henry I. She was a very learned woman while her husband, the first Ottonian, was not able to read or write. Maud trained her son, the emperor Otto I, to become a learned person, too. This is symptomatic for this period. Knowledge was transmitted by learned women and learned monks and priests. When the first universities were founded in the 13th century women were excluded from knowledge. German queens and later empresses were crowned like their husband, a fact which emphasises their importance. Maud was even called in documents *co-regnante*; the queen was considered to be the *consors regni*.

The wife of emperor Otto I, Adelaide (†999), born a Burgundian princess and widow of king Lothar I of Italy, was actively engaged in politics. Her name is mentioned in many official documents and she acted as a governor in Italy on behalf of her husband. When Otto I died in 973, she continued to reign as a regent despite the fact that her son was eighteen years old. Medieval princes normally came of age at fourteen. Shortly afterwards, Otto II forced Adelaide to resign as a regent. But Otto III was married to a strong woman as well, Theophano (†991), a Byzantine princess who became one of the most important empresses of the Middle Ages. When Otto III died in 983, Theophano, with her mother-in-law Adelaide, and her sister-in-law Maud, an abbess, took over the government of the Empire to secure it for her little son Otto III against his enemies. Otto was just three years old when his father died. The clergy, princes and barons of the Empire mainly supported Theophano.

The empress was quite successful and acted as a very self-confident person who was very sure of herself and her imperial rank. This can be seen in many documents; she did not sign using the title of a widowed empress or regent but she called herself frequently *Theophano divina gratia imperatrix augusta* and in an even more important manner *teophanius divina gratia imperator*. Hence Theophano took a male name and title. The dates indicated in the document mention the number of years since her own coronation as an empress and not those of the reign of her son. It is possible that Theophano followed a Byzantine example because Byzantine empresses like empress Irene in the 9th century signed documents as *Eirene basileus*. But it is possible that Theophano wanted to stress as well in the Western Empire that she was reigning by her own right, independently. But after having reigned during eight years, Theophano died suddenly and her mother-in-law Adelaide took over the government alone. When Otto III came of age in 994, he took over the government and sent his grandmother back to her native country of Burgundy [4].

During the following centuries other empresses like Kunegunde (†1033), the wife of Henry II (†1024), participated actively in politics [5]. Politically active female members of the Salian dynasty were for example Gisela of Swabia (†1043), wife of emperor Conrad II (†1039), and Agnes of Aquitaine (†1077), the widow of Henry III (†1056) and mother of emperor Henry IV (†1106). Agnes became regent after the death of her husband. But then an opposition formed by princes and clergy acted against her. Some bishops openly stated that women were on the same intellectual level as children and that they should not and could not govern a kingdom or empire. Finally, Agnes resigned in 1062 and went to live in a monastery in Rome where she died [6].

A hostile attitude towards the active participation of queens and empresses in politics can still be seen in the following decades and centuries. In the middle of the 12th century, empresses of the Holy Roman Empire no longer played an important role in politics, except in exceptional cases. They were slowly excluded from politics and only allowed to govern their own possessions. In the 14th century, emperor Charles IV (†1378) decided that during official festivities the empress should walk behind the emperor. Her table should be smaller and not so high as that of the emperor. Some historians say that the weakness of the royal power in Germany and the development of territorial states had a negative effect on the role of the empress. The position of the queen and/or empress changed. When at last trained administrators came to live and work in the palaces, the help of the queen in governing the kingdom/empire was no longer needed. She was forced to concentrate her energies on her personal "court", belongings and estates [7].

3. QUEENS OF ENGLAND

The situation in other parts of Europe was quite different. Here we wish to analyse some examples of medieval queens in England. Only a few queens like Isabella of Gloucester, first wife of king John I (†1216) or Mary de Bohun (†1394), wife of king Henry IV (†1413) were members of English feudal families: many English queens came from the kingdom of France and a smaller number of queens were born in other European countries like Scotland, Flanders, Hainault, Navarre, Castile, Provence and Bohemia. Some of these queens became quite famous because of their involvement in politics [8].

One of the most important English queens was Eleanor of Aquitaine (†1204), wife of king Henry II (†1189), and the subject of many studies and even contemporary motion pictures [9]. Still today Eleanor is considered by many historians one of the most important female personalities of the Middle Ages and one of the most active queens in politics. She was born in 1122 as the heiress of the mighty duke of Aquitaine and eventually became the first wife of king Louis VI of France in 1137. She was immediately interested in politics, but found an enemy in Abbot Suger of Saint-Denis who influenced her husband as well. Eleanor took part actively in the crusade of 1146 and accompanied her husband. Eleanor gave the king two daughters but no male heir and finally the marriage was dissolved in 1152. The duchess of Aquitaine returned to her homelands and then married the young Henry of Anjou in the same year. Two years later he became king of England and Eleanor was queen for the second time. Their combined territories were much larger than those of the French king. During her English marriage she gave birth to five sons and three daughters and assured the royal succession in England. King Richard I "the Lionhearted" (†1199) and John I Lackland (†1216) succeeded their father. Eleanor was clearly involved in the government of the kingdom of England and her own duchy of Aquitaine and acted as regent when her husband was absent.

In her later years, Eleanor and her husband became estranged. The restless queen finally left for Aquitaine where she governed for a time, but then she started a rebellion against her husband and was supported by her sons. But Henry II was able to defeat his wife and he imprisoned her in 1173. She was kept as a royal prisoner more or less until the death of the king in 1189. Then she started a new political career at the age of sixty-seven and governed England on behalf of her son Richard who was on a crusade. After the death of Richard in 1199, she was able to secure the throne for her youngest son John I. She even managed to travel a lot. For example she visited Cyprus, where the wedding of Richard and Berengaria of Navarre took place, and Castile, where her daughter Eleanor was married. The Queen decided to marry her grand-daughter Blanche to the future king Louis VII of France and accompanied the bride personally to France in 1201. Finally, she retired and died in the abbey of Fontevrault in 1204 [10]. [See Plate 1]

Quite a few of Eleanor's successors as queen of England continued to be involved directly in politics. Let us just mention some examples. Queen Eleanor of Provence (c. 1220-1293) was born the daughter of Raymond Berengar, count of Provence. She was married in 1236 to king Henry III of England (1207-1272) who became king in 1216 as heir of king John I Lackland. The king and queen had a happy marriage. One of Eleanor's sisters was Margaret of Provence, wife of king Louis IX of France. Like her sister, Eleanor was a very ambitious woman and because of her activities she became quite unpopular in England. Eleanor was able to gain a strong influence on her husband and therefore she managed to provide many members of her French and Savoy family with huge possessions, fiefs and honours in England. As a consequence of this widely discussed misbehaviour, in later centuries foreign princesses who married English kings were no longer allowed to include their relatives or other foreigners in their household.

Queen Eleanor administered her own possessions, which increased enormously during the years of her marriage. Nevertheless, she needed a great amount of money because her expenditure was much higher than her income. Naturally her attempts to get it also contributed to her unpopularity. Queen Eleanor supported her husband in his political tasks and at a certain moment she was named regent of Gascony, an English possession on the Continent. When her husband had to fight against the rebellious barons in England and was defeated in Lewes, Eleanor was forced to go to France to find refuge, but she tried to use her jewels and money to build up a fleet and an army to support her husband. She was in continuous contact with her sister Margaret and other relatives in order to continue her involvement in English politics. At her husband's death in 1272, she became regent for her son, who took over the government when he came back to England. Eleanor changed her life slowly and finally, after a couple of years, she went to live in a nunnery where she died in 1291 [11].

Her daughter-in-law was Eleanor of Castile. This wedding was arranged while Eleanor of Provence was regent of Gascony. The marriage was part of a peace treaty between England and Castile, which also claimed possessions in Gascony. Eleanor of Castile (c. 1240-1290), half-sister of king Alfonso X the Learned of Castile (†1284) was married to Edward (1239-1307), eldest son of Eleanor and Henry, in 1254. When Edward succeeded to his father in 1272, Eleanor of Castile became queen of England but she never became as powerful as Eleanor of Provence and was never officially named regent by her husband [12].

Eleanor of Castile´s son, king Edward II of England (1307-1327), was born in 1284 and in 1308 married Isabella of France (1296-1358), daughter of king Philip IV the Fair of France. This marriage proved to be a very unhappy union because of the homosexuality of the king, but eventually a male heir, the future king Edward III, and three other children were born. In 1324 Isabella was sent as an intermediary by her husband to France to negotiate a peace

Fig. 1
Philippa of Hanault.

between the kingdoms. Isabella decided to stay in France with her son and soon afterwards decided to take a lover, Roger Mortimer, and to start her own political career. She was a very independent woman, openly committing adultery and living with her lover. When she was forced to leave France, she returned to England with an army. Isabella had assembled a great number of supporters and managed to govern the kingdom for a short period on behalf of her son. During the minority of Edward III, Isabella and Mortimer reigned until 1330. That year, the new king turned eighteen and was able to take over the government, supported by several courtiers. He ordered Mortimer to be executed and kept his mother as a prisoner but did not dare let her face a public trial. At first Isabella was deprived of all her possessions but gradually she succeeded in regaining them. She was never able to act again on the political scene but she led a comfortable life as a noble lady in Norfolk and died peacefully in 1358. Still today queen Isabella is known as the "she-wolf of France" and described as a very unpopular queen [13].

Isabella's daughter-in-law proved to be quite a different personality but nevertheless she was also influential, although she stayed a bit more behind the scenes. The son of Edward II and Isabella of France, king Edward III (1327-1377), was born in 1312 and married in 1328 to Philippa of Hainault (c. 1315-1369) (Fig. 1). This union was a quite happy one and Philippa was later well known as a patron of the famous chronicler Jean Froissart. But she was also actively interested in politics and able to act some times on the political scene, exerting some influence. She accompanied her husband on many travels. For example, we may mention her intervention in Calais, pleading for the burghers of Calais condemned to death by her husband [14].

As a final and also striking example let us consider Queen Margaret of Anjou (1429-1482) (Fig. 2) who was born as the daughter of René, duke of Anjou and married to king Henry VI of England in 1445 to secure peace between France and England at the end of the Hundred Years War. Margaret was a very determined woman and exercised considerable political influence at the royal court. When her husband started suffering from a mental illness in 1453, Margaret's political influence became more important as she tried to support her husband and young son during his minority in her fight against her rival, duke Richard of York. She led the royal forces against the duke of York, who was killed on the battle-field in 1460, but finally the son of the deceased duke, Edward, continued the fight against Margaret and her family and took the throne in 1461 as king Edward IV (†1483). Henry VI was captured by his enemies in 1463 and murdered in 1471, his son Edward was killed in a battle in the same year. Queen Margaret was kept as a prisoner and finally released in 1475 after the French king had paid a ransom. She had to renounce all her rights and return to France, where she died quite miserably in 1482 [15].

4. QUEENS OF FRANCE

Let us have a brief look at the kingdom of France. In the kingdom of France we cannot find queens reigning in their own right, by birth [16]. Until the 14th century, this would have

Fig. 2
Mrgaret of Anjou.

been possible in theory, but in fact never happened because all the French kings left male heirs. But we can find many French queens who were politically very active, such as, for example, queen Constance of Arles (†1032), the second wife of king Robert the Pious (†1031). She came from Provence and wanted to support people from that region. Chronicles show us that the pious king feared his wife because of her character. Queen Anne of Kiev (†after 1075) came from Russia and acted successfully as a regent for her son Philip I (†1108).

But the most famous French example of a successful female regency is that of Blanche of Castile (†1252). It is interesting to note that Blanche was the grand-daughter of the famous Eleanor of Aquitaine, the exceptional queen who was first married to king Louis VII of France, then to king Henry II of England. Blanche was the daughter of Eleanor of England and Alphonse VIII of Castile. Obviously she had inherited her political ambitions from her grand-mother. Eleanor travelled personally to Castile to choose her as a bride for the son of the French king, the future Louis VII. King Louis VII (†1226) died after a few years and Blanche became the regent for her son, the new king Louis IX (†1270), the future Louis the Saint. Blanche reigned over the kingdom with only the help of advisers; when her son came of age, she still continued to be involved actively in politics and again became a regent when her son left France to lead a crusade. Blanche was especially successful in establishing the inner stability in the kingdom [17].

King Louis (†1270) himself was married to Margaret of Provence (†1295) who also had strong political ambitions like her sister, Eleanor of Provence, the wife of king Henry III of England (†1272). In Margaret's case we can see that quite often young queens had only limited possibilities to act on the political scene while their mothers-in-law were still alive and also actively involved in politics. Blanche controlled even the private life of the young couple who had to live on separate floors; eventually Louis gave orders to construct a hidden staircase so that he could meet his wife secretly; they were finally able to have many children.

The memory of the famous queen Blanche was still alive long after her death. In a miniature of the 14th century, Blanche is represented a powerful queen and a regent. She is shown as crowned queen sitting on a throne while her little son king Louis is sitting in front of her reading a book; he is accompanied by his teacher, a friar. It is clear that Blanche was supervising the education of her son. In a second contemporary image [See Plate 2], which was made around 1235, we can see both protagonists, Blanche and Louis, again. They are sitting on thrones placed on the same level, although only Louis is holding a sceptre. It is interesting to see that Louis, who was already married at that time to Margaret of Provence, is still represented sitting on the throne beside his mother, the dowager queen, and not beside his wife, the young queen. His mother was the dominant character on the political scene, meanwhile Margaret had to stay in the background. Only after Blanche's death in 1252 can we find Margaret depicted regularly with her husband. Margaret had no official political life before the death of her mother-in-law, as is clearly demonstrated by the royal iconography.

Queen Margaret accompanied king Louis on crusades, but until 1252, the year in which Blanche died, the young queen was not allowed to be openly involved in politics. Her personal dream was to become a successful regent like Blanche. Margaret wanted to take power after the death of Louis, who was not healthy. Finally he died on a crusade in 1270. But Margaret was not appointed regent: not only because her son was already of age but also because she had committed a fatal error years before. Long before the death of her husband, she had forced her son Philip, at that time already eighteen years old and of age, to secretly swear that he would accept her as a regent until he was thirty. This was totally unusual and legally not allowed. Soon after having made this oath, Philip realised what he had done and informed his father who became furious and immediately wrote to the pope, the only person who could release a person from an oath. From that time on, king Louis never named Margaret regent when he left France. After his father's death in 1270, Philip III (†1285) took over the government without any problems. Margaret had to retire and spent her last years in a monastery where she died in 1295 [18].

Let us mention briefly the changes that took place in France concerning queenship during the 14th century. Until 1316 it would have been theoretically possible, as we have seen, for a French royal princess to inherit the kingdom, although this never happened in reality because until that year every French king left a male heir. In 1316 king Louis X died leaving only a daughter and a pregnant wife. His brother Philip became regent during the pregnancy. A little boy, king John I, was born, but he died after a couple of days. The regent was interested in becoming king himself and did not want to see his niece Joan, the legal heiress, on the throne. He asked several lawyers who taught at the Sorbonne to declare that female persons were not allowed to succeed to the kingdom and to reign or even to pass the heritage on to their male children. This so-called Salic Law, made at that time, was presented as very ancient, dating back to the Franks.

Philip V (†1322) and his younger brother Charles IV (†1328) finally died without leaving a male heir, which meant the end of the male succession in the Capetian family. The Valois dynasty became the new royal family of France. No further French king changed this law. In later centuries experts expressed their fear of a reigning French queen. They believed that a woman would be too weak to reign or would marry a foreign prince who might gain influence in the kingdom of France. In 1374 and 1407 royal orders were published which defined exactly the role of a queen as a regent [19].

The political importance of queens nevertheless remained. Several queens acted as regents and were quite powerful, like Isabeau of Bavaria (†1435) (Fig. 3), who however was not a very popular queen and regent. She was born in 1370 in Munich as the daughter of duke Stephan III of Bavaria and the Italian princess Taddea Visconti of Milan. In 1385 Isabeau was married to king Charles VI of France (†1422) who suffered from a mental illness from 1392 on and was incapable of reigning. Isabeau was involved not only in familiar conflicts but in the troubles of the Hundred Years War and the struggle over succession between her son and the English king Henry V as well. Her fate proved quite unhappy and dramatic and has been the subject of scientific studies and of novels and so forth. Especially in novels and drama Isabeau is depicted as an immoral and evil woman [20].

When king Louis XI died in 1483, his son and successor Charles VIII (†1498) was too young to reign but his widow was not appointed regent. The king did not want his wife, queen Charlotte, to be regent but left the regency instead to his eldest daughter Anne de

Fig. 3
Isabeau of Bavaria.

Beaujeu (†1522) who indeed was a very efficient regent. She was a very intelligent woman who proved capable of assuming this task in difficult times. Charles VIII himself married another important woman, Anne of Britanny (†1514), the heiress of the duchy of her birth. She was directly involved in politics during her times, at the end of the Middle Ages and the beginning of the modern period, as queen of France and especially as duchess of Britanny. After the Charles' death she married his successor Louis XII (†1515). When Anne died in 1514 she left her duchy to her daughter Claude (†1524) who became the wife of king Francis I of France (†1547). From that time on Britanny was part of the kingdom of France. Her second daughter, Renée, was married to the duke of Ferrara and became well known as an intellectual woman involved in the Reformation movement [21].

5. QUEENS OF CASTILE AND ARAGON

Let us now consider the Iberian Peninsula in the Middle Ages mentioning a few examples of the political activities of medieval queens. Queen Urraca of Castile (†1126) (Fig. 4). inherited the kingdom in 1109 after the death of her father. After the death of her first husband, a prince of Burgundy who had come to Castile to fight against the Muslims, she married King Alfonso I of Aragon called "the Fighter". This marriage could have been the first step towards a reunification of Aragon and Castile but the couple continued to reign sep-

Fig. 4
The *signum* of Queen Urraca.

arately and independently in their own kingdoms. Especially Urraca's son Alfonso from her first marriage was very reluctant to see his step-father involved in Castilian politics. Husband and wife were both strong personalities and finally the marriage ended up in a divorce granted by the pope. Urraca continued to reign as a queen and later married a local nobleman [22].

King Alfonso I of Aragon died without leaving children and in his testament stated that he wanted to give the whole kingdom to the military orders. His family refused to accept his last will and therefore his brother Ramiro, who was at that time a Benedictine monk, was forced to leave his monastery and marry a princess of Aquitaine to produce heirs. Finally, a daughter named Petronilla was born, but Ramiro obviously preferred the monastic life and engaged his baby-daughter to the much elder count of Barcelona, proclaimed her queen of Aragon and returned to his monastery.

Petronilla became queen of Aragon at the age of two; at the age of fourteen she married her fiancé, count Ramon Berenguer IV of Catalonia who lived in Barcelona. It is interesting to see that she was raised in the household of her husband in a traditional manner and during her marriage she was never really independently active in politics. Officially she was the queen and had to sign all necessary documents, but the decisions were obviously made by her husband. Ramon Berenguer never became king of Aragon, it was still Petronilla who held the *regnum* and the *potestas*. But he acted as tutor and as regent for his wife. In her testament she declared that her only son – not her husband – should be the next king of Aragon. Only in case of the premature death of her son Alfonso, should her husband become king. When Ramon Berenguer IV finally died in 1162, Petronilla appeared on the political scene on her own and acted as a queen although only for brief time. Then she transmitted her power directly to her grown-up son, retired from politics and died in 1173 [23].

It seems quite clear that Petronilla had political abilities, but she had never been trained to live her ambitions openly. She had been raised since she was a baby to be a perfect wife and mother. Furthermore this education had taken place in the household of her future husband who was not interested in having an independent wife. By contrast, Urraca of Castile had been prepared carefully for many years to take power and reign as an independent queen.

In Castile we can find a similar situation concerning the transmission of the royal power from mother to son, but this case is somewhat different. Berenguela of Castile (†1246) was the eldest daughter of king Alfonso VIII and Eleanor of England, a daughter of the famous Eleanor of Aquitaine. Her sister was Blanche of Castile, the above-mentioned queen of France. Like Blanche, Berenguela was a very intelligent woman who was deeply interested in politics. She was married to king Alfonso IX of León and had a son, Fernando, and several other children. Because of consanguinity, her marriage was finally dissolved. After the death of her father and her mother in 1214 she acted as a regent for her younger brother Henry who died in 1217. At that moment, Berenguela became the official heiress of the crown of Castile and possessed the *regnum* and the *potestas* and would have had the possibility to reign as a queen of Castile like Urraca. But Berenguela decided otherwise and transferred her power directly to her seventeen-year-old son Fernando because she wanted him, as heir of the kingdom of León, to unify both kingdoms in the near future. This actually happened in 1230 after the death of Alfonso IX. Berenguela resigned but continued to be active in politics helping her son in all aspects of political life in Castile and abroad by maintaining close relations with many neighbours. It was her decision to marry Fernando III to a grand-daughter of the emperor Frederick Barbarossa in 1219 and to reinforce the international position of the kingdom of Castile in Europe. This German heritage would later help her grandson, king Alfonso X, to be elected emperor [24].

But Berenguela was not the only queen in her family to be involved in politics. Another case of a very active Castilian queen is that of Violante of Aragon, a daughter of king James I the Conqueror of Aragon. She was married to king Alfonso X of Castile, son of the above-mentioned Fernando III and Beatrice of Swabia. During the first years of her marriage she travelled a lot to help maintain peace between Castile and Aragon. In later years, she also founded monasteries and promoted the rise of the Mendicant Orders. In 1275 her eldest son Fernando died suddenly, leaving behind a wife Blanche, daughter of the above-mentioned king Louis IX of France, and several children. Normally, their eldest son would have become the next king of Aragon, but king Alfonso preferred to recognize his second son Sancho as heir. Violante and her daughter-in-law did not share his opinion and protested, but finally the situation took a dramatic turn and as the two women were afraid to stay in Castile, they took the children and escaped to Aragon, where Violante's brother was king. This caused a great scandal in Europe.

Violante and Blanche tried to find supporters everywhere in Europe who would be able to defend the rights of the young children. They started to build up a political network by writing letters to Blanche's mother Margaret, the French dowager queen, her brother the French king, to the English king, to the English queen, a Castilian princess, to Isabel, queen of Portugal, to the pope and other important personalities. It is interesting to see that Blanche received open support from the queens and princesses, creating thus a kind of female network in politics. Finally, after negotiating, Violante returned home but never was really reconciled with her husband. Blanche stayed behind and continued her fight until her brother signed a peace treaty with king Sancho IV of Castile and recognised him as king. She was forced to ratify that treaty as well and then she retired to a French nunnery where she died in 1323. Violante spent several years in Castile consecrating her life to pious works, but occasionally made her way back to the political scene supporting for example her son Sancho, who had started a rebellion against her estranged husband, the king. She died probably in 1300.[25]

In those conflicts between the future king Sancho IV and his father king Alfonso X, it was not Violante who acted as an intermediary but her daughter-in-law, the famous Mary of Molina (†1321) who tried to reconcile father and son. Since the first moments of her marriage to Sancho, Mary is shown in the documents and chronicles as a very active person and strong assistant of her husband. When he died quite young in 1295 she became the official regent for her son Fernando IV (†1312) and later for her grandson Alfonso XI (†1350) during their minority. She was able to secure the throne for her offspring in a period of continuous civil war within the royal family involving their relatives; she reinforced the position of Castile against the attacks of its Christian and Muslim neighbours and played as well an important role in international relations signing for example treaties with Portugal and France and by arranging marriages for her children to maintain peace. In Spain Mary of Molina is still today known as a very capable politician and the most prominent medieval Castilian queen.[26]

6. Conclusion

As a conclusion we can stress that in many countries medieval empresses and queens had the possibility of participating actively in politics. But this participation could be limited due to national practices and laws and changing times. In some countries princesses could inherit the kingdom and rule as queens, although in fact this was not very often the case because in general there were male heirs when the king died. More frequently queens were involved in politics as the wives of a king, or as a dowager queens and regents for their young sons. In those cases their power was in many cases quite important and their tasks theoretically often not limited, although in practice the queens had to find "their place" on the political stage. Some queens were not interesting in politics but most princesses were brought up to take their responsibilities. They received a good education and especially were trained to act as ambassadors of their home-country when they were married to foreign princes. We can meet these queens in situations of conflicts as intercessors, as mediators or match-makers for their children. They acted like men, led wars, made peace treaties, raised children, and took decisions concerning all fields of politics.

 Selected bibliography

Anderson B.S., Zinsser J.P., *A history of their own: Women in Europe from Prehistory to the Present*, 2 vol., New York 1988.

Duggan, A. (ed.), *Queens and queenship in Medieval Europe*, Woodbridge 1997.

Erler M., Kowaleski M. (eds.), *Women and Power in the Middle Ages*, Athens (USA) 1988.

Fößel A., *Die Königin im mittelalterlichen Reich*, Stuttgart 2000.

Garrido E., Folguera P., Ortega M., Segura C., *Historia de las mujeres en España*, Madrid 1997.

Gies F., Gies J., *Marriage and Family in the Middle Ages*, New York 1987.

Gies F., Gies J., *Women in the Middle Ages*, New York, 1987.

Klapisch-Zuber Ch. (ed.), *Histoire des femmes*, vol. 2, *Le Moyen Age*, Paris 1991.

Leyser H., *Medieval Women. A social history of women in England 450-1500*, London 1995.

McCash J. (ed.), *The cultural patronage of medieval women*, Athens (USA) 1996.

Mirrer L. (ed.), *Upon my Husband´s Death. Widows in the literature and histories of Medieval Europe*, Ann Arbor 1992.

Mitchell L.E. (ed.), *Women in Medieval Western European Culture*, New York - London 1999.

Parsons J.C. (ed.), *Medieval queenship*, Stroud 1994.

Shahar Sh., *The fourth estate. A history of women in the Middle Ages*, London-New York 1983.

Stafford P., *Queens, concubines and dowagers. The King's wife in the Early Middle Ages*, Athens 1983.

Vann Th. (ed.), *Queens, regents and potentates*, Cambridge 1993.

Ward J. (ed.), *Women of the English Nobility and Gentry: 1066-1500* (Manchester Medieval Sources Series) Manchester-New York 1995.

 NOTES

[1] See general information about medieval women, queens and queenship, in Shahar Sh., *The fourth estate. A history of women in the Middle Ages*, London-New York 1983; Stafford P., *Queens, concubines and dowagers. The King's wife in the Early Middle Ages*, Athens 1983; Anderson B.S., Zinsser J.P., *A history of their own: Women in Europe from Prehistory to the Present*, 2 vol., New York 1988; Erler M., Kowaleski M. (ed.), *Women and Power in the Middle Ages*, Athens 1988; Brooke C.N.L., *The Medieval Idea of Marriage*, Oxford 1989; Gies F., Gies J., *Marriage and Family in the Middle Ages*, New York 1987; Gies F., Gies J., *Women in the Middle Ages*, New York 1987; Duggan A. (ed.), *Queens and queenship in Medieval Europe*, Woodbridge 1997; Klapisch-Zuber Ch. (ed.), *Histoire des femmes*, vol. 2, *Le Moyen Age*, Paris 1991; Mirrer, L. (ed.), *Upon my Husband's Death. Widows in the literature and histories of Medieval Europe*, Ann Arbor 1992; Vann Th. (ed.), *Queens, regents and potentates*, Cambridge 1993; Parsons J.C. (ed.), *Medieval queenship*, Stroud 1994; McCash J. (ed.), *The cultural patronage of medieval women*, Athens (USA) 1996; Mitchell L.E. (ed.), *Women in Medieval Western European Culture*, New York-London 1999; Nelson J.L., *Medieval Queenship*, in Mitchell L.E. (ed.), *Women in Medieval Western European Culture*, New York-London 1999, pp. 179-208.

[2] This is an introduction to this subject and a brief overview of the political aspects of medieval queenship by presenting various examples from different European countries. Footnotes are used to give special reading indications. General readings are as well indicated in a "Selected Bibliography", see above.

[3] See especially concerning the Merovingian, Carolingian period and the Holy Roman Empire Vogelsang T., *Die Frau als Herrscherin im hohen Mittelalter. Studien zur "consors regni" Formel* (*Göttinger Bausteine zur Geschichtswissenschaft 7*) Göttingen-Frankfurt-Berlin 1954; Konecny S., *Die Frauen des karolingischen Königshauses. Die politische Bedeutung der Ehe und die Stellung der Frau in der fränkischen Herrscherfamilie vom 7. bis zum 10. Jahrhundert* (Dissertationen der Universität Wien 132) Wien 1976; Nelson J., *Queens as Jezebels: The Careers of Brunhild and Balthild in Merovingian History*, in *Medieval Women*. Dedicated and presented to Professor Rosalind M.T. Hill on the Occasion of her seventieth birthday, ed. by D. Baker, Oxford 1978, pp. 31-77; Wemple S.F., *Women in Frankish society. Marriage and cloister (500 to 900)*, Philadelphia 1981; Ketsch P., *Aspekte der rechtlichen und politisch-gesellschaftlichen Situation von Frauen im frühen Mittelalter (500-1150)*, in Kuhn A., Rüsen J. (eds.), *Frauen in der Geschichte*, vol. 2 (Geschichtsdidaktik. Studien, Materialien 8) Düsseldorf 1982, pp. 11-71; Ketsch P., *Die Beteiligung von Frauen an der politischen Herrschaft*, in Kuhn A. (ed.), *Frauen im Mittelalter, vol. 2: Frauenbild und Frauenrechte in Kirche und Gesellschaft. Quellen und Materialien* (Geschichtsdidaktik. Studien, Materialien 19), Düsseldorf 1984, pp. 361-426; Ennen E., *Frauen im Mittelalter*, München 1984; Affeldt W. (ed.), *Frauen in Spätantike und Frühmittelalter. Lebensbedingungen – Lebensnormen – Lebensformen*, Sigmaringen 1990; Uitz E., Pätzold, B., Beyreuther G., *Herrscherinnen und Nonnen. Frauengestalten von der Ottonenzeit bis zu den Staufern*, Berlin 1990; Jäschke K.-U., *Notwendige Gefährtinnen. Königinnen der Salierzeit als Herrscherinnen und Ehefrauen im römisch-deutschen Reich des 11.*

und beginnenden 12. Jahrhunderts, Saarbrücken 1991; Folz R., *Les saintes reines du Moyen Age en Occident (VIe - XIIIe siècles)* (Subsidia Hagiographica 76), Bruxelles 1992; Goetz H.-W., *Frauen im frühen Mittelalter. Frauenbild und Frauenleben im Frankenreich*, Köln-Weimar-Wien 1995; Schnith K. (ed.), *Frauen des Mittelalters in Lebensbildern*, Graz-Wien-Köln 1997; Fößel, A., *Die Königin im mittelalterlichen Reich*, Stuttgart 2000.

[4] See concerning the empress Adelaide and her daughter-in-law empress Theophano Beyreuther G., *Kaiserin Adelheid. "Mutter der Königreiche"*, in *Herrscherinnen und Nonnen*, pp. 43-79; Gussone N., *Trauung und Krönung. Zur Hochzeit der byzantinischen Prinzessin Theophanu mit Kaiser Otto III.*, in *Kaiserin Theophanu. Begegnung des Ostens und Westens um die Wende des ersten Jahrtausends. Gedenkschrift des Kölner Schnütgen Museums zum 1000. Todesjahr der Kaiserin*, ed. by A. v. Euw, P. Schreiner, vol. 2, Köln 1991, pp. 161-173; Leyser K., *Theophanu divina gratia imperatrix augusta: Western and Eastern Emperorship in the later tenth century*, in Reuter T. (ed.), *Communications and power in medieval Europe. The Carolingian and Ottonian Centuries*, London 1994, pp. 143-164; Davids A. (ed.), *The empress Theophano. Byzantium and the West at the turn of the first millennium*, Cambridge 1995.

[5] See concerning Kunegunde p. ex. Baumgärtner I. (ed.), *Kunigunde – eine Kaiserin an der Jahrtausendwende*, Kassel 1997.

[6] See Bulst-Thiele M.-L., *Kaiserin Agnes (Beiträge zur Kulturgeschichte des Mittelalters und der Renaissance 52)* Leipzig-Berlin 1933, repr. Hildesheim 1972 and Black-Veldtrup M., *Kaiserin Agnes (1043-1077). Quellenkritische Studien (Münstersche Historische Forschungen 7)*, Cologne-Weimar-Vienna 1995.

[7] Ketsch, *Aspekte*, p. 44; Fößel, *Königin*, pp. 385ss.

[8] See in general Jewell H., *Women in medieval England*, Manchester 1996. *in the middle ages*, London-New York 1990; Ward J. (ed.), *Women of the English Nobility and Gentry: 1066-1500* (Manchester Medieval Sources Series), Manchester-New York 1995; Leyser H., *Medieval Women. A social history of women in England 450-1500*, London 1995 and for more details especially *Letters of the Queens of England, 1100-1547*, ed. by A. Crawford, Stroud 1994; Jones M.K., Underwood M.G., *The King's Mother: Lady Margaret Beaufort, Countess of Richmond and Derby*, Cambridge 1992; Ward J.C., *English Noblewomen in the Later Middle Ages*, Harlow 1992; Chibnall M., *The Empress Matilda*, London 1991; Stafford P., *Queens, Concubines and Dowagers: the king's wife in the early middle ages*, London 1983.

[9] Concerning Eleanor of Aquitaine just a few studies can be mentioned: Kibler W.W. (ed.), *Eleanor of Aquitaine: Patron and Politician*, Austin 1977; Pernoud R., *Eleanor of Aquitaine*, London 1967; Kelly A., *Eleanor of Aquitaine and the Four Kings*, London 1950; Bagley J.J., *Margaret of Anjou, Queen of England*, London 1948 and especially Crawford, *Letters*, pp. 30-43.

[10] Crawford, *Letters*, pp. 30-34.

[11] Concerning Eleanor of Provence see Crawford A. (ed.): *Letters of the Queens of England, 1100-1547*, pp. 54-67 and Howell M., *Eleanor of Provence, Queenship in Thirteenth-Century England*, Oxford 1998.

[12] Concerning Eleanor of Castile see Crawford, *Letters*, pp. 68-75 and especially Parsons J.C., *Eleanor of Castile. Queen and Society in Thirteenth-Century England*, New York 1995.

[13] Concerning Isabella of France see Crawford, *Letters*, pp. 81-92, a new biography about Isabella is still missing but her life was described in the cycle of novels written by M. Druon.

[14] Concerning Philippa of Hainault see Crawford, *Letters*, pp. 92-100. An exhaustive biography about Philippa has not been written yet.

[15] See Crawford, *Letters*, pp. 119-129 and also Bagley J.J., *Margaret of Anjou, Queen of England*, London 1948.

[16] See concerning the French queen Barry F., *La reine de France*, Paris 1964; Facinger M.F., *A study of medieval queenship: Capetian France. 987-1237*, in "Studies in Medieval and Renaissance History", 5 (1968) pp. 1-48; Bertière S., *Les Reines de France au temps des Valois*, Paris 1994; Cosandey F., *De lance en quenouille. La place de la reine dans l'Etat moderne (14e - 17e siècles)*, in *Annales HSS, juillet-août 1997*, n. 4, pp. 799-820; Cosandey F., *La reine de France. Symbole et pouvoir. XVe - XVIIIe siècles*, Paris 2000.

[17] See Pernoud R., *La reine Blanche*, Paris 1972 and LeGoff J., *Saint Louis*, Paris 1996; Richard J., *Saint Louis*, Paris 1983.

[18] See Sivéry G., *Marguerite de Provence*, Paris 1987.

[19] Cosandey, *Lance and Cosandey*, Reine, 20ss., 36-43.

[20] For Isabeau see Saller M., *Königin Isabeau*, München 1979; Verdon J., *Isabeau de Bavière*, Paris 1981; concerning Isabeau and her husband Charles VI see Autrand F., *Charles VI*, Paris 1986.

[21] For Anne see *Anne de Bretagne et son temps*, catalogue d'exposition, Nantes 1961. To avoid repetitions, this part of our paper had been shortened considerably, see for further information on the French queens and princesses the chapter in this volume by Anne Lemonde.

[22] See in general Garrido E., Folguera P., Ortega M., Segura C., *Historia de las mujeres en España*, Madrid 1997 and especially concerning Urraca Reilly B.F., *The Kingdom of León-Castilla under Queen Urraca 1109-1126*, Princeton 1982; Lacarra J. M., *Vida de Alfonso el Batallador*, Zaragoza 1971.

[23] See Vajay S., *Ramire II le Moine, roi d'Aragon et Agnès de Poitou dans l'histoire et la légende*, in *Mélanges offerts à René Crozet*, ed. by Gallais P., Riou Y.-J., 2 vol., Poitiers 1966, vol. 2, pp. 727-750; Bagué E., Cabestany J., Schramm P.E., *Els Primers Comtes-Reis*, Barcelona 1960 (Història de Catalunya. Biografies catalanes 4), pp. 9-51; Stalls W.C., *Queenship and the royal patrimony in the twelfth-century Iberia: the example of Petronilla of Aragon*, in Vann Th. (ed.), *Queens, Regents and Potentates*, Cambridge 1993, pp. 49-62.

[24] No actual biography of Berenguela exists, but see works concerning her father and son where she is mentioned: González J., *El reino de Castilla en la época de Alfonso VIII*, 3 vol., Madrid 1960; González J., *Reinado y diplomas de Fernando III*, 2 vol., Córdoba 1983; and concerning the cultural influence of Berenguela, her mother and sister Blanca or in French Blanche see Shadis M., *Piety, politics and power: the patronage of Leonor of England and her daughters Berenguela of León and Blanche of Castile*, in McCash J. (ed.), *The cultural patronage of medieval women*, Athens 1996, pp. 202-227.

[25] The studies concerning king Alfonso X are numerous, especially concerning queen Violante and her struggle see Ballesteros Beretta A., *Alfonso X el Sabio*, Barcelona 1963; Vann Th., *The theory and practice of medieval Castilian queenship*, in Vann Th. (ed.), *Queens, Regents and Potentates*, Cambridge 1993, pp. 125-148.

[26] See the excellent biography by Gaibrois de Ballesteros M., *María de Molina, tres veces reina*, Madrid 2nd ed. Madrid 1968.

 SOURCES

Christine de Pizan, in her *Livre des trois vertus* (or *Treasure of the City of Ladies*) describes the activities appropriate to a queen or princess. The critical edition of the text is pubblished by C.C. Willard (Paris 1989). Christine wrote it in 1404 for Margaret of Burgundy.

CI DEVISE LA MANIERE DU VIVRE DE LA SAGE PRINCESSE ET PAR L'ADMONNESTEMENT DE PRUDENCE

Prudence, si que j'ay dit devant, avertira la sage princepce comment l'ordre de son vivre sera riglee, et par elle et par son enortement tendra telle maniere: elle se levera tous les jours assez matin, et seront ses premieres paroles adreçans a Dieu, en disant: Daigne nous, Sire, garder ceste journee de pechié, de mort soubdain, et de toute mauvaise aventure. Ainsi soit il a tous nos parens et amis, aux trespasséz pardon, et a noz subgiéz paix et transquillité. Amen. Pater Noster. Et du surplus d'oroisons ce que devocion lui admenistrera, ne querra entour elle avoir moult grant affaire de service; et ceste voye tenoit, n'a pas moult de temps qu'elle vivoit, la bonne et sage royne Jehanne, femme jadis du roy Charles de France, iiiie du nom, qui se levoit tous les jours ains l'adjournant, alumoit elle meismes sa chandelle pour dire ses heures, et ne souffroit que femme que elle eust se levast ne perdist son somme. Après ce que elle sera preste, yra ouïr ses messes, tant et en tel quantité que sa devocion sera, ou que loisir et temps luy donra: car n'est mie doubte que se ceste dame a qui soit commis grant gouvernement, comme plusieurs font et ont fait a leurs femmes quant les veoyent bonnes et sages et ilz aroyent hors, ou ilz estoient occupéz ailleurs, ilz bailloient la charge a elles et auctorité de governer tout le fait de leur seigneurie et estre le chief du conseil, – et telles dames font a excuser plus meismes vers Dieu se tant n'employent de temps en longues oroisons que celles qui plus ont loisir, ne elles n'ont pas moins de merite de bien et justement entendre a la chose publique et au bien de tous a leur pouoir que elles aroyent de plus longuement vaquer en oroisons, s'ainsi n'estoit que elles voulsissent du tout entendre a la vie contemplative et laissier la vie active, si que j'ay dit. Car la contemplative puet bien sans l'active, mais la droicte bonne active ne puet sans aucune partie de la contemplative.

Ceste dame aura tele ordonnance que a l'issue de sa chapelle, elle meismes par humilité et devocion, en memoire et signe que elle ne doit mie desprisier les povres, donra de sa main l'aumosne; et la endroit se aucunes piteuses requestes lui sont a faire, elle les orra benignement, donra a chascun gracieuse responce, et ceulz que elle pourra en brief temps expedier ne tendra par longue dilacion: et de ce faire accroistra l'aumosne, et aussi sa renommee. Si y aura aucuns preudommes, pour ce que elle ne pourroit par aventure entendre a tout les requestes qui lui venront, qui seront commis a y entendre, et vouldra que yceulx soient / charitables et expediens, et elle meismes de leurs meurs se prendra garde.

Ces choses faictes, se elle est dame qui se mesle du gouvernement, comme dit est, yra au conseil aux jours que tenir se devra; la aura tel port, tel maintien et telle contenance, quant en son hault siege sera assise, que elle semblera bien estre dame de tous, et chascun l'aura en grant reverence, comme leur sage maistresse et de grant auctorité.

Fig. 5
Christine de Pizan with a prince.

Si orra diligemment ce qui sera proposé, et l'oppinion de tous, et tant bien y aura son entente que elle en retenra les principaulx poins des matieres et des conclusions; et bien nottera lesquelx diront mieulx, et par la meilleur consideration et avis et qui lui apparont les plus sages et de la plus vive opinion, et aussi nottera la diversité des opinions, quelz causes et quelz raisons pourroit mouvoir les disans, et ainsi en toutes choses sera avisee. Et quant venra a elle a parler ou respondre, selon le cas qui escherra, si sagement / s'avisera du faire que elle ne puisse estre reputee simple ne ingnorante. Et se avant la main elle puet estre informee de ce que on devra proposer au conseil, et que sur ce, se choses pesantes sont, se pourvoye par sage conseil de response, ce n'est que bien.

Avec ce, ceste dame aura establi sages preudeshommes certaine quantité, qui seront de son conseil, que elle sentira bons, loyaulx, de bonne vie, et non mie moult convoiteux, car c'est ce qui honnist tout entour plusieurs princes et princepces que conseilliers remplis de convoitise, car selon leur inclinacion ilz enduisent et enortent ceulz qu'ilz conseillent, et sans faille ceulx qui habondent en tel vice ne pourroient bien ne loyaument ne au prouffit de ame et honneur de corps conseillier, / et que ilz soient de bonne vie, et de ce doit bien enquerir la prudent dame. A ceulx elle se conseillera par chascun jour a certaine heure des besoignes que elle aura a faire. Après ce conseil du matin yra a table, / qui sera par especial aux jours solennelz et aux festes, voire le plus communement, en sale ou seront assises toutes les dames et damoiselles et les personnes a qui il apertendra, par ordre selon leurs estaz. La sera servie selon qu'il affiert a tel estat, et tandis que l'assiete durera, selon la belle ancienne coustume des roynes et des princepces, aura un preudomme en estant au chief du dois qui dira dictiéz d'anciennes gestes des bons trespasséz, ou d'aucunes bonnes moralitéz ou exemples. La n'aura mie grant noyse menee. Et après les tables levees et dictes graces, s'il y a princes ou seigneurs, chevaliers, escuiers ou damoyselles, ou aultres estrangiers venus vers elle, adonc comme celle qui sera en toutes choses enseignee et apprise, recevra chascun en tel honneur *comme a lui apertendra, si que tous s'en tendront pour contens: parlera a eulx par maniere rassise a joyeux visage, aux anciens d'une guise plus / pesante, et aux joennes d'une aultre plus riant. Et se adonc vient la a parler ou ouïr de aucuns esbatemens ou d'aucunes joyeusetéz, elle s'i saura contenir par si plaisant maniere que tous diront que c'est une gracieuse dame et qui bien scet son maintien en tous endroiz.*

Aprés les espices prises et que il sera temps de retraire, la dame s'en yra en sa chambre. La un petit se reposera, se besoin en a; puis après, s'il est jour ouvrier et elle n'a aucune aultre occupacion plus grant, pour eschiver oiseuse se prendra a faire aucun ouvrage, et environ elle fera semblablement ouvrer ses filles et ses femmes; et la a privé vouldra que hardiement chascune devise de toutes honnestes joyeusetéz si que il lui plaira, et elle meismes rira avecques elles et s'esbatra en devisant si famillierement que toutes loueront sa grant priveté et benigneté et l'aimeront de tout leur courage. Ainsi fera jusques a heure de vespres que elle yra ouïr / en sa chappelle, se il est jour de feste, se aucune autre grant occupacion ne l'empesche, ou les dira sans faillir avec sa chappellaine. Et apprés ce fait, s'il est en esté, s'en yra esbatre en aucun vergier jusques a heure de soupper. La yra et venra pour sa santé, si vouldra que se aucuns ont a besoingnier a elle pour certaines causes que ilz soient laisséz entrer et les orra. Aprés son soupper, vers le couchier, son retour sera a Dieu en oroisons, et ainsi se finera l'ordre des communes journees de la prudent princepce vivant en bonne et saincte activeté.

THE WAY OF LIFE OF THE WISE PRINCESS

Prudence, as I have said before, will advise the wise princess how her life should be ordered, and as a result she will adopt the following way of life. She will rise quite early every day and address her first words to God, saying, "Lord, I beseech thee to guard us this day from sin, from sudden death and from all evil mischance, and also protect all our relatives and friends. To those who have passed on, pardon, and to our subjects, peace and tranquillity. Amen, Pater Noster.". She will say such additional prayers as her devotion may prompt her to, but she will not insist on having a great attendance of servants around her. (The good and wise Queen Jeanne, the late wife of King Charles V of France, followed this course when she was alive. She rose every morning before daylight, lit her candle herself to say her prayers, and did not allow any woman of hers to get up or lose sleep on her account.)

When the lady is ready she will go to hear her Masses, as many as accord with her devotion and as time and leisure will permit her. For there is no doubt that this lady, to whom great powers to govern are entrusted, will merit the trust that many lords have, and have had, in their wives when they see that they are good and prudent and they themselves have to go away to be occupied elsewhere. The husbands give them the responsibility and authority to govern and to be head of the council. Such ladies are more to be excused in the eyes of God if they do not spend so much time in long prayers as those who have more leisure, nor do they have less merit in attending conscientiously to public affairs than those who occupy themselves more with prayers (unless they intend devote themselves to the contemplative life and leave the active life).

But as I have said before, the contemplative life can manage quite well without the active, but the good and proper active life cannot function without some part of the contemplative. This lady will have such a good, orderly system that as she leaves her chapel there will be some poor people et the door to whom she herself with humility and devotion will give alms from her own hand, and if any deserving petitions are made to her, she will hear them kindly and give a gracious reply. She will not detain those that she can deal with quickly, and she will therefore increase her alms and also her great renown. If she perhaps cannot consider all the requests that are made to her, certain gentlemen will be appointed to hear them. She will wish them to be charitable and work quickly, and she herself will watch over their conduct.

When she has done these things, if she has responsibility of government, she will go to the council on days when it is held. There she will have such a bearing, such a manner and such an expression when she is seated in her high seat that she will indeed seem to be the lady and mistress over all, and everyone will hold her in great reverence as their wise mistress with great authority. She will conscientiously hear the proposals that are put forward and listen to everyone's opinion. She will be so attentive that she will grasp the principal points and conclusions of matters and will note carefully which of her counsellors speak better and with the best deliberation and advice, and which seem to her the most prudent and intelligent. And she will also note, in the diversity of opinion, which causes and which reasons most stir the speakers. In this way she will attend to everything, and when someone comes to her to speak on a subject or to reply, according to the circumstances, so wisely will she consider the matter that she cannot be thought simple or ignorant. If she can find out in advance what someone is going to propose and what the ramifications of it may be, and if she can with wise counsel think of a suitable reply, it is all to the good. Furthermore, this lady will establish a certain number of wise gentlemen who will sit on her council, who she will deem good, loyal, virtuous and not too covetous. A great many princes and princesses are put to shame by counsellors filled with covetousness, for according to their own inclinations they incite and encourage those whom they counsel. Inevitably, those who indulge in such vice counsel neither well nor loyally, neither to the profit of their souls nor to the honour of their bodies, and so the prudent lady must inquire whether they lead virtuous lives. She will be counselled every day by these gentlemen at a certain hour about the necessary matters that she has to deal with.

After the morning council she will have her midday meal, which ordinarily and especially on solemn days and on feast will be in the hall, where the ladies and maidens are seated, and other suitable persons ranked according to their positions at court. There she will be served in a manner befitting her rank, and while the plates are still on the table (according to the fine old custom of queen and princesses) she will have a gentleman at hand who will speak of the deeds of some good deceased person, or will speak on some excellent moral subject or tell stories of exemplary lives. No dispute will be conducted there. After the tables have been taken up and grace has been said, if there are any princes or lords present, if there are any ladies or damsels or other visitors around her, then she will receive each of them in such honour as is fitting so that everyone will feel contented. She will speak to them in a thoughtful manner, with a pleasant expression; to the elderly people in a more serious manner, to the young people in a different and merrier one. And if one happens to say or to hear any amusing thing or any merriment she will know how to contain it with such a pleasant manner that everyone will say that she is a gracious lady and one who well knows her manners in all places.

After the spices have been taken and it is time to retire, the lady will go to her chamber, where she will rest for a short while if she feels the need to. Then afterwards, if it is a weekday and she has no other more important occupation with which to avoid idleness, she will take up some work, and she will have the women and girls around her to choose freely whatever she likes from all respectable kinds of merriment, and she herself will laugh with them and divert herself in private gatherings so unconstrainedly that they will all praise her great liberty and indulgence and they will love her with all their hearts. She will be occupied like this until the hour of vespers, when she will go to hear them in her chapel if it is a feast day and if no weighty business prevents her, or otherwise she will say them without fail with her lady chaplain. After doing this, if it is summer, she will go off to amuse herself in a garden until suppertime, walking up and down for her healt. She will wish that if any persons need to see her for any reason they will be allowed to enter and she will hear them. At bedtime she will pray to God. And that concludes the schedule of the ordinary day of the prudent princess living in good and holy occupation.

SEE PLATES 1-2

Nationbuilding and Gender in 19th-century Germany

Sybille Küster

Universität Hannover

Aus geschlechtergeschichtlicher Perspektive erhalten die gleichursprünglichen Prozesse der Inklusion und Exklusion, welche die moderne europäische Nation historisch gekennzeichnet haben, eine spezifische Ausprägung. Diese These wird am Beispiel des Konstitutionsprozesses der deutschen Nation im 19. Jahrhundert in Hinblick auf zwei Themenfelder entwickelt: (1) Die Formierung nationaler Identität in Kategorien des Krieges, der Feindschaft und der nationalen Verteidigung trug zu der diskursiven Konstruktion eines asymmetrischen Geschlechterverhältnisses bei, in desssen Kontext die politische Teilhabe an der Nation an Attribute militarisierter Männlichkeit bzw. männlichen Soldatentums geknüpft wurde. (2) Gleichzeitig idealisierte und legitimierte der Aufstieg Deutschlands als Volks- und Kulturnation die Trennung der Geschlechtersphären als Ausdruck einer angeblich überzeitlichen deutschen Kulturtradition. Gleichwohl schloss die nationale Mobilmachung Frauen nicht gänzlich aus. Die symbolische Zusammenfügung von Vaterland und heimischem Herd – die Sicht auf die Familie als Keimzelle der deutschen Nation – bedingte, dass die Beteiligung beider Geschlechter an der Nationsbildung unabdingbar war. Während diese integrative Dynamik weibliche Handlungsspielräume erweiterte und Frauen aus zumeist bürgerlichen Schichten vielfältige Möglichkeiten des öffentlichen Engagements im nationalistischen Sinne erschloss, verstärkte die asymmetrische Konstruktion der Geschlechter-Differenz das Bild einer 'männlichen' Nation und begründete historisch folgenreiche soziale Hierarchien und Ungleichheiten im Zugang zu politischer Macht. In dieser Konstellation wurden Frauen nicht als Staatsbürgerinnen oder politisch autonome Subjekte, sondern als letztlich untergeordnetes Komplementär-Geschlecht, als dem männlichen Part zugeordnete Ehefrauen, Mütter, Schwestern oder Töchter in die Nation einbezogen. Die emanzipatorische Dimension des Nationenkonzepts, die in der prinzipiellen Gleichstellung seiner Angehörigen liegt, ist somit von Anfang an durch ein Moment der internen Abgrenzung und Ausschließung entlang der Demarkationslinie 'Geschlecht' gebrochen.

Sybille Küster, born in 1963, studied history, political science and literature at Washington State University, the University of Zimbabwe in Harare, the School of Oriental and African Studies (SOAS) in London and the University of Hannover, Germany, where she received her PhD in 1998. She now teaches African colonial and modern German history at the University of Hannover. She is the coordinator of the Gender Studies program at the University of Hannover and one of the regional coordinators of the German Federation for Research in Women's History. Her fields of research and publication include the history of colonial education in southern Africa, gender history in 19th and 20th century Germany as well as current debates in postcolonial criticism and theory.

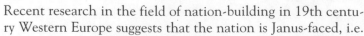

INTRODUCTION

Recent research in the field of nation-building in 19th century Western Europe suggests that the nation is Janus-faced, i.e. that the nation is a two-sided affair. From the moment of its inception the nation rests on two elements which are central to its development: the promise to include all its members as equal participants on the one hand, and the propensity for violence on the other hand. It is arguably the most characteristic trait of the nation to combine opportunities of integration and identification with mechanisms of exclusion, the drawing of physical and discursive boundaries and the definition of who is considered to be the nation's enemy or antagonist. On the one hand the 'democratization' of the nation implied that social boundaries would be overcome and that the bourgeois claim to civil rights would undergo a process of continuous dilution. According to Hans-Ulrich Wehler, "in the long run the egalitarian national democracy, that comprehended everyone without exception as a fully eligible political citizen, proved to be a demand that could not be put on hold" [1]. On the other hand national sovereignty could only be determined by way of comparison, through a process of demarcation. This external demarcation corresponded with the construction of unity within, which at the same time worked towards excluding those groups that were not regarded as belonging to the nation—be it for religious, ethnic, political or cultural reasons.

Here I would like to explore the articulation of these simultaneous processes of inclusion and exclusion – arguably the founding principles of the nation – by looking at them from a gender perspective. How are gender and nation-building related in 19th-century Germany? Do women belong to the nation? Is the nation a male domain? Or is it a neutral, an ungendered area that has nothing to do with the way in which gender difference and gender relations are formulated and structured? The suggestion I would like to put forward follows the work of Ute Frevert, Charlotte Tacke, Mechthild Rumpf and others, according to whom the nation cannot be conceptualized or understood without reference to gender constructions and gender relations. I will develop this argument with respect to the way in which the German nation was constituted. Social relations as well as the self-perception of the German nation in the 19th century embrace women *and* men; however this process of inclusion unfolds in a specific manner which postulates an asymmetrical system of gender relations that is consolidated in the course of time. Contrary to men, in this constellation women are incorporated into the nation not as political citizens or politically autonomous subjects, but as a subordinated, complementary gender; as wives, mothers, sisters or daughters to their male counterparts. In this immediate sense the nation can be described as 'male'. And yet, women were not wholly excluded from the process of nationbuilding. Times of political change and nationalist transformation provided women with manifold opportunities to participate in national affairs and extend their scope of activities.

Here of course I can only begin to address the complexity inherent in this contradictory constellation of being included and excluded at the same time. I would like to introduce two perspectives on the connection between nationbuilding and gender. The first perspective relates to the militarization of German society in the 19th century, in the course of which the suggestive power of 'war' rises to dominate collective memory and perception.

The second perspective centers around the model of nation building that determined the development of the German nation as a *Volks- or Kulturnation.*

Let me start with the first perspective.

NATIONALISM, WAR AND GENDER

Recent studies emphasize the significance of the means of violence and force as constitutive factors in the origin of nations in Western, Southern and Central Europe. In this vein Hagen Schulze states that "if not the origin of nation, war might very well be considered its catalyst. From the beginning European nations came into their own by way of marking themselves off against their neighbors through hostility and through military combat". Dieter Langewiesche adds that, "as far as the origin of nation states is concerned we will have to take this argument a step further: war as the father of nation states, not only [as] their catalyst. [...] All European nation states of the 19th century – not only the German and the Italian nation state – originated as the children of war, and in the 20th century it was the two world wars that triggered both of the great founding movements of nation states" [2].

In Germany, the Prussian defeat of 1806 at Jena and Auerstedt, the invasion of Berlin by Napoleon and the humiliation connected with these events set off a patriotic revival. Subsequently, a national movement developed that surpassed territorial boundaries and that reached its first climax with the voluntary participation in the so-called *Freiheitskriege* (liberation wars) from 1813-1815. According to Hagen Schulze [3], at the time mobilization in a nationalist sense did not reach much beyond the educated and propertied citizens and artisans in the cities. The motivation of nationalist euphoria was of a negative kind: the hatred against Napoleon and the cry for national freedom, not in the sense of liberal claims for constitutional reform but in the sense of freedom from French oppression. The mass experience of national unity and solidarity manifested itself solely with regard to the image of an enemy which in turn produced an idea of national identity. As Schulze remarks, even if it still took one or two generations for this national sentiment to grip the masses and become deeply and permanently entrenched, a specific combination of national identity and belligerent militancy had come to the fore. This combination was to be consolidated in the following decades.

This conception of the German nation – emerging with the liberation wars at the beginning of the 19th century – remained bound to the experience of war and thus to a specific image of belligerent masculinity and a complementary, self-sacrificing ideal of femininity. The nation was portrayed as a brotherhood of warriors; according to Ute Frevert [4], in German national discourse of the 19th century all adjectives relating to the nation (belligerent, strong, prepared) referred to 'male' qualities. The postulation of equality within the confines of the nation was directly deduced from the preparedness to defend the nation outwardly and to sacrifice one's life for this cause if need be. It was a widespread conviction that the unity of the nation grew out of struggle and war; in this fashion the liberation wars were interpreted as the regeneration of the nation while the coming into being of the German *volk* (people) was intimately linked to the defense against an external enemy. With the introduction of universal compulsory military service, military combat was performed by 'national warriors' and 'civilian soldiers', and no longer by mercenaries or by men subjected to life-long servitude. The national army represented the 'people in arms', and in contemporary national propaganda there was no longer any substantial difference between the army and the nation [5]. Universal conscription and political participation, equality in war and equality in the national community presupposed each other [6]. This equation of political participation and militarized masculinity effectively excluded women; participation in the nation was linked to the defense of the nation and thus reserved for male warriors.

And still, national mobilization did not entirely exclude women although the scope of women's activites was decidedly different from that of their male counterparts: in the case of war women did not potentially sacrifice themselves but rather their male next of kin: their husbands, sons or brothers. Women's engagement ranged from the individual, material and financial support of war volunteers to the founding of the so-called patriotic women's associations that took care of war casualties and often provided financial relief for widows and orphans. In nationalist discourse female love, devotion and sacrifice constituted the necessary counterpart of male belligerence. The character traits ascribed to women predestined them to their tasks of strengthening the *volk* on the home front: their responsibilities within the national community encompassed the sphere of reproduction, rearing children, in particular boys to become warriors, nursing the wounded and the sick, and sustaining their men's war morale [7].

Summing up we can say that the formation of national identity in categories of war, antagonism and national defense worked towards consolidating the polarity of gender characters; the dead soldier becomes the mythic symbol of the nation whose sense of self is crucially shaped by the discursive construction of an asymmetrical gender system.

I would like to mention only briefly the consequences that this constellation harbored in terms of an emerging understanding of national politics. In the course of the 19th century the tying together of war and nation, of military force and national 'male' politics resulted in a far-reaching militarization of political culture in Germany. Ideas on how politics worked, on how political decisions were to be made and conflicts were to be solved were closely bound to ideas about the essence of war and soldiery. To be in politics meant to distinguish between friend and foe, to arrive at clear decisions without 'ifs, ands or buts', and to beat one's adversary. The dichotomizing military principle of 'victory or defeat' became constitutive for patterns of interpretation in the field of politics. Democracy was equated with pettycoat-government, Western civility, effeminate self-indulgence and so forth, whereas the German state was celebrated as a brotherhood of soldiers and heroes. According to Thomas Kühne, the ability and preparedness to 'decide' became the core of the ideal of masculinity, and it remained one of the key elements of hegemonic masculinity in Germany up to the end of the 'Third Reich'. Widely propagated, "habitually strengthened and practiced on a daily basis, ['decisionism'] defined the seemingly 'self-evident' framework of national politics" [8].

KULTURNATION AND GENDER

I would now like to discuss the second perspective on the way nationbuilding and gender are interrelated, that is, the model of nationbuilding that shaped the development of Germany as a *Volks-* or *Kulturnation*.

It was not until 1871 that the German nation became a nation state. It was constituted not through the sovereignty of the people, i.e. the claim for equal rights of all citizens, but through Bismarck's 'blood-and-iron' politics and a national, racial or ethnic understanding of what it means to be German [9]. The German counterpart to the nation of citizens, brought about by the French Revolution, was the model of the *Kulturnation*: an imagined unity without a centralized state and without democracy. The main protagonists in projecting this *Kulturnation* in the 19th century were a group of German scholars in the emerging field of national historiography and the intellectual and cultural elite of the rising middle classes. The concept of the *Kulturnation* centered around ideas of a common racial descent and a legacy of a German 'high' culture and a moral-ethical community that could be traced back over centuries. As Rumpf [10] remarks, intimately related to this notion of the *volk* was an essentialist definition of the nature of the German people and their collective identity. This definition worked towards creating the German Nation on a symbolic level and teleologically projected it into the future. The revolution of 1848 could not reverse this tendency as it did not succeed in establishing an egalitarian model of a nation of citizens. Consequently, the cultural homogenization of the German people and the subsequent unity of the nation state were legitimized in a *völkisch* or national fashion, with reference to the principle of an alleged common racial descent.

Contrary to the nation of citizens, this cultural or *völkisch* construct did not rely on theories of democracy for its foundation. From the beginning and as a crucial part of its conception, an asymmetrical gender system was idealized and legitimized as the cultural heritage of the *volk*, "as an expression of the will of the people or of collective popular sentiment" [11]. At the beginning of the German history of the nation, Arminius (*Hermann der Cherusker*) stood as the shining example of the German man: ever since Arminius rallied the Germanic tribes around himself and led them against the Roman invaders – so it was argued in the 19th century – German warriors defended their 'nation' against the external enemy over and over again. Whereas the Germanic or German man excelled by virtue of his belligerence – his bravery, his physical strength, his fearlessness – his helpmate in the struggle, the German woman, was depicted as faithful, humble and self-sacrificing. In the *Ladies' Universal Encyclopedia* published in the 1830s under the headword 'Germany (women)' we can read the following, "The inner character of the German woman – we confess it with pride! – has remained essentially the same from the oldest to the most recent times [...] She is still filled with the gentleness, the faithfulness, the generosity, the humbleness, the chastity, the self-sacrifice, the sweet modesty that inspired her in the times of Tacitus... Together with their men they raised their children to become warriors... They accompanied their men to the battlefields, encouraged them from above through chants and cheers, dressed their men's wounds and nursed them... They rarely adorned themselves with rings or bracelets, and if they did the jewellery had surely been taken as booty in battle by their loyal husbands... Respectability was their highest virtue, and just as the man's religion was bravery, the wife's religion was chastity... Her heart belonged to her husband, her love to her fatherland" [12].

In this way gender characteristics were historically legitimized and portrayed as an expression of an allegedly timeless German cultural tradition. They in turn became a crucial element of German national identity, especially when the line was drawn between Germany and the 'archenemy' France. The moral elevation of the German *volk* corresponded with the tying together of national gender characteristics and national stereotypes. As Tacke remarks, in nationalist discourse not only did German culture stand in hostile opposition to French civilization, this demarcation was reinforced by the insurmountable opposition of national gender characteristics: "The idea of a German nature was closely connected with the image of the German woman as the one who defends German culture and, with her feminine virtues, constituted a bulwark against 'French trumpery' and 'foreign influences'. Sensuality and lasciviousness, frivolity and carelessness, coquetry and love of pleasure were all seen as French vices conveyed through the female gender and from which the German woman as well as the German nation had to be protected" [13]. The difference between the German and the French woman underlined the national antagonism between Germany and France.

To quite an extent, these discursively constructed oppositions between male and female, public-belligerent behavior and domestic-supportive behavior determined not only the thinking but also the spheres of activity of nationalistically-minded men and women. As Frevert [14] remarks, men and women both made sacrifices on the altar of the fatherland, however they did so within the scope of different patriotic practices. Men demonstrated their national allegiance through rendering military service, through defending their fatherland in case of attack, through their work in national and civil associations and through their still oftentimes indirect participation in national politics. Even if women were barred from the most noble national rights and duties such as military service, participation in war and political activities, in the course of the 19th century they nevertheless took part in the national awakening and expressed their patriotic convictions in a variety of ways. As an exceptional case, the women who actively battled on the streets during the revolution of 1848 have become famous. The majority of middle-class women, however, demonstrated their patriotism in a less militant way: as early as during the time of the liberation wars at the beginning of the 19th century they founded a number of patriotic women's associations. In the 1840s women paid tribute to the national cause by boycotting 'foreign-made textiles' and instead wearing the 'beautiful feminine dress of the new German fatherland'. Having been excluded from the places of major national and public activity, the spaces where women got involved were the marketplace, the streets, the schools, the sewing-table, the honorary grandstand at public celebrations, the ballroom, the choral society and the women's associations [15]. During the period of war from 1866 to 1871 the *Vaterländische* women's association was founded, the patriotic aspirations of which were already evident in its name and whose membership was to increase to 600,000 by 1914 [16]. I have already mentioned the involvement of women in war activities in the form of nursing the wounded and collecting financial and material donations as a part of their engagement in charity work. Although these activities were hardly ever linked to a demand for political participation and civil rights, women still documented that they were very much aware of having their place in the German nation as 'daughters of the *volk*', as 'German' women who participated with a great deal of enthusiasm in the multitude of patriotic processions and national commemorations that permeated the 19th century. On these occasions, as symbols of the chaste, loyal woman who complemented the German warrior-soldier, dressed in white and adorned with flowers, they often presented the men with self-made and embroidered banners and thus became an indispensable part of the image conjured up to represent the 'German national body'. In the German version of female patriotic participation in national affairs, the extension of the scope of women's activities went hand in hand with a fundamental self-restriction inherent in an emphasis on the duty, not the rights, of women to serve their fatherland.

CONCLUSION

Let me draw my arguments together. The picture that emerges is to some extent an ambivalent one. On the one hand social realities and the way in which the German nation of the 19th century came to perceive itself opened up additional opportunities of participation for both men and women. The symbolic merging of fatherland and domestic hearth as well as the combination of the concept of nation with allegedly timeless German cultural traditions meant that the process of nationbuilding required the participation of both genders. In the context of the national mobilization that permeated all of society, the physical, material and spiritual reproduction of the German nation relied to a remarkable extent on women's contributions. On the other hand, this mechanism of integration was structurally accompanied by an almost hermetic discursive segregation of gender', spheres. This discursive segregation became stronger over the years as it gained legitimacy through the commonly made reference to the construct of a specifically German cultural and gender order traceable to times immemorial. As the 'complementary gender' women were overwhelmingly pushed towards the performance of emotional and material auxiliary services. The distinctly male connotation of the concept of the nation – the equation of nation with male belligerence – shaped an asymmetrical system of gender relations and excluded women from participation in the political realm. The nation cannot be understood – and here I am taking up the point that I made at the beginning – without reference to the construction of gender differences and gender relations. And vice versa: the way in which men and women are positioned in relation to each other in a certain society cannot be understood without reference to the constitution of the nation state. For comparative purposes, which become more and more important with the growing together of the countries of Europe, the category of 'gender' is therefore a structuring principle which we can use to determine relations of similarity and difference.

In Germany the founding principle of the nation state, which embraces processes of inclusion and exclusion occurring at the same time, acquires a specific twist: the nation essentially constitutes itself through the asymmetrical construction of gender differences. These in turn worked towards establishing social hierarchies and inequalities that prevented women from gaining full status as politically eligible German citizens. This basic constellation, which works on a structural as well as on a symbolic level, survived and continued to be effective long after women gained the right to vote in 1918. From its very beginning, the emancipatory dimension of the nation concept, which lies in the essential equality of all people belonging to the nation, is curtailed by a founding structure of internal division and exclusion along gender lines. While the antagonism towards France is crucially played out in the construction of national gender characteristics, the German political nation is constituted as a brotherhood of warriors and soldiers.

 NOTES

[1] Wehler H.-U., *Deutsche Gesellschaftsgeschichte*, vol. 1, *Vom Feudalismus des Alten Reiches bis zur defensiven Modernisierung in der Reformära, 1700-1815*, Munich 1987, p. 508 (this translation and those below are my own). In general, on gender and nationalism, see Hagemann K., *Heldenmütter, Kriegerbräute und Amazonen. Entwürfe 'patriotischer' Weiblichkeit zur Zeit der Freiheitskriege*, in Frevert U. (ed.), *Militär und Gesellschaft im 19. und 20. Jahrhundert*, Stuttgart 1997, pp. 174-200 and, by the same Author, *Der Bürger als 'Nationalkrieger'. Entwürfe von Militär, Nation und Männlichkeit in der Zeit der Freiheitskriege*, in Hagemann K., Pröve R. (eds.), *Landsknechte, Soldatenfrauen und Nationalkrieger. Militär, Krieg und Geschlechterordnung im historischen Wandel*, Frankfurt a. M., New York 1998, pp. 74-102.

[2] Schulze H., *Staat und Nation in der europäischen Geschichte*, Munich 1999, p. 126; Langewiesche D., *Nation, Nationalismus, Nationalstaat. Forschungsstand und Forschungspersektiven*, in "Neue Politische Literatur", 40, 1995, p. 195.

[3] Schulze H., *Staat und Nation in der europäischen Geschichte*, pp. 200-203.

[4] Frevert U., *Nation, Krieg und Geschlecht im 19. Jahrhundert*, in Hettling M., Nolte P. (eds.), *Nation und Gesellschaft in Deutschland. Historische Essays*, Munich 1996, p. 154.

[5] Ibid., p. 155.

[6] Tacke C., *Nation und Geschlechtscharaktere*, in *Frauen und Nation*, Tübingen 1996, pp. 38, 42.

[7] Ibid., pp. 42, 43.

[8] Kühne T., *Staatspolitik, Frauenpolitik, Männerpolitik: Politikgeschichte als Geschlechtergeschichte*, in Medick H., Trepp A.C. (eds.), *Geschlechtergeschichte und Allgemeine Geschichte. Herausforderungen und Perspektiven*, Göttingen 1998, p. 218.

[9] Rumpf M., *'Teures Vaterland, die Wiege alles Großen und Guten'. Die Befreiungskriege 1813-1815 als Altar für deutschen Volksgeist*, in Eifler C. (ed.), *Militär – Gewalt – Geschlechterverhältnis*, Frauenbündnis Projekt Osnabrück, Osnabrück 1999, pp. 45, 46.

[10] Ibid., p. 49.

[11] Ibid., p. 50.

[12] Tacke C., *Nation und Geschlechtscharaktere*, pp. 39-40.

[13] Ibid., pp. 42-43.

[14] Frevert U., *Nation, Krieg und Geschlecht im 19. Jahrhundert*, p. 161.

[15] Lipp C., *Vorwort*, in Lipp C. (ed.), *Schimpfende Weiber und patriotische Jungfrauen. Frauen im Vormärz und in der Revolution 1848/49*, Baden-Baden 1998, p. 9.

[16] Frevert U., *Nation, Krieg und Geschlecht im 19. Jahrhundert*, p. 162.

SOURCES

Würde der Frauen

Ehret die Frauen! sie flechten und weben
Himmlische Rosen ins irdische Leben,
Flechten der Liebe beglückendes Band,
Und in der Grazie züchtigem Schleier
Nähren sie wachsam das ewige Feuer
Schöner Gefühle mit heiliger Hand.

Ewig aus der Wahrheit Schranken
Schweift des Mannes wilde Kraft,
Unstet treiben die Gedanken
Auf dem Meer der Leidenschaft.
Gierig greift er in die Ferne,
Nimmer wird sein Herz gestillt,
Rastlos durch entlegne Sterne
Jagt er seines Traumes Bild.

Aber mit zauberisch fesselndem Blicke
Winken die Frauen den Flüchtigen
        zurücke,
Warnend zurück in der Gegenwart Spur.
In der Mutter bescheidener Hütte
Sind sie geblieben mit schamhafter Sitte,
Treue Töchter der frommen Natur.

Feindlich ist des Mannes Streben,
Mit zermalmender Gewalt
Geht der Wilde durch das Leben,
Ohne Rast und Aufenthalt.
Was er schuf, zerstört er wieder,
Nimmer ruht der Wünsche Streit,
Nimmer, wie das Haupt der Hyder
Ewig fällt und sich erneut.

Aber, zufrieden mit stillerem Ruhme,
Brechen die Frauen des Augenblicks
        Blume,
Nähren sie sorgsam mit liebendem Fleiß,
Freier in ihrem gebundenen Wirken,
Reicher als er in des Wissens Bezirken
Und in der Dichtung unendlichem Kreis.

Streng und stolz sich selbst genügend,
Kennt des Mannes kalte Brust,
Herzlich an ein Herz sich schmiegend,
Nicht der Liebe Götterlust,
Kennet nicht den Tausch der Seelen,
Nicht in Tränen schmilzt er hin,
Selbst des Lebens Kämpfe stählen
Härter seinen harten Sinn.

Aber, wie leise vom Zephir erschüttert
Schnell die äolische Harfe erzittert,
Also die fühlende Seele der Frau.
Zärtlich geängstigt vom Bilde der
        Qualen,
Wallet der liebende Busen, es strahlen
Perlend die Augen von himmlischem
        Tau.

In der Männer Herrschgebiete
Gilt der Stärke trotzig Recht;
Mit dem Schwert beweist der Skythe,
Und der Perser wird zum Knecht.
Es befehden sich im Grimme
Die Begierden wild und roh,
Und der Eris rauhe Stimme
Waltet, wo die Charis floh.

Aber mit sanft überredender Bitte
Führen die Frauen den Zepter der Sitte,
Löschen die Zwietracht, die tobend
        entglüht,
Lehren die Kräfte, die feindlich sich
        hassen,
Sich in der lieblichen Form zu umfassen,
Und vereinen, was ewig sich flieht.

Friedrich Schiller (1795)

Dignity of Women

Honor the women! They're roses celestial
Twining and weaving in lives terrestrial,
Weaving the bond of the most blessed love
Veiled in the Graces' most modest attire
Nourish they watchful the e'erlasting fire
Of lovely feelings with hand from above.

To truth's limits ever endless
Man with wild force doth flee,
Thoughts do drive him ever restless
Onto passion's stormy sea.
Greedy grasps he the eternal,
Silent will his heart be ne'er,
Restless through the stars supernal
Hunts he his dream's image e'er.

But with their glances so magicly chaining
Beckon the women the fug'tive restraining,
Warning him back in their presence anew.
In the mother's most moderate quarters
They have remained yet with modesty's manners,
Nature's daughters, with piety true.

Hostile e'er the man is striving,
With a crushing force doth roam,
Wildly through his life surviving,
Without rest and without home.
What he builds, he ruins later,
Never rests the wishes' strife,
Never, as the head of Hydra
Falls and e'er renews its life.

But they, contented with quieter honor,
Pluck now the women the moment's fine
flower,
Nourish it lovingly and diligently,
They have in their bounded work greater freedom,
Richer than man, too, in districts of wisdom
And in the unending sphere, poetry.

Stern and proudly self-depending,
Knoweth man's cool breast thereof,
Heartily to beat though bending,
Not the godly joy of love,
Knows he naught of souls exchanging,
Not in tears melts he e'er hence,

Steels he in life's battles raging
Harder yet his hardened sense.

But, just as softly, from zephyr doth shiver,
Quick as Aolian harp-string doth quiver,
Thus so the feeling-full woman's soul, too.
Image of pain makes her tenderly fearful,
Heaves then the e'er-loving bosom, and tearful,
Beaming the eyes are from heavenly dew.

In the realm where men are ruling
Might defiant right doth have,
With his sword the Scyth'an's proving
And the Persian will enslave.
War be they in fury waging,
The desires both wild and rude,
Eris's voice is hoarsely raging,
Governing, where Charis fled.

But now, so softly, persuasively pleading,
Women with scepter of morals are leading,
Smother they discord, all raging enlight,
Teach they the powers, that hateful develop,
Each in a more loving form to envelop,
And what forever would flee, they unite.

[Translated by Marianna Wertz, in *Friedrich Schiller, Poet of Freedom*, Vol. II. Schiller Institute, Washington, D.C., 1988, pp. 27-28]

Sybille Küster

A polemic response by an anonymous male author/journalist in the "Nürtinger Wochenblatt" (a newspaper published in Nürtingen, a town near Stuttgart) to the women who had tried to become politically involved in the 1847/8 revolution:

„Der Humorist hält den demokratischen (Wiener) Frauen eine Vorlesung.

Meine sehr verkehrten Hörerinnen! Wundern Sie sich nicht, daß ich die Ehre habe, Ihnen von rückwärts Etwas vorzulesen, denn ich denke so: wenn man verkehrte Dinge von dem verkehrten Gesichtspunkte betrachtet, so erhält man die richtige Ansicht der Dinge. Überdem glaube ich, meine sehr verkehrten Hörerinnen, daß wir uns gegenwärtig nur gratuliren sollen, daß wir uns nicht sehen; wir haben Beide dabei nichts verloren; denn die Sage geht im Volke, daß die Mitgliederinnen des ‚demokratischen FrauenClubbs' in Bezug auf ‚Schönheit' unschuldig an jeder Anregung und Aufreizung des Volkes sind und daß im Durchschnitte Elisabeth's Worte: ‚Die verführt mir keine Unterthanen mehr' auf jede Einzelne von Ihnen anzuwenden sind. Von der anderen Seite aber, meine sehr verkehrten Hörerinnen, verlieren Sie auch nichts, daß Sie ihrem ‚Humoristen' nicht in's Angesicht sehen, denn – ohne ihm im Entferntesteen schmeicheln zu wollen – was ‚Schönheit' betrifft, könnte er alle Augenblicke die Ehre haben, eine ‚Demokratin' zu sein. Mein jetziger Stand- oder vielmehr Sitzpunkt ist eben schon deshalb gut gewählt, weil Sie wissen, daß man nur hinter dem Rücken der Menschen die Wahrheit von ihnen sagt. Der Text meiner heutigen Vorlesung findet sich bei Schiller und heißt:

‚Ehret die Frauen, sie flechten und weben
Himmlische Rosen ins irdische Leben,
Flechten der Liebe beglückendes Band;
Und in der Grazie züchtigem Schleier
Nähren sie wachsam das ewige Feuer
Schöner Gefühle mit heiliger Hand.'

Nun frage ich Sie, meine sehr verkehrten Hörerinnen, was haben Sie ‚geflochten', was ‚gewoben', wo sind Ihre ‚himmlische Rosen', wo befindet sich Ihre ‚züchtige Grazie' mit oder ohne ‚Schleier', was für ‚ewiges Feuer' nähren Sie, wo sind Ihre ‚schönen Gefühle', wo ist besonders Ihre ‚heilige Hand'? Anstatt ‚sie flechten und weben', muß es von ihnen heißen: ‚sie schnattern und tratschen'; anstatt ‚flechten der Liebe beglückendes Band', muß es heißen: ‚entwürdigen des Weibes natürlichen Stand' anstatt im ‚züchtigen Schleier der Grazie', sehen wir Sie im unzüchtigen Hute der Burschenschaft; an der Stelle des ‚ewigen Feuers schöner Gefühle' schüren Sie ‚stinkende Zigarren roher Gesellen' und das nicht mit ‚heiliger Hand', sondern mit ‚entweihtem Schnabel'. Sie wollen Freiheit? Die erringt man nicht durch Frechheit. Gehen Sie nach Hause, meine sehr verkehrten Hörerinnen! Stopfen Sie die Löcher Ihrer Strümpfe, bevor Sie die im Staate stopfen wollen; waschen Sie Ihre schmuzige Wäsche, ehe Sie die Landeswäsche waschen wollen; flicken Sie Ihrem Manne oder Ihren Kindern die Hemden, ehe Sie der Politik was anflicken wollen; machen Sie Ihre Familie glücklich, ehe Sie das Volk glücklich machen wollen, krönen Sie vorerst ihre Männer nicht, bevor Sie alle anderen Kronen abschaffen wollen; kurz, seien Sie des Namens ‚Weib' würdig und nicht des Ausdrucks ‚Weibsbilder', dann, dann will ich Ihnen wieder in's Gesicht sehen. Adieu. Saphir." (NWB 3.4.49)

The humorist holds a lecture for Vienna's democratic women

My very queer Ladies! Do not marvel that I have the honour of reading aloud something behind you, because I think thus: if one looks at backward things from a backward point of view, one sees the things correctly. Aside from this I think that, my very queer listeners, you are wrong, we should congratulate ourselves that we do not see each other; neither of us will have lost anything, because there is the saying of the people, that the members of the "Democratic Women's Club" are not guilty of any stimulation and attraction of the people in reference to beauty, and in general Elisabeth's words can be used for every single one of you "she no longer seduces any of my loyal subjects ". But on the other hand, my very queer listeners, you aren't missing anything by not seeing your humorist in the face, because (as to beauty) – without wanting to flatter him at all – he could at any moment have the honour of being a democratic lady.

Where I am today – or better, where I am sitting now, is well chosen even just for this reason, because you know that the truth is only said behind people's backs. The text of my lecture for today comes from Schiller and is called:

Honor the women! They're roses celestial

Twining and weaving in lives terrestrial,

Weaving the bond of the most blessed love

Veiled in the Graces' most modest attire

Nourish they watchful the e'erlasting fire

Of lovely feelings with hand from above.

Now I ask you, my very queer listeners, what have you 'twined', what have you 'woven', where are your 'celestial roses', where is your 'grace full of virtue', with or without a 'veil', what 'everlasting fire' do you nourish, where are your 'lovely feelings'? Above all, where is your 'holy hand'? Instead of "they are twining and weaving" we should say they "chatter and quack", instead of "they weave the bond of the most blessed love" we should say "they disdain the natural position of women", instead of the veil full of virtue, of grace, we see you with the lusty hat of the student association, instead of "the everlasting fire of lovely feelings" you stoke up "stinking cigars of rough workmen" and this not with a holy hand, but with an unholy beak!

Do you want liberty? That cannot be won with impudence! Go home, my very queer audience! Repair the holes in your stockings before wanting to repair those of the state; wash your dirty laundry before wanting to wash the laundry of the country; patch your husband's and your children's shirts before wanting to patch up something in politics; make your family happy before trying to make the people happy; do not crown your husbands before wanting to overthrow all the other crowns; in brief, be worthy of the name "woman" and not of the name "bad woman", then I want to look you in the face again. Adieu. Saphir.

SEE PLATE 3

To Become a Man: The Ambiguities of Gender Relations in late 19th and early 20th century Iceland

Gudmunður Hálfdanarson

Háskoli Íslands, Reykjavik

Árið 1863 tók kona í fyrsta skipti þátt í lýðræðislegum kosningum á Íslandi að því að vitað er. Þetta var Vilhelmína Lever, fráskilin og ágætlega stöndug veitingakona á Akureyri, en hún uppfyllti öll skilyrði sem sett voru fyrir því að kjósa til bæjarstjórnar – nema hvað hún var kona. Þetta er skýrt hér með því að annars vegar hafði orðið maður í lögunum aðra merkingu í íslensku en danska orðið mand í dönsku máli, þ.e. fyrir Íslendingum eru konur einnig menn. Hins vegar stafaði þetta sennilega einnig af því að konur höfðu ávallt haft ákveðin réttindi í stjórnun hreppa á Íslandi, þ.e.a.s. ef þær stóðu fyrir búi. Slíkt var nokkuð algengt þar sem ekkjur tóku oft við búrekstrinum eftir að eiginmenn þeirra létust. Þessi staða kvenna kom skýrt fram í því að slíkum ekkjum var veittur kosningaréttur í hreppsnefndarkosningum með lögum sem gengu í gildi árið 1882, þótt þeim væri ekki veitt kjörgengi í það sinn. Í lögunum birtist vel afstaða íslenskra ráðamanna til stöðu kvenna í samfélaginu. Þeir höfðu yfirleitt lítið á móti því að veita sjálfstæðum konum (þ.e. þeim konum sem ekki töldust undir karla settar sem dætur, vinnukonur eða eiginkonur) rétt til að tjá hug sinn í stjórnmálum, en þeim var þó mjög í nöp við að þær tækju beinan þátt í stjórn samfélagsins og þeir þyrftu þannig hugsanlega að lúta valdi kvenna. Þegar kosningaréttur var smám saman rýmkaður á fyrstu áratugum 20. aldar gekk konum því vel að fá rétt sinn viðurkenndan til jafns á við karla sem töldust ekki sjálfstæðir (s.s. vinnumenn), en þegar þær notuðu þessar breytingar á virkan hátt í kosningum til bæjarstjórnar í Reykjavík árið 1908 runnu tvær grímur á marga þingmenn. Töldu þeir sig því knúna til að takmarka kosningarétt og kjörgengi kvenna í alþingiskosningum við hærri aldur en karla, a.m.k. um stundarsakir. Þessi ótti reyndist þó ástæðulaus vegna þess að þegar til kom tóku konur mjög óvirkan þátt í íslenskum stjórnmálum um langan aldur og réttindi þeirra ógnuðu því ekki karlaveldinu – a.m.k. ekki fyrr en langt var liðið á 20. öldina. Formleg mismunun karla og kvenna í stjórnmálum á Íslandi var því afnumin með öllu með stjórnarskrárbreytingu árið 1920.

Guðmundur Hálfdanarson (1956) was educated at the University of Lund, Sweden, University of Iceland, Reykjavík, and Cornell University. He is a professor of history at the University of Iceland, specializing in European social and intellectual history, with special emphasis on the history of nationalism. He edited (with Prof. Svanur Kristjásson) *Íslensk þjóðfélagsþróun 1880-1990* (Icelandic social development, 1880-1990), and his other publications include *Íslenska þjóðríkið - upphaf og endimörk* (The Icelandic nation-state-origins and limits) and a number of articles in Icelandic and international journals.

 In the late winter of 1863 the people of Akureyri, a small town in northern Iceland, voted for the town council for the first time. Among the voters was Mrs. Vilhelmina Lever, an innkeeper and a well-known member of the community. This is the first known case where a woman took an active part in Icelandic politics, thus transgressing the traditional exclusion of women from the democratic process. What makes this incident even more remarkable is the fact that it occurred some eighteen years before Icelandic women were enfranchised at all. Naturally, Mrs. Lever's action was, for that reason, entirely illegal, as the royal decree on the township of Akureyri, issued the year before in Copenhagen, gave only men of certain status the right to vote [1]. On the surface, this seems to amount to a bold attack on a cherished male institution. But the records do not indicate that anyone questioned Mrs. Lever's right to cast her ballot. As it turns out, three of the 25 individuals listed in Akureyri's register of voters, fulfilling the strict property restrictions on voting in local election in the town, were women, although Mrs. Lever was alone in actually casting her ballot.[2] The question is, then, if the inhabitants of Akureyri belonged to the small avant-garde movement of those who thought that women and men should have equal rights in politics.

Actually, there is not much evidence to support this suggestion. At that time, Akureyri was a small and sleepy provincial town, with little over 500 inhabitants, and certainly not known for either social or political radicalism. The only explanation for Mrs. Lever's political participation was, therefore, that the royal decree defining the right to vote in the town, originally written in Danish, became very ambiguous when it had been translated into Icelandic. In the original Danish version it was clearly stated that "all men who have achieved their majority" – "alle fuldmyndige Mænd" is the Danish term – who paid a certain amount in communal taxes, had the right to cast their ballot. In Danish the term *mænd*, has the same meaning as in English word "men", while in Icelandic the corresponding word, *menn*, is a generic term, referring to both men and women (that is, it is roughly synonymous to the word "human" in English). Understood in this way, Mrs. Vilhelmína Lever, as a divorced woman, and therefore not under the authority of a husband, a property owner, and a taxpayer, fulfilled all the requirements requested for a prospective voter.

This semantic confusion does not, however, fully explain Mrs. Lever's political act. The very fact that female participation in the election process was not rejected out of hand, as an absurd idea or a threat to good social order, is interesting in itself. And, to a certain degree, it reflects the ambiguities and contradictions in the definition of gender roles in Icelandic politics at the time. Thus, because of the social prominence of the peasant wife, her authority in the home, and her centrality in the peasant economy, it seemed only natural that women who headed independent households should be allowed to select those who governed the local community. At the same time, the strict boundaries of the female sphere of influence, that is, their seclusion in the home and their exclusion from the public world, inhibited women from taking active part in the male dominated society. Mrs. Lever would, therefore, never have been voted to the local council of Akureyri, although she was allowed to take part in the voting itself.

The story of female participation in politics in Iceland has to be studied in this context.

Gudmundur Hálfdanarson

Here I want to discuss the complex history of gender definition in Icelandic politics in the period when women received full citizen rights in Iceland, outlining the difference and tensions between what we can call "substantive" and "formal" citizenship, where the first means "full and equal rights and opportunities", while the latter indicates legal rights to political participation [3].

In 1863, Iceland was a peasant society above all. Of the 67,000 souls that inhabited this large island, almost 90 percent lived on small and isolated farmsteads scattered around the inhabitable area. At this time, almost no towns or villages existed in Iceland, and the population was almost entirely rural [4]. The primitive fisheries in Iceland were, for the most part, a subsidiary economy for the farming households, with peasants and their servants moving to the fishing stations on the coast during the slack-season in the countryside. Fish was certainly important in the overall economy but a primitive animal husbandry was, nevertheless, its primary basis, as unfavorable climatic conditions rendered grain growing more or less impossible. This was a land-extensive economy, as the precious flocks of sheep needed ample space to graze but relatively few people were needed to tend them. For this reason, large distances usually separated one farm from another, making each farm almost a complete social universe.

As in most peasant societies, there was a clear gender division of labor in Iceland, making both men and women essential for the working of the farm. In general, men tended the sheep, went fishing, and brought the production of the farm to the market, while women took care of the cows, milked the ewes in the summer, and processed the milk. Thus, men controlled access to the market and relations to the world outside of the home, while women procured the food for the home. Moreover, the peasant wife had a total control over the food rationing on the farm, which was a position of considerable authority in a poor society. A home where the wife was generous attracted the best servants, because all wanted to serve a good *matmóðir* – or a "food mother" in literal translation – but she could also use her authority to punish those who fell out of her favor by reducing their ration of food.[5] Finally, hiring of female servants was entirely in the hands of the peasant wife, while the peasant hired the male servants.

In general, therefore, women played a crucial role in the peasant economy of 19th-century Iceland, and they had considerable authority in the home. This position of power and importance was circumscribed, however, in two respects. First, it was the family status of the woman that determined her authority on the farm, as the position of authority was entirely limited to the peasant wife. Female servants, for example, were totally subjugated to their masters, and it is clear from the numerous cases of births out of wedlock in nineteenth-century Iceland that they did not even have full authority over their bodies. Second, the authority of the peasant wife was entirely centered on the private world of the home, while her contacts with the outer world were for the most part limited to sporadic visits to church.

Farming widows posed a serious challenge to this gendered division of social roles in 19th-century Iceland. When a peasant passed away, it was a normal practice for his widow to replace him, and for her to remain as the head of the household until her retirement. In this position she administrated the male servants, and participated in the communal affairs

– at least to a certain degree. Hence, in the home the widow took on a traditional man's role, with all the authority and responsibility that came with it – i.e. she became virtually a man. In the first years of parliamentary elections, many even assumed that these women could participate in the political process. As most peasants had the right to vote, it seemed only natural that farming widows had the same right – that is, political right should be determined by status rather than gender. It was only with more experience that Icelandic men learned that this was not a "proper" way of arranging their political affairs, and gradually women were barred from all political participation.

Petitions to parliament from this period bear testimony to this ambivalence. In the early years of parliamentary politics – that is, from the foundation of the modern parliament in Iceland in 1845 and onwards – this was the normal method of the peasant communities to express their opinions on issues of particular interest to the voters. The common practice was to collect signatures from the heads of households on original forms, circulating from one farm to another, following the customary order of the farms in each community. Later, these originals were collected in the capital, Reykjavík, where they were copied before they were introduced to the parliamentary discussions. Finally, the original documents were stored in the parliamentary archives, while the copies were dispatched to Copenhagen to be presented to the king and his government. In the beginning, the organizers of such petition campaigns clearly felt it was appropriate for farming widows to sign these political declarations, in the same way as other farmers. For that reason, women's names are frequently found among the signatories on the original documents. When the petitions were copied in parliament, however, the more "knowledgeable" scribes changed the female names into common male names. Thus, Valgerður Eiríksdóttir became V. Eiríksson, Guðrún Guðnadóttir became G. Guðnason, or even Hallur Grímsson, and so on [6]. This gender confusion did not last for long as women's names are only found on petitions to the first sessions of parliament, meaning that Icelanders learned fairly quickly that women had no right to participate in parliamentary politics [7].

In this light Vilhelmína Lever's case becomes more comprehensible. It is clear that even if her gender was certainly of social significance, it did not alone determine her position in society. Here her status as an independent property owner and a taxpayer played also a significant role. As such, she was allowed to vote in local elections, and did so at least twice – that is, in 1863 and 1866. This is not to say, however, that women had equal status in Icelandic politics to men as Mrs. Lever's right to vote was entirely determined by the fact that she was not married at the time and, therefore, not under the "natural" authority of a husband.

Questions of how to translate gender discrimination into political practice continued to puzzle Icelandic lawmakers for the remainder of the 19th century. Thus, the first general legislation on local elections in Iceland, issued in 1872, specified that "each farming person [maður] in the community had the right to vote in communal elections and to be voted to local councils" [8], using similar language as in Akureyri a few years earlier. To begin with, the phrase was generally interpreted as including only men among voters, but a few years later, the president of the Icelandic High Court pointed out that this was far from clear. Thus, in discussions in parliament on proposed law on elections of vestries, he commented that by using the term maður, the bill opened the way for women to take part in the elections and to sit in church councils. Mockingly, he claimed that he found the "bill good and liberal, indeed", although he "could not deny that he would object to seeing a woman serve as a deacon ..." [9].

In 1881, the Icelandic parliament decided to clear up the issue. After heated discussions, where some representatives called for full political rights of farming women in local politics, the majority concluded that "widows and other unmarried women, who head a farming household, or who in some other way are independent householders" should have the right to vote in local elections, "provided that they fulfill all the other legal requirements for this right." This solution specifically denied women the right to sit in councils themselves, because, as one representative in parliament commented, if elected they would have to "travel around the community and venture out in snowstorms on treacherous roads in the winter." In order to save women from the hazard of public life they had, therefore, to be denied direct participation in the communal administration [10].

In spite of its shortcomings, the Icelandic election law, confirmed by the Danish king in 1882, might be considered as progressive and a sign of changing times in European politics. Voting rights for women, however limited, were rare in the early 1880s. For this reason, claimed the lawyer and crown official Páll Briem, one of the early advocates of women's rights in Iceland, the law drew attention to Icelanders as liberal people and made them famous and popular among liberals abroad" [11]. This interpretation of the election laws of 1882 is hardly warranted, as it was rather a confirmation of traditional gender relations in Iceland than a leap toward a "gender blind" future. Its underlying premise was, in fact, to defend the political hegemony of household heads on one hand, and to protect the male dominance in the public arena on the other. The law had the effect, however, of making gender discrimination in politics more difficult than before, simply because by acknowledging the right of some women, it became harder to draw the line between those who had the right to vote and those who did not.

The last decades of the 19th century and the beginning of the 20th were a period of a rapid social and political change in Iceland, disrupting the traditional social structures – including gender roles and the relations between men and women. This was also a period of an intense nationalist struggle in Iceland, where the great majority of those involved in politics demanded autonomy for Iceland from Danish rule, using the claim that this was the inherent right of the Icelandic nation. In the last decades of the 19th century, parliament repeatedly passed amendments to the constitution, calling for more independence from Denmark, but the conservative government in Copenhagen turned them all down and the king refused to sign them into a law. Finally, in 1904, soon after a more liberal majority came into power in Denmark, the Danish government gave in and granted Iceland home rule.

This was also a period of radical change in the definition of citizen rights in Iceland, or a change from what the American sociologist Reinhard Bendix calls "functional representation" to a "plebiscitarian principle." According to the first notion, participation in society is determined by people's status and functions, and dependent persons are generally excluded from public life—including political participation. According to the second, "all powers intervening between the individual and the state must be destroyed ... so that all citizens as individuals possess equal rights before the sovereign, national authority" [12]. Thus, membership in the political community becomes an individual rather than a collective right, although political participation is usually mediated through political parties, labor unions, or other collective bodies.

The theoretical foundation of modern citizenship can be traced to two distinct sources; on the one hand, it springs from the liberal idea of the individual, who has both an inherent or natural capacity for reason and possesses universal human rights, providing him—and in more recent times also her—with a certain autonomy in relations with other individuals [13]. On the other hand, it originates in the Rousseauist ideal of popular sovereignty, claiming that law cannot have any legitimate foundation except for the general will of the people [14]. This twin ideal came to Iceland through Copenhagen, as the Danish constitution of 1849 established democratic rule in the Danish part of the monarchy, forcing the periphery to re-evaluate its relations with the center and the internal organization of its own society. The first reaction in Iceland was an attempt to adapt the democratic principles to the old perception of the independent farming household, where the "húsbóndi"—the master of the house—reigned supreme, and where servants were treated as children. In this order, a clear division was made between the private life of the household and the public life of society—a division reminiscent of Aristotle's distinction between the *oikos* and the *polis*.[15] The former was arranged on a strict hierarchical principle, while the latter was more democratic, allowing all farmers to take part in the public arena.

Throughout the 19th century, the right to vote in Iceland followed the rules of functional representation mentioned earlier, limiting political citizenship to peasants in the countryside and to men who paid a certain amount in taxes in the towns. In the first decades of the 20th century, the Icelandic election laws moved gradually toward the plebiscitarian principle, where all adults had the right to vote. The first step was taken in communal elections in 1907, when all adults, except for paupers, were enfranchised, and in parliamentary elections in 1915, with similar restrictions. The final step was taken in 1934, when paupers finally received full citizen rights, including the right to vote.

The democratic ideal challenged the political position of women in a fundamental way, because in traditional society most women were placed in a subordinate position in the home—be it as daughters, maids or wives. As the right to vote became an individual right rather than the prerogative of "independent" persons, the exclusion of women from political participation became much more problematic than before. The question was discussed thoroughly in the constitutional debates in the 1890s, and the majority in the Icelandic parliament was usually quite open to the idea of enfranchising women. When reforming the local election laws in 1907, parliament did not hesitate, therefore, to give women equal rights to men, both regarding voting in elections and serving in local councils. As it turned out, women did not hesitate to use that right, presenting an all-female list in the council elections in Reykjavík in 1908. The initiative was a resounding success, as the list received over a quarter of the votes cast and had four women elected to the city council [16].

This was clearly more than the representatives in parliament had bargained for. Thus, in discussions leading to constitutional reform of 1915, many expressed reservations about enfranchising women. "If we consider", exclaimed one representative in 1911, "how women utilized the suffrage in the last municipal elections in Reykjavík ... [I think] it would be proper to expand this right gradually. Even if I am fond of women, I do not like the idea of having, all of a sudden, twenty women in parliament" [17]. For that reason, the constitution of 1915 restricted the suffrage to women over forty years of age, with the age going down by one year every year until it had reached the same level as for men. Anyway, women did not invade parliament in massive numbers and, for that reason, this peculiar rule was abolished in 1920, granting Icelandic women the same political rights as men.

Although Iceland was a poor and fairly backward peasant society until the first half of the 20th century, it became one of the first countries in the world to grant women the right to vote in local and parliamentary elections. In many ways, it was only logical that women received this right at the same time as political citizenship was extended to men in subordinate positions (primarily servants), because women had not been excluded from Icelandic politics primarily on the basis of their gender, but rather because they were in most cases dependent upon a male relative or an employer. Receiving formal rights was very different, however, from becoming active participants in political life. From the beginning, men feared that women would take over their institutions of power once political equality was established, and thus women would abandon their homes and children. This did not happen, of course, as very few women were elected to parliament in Iceland until the 1970s, and it was only at the end of the 20th century that they began to play important role in the traditional political parties.

 NOTES

[1] "Anordning angaaende Handelsstedet Akureyris Oprettelse til en Kjöbstad", 29 Aug. 1862, *Lovsamling for Island* vol. 18, Copenhagen 1884, pp. 385-412, § 3.

[2] See Jónsson G., *Konur og kosningar. Þættir úr sögu íslenskrar kvenréttindabaráttu*, Reykjavík 1977, pp. 7-8 and Hjaltason J., *Saga Akureyrar í landi Eyrarlands og Nausta, 890-1862*, Akureyri 1990, pp. 160-164 and 205-208.

[3] See also Hálfdanarson G., *Defining the Modern Citizen: Debates on Civil and Political Elements of Citizenship in Nineteenth-Century Iceland*, "Scandinavian Journal of History" 24, 1999, pp. 103-116.

[4] *Hagskinna. Icelandic Historical Statistics*. Jónsson G. and Magnússon M.S. (eds), Reykjavík 1997, pp. 64-74.

[5] A good description of this role of women is in Björnsson J., *Æskustöðvar*, Reykjavík 1954, pp. 73-83.

[6] In Iceland, it is easy to distinguish between the names of most men and women, because male last names are made of the first name of the father with the suffix *son* added to it, while for women the suffix *dóttir* (that is, daughter) is added to the father's first name. This patronymic system is still in use in Iceland.

[7] Karlsson G., *Frelsisbarátta suður-þingeyinga og Jón frá Gautlöndum*, Reykjavík 1977, pp. 42-43.

[8] "Forordning om de islandske Landkommuners Styrelse," 4 May 1872, *Lovsamling for Island*, vol. 21, Copenhagen 1889, pp. 354-408, § 3. At least in one instance, women voted in local elections after the passing of this law, see Kristjánsson Ó.P., *Tvær konur kjósa í hreppsnefnd 1874*, "Ársrit Sögufélags Ísfirðinga", 22, 1979, pp. 149-152.

[9] *Alþingistíðindi* II, Reykjavík 1879, p. 658.

[10] *Alþingistíðindi* II, Reykjavík 1881, p. 401.

[11] Briem P., *Um frelsi og menntun kvenna. Sögulegur fyrirlestur*, Reykjavík 1885, p. 32.

[12] Bendix, *Nation-Building and Citizenship. Studies of Our Changing Social Order*, New edition, Berkeley 1977, pp. 89-91.

[13] See for example, Arblaster A., *The Rise and Decline of Western Liberalism*, Oxford 1984, pp. 15-91.

[14] Cf. Rousseau J.-J., *Du contrat social*, 1762, book II.

[15] Cf. Pocock J.G.A., *The Ideal of Citizenship Since Classical Times*, in Beiner R. (ed), *Theorizing Citizenship*, Albany 1995, p. 32.

[16] Styrkársdóttir A., *From Feminism to Class Politics: The Rise and Decline of Women's Politics in Reykjavík, 1908–1922*, Umeå 1998.

[17] *Alþingistíðindi* B: II, Reykjavík 1911, col. 927.

 SOURCES

Two visions of women's suffrage in 1911

Jón Jónsson, representative in the Lower House of the Icelandic Parliament, on women's right to vote:

Staða konunnar er aðallega sú, hér eins og annarsstaðar, ad vera móðir og húsmóðir, og eg geri ráð fyrir, að enginn sé svo djarfur að halda því fram, að það sé þýðingarminna að ala upp börn og standa fyrir heimili, en að halda misjafnar ræður á alþingi. það er því einfalt og auðsætt, að sérhvað það, sem dregur huga konunnar frá heimilinu, er úr lakari átt, og þarf mikið gott að koma, ef ábati á að vera af því.

Eg vil líka benda á það, sem eg hygg vera flestra manna reynslu, að pólitisk störf eru ekki vel löguð til þess að auka hina fínni og viðkvæmari kosti nokkurs manns. Og eg hygg, að ef það væri á nokkurn hátt unt, þá væri það þarft verk að aftra konum frá því að gefa sig í hið pólitíska skítkast og gera sig þannig konur að verri. Eg fyrir mitt leyti er öldungis viss um, að það mundi leiða til þess, að lífsfarsældin yrði minni, og mæla þó margir, að hún megi ekki minni vera. Sá eðlismunur, sem er, má ekki missa sig. þegar fram í sækir og til lengdar lætur má vera að hugsunarháttur kvenna breytist, en þá leysast líka heimilin upp. þetta kalla menn nú fjarmæli, en margir vitrustu menn heimsins eru nú samt á þessari skoðun.

Alpingistídindi B:II (Reykjavík, 1911), col. 934–935.

The place of the woman is here, as everywhere else, to be a mother and a wife, and I assume that no one is so bold to claim that it is less important to raise children and to be in charge of a home than to deliver speeches of unequal quality in the parliament. It is, therefore, simple and obvious that everything that draws the woman's attention from the home is rather harmful, and it has to lead to something very good if it is to be of any benefit.

I also want to point out what I think is most people's experience, that is, that political activity is not well suited to increase any person's finer and more delicate qualities. And I think that if it were in any way possible, then it would be beneficial to prevent women from par-

Gudmundur Hálfdanarson

ticipating in the political invective, which damages women. I am, for my part, totally convinced that this would decrease human happiness, and it is often said that it must not be less than it already is. The natural difference that exists is absolutely necessary. In the future, as time progresses, women's way of thinking may change, but then the homes will also dissolve. People say now that this is absurd, but many of world's wisest men are of this opinion all the same.

Bjarni Jónsson, another representative in the Lower House, responding to the statement above:

Háttvirtur … þingmaður … var ærið þungorður í minn garð út af kvenfólkinu, og sagði, að eg hefði ekki komið með annað en tómar fullyrðingar, engin rök fært fyrir mínu máli. Að eg ekki kom með rök fyrir mínu máli, stafar af því, að eg hélt, að eg þyrfti þess ekki; þar sem hér er um skylausan rétt kvenfólksins að ræða, þótt við ekki höfum viðurkent hann fyr en nú, þótt þær að sjálfsögðu hefðu átt að vera búnar að fá hann viðurkendan fyrir löngu. … þá mintist háttv. þm. á, að kvenfólkið hefði ekki tíma til að taka þátt í stjórnmálum, … en eg held, að þeim tíma sé ekki ver varið en hjá karlmönnunum, og þó að þingmaðurinn talaði um, að kvenfólkið hingað til hefði mest gegnt húsmóður- og uppeldisstörfum, þá vil eg halda því fram, að þær muni alveg halda því áfram að vera mæður og hugsa um menn sína og heimili, þótt þær fái réttindi sín, nema hvað þær muni vera mikið færari um það að veita börnum sínum gott uppeldi, ef þær sjálfar hafa tekið þátt í almennum málum, með fullu jafnrétti á við karlmenn. Hinsvegar skal eg játa það rétt hjá hinum h. þm., að það er fyllilega eins veglegt starf að annast um barnauppeldi og húsmóðurstörf eins og standa hér á þingi og halda misjafnlega góðar ræður, og hann heldur því fram ennfremur, ad þær væru of góðar til þess ad kasta þeim inn í hið pólitíska skítkast, en þm. gætir ekki að því, að þar eru einmitt þær sjálfar, sem vilja takast þetta á hendur, og trúa mín er sú, að hið pólitíska skítkast muni þverra, þegar þessi kurteisari helmingur mannanna tekur þátt í stjórnmálastörfum ásamt karlmönnum, því það verður til þess, ad karlmennirnir munu temja sér meiri kurteisi bæði í orði og verki.

Ibid, col. 939–942.

The Honorable … Representative … reprimanded me for what I said about the women, and maintained that I had made all kind of claims, but without any support for my case. The reason for not supporting my case was that I thought that it was not needed, because this was so obviously the women's right, although we have not admitted it until now, and although we should have acknowledged it long time ago. … Then the Hon. Rep. mentioned that women do not have time to take part in politics … but I think that the time that they spent in this way would not be of less use than the time men spend on the same activity, and although the representative mentioned that women have so far primarily served as wives and mothers, I should like to claim that they will continue to be mothers and to take care of their husbands and homes even if they will be granted their rights, except for the fact that they will be much better qualified to raise their children properly if they themselves have taken part in public affairs, in total equality with men. On the other hand I must admit that I am in total agreement with the H. Rep. that it is just as important to raise children and to take care of the home as to stand here in parliament and deliver speeches of unequal quality, and he also claims that they are too good to be thrown into the political invective, but the Rep. does not consider that it is exactly they themselves that want to take on this responsibility, and I am convinced that the political invective will decrease when this more polite part of humanity will take part in politics with the men, because men will, as a consequence, become more polite both in what they say and how they act.

What difference did the vote make?

Pat Thane

University of Sussex

 In 1918 the British parliamentary franchise was extended to women aged 30 years and over who were occupiers, or wives of occupiers, of land or premises of not less than £5 annual value and to women of 30 and over who held university degrees. The local government franchise, which since 1869 had included all women aged 21 or above who held property on which they were liable to pay local taxes ('rates') – mainly unmarried or widowed women – was extended to include the wives of male electors.

A conventional narrative has developed about the outcome of this partial concession of the vote to women in 1918: the previously active and united movement became splintered, divided, less publicly and dramatically effective; the impact of women as voters on politics and policy was slight, except possibly to reinforce conservative and Conservative Party values, including traditional values of domesticity; there was a backlash against the small shift in gender relations so far achieved. After women obtained the vote on equal terms with men in 1928, women's political involvement declined still further, reinforced by powerful and effective social pressure upon women to give primacy to their domestic roles. The second world war brought only short-term and ambiguous gains for women, followed speedily by a reimposition of domestic values. Traditional gender roles were not seriously challenged again until the late 1960s, but even then with only limited and short-term effects [1].

This narrative is not wholly mistaken, but it is far from being a complete representation of a complex set of processes. Just as other contributions to this volume argue for new understandings of women's political roles in earlier periods, this chapter argues that we need a more complex understanding of the 20th century, which recent research is beginning to make possible. A large part of the problem historians have encountered in interpreting events after 1918 relates to expectations. How soon could women have expected to overthrow thousands of years of male predominance in the political culture ? Too much writing on this theme assumes that because there were not dramatic changes in gender roles shortly after the partial attainment of the vote, therefore there were no significant changes. There is a danger of measuring the impact of the vote by impossible standards, of expecting change to be unrealistically rapid, and of underestimating, by applying the values of later generations, shifts which were more significant in the context of the 1920s and 1930s than they appear with hindsight. Martin Pugh has pointed out that the middle classes did not dominate British politics for many decades after they obtained the vote in 1832, or working men for almost 50 years after some of them gained the vote in 1867. "If these precedents are a real guide" he suggested in 1992 "we may be on the verge of a take-off by women in the 1990s" [2]. And indeed the general election of May 1997 brought an unprecedented number of women into the House of Commons and into ministerial office, as a result of a commitment to greater gender equality on the part of influential sections of the victorious Labour Party. Following the election one third of Labour parliamentary seats were held by women compared with a little over one-seventh in the previous parliament; the proportion of Conservative seats held by women barely changed. We need to think in terms of long as well as short-term outcomes. However, the resistance to the policy of promoting female candidates suggests the resilience of opposition to women in political life even at the beginning of a new millennium.

But presence in parliament is only one possible measure of women's roles in British political culture. Others have measured this primarily by the achievement of legislation which directly promotes gender *equality* [3]. *This, surely, is also inadequate. Women can play a role in other areas of politics, and if equality with men is their aim, they should surely do so. The search for a more satisfactory picture can best start by asking what the suffragists themselves expected to follow from the vote.*

Pat Thane (MA Oxford, PH.D.LSE) from October 2001 will be Professor of Contemporary British History, Institute of Historical Research, University of London. Her main publications are: *The Foundations of the Welfare State* (1982, 2nd ed. 1996); *Women and Gender Policies. Women and the Rise of the European Welfare States, 1880s-1950s*, co-ed with Gisela Bock (1990); *Old Age from Antiquity to Post-Modernity*, co-ed with Paul Johnson (1998); *Old Age in England. Past Experiences, Present Issues* (2000); *Women and Ageing in Britain since 1500*, co-ed with Lynne Botelho (2001); *Labour's First Century. The Labour Party 1900-2000* co-ed with Duncan Tanner and Nick Tiratsoo (2000).

WHAT DID THE SUFFRAGE CAMPAIGNERS EXPECT?

It is often argued that suffrage campaigners themselves had high expectations of the extent of social and economic as well as of statutory change that gaining the vote would bring about, and were disappointed by what followed. Maybe this was true of some, but many influential suffragists were shrewd enough politically and had enough experience of the extent of opposition to their cause to be less optimistic, to expect the struggle to continue and change to be slow. The militant suffragist, Viscountess Rhondda, commented in 1921 that, in gaining the vote, women "had passed the first great toll-bar on the road which leads to equality", but "it is a far cry yet to the end of the road" [4]. Her biographer suggests that "while welcoming the [1918 Representation of the People Act] she was neither naive enough nor complacent enough to expect that such a limited measure would break down the still significant barriers to full emancipation" [5]. In 1920 Lady Rhondda founded and edited the weekly journal *Time and Tide*, which was produced wholly by women, and gave broad coverage to political and cultural issues, most of them not directly concerned with gender equality, in order to promote such equality both by demonstrating the capacities of women and by informing and educating newly enfranchised women. It also gave prominence to the issues of central importance to feminists until women obtained the vote on equal terms with men in 1928. Thereafter Lady Rhondda felt free to shift the emphasis to what she defined as "the real task of feminism", to "wipe out the overemphasis on sex that is the fruit of the age-long subjection of women. The individual must stand out without trappings as a human being " [6]. In the 1930s the journal employed and published a balance of men and women and became one of Britain's most influential reviews of politics, the arts, and social questions. Despite Lady Rhondda's own increasing conservatism, *Time and Tide* continued to be a strong advocate of all forms of social equality, including gender equality.

Lady Rhondda appears in the historiography as a leading standard bearer of egalitarian "old" feminism, self-consciously promoting what is seen as the predominant commitment of the pre-1914 suffrage campaigners to complete equality between the sexes. Eleanor Rathbone, on the other hand, is represented as a leader of welfare-oriented "new" feminism [7]. This recognized that women and men had some different needs and that, at least in the short run, women needed support in their roles as mothers. Some see "new" gradually replacing "old" feminism in the inter-war years, though in reality the distinction between them was by no means clear-cut. Rathbone also recognized the struggle ahead. She believed that if women were to take advantage of their new political rights, new methods were needed, for women were no longer seeking "a big, elemental ... simple reform", such as enfranchisement, but the "difficult re-adjustments of a complicated ... antiquated structure of case law and statute law" which required sober and tricky negotiation [8].

From another perspective again, Sylvia Pankhurst, from the family that had led militant suffragism before the First World War, had moved far to the left of her mother and sisters during the war. Unlike them, she was strongly committed to equal adult suffrage: the granting of the vote to all males and females at age 21. She was deeply disappointed that this was not achieved in 1918, that "masculine timidity entrenched itself against the dangers of majority rule" [9]. Indeed recognition that there were more women than men in Britain over the age of 21 had strongly influenced the framing of the Representation of the People Act [10]. Reflecting in 1931, she believed that, nevertheless, "a breach in the sex barrier had been made" in 1918, but that its occurrence while a terrible war continued explained the sober response:

> The pageantry and rejoicing, the flaming ardour, which in pre-war days would have greeted the victory, were absent when it came. The sorrows of the world conflict precluded jubilations...
>
> The Suffrage movement, which lived through the vast holocaust of peaceful life, was a more intelligent and informed movement than that which, gallant as it was, had fought the desperate, pre-war fight. Gone was the mirage of a society regenerated by enfranchised womanhood as by a magic wand. Men and women had been drawn closer together by the suffering and sacrifice of the War. Awed and humbled by the great catastrophe and by the huge economic problems it had thrown into naked prominence, the women of the Suffrage movement had learned that social regeneration is a long and mighty work. The profound divergences of opinion on war and peace had been shown to know no sex [11].

Sylvia Pankhurst's notably sober assessment calls in question not only the belief that suffrage campaigners expected the franchise to deliver instant transformation of gender roles but also the argument, based upon a limited range of literary sources, that the "Great" War so undermined masculine confidence that it bred a backlash against women's aspirations for change [12]; she believed, rather, that the war had drawn men and women closer together. It is questionable whether the concept of 'backlash' is appropriate for the interpretation of this period, when it is not clear that the hostility to women's aspirations, which had long existed, was greater or more effective or had different sources than at previous times.

When sections of the press commented slightingly on the small number of women candidates in the General Election of 1922, the Women's Freedom League (WFL) retorted that since men had been involved in the political process since 1265 and women for only four years, 33 female candidates was not an inconsiderable achievement, especially in view of the extent of opposition in political parties to women as candidates [13]. WFL was a radical group, which before the war had split from the Pankhursts' Women's Social and Political Union (WSPU) because it wished to campaign for broader social and economic change than for the vote in itself. It had about 5,000 members in the 1920s and was very active [14]. WFL also had few illusions about how easy the way forward would be. After the vote was extended to all women in the same terms as men in 1928 its journal stated: "For sixty-one years women have striven to win an equal footing with men; it is only an equal footing they have gained, not equal political power" [15].

Prominent suffragists appear to have greeted the partial success of their cause with sober realism, but not to have given up the fight for further advance. The belief that women generally ceased to campaign after 1918 is often derived from a comparison of the sobriety of their politics after the war compared with pre-war suffragette militancy. Of course a substantial and indispensable component of the pre-war campaign, embodied especially in the National Union of Women's Suffrage Societies (NUWSS), was peaceable and constitutional.[16] The most prominent figure in NUWSS, Millicent Garrett Fawcett, wrote of her reaction in November 1919 in the final chapter of her memoir *The Women's Victory-and After*, "The Difference the Vote Has Made". She challenged those who argued that it would make no difference:

> If the vote makes no difference, why have our race all over the world attached such enormous importance to it?... the possession of the franchise is the very foundation stone of political freedom. Our fifty years struggle for the women's vote was not actuated by our setting any extraordinary value on the mere power of making a mark on a voting paper once in every three or four years. We did not, except as a symbol of free citizenship value it as a thing good in itself...but for the sake of the equal laws, the enlarged opportunities, the improved status of women which we knew it involved. We worked for it with ardour and passion because it was the stuff of the conscience with us that it would benefit not women only, but the whole community...it was the cause of men, women and children [17].

Garrett Fawcett described how, immediately the extension of the franchise was decided, the Council of NUWSS decided to extend its aims. They retained the old single objective, "to obtain the parliamentary franchise for women on the same terms as it is or may be granted to men", but added two more: "to obtain all other such reforms, economic, legislative and social, as are necessary to secure a real equality of liberties, status and opportunities between men and women", and "to assist women to realize their responsibility as voters".

In assessing the impact of the vote it is also important not to abstract the experience of women in politics from the wider political context. The quieter public engagement of women activists in the 1920s compared with the drama of the pre-war campaign of the suffragettes is commonly interpreted as a change specific to women's politics [18]; yet, as Jon Lawrence argues persuasively, this preference for sobriety was a general feature of British politics at this time in which women shared. Contemporaries commented, with surprise, that there were so few 'scenes' in post-war elections. The *Times* described the "almost cloistral calm" that prevailed in London on the day of the October 1924 election, but denied that this was due to lack of interest among women or men: "There is still a belief abroad that Eatanswill is characteristic of our election scenes and it is hard to convince the foreigner that voting does not necessarily mean more bloodshed and that British phlegm does not necessarily mean apathy" [19]. Perhaps, as Sylvia Pankhurst suggested, this calm response to politics was a reaction to the violence of the war. Rathbone thought that on the part of women it was a response to a new political situation which required changed tactics. She answered critics who complained that the passion had gone out of the movement after 1918, and that she and her associates had become too cautious, by saying:

> We knew when it was necessary to compromise. There is a school of reformers which despises compromise... we acquired by experience a certain flair which told us when a charge of dynamite would come in useful and when it was better to rely on the methods of a skilled engineer [20].

The violence of a strand of pre-war suffragism had been bred by frustration at the intransigence of resistance to the reasonable claim of women for the vote. Partial attainment of the vote led to calmer forms of political pressure, though not, as we shall see, to the cessation of demonstrations by women. Nor did violence wholly disappear from British public discourse about gender roles; rather it survived longer among anti-feminists than among feminists. In 1921 Cambridge, "that perverse university", as the suffragist and Cambridge mathematics graduate Ray Strachey described it [21], refused to follow the example set by Oxford in the previous year, and other British universities long before, and voted against admitting women to full membership of the university as students and faculty. A gang of male undergraduates at Cambridge celebrated their victory by smashing up the bronze gates of Newnham, one of the two women's colleges at Cambridge. A reason for the low expectations of suffragists of the outcome of the extension of the franchise was their awareness of the continuing strength of hostility to women's claims.

WOMEN AS VOTERS

How did women use their vote when they acquired it? It has been claimed that "once the vote was gained it became clear that large numbers of women really had little interest in it" [22]. There is no evidence to support this claim. Rather, contemporaries commented on how eager women were to vote. Ray Strachey, a leading member of the NUWSS and a close friend and colleague of Millicent Garrett Fawcett, wrote in 1928 that in the preceding decade feminists "had regarded the vote not as an end in itself, but as an instrument for securing other reforms; and now they proceed to use it" [23]. Strachey herself stood unsuccessfully for Parliament as an Independent, in 1918 and 1922: became political adviser to the first woman Member of Parliament, the Conservative Lady Violet Astor; and was active in a range of causes until her early death in 1940.

Certainly the percentage turnout of eligible electors in normal elections after women obtained the vote was not unduly low [24]. The first General Election after the Representation of the People Act, that of December 1918, followed too soon on the change in the law and after the war (which had ended only one month previously) to be a reasonable test of the effects of the franchise changes for women and for men (for this was also the first occasion on which all adult men, from age 21, had been enabled to vote, previously about 40 percent of males were disfranchised). Many who had newly gained the right to vote were not yet on the voting register by the time of the election. The turnout was only 58.9 percent in 1918 compared with an average of 73.5 percent in the seven ensuing elections.

The next general election, in 1922, was a more realistic test of the effects of the change in the franchise. On the day following the election, the *Times*, which had no obvious commitment to the cause of women, commented:

> The greatest surprise which those in charge of the polling booths had yesterday was the number of women who appeared to vote immediately after the booths were opened.

In 1918, wrote the reporter, women had been uncertain and diffident, "many of those who did vote were accompanied by men and their views were probably influenced by them." But:

> Yesterday the contrary was the case... canvassers found themselves questioned alertly and adroitly on matters not usually considered women's questions. Foreign policy was a strong point in moving women in constituencies.

> Women's questions as such played a small part in this election; women in many constituencies attended meetings especially called for them when they were held in private houses, but it may be doubted whether any candidate, woman or man, polled a large vote purely on his or her stand on these matters... in every constituency it was the big issues that counted and men's questions were undoubtedly also women's questions.

> So far from married women voting as their husbands told them to, it was quite evident that where there was influence, it was not necessarily wielded by the man... the percentage of women electors who voted may be taken as possibly greater than that of men and their vote must have influenced if it did not secure the election of the majority of candidates [25].

The *Times* similarly commented following the next election, of December 1923, that women had polled heavily [26], and that it believed that the Conservatives lost partly on the "dear food" issue... especially with the women:

> At the last election the Labour Party was very disappointed at the fact that it did not poll more than about 35-40 per cent of the women's vote, but on this occasion the proportion seems to have been much higher [27].

On the next polling day, October 30, 1924, which brought an end to the first, short-lived Labour government,

The women in most of the London constituencies seemed to be mustering in great force in the earlier hours and in widely separated constituencies there was no doubt that they were far more interested than last year in the election. At Marylebone, in Battersea and at Bromley there were more women voters than there have been since they obtained the franchise [28].

After 1928, when all women obtained the right to vote at age 21 on the same terms as men, women made up 53% of the electorate. Women voted on equal term with men for the first time in May 1929, the election which brought the Labour party into government for the second time. Before polling there was extensive press comment on "the sphinx of the election", "the enigma presented by the new woman voter" [29]. There were predictions from some parts of the country that "there may be a great deal of indifference to political questions among the newly enfranchised women" [30]. In Greater London it was reported that "there has been a remarkable absence of rowdyism" and that

Women form the majority of the electorate in all save one or two constituencies and in many places they largely preponderate. This is one of the factors which all the parties have kept very steadily in view. So far as meetings are any guide, the women, including the new voters, have displayed quite as much interest as the men and they have shown great willingness to render voluntary assistance as canvassers and so forth [31].

In the Midlands there was a "lack of excitement" about the election, but there were well attended meetings:

Women only are wearing party favours and women have carried on most of the canvassing... There is no doubt in the minds of any organiser that the electors – and particularly the women – are taking the election seriously... Women are expected to poll heavily but no-one can form any opinion of how the woman's vote was going [32].

The *Times* reporter in Scotland commented:

The greatest riddle of the election is still the vote of the newly enfranchised young women. Nothing has arisen to entitle any party to expect a monopoly of favour from this source or to disturb the conjecture that the vote of the women will be distributed among the three parties in measurable proportion to that of men [33].

When the poll was completed,

There was every sign in many constituencies that [the new woman voter] had risen admirably to the occasion. Though stories were told of her nervous uncertainty about polling procedures, general observation suggested that she had no need to ask her way, but displayed the coolness attributed to the modern generation.

Women were said to have polled well all over London, and

in South Kensington, where women largely outnumber men, no time was lost in going to the polling stations. The chances seemed that the division would poll a larger proportion of the register than had been its custom [34].

The local press in the northern port city of Liverpool reported that women had polled in large numbers and that their votes appeared to have favoured Labour [35].

Nevertheless, the belief that women do not vote with the same frequency as men has become a conventional wisdom of British political science [36], despite a striking absence of supporting evidence. No statistical surveys exist for the inter-war years. Studies for the later 20th century (1960s to 1990s) support the journalistic observations of the 1920s that there were no significant differences in the tendency of males and females to vote in national elections [37].

The comment of the *Times* in 1922 that women's voting preferences did not appear to be dictated by their close male relatives was a response to a commonplace assertion at the time, repeated in the historiography and more insistently in works of political science, that women largely followed the political preferences of men who were close to them. There is considerable biographical evidence that women as often led as followed the politics of their partner, or that couples were drawn together by a shared political preference [38]. The 1993 annual British Household Survey (of a nationally representative sample of British households) found that Labour-supporting women were more effective in persuading their husbands and families to follow their voting preferences than were Labour-supporting men. It would be unwise to generalize these findings to all political parties throughout the 20th century, but, together with other evidence, they suggest that we should hesitate before assuming that female voters at any time simply stood by their man.

Newspaper comment on inter-war elections suggests that "women" were not immovably wedded to a single party but shifted their allegiance according to their assessment of salient political issues. In this women do not seem to differ from male voters. The electorate as a whole appears to have been volatile in the uncertain conditions of the 1920s and 1930s. Nevertheless it has become another axiom of British political sociology that women since 1918 have been more inclined than men to support the Conservative Party [39]. This has been put forward as one explanation for the success of the Conservative Party in remaining in office for most of the period since 1918. As one group of female political scientists has put it: " had there been no women's franchise... Labour would have been continuously in office between 1945 and 1979 " [40]. If this is so, of course, it suggests that women's votes have made a difference to British politics, if an unwelcome one in the eyes of many commentators. But David Jarvis suggests that this assumption also is insecurely based. It has been derived from statistical calculations which are riddled with unexamined technical problems [41]. A more careful analysis of all Liverpool parliamentary elections between 1924 and 1935 and of voting turnout in all of the English parliamentary divisions in May 1929, which takes account of socio-economic variations among constituencies, suggests that class was a more important influence upon voting than gender. The evidence does not support a stronger conclusion than that women's voting behavior in this period "remains an open question".[42] The voting preferences of women and men have fluctuated throughout the 20th century; and women, like men, do not vote as a bloc, undifferentiated by class, religion, or any other variable [43]. Nor is there any sign that women have been uninterested in voting.

WOMEN AND POLITICAL PARTIES

Nor have substantial numbers of women been averse to joining political parties, though this has always been a minority pursuit among both men and women. Women joined the Labour Party in significant numbers immediately on attaining the vote. By 1927 about 300,000 women were members. This was about half of the individual membership of the party and in some constituencies the female proportion was higher still [44]. This proportion did not however give women as much power within the party as might appear. In accordance with the constitution of the Labour Party, the votes of individual members in the local branches were hugely outnumbered at the powerful annual party conference by the trade unions each of whom wielded a number of votes, in proportion to the size of their membership, whereas as each party branch had just one vote. Labour women could, however, make effective use of their numerical force in local politics, especially perhaps in areas with a strong tradition of women's public activity, possibly combined with paid employment, such as in parts of Lancashire [45], though there is no study of women in local government after 1918 to compare with Patricia Hollis' work on the previous period [46]. One of the few local studies, by Michael Savage, describes how the textile town of Preston, Lancashire, was transformed from a Conservative to a Labour stronghold in the 1920s, when working women formed a strong Woman's Section of the local party and persuaded an initially unsympathetic local party to adopt a program advocating improvements in education, maternity and child welfare, health care, housing, and the provision of such public amenities as baths and wash-houses [47]. In Liverpool, women were made more welcome in the local party in the early 1920s, though they later met resistance from an increasingly powerful group of Roman Catholics in the party. Nevertheless Liverpool Labour women campaigned successfully for increased local provision of education, maternity and child welfare, baths, libraries, and recreation. The success owed much to the energy of Bessie Braddock who was a city councillor throughout the 1930s and later a respected local MP, though she would never have described herself as a feminist [48]. In other areas, however, women met stronger resistance in local Labour Parties [49].

There were about one million women in the Conservative Party in the 1920s [50]. The female membership of both parties appears to have declined a little during the 1930s [51]. Even the Liberal Party, which, in view of its leaders' lack of support for the suffrage movement before 1918, had done little to attract women, and which was weak and divided in the 1920s, attracted increasing numbers of women members, reaching about 100, 000 by 1928 [52]. Many women found Liberalism attractive philosophically and in terms of its broad policy commitments and believed that the ideas of the party of John Stuart Mill continued to be consistent with support for gender equality. A prize-winning essay by Mrs Penberthy of Exeter published in *Liberal Women's News* in 1925, "Why I am a Liberal", expresses the blend of 'equal rights', welfare and other political issues which attracted women of no particular prominence or distinction into politics:

I am a Liberal because I wholeheartedly believe in Free Trade, in the League of Nations, in drastic Temperance Reform, Equal Suffrage, Religious Equality, Disestablishment, Revision of the Land Laws and Divorce laws and a host of kindred reforms which can only become possible when better housing obtains [53].

The Labour Party Constitution of 1918 provided a structure for the organization of women within the party. A permanent Chief Woman Officer was appointed to preside over a network of Women's Sections of the party branches. She was assisted by regional women's officers. Women had four reserved places on the powerful National Executive Committee of the Party, which was elected by the annual conference. Delegates of the Women's Sections met at an annual Women's Conference, but there was no obligation upon the Annual Party Conference or the National Executive Committee to take account of their decisions. Women often felt that they had the appearance rather than the substance of power within the Labour Party and they had certainly to struggle, often unsuccessfully, to be heard. But they were not wholly ignored and the Women's Sections and the Women's Conference did provide environments in which women could develop their political ideas and their skills of organization in a manner which had not previously been possible [54].

In 1918 the Conservative Party similarly reconstructed its machinery and sought to develop a mass organization in which women had a recognized place. Women were to have one third representation at all levels of party organization, presided over by a Women's Advisory Committee at Conservative Central Office. The activities of the Conservative women are discussed by Jarvis in this volume [55]. Liberal women were organized in the Asquithian Women's National Liberal Federation (WNLF), which played an important part in organizing women and in campaigning for the party. However, having been established some decades before women gained the vote, unlike the Labour and Conservative bodies, the WNLF had no secure position in the constitution of the Liberal Party and experienced continual frustration at the unwillingness of the Party leaders to take account of the views of the Council of the WNLF.

The women in all three major political parties in the inter-war years, and for long after, expressed frustration at the unresponsiveness to their views of their male-dominated parties, and at the difficulty experienced even by women with long records of party activity in achieving selection for winnable parliamentary, or even local government seats [56]. The table below (Table 1) shows how few women stood for parliament, and the still smaller numbers who were successful between 1918 and 1992.

The women's organizations of the political parties did, however, provide an opportunity for women to develop their political ideas and their organizational skills. All three aimed to educate women in the use of the vote. It is easy to caricature these organizations as subordinate to male-dominated parties, providing no more than domestic support to the real work of politics, providing the tea at meetings rather than the substance of policy-making. Such comments underestimate the importance of sociability in political culture, in the building and sustaining of political parties; and they also underestimate the political impact of the women's presence in certain areas of policy, as we will see.

Table 1. Women Candidates and MPs

	Conservative		Labour		*Liberal & Alliance		Other		Total	
	Cands.	MPs	Cands	MPs	Cands.	MPs	Cands.	MPs	Cands.	MPs
1918	1	-	4	-	4	-	8	1	17	1
1922	5	1	10	-	16	l	2	-	33	2
1923	7	3	14	3	12	2	1	-	34	8
1924	12	3	22	1	6	-	1	-	41	4
1929	10	3	30	9	25	1	4	1	69	14
1931	16	13	36	-	6	1	4	1	62	15
1935	19	6	35	1	11	1	2	1	67	9
1945	14	1	45	21	20	1	8	1	87	24
1950	28	6	42	14	45	1	11	-	126	21
1951	29	6	39	11	11	-	-	-	74	17
1955	32	10	43	14	12	-	2	-	89	24
2959	28	12	36	13	16	-	1	-	81	25
1964	24	11	33	18	25	-	8	-	90	29
1966	21	7	30	19	20	-	9	-	80	26
1970	26	15	29	10	23	-	21	1	99	26
1974	33	9	40	13	40	-	30	1	143	23
1974	30	7	50	18	49	-	32	2	161	27
1979	31	8	52	11	51	-	76	-	210	19
1983	40	13	78	10	(115)	-	87	-	280	23
1987	46	17	92	21	(106)	2	85	1	329	41
1992	59	20	138	37	144	2	227	1	568	60

* including Social Democrat & Lib Democrat candidates

(Source: David Butler and Gareth Butler, *British Political Facts, 1900-1994* (London, 1994), 243.)

WOMEN AND NON-PARTY ORGANIZATIONS

Apart from the large numbers of women who joined and were active in political parties, possibly larger numbers belonged to non-party political organizations that were dedicated to educating women in the use of their civil rights and that worked to achieve highly political goals of particular importance to women. These organizations were distinctive to the decades between the wars, when women first had the vote, though some were continuations of older associations in new forms and some survived long after the 1930s in new guises.

Even before the passing of the Representation of the People Act, suffrage societies began to organize to raise political awareness among women, to inform them about important political issues, to train them in procedures of campaigning, public speaking, committee work, and other essential skills of public life. Once women had the vote, they believed, it was important that they use it. In 1917 the National Union of Women Workers and the National Council of Women decided to form a network of Women's Citizens Associations (WCAs) throughout the country to provide this training. The first of these had been formed by Eleanor Rathbone in Liverpool in 1913. Membership was open to all women at age 16, so that political education could begin early in life. Women could join a WCA branch or a society which affiliated to it, as many local suffrage societies did. The role of WCAs was to "foster a sense of citizenship in women. Encourage the study of political, social and economic questions; secure the adequate representation of the interests and experience of women in the affairs of the community" [57].

The NUWSS moved smoothly from its major role in helping to bring about the Representation of the People Act to that of putting it into practice. It published pamphlets guiding women through the complexity of getting themselves onto the voting register and of using the vote, such as: *And Shall I have the Parliamentary Vote? Six Million Women Can Vote. The New Privilege of Citizenship and How Women Can Use the Vote.* It changed its name accordingly to the National Union of Societies for Equal Citizenship (NUSEC), and in 1924 it merged with the WCAs. Both organizations were determinedly non-party. This did not mean that they were necessarily wholly hostile to political parties. A substantial section of the pre-First World War women's movement – as of other sections of British society – was hostile to the party system, believing that party organization and discipline undermined the democratic process. When pre-war suffragists were asked what difference the vote would make, some of them replied: "the automatic disappearance of party government" and "the subordination of party considerations to principle" [58]. In consequence many women ran for election as independents. Eleanor Rathbone was an independent member of Liverpool city council from 1910 until the mid 1930s and an independent Member of Parliament from 1929 until her death in 1946. She held one of the anomalous university seats [59] which regularly returned independents to parliament. Until 1948 university graduates held a second vote which returned members of parliament for a small number of university seats. Unusually in the British electoral system they were elected by proportional representation. It was almost impossible for an independent to be returned for a non-university constituency at any other point in the 20th century, in peacetime [60].

The relationship of women's non-party organizations with the political parties was a source of debate and tension. However the WCAs and NUSEC were prepared to give support in elections and to work with party candidates, mainly female, but also male, who were active in causes favored by the women's movement. They were anxious in principle to promote and to support women as candidates in national and local elections and they had to acknowledge that the political culture in some parts of the country was more receptive of independent candidates than it was in others. For example of the 13 women elected to Cambridge City Council between 1918 and 1930, 10 were independents. All of the 39 women elected to Manchester City Council between 1908 and 1939 were party representatives [61]. Of the 52 women elected to Liverpool City Council between the wars, 17 were not representatives of the three major parties. Four were independents, the remainder were scattered among a variety of causes including the Co-operative Party (4), the Communist Party (1), the Protestant Party (2) and 'Anti-Waste'(1) [62]. Many female local candidates had support from the NUSEC. As the parties recruited more women, and were often hostile to the non-party women's organizations [63], the women's organizations had little to gain from withdrawal from electoral politics, and they recognized that beleaguered party women needed and appreciated support from women who shared many of their sympathies but were outside their party. There was frequent collaboration between party and non-party women at local level despite the disapproval of national party leaders.

A formal attempt to co-ordinate the activities of party and non-party women was made by the Consultative Committee of Women's Organizations (CCWO). This was initially formed by the NUWSS in 1916 to co-ordinate the demand for the vote and then to mobilize women voters. It became more active in 1921 when Lady Astor reorganized it to provide a link between members of parliaments and women's organizations. Forty-nine women's societies affiliated, including the NUSEC, the National Council of Women (NCW), the Six Point Group; and the Liberal and Conservative, but not the Labour, women. It had the support of a number of male MPs and campaigned against parliamentary candidates hostile to women's demands and for the supporters. It promoted networking, often at parties thrown by the wealthy Lady Astor, among women activists and politicians, seeking to draw women into the normal processes of political lobbying. It had some success in the 1920s but declined somewhat in the 1930s, as Lady Astor's concern to appease Nazism diverted her attention and lost her much support in women's associations [64].

Alongside the women's organizations, such as NUSEC, which were primarily dedicated to encouraging women to use the vote, other women's organizations with either broader, or more specific, single-issue, objectives, were also committed to the political education of the new female voters. The Women's Institutes (WIs) were founded in 1915 by suffragists, some of them former militants, to provide the large numbers of British countrywomen with opportunities for personal and political development, partly by providing them with a social space which was under their own control and independent of the traditional rural social hierarchy, in which the squire's wife was at the apex, and the wife of the parish clergyman a little below. The democratically elected committees of the WIs aimed at initiating a shift in rural power relationships among women, while also providing experience of political organizing. Equally importantly, they encouraged women to value their work and their skills, both in and outside the home, as men did, and to seek to improve their conditions of work in the home. They encouraged recognition of the value of women's products through sales of jams, chutneys, home-made garments, and other products at WI meetings and markets. These aims they held in common with the women of the Labour Party. The two organizations co-operated on campaigns to improve the quality of housing and to press their local authorities to take advantage of the inter-war housing legislation to build more and better houses. The WIs encouraged women, as men were doing at the time, to seek reduced hours of work and a wider range of leisure activities, encouraging sociability and activities such as drama and craft work and day trips. Equally importantly, they sought to provide country women with encouragement and training in using the vote and in campaigning for political changes of importance to them, such as improvement in the appalling state of rural housing, and access to piped water and electricity supplies, which were still absent from much of the countryside in the 1930s. The gradual spread of improvements in such essential facilities owed something to pressure from the WIs, though it is difficult to assess their precise input. It would be mistaken to overrate the political or the cultural influence of the WIs, but they had an undeniable role in improving the living and working conditions of countrywomen and in increasing their sense of empowerment. They should not be overlooked within the large network of organizations seeking to encourage women to exert their civil rights [65].

In 1932 the NUSEC established Townswomen's Guilds (TGs) as small town analogues of the WIs, in acknowledgement of the success of the WIs in providing a space for women previously excluded from the political culture. The TGs had an impressive 54,000 members by 1939 [66]. A similar role of encouraging political awareness and political education among women, alongside other goals, was performed by women's trade unions, professional, confessional, and single-issue groups such as the National Union of Women Teachers, the Council of Women Civil Servants, the (Roman Catholic) St Joan's Social and Political Union, the Union of Jewish Women, the Women's Sanitary Improvement and Health Visitors' Union, the working class Women's Co-operative Guild, and many others. At least 130 such organizations were active in the 1920s, almost certainly drawing into public life a larger number and a wider social range of women than ever before [67]. The impact of many of them is only beginning to be explored [68]. For example, women challenged with a new vigor the established gender order in one of the key institutions of the English cultural hierarchy: the Church of England. The Church League for Women's Suffrage (CLWS) had been founded in 1909 as a democratic organization, including both men and women, initiated mostly by individuals with backgrounds in Christian Socialism. In 1919 it renamed itself the League of the Church Militant, protesting, convincingly, that the Church was "not half militant enough" [69]. The League campaigned thereafter for greater representation of women within the Church and, particularly, for the ordination of women. The latter objective was not achieved until 1994. More immediately, in 1919, women were granted equal representation for the first time on the newly reorganized lay councils of the Church. The League carried on campaigning, especially among young women, for equal rights within the Church of England and on broader issues concerning women. Women were admitted more readily to the Ministry of Non-Conformist religious institutions: by the Congregationalists in 1917 and by Baptists in 1926 [70].

The League was one of many organizations which both campaigned on single issues and also worked with others in support of causes in which the variety of women's associations felt a common interest, especially the campaign between 1918 and 1928 to equalize the franchise and the longer struggle against the marriage bar. In the 1930s women showed a distinct preference for membership of more specialized women's organizations over those whose rationale was gender equality. The membership of professional, confessional, and other organizations grew as that of the NUSEC (from 1932 the National Council for Equal Citizenship) declined. The number of societies affiliated to the NUSEC fell from 2220 in 1920 to 48 in the later 1930s, while the membership of the TGs reached 54,000 in 1939. [71] This proliferation of women's organizations was not a splintering of the women's movement, rather it illustrates how women's organizations came to permeate public life in the decades after the vote was gained while continuing to co-operate on key issues.

In all three major political parties and in non-aligned organizations women worked hard to help women acquire the skills of political campaigning. This finding conflicts with assertions that since the political parties showed no strong inclination to support the issues on which many women felt strongly, women held aloof from the whole representative process.[72] It would indeed have been odd (as the above quotation from Millicent Garrett Fawcett suggests) if women, having fought so hard for the vote on the grounds that it would benefit them, had immediately refused to use it on the grounds that it could not. Rather, many women argued that in a political system so dominated by political parties as the British, there was no alternative but to seek to influence the parties and to use the potential power of the vote to pressurize them, fully aware of how difficult this would be. The argument that "the attainment of at least a measure of enfranchisement for women meant that legal and political rights ceased to be a dominating issue and were replaced by economic and cultural questions" [73] oversimplifies the perceptions of many new voters and of the leaders of women's associations. By the end of the 1920s many, including the leadership of the NUSEC, had come to realize, if they had not before, that a focus simply upon parliamentary lobbying and legislation by a small minority of women and their male supporters could not achieve gender equality or, at least, would not achieve it soon; rather, there was a need for cultural change, drawing more women and men into awareness of the need for transformation, or at least modification, of gender roles and into awareness of their own power to effect change. This was the role of organizations such as the WIs and TGs. But at the same time it was not forgotten that much remained to be fought for, that could only be achieved by legislative change: the divorce law and other aspects of family and property law, for one example. Making a reality of civil rights, putting them to use, remained as challenging as gaining them in the eyes of many women at the time.

But women found it difficult to reach positions of overt power from which they could promote these causes. We have seen (see above, Table 1) how slowly they acquired access to parliamentary seats. When they were successful the House of Commons was inhospitable to women. Even Lady Astor, was taken aback by the hostility she experienced. She later admitted: "If I'd known how much men would hate it, I would never have dared do it".

Table 2. Women in Local Government

	1914	1923	1930	1937	% of total
County Councils	7	68	138	242	5
City & Boro' Councils	19	213	439	599	5
London Boroughs	22	116	289	253	15.8
UDCs	11	104	308	255*	4.5
RDCs	200	353		334*	4.6
Total	259	754	1174	1653	5.4
Board of Guardians	1536	2323	-	-	

* Returns incomplete. If women had been represented in the same proportion as on bodies for which returns were made there would have been an additional 684, giving a total of 2346.

(Source: Martin Pugh, *Women and the Women's Movement in Britain, 1918-1950*, London 1992, p. 57)

Local government, which was still of great importance especially concerning social policy questions in the inter-war years, was only slightly more receptive (Table 2).

There is, however, as the above account suggests, another level on which women's role in the political culture needs to be assessed: as members of interest groups lobbying, often successfully, for legislative change.

WOMEN AND PUBLIC POLICY

The years immediately following 1918 saw a strikingly rapid flow of legislation for which women's associations had exerted organized pressure and which favorably affected women's lives. Millicent Garrett Fawcett judged that between 1902 and 1914 "only two really important Acts bearing especially upon the welfare and status of women had been passed - namely the Midwives Act, 1902, and the group of Acts dating from 1907 to 1914 dealing with the qualification of women as candidates in local elections",[74] but she stated that in the year following "the passing of the Reform Act of 1918 at least seven important measures effecting large improvements in the status of women have rapidly gone through all their stages in both Houses of Parliament".[75] Among these measures was the rapidly approved and largely unopposed legislation of November 1918, put into effect three weeks before the election, which enabled women to be elected to Parliament. Even suffragists were surprised that this came so soon and without a struggle, the more so because women were allowed to sit in parliament before they could vote, at age 21.

Fawcett also included in her triumphal list the doubling, also in 1918, of the sum fathers could be obliged to pay towards the maintenance of an illegitimate child (from 5s to 10s a week); and in the same year the Midwives Amending Act which improved midwife training, followed by measures to improve nurse training [76]. These improved both the professional status of women and the quality of care available to them. Curiously Fawcett did not include the Maternity and Child Welfare Act, 1918, which facilitated improvement in the care available to women – before during and after childbirth – and to their children. This was the outcome of campaigns by women, especially of the Women's Co-operative Guild (WCG), before and during the war. Further campaigning by women, at local government level especially, ensured the implementation of a measure which, like much social legislation, was permissive – that is, local authorities had discretion as to its implementation [77]. Improvement of the conditions of childbirth and childrearing were important preoccupations throughout the inter-war years, especially of organizations with a substantial working class membership, such as WCG and the Women's Sections of the Labour Party. These included a desire to make birth control information easily available to women. Voluntary organizations opened birth control centers throughout the 1920s, but they were relatively few and scattered and generally required payment. Women and men campaigned that local authority health and welfare clinics should be enabled to give free advice. Governments were reluctant to take up an issue which was highly controversial in Britain, but in 1930 the Labour government granted permission for local authority centers to give advice to married women for whom pregnancy would be detrimental to health. This qualification was widely ignored and later modified. The response to this new dispensation was regionally variable and difficult to assess, but the decline of the national campaign gives substance to

Pat Thane

suggestions that many local medical officers and health visitors felt free to give birth control advice [78].

Fawcett did include in her list of victories for women the Sex Disqualification (Removal) Act, 1919, which in principle abolished disqualification by sex or marriage for entry to the professions and universities and the exercise of any public function (such as jury service or appointment to the magistracy). She regretted that this Act was less comprehensive than the Women's Emancipation Bill put forward by the Labour Party which had passed all stages in the House of Commons, but was opposed by the government and rejected in the House of Lords, because, she believed, credibly enough, it included an equal franchise clause. In practice considerable obstacles remained in the path of women seeking to enter such professions as law and medicine or the higher levels of the civil service; they were the object of persistent campaigning by women through the 1920s, 1930s and 1940s [79]. Nevertheless, in 1920, 200 women, including Fawcett herself, were appointed magistrates, presiding over the lowest but most active level of the judicial system. As well as admitting women to an influential area of public life, this change brought to an end the situation in which, throughout time, women involved in legal processes, such as those concerning marital or family matters or cases of physical or sexual assault, had faced courtrooms wholly composed of men. This was an experience against which organizations such as the NCW (founded in 1895) had long campaigned. There were 1600 female magistrates in England and Wales by 1927, out of a total of 25,000.

Fawcett noted also improvements in the inheritance rights of women under Scottish law (which was distinct from that of England and Wales); and the Industrial Courts Act, 1919 which, due to an amendment put forward by the Labour Party, allowed women to sit in these newly established courts of arbitration on such matters as pay and conditions in the workplace. Fawcett also, with good reason, claimed as a victory the inclusion in the Charter of the newly formed League of Nations of a clause enabling women to be eligible for all appointments in connection with the League. This followed a deputation from representatives of suffragists of the allied nations and the USA. Women indeed became active and effective within the League, especially on industrial and social questions. As Fawcett put it, by 1920, "The walls of our Jericho have not fallen at the first blast of our trumpet, but we have made great progress" [80].

The progress appeared to continue. In 1919 the NUSEC decided to focus upon a limited number of objectives at one time, for "we had learned that the field was so vast that success was jeopardised if we scattered our energies over the whole of it" [81]. The NUSEC chose as its immediate objectives, equal pay for equal work; reform of the divorce law and laws dealing with prostitution and the establishment of "an equal moral standard"; pensions for civilian widows (they had been granted to war widows for the first time during the Great War); equal rights of guardianship of children; the opening of the legal profession to women. By 1926 there had been decisive movement on all of these, with the exception of equal pay.

The Deceased Brother's Widow's Marriage Act, 1921, enabled a woman to marry her deceased husband's brother, removing the oddity that this had previously been prohibited, whilst men had the right to marry a deceased wife's sister. This change was supported by the Women's Freedom League and the Women's National Liberal Federation. It was a measure which promoted gender equality and also one of many of the period designed to stabilize family life, in this case by enabling a brother to support the family of a dead sibling [82].

A important cause for a range of women's associations in the inter-war years was 'the equal moral standard', essentially the protection of women and children against sexual and physical exploitation and abuse, within and outwith marriage. Their campaigns contributed to the passing of the Criminal Law Amendment Act, 1922, which raised the age of consent from 13 to 16 and extended from six to nine months the period during which proceedings could be taken in cases of criminal assault. In 1929 an anomaly was removed when the age of marriage for both sexes was raised to match the age of consent. Previously the age at which marriage was permissible was twelve for females (though consummation was prohibited until age thirteen) and fourteen for males. In the 1920s about 24 girls each year were married before the age of sixteen, most of them pregnant. This legal change owed much to the work of NUSEC, the St Joan's Social and Political Union (as CWSS had become) and the YWCA [83]. In 1922 the level of maintenance allowed to a woman and her children under a separation order was increased, giving further support to women needing to escape from intolerable marriages. Further legislation in 1925 extended the grounds on which either partner could obtain a separation, to include cruelty and habitual drunkeness, and abolished the requirement that the wife must leave the marital home before applying for a separation order. NUSEC believed that separation, with adequate financial safeguards, was 'the women's issue par excellence', because economic dependence upon men made women vulnerable to abuse. These legislative changes were supported by a diverse set of women's associations including the Catholic Women's Suffrage Society (CWSS), the Conservative Women's Reform association, the Labour supporting Women's Group of the Fabian Society, the Standing Joint Committee of Industrial Women's Organizations and the Women's Co-Operative Guild, the radical Women's Freedom League and the Union of Jewish Women [84].

The Infanticide Act, 1922, removed another grievance highlighted by the women's organisations by eliminating the charge of murder for a woman guilty of killing her child, where it was shown that she was suffering from the effects of her confinement. Also the long process of equalising property rights went a step further in the Law of Property Act, 1922, which enabled a husband and wife equally to inherit each other's property and granted them equal rights to inherit the property of intestate children. The New English Law of Property, 1926, allowed both married and single women to hold and dispose of their property, real and personal, on the same terms as men. Further legislation in 1935 empowered a married woman to dispose by will of her property as though she were single; and, taking gender equality a logical step further, abolished the husband's liability for his wife's debts.

The Matrimonial Causes Act, 1923, relieved wives of the necessity to prove desertion, cruelty or other faults in addition to adultery as grounds for divorce, thus bringing gender equality in the divorce courts closer. Divorce was a divisive issue, denominational associations affiliated to NUSEC such as CWSS being opposed to it. Nevertheless this was an instance in which NUSEC was 'unequivocally... successful in the implementation of its policy' [85] having played an important role in drafting and promoting the legislation. Further legislation in 1937 and 1950 extended the grounds for divorce. Women supported equal divorce legislation not only to enable women, and men, to escape from miserable marriages, but also in order to encourage higher expectations of, and behaviour within, an institution which had encountered widespread criticism since the later 19th century. Similarly, the Bastardy Act, 1923, sought to promote stable family life and to remove a painful anomaly by enabling children to be recognized as legitimate on the subsequent marriage of their parents. It sought also to improve procedure to enable unmarried mothers to claim maintenance from the fathers of their children. The National Council for the Unmarried Mother and her Child had been founded in 1918 primarily to promote such changes, with the support of prominent women's organizations. Similarly the Adoption Act, 1926, which introduced the principle that a court must satisfy itself with the circumstances of an adoption, sought to protect adopted children who were often 'illegitimate'. The Intoxicating Liquors (Sales to Young Persons under 18) Act, 1923, was a further outcome of the campaign of many women's groups for the protection of young people.

In 1924 women acquired equal guardianship rights over infants following the break-up of a marriage. In the following year Widows and Orphans Pensions were introduced. By 1933 these gave pensions to 725,000 women and 340,000 children, for the first time enabling these exceptionally poor people to escape from the Poor Law. This was an important campaigning issue for NUSEC and other groups and was seen as the first step towards the objective of family allowances, granting unconditional payments to the poorest mothers. Family Allowances, which had been Eleanor Rathbone's special cause, were introduced in 1945 [86].

In 1928 NUSEC felt that women had achieved a major victory when voting rights were extended to all women on equal terms with men.

Legislation was occasionally a cause of conflict. Legislation specifically protecting women in the workplace had long been a source of dissension. Some feminists argued that such legislation when applied only to women restricted their work opportunities; and that all workers, male and female, deserved protection from hazardous conditions. Others, especially female trade unionists, recognized the strict gender division of labour and believed that the working conditions of many women were so poor, and that women were so little supported by trade unions, that any legal protection was to be welcomed. Conflict broke out over the Factory Act, 1927 and led to the resignation of a number of members of the Council of NUSEC [87].

Women's organizations played an active part in bringing about these changes. NUSEC send a questionnaire to all candidates in the general election of 1922 soliciting views on the issues it was committed to. They included: equal franchise, equal pay and opportunities, equal guardianship of children, the equal moral standard, protection and maintenance of illegitimate children, the appointment of women police, admission of women to the House of Lords, improved separation and maintenance arrangements, admission of women to juries, widows pensions, the granting of full degree status to women at Cambridge University [88] and proportional representation. Only on proportional representation were there no change by the later 1950s. The principle of equal pay was accepted in the public service in 1954, though not in the private sector until 1970. Women were admitted to the House of Lords as Life Peers when this new category was introduced in 1958, though not until 1963 were female holders of hereditary peerages admitted to membership of the House of Lords.

At the election of 1922 the Women's Freedom League also distributed a questionnaire to candidates. This gave priority to the franchise, admission of women to the House of Lords, equal pay and opportunities, equal legal status for men and women and equal training and relief for the unemployed (which NUSEC also supported) [89]. Most women's organizations agreed on a cluster of objectives, though they differed in the salience they gave to individual items. They agreed on issues of welfare and income maintenance, mainly affecting poorer women including housing, education, maternal and child health and welfare, widows pensions, family allowances and equal pay; legal matters concerning property and taxation which mainly concerned better off women; wider access to employment, pay and promotion for women at all levels; issues around marriage and divorce and rights over children; the protection of women and children from sexual and physical abuse. There was not the clear division historians once perceived between 'old' 'equal rights' feminists fighting for full gender equality and 'new' 'welfare' feminists concerned with more limited social improvements in women's lives. These goals could be held simultaneously and were complementary. For example, the active campaign, for example by WCAs for the appointment of policewomen, was as much a product of the fight for an equal moral standard as for wider employment opportunities for women. Victims of abuse were thought more likely to report their problems to policewomen than to men and in a range of situations, for example when confined to police cells, vulnerable women and children were thought to need the protection of other women. Policewomen had first been appointed during the Great War and local police authorities were reluctant to continue the practice after the war. In 1939 43 out of 183 police authorities employed policewomen, but only 174 of them in a total force of 65,000.

Women's organizations lobbied skilfully for many of the legal changes of the inter-war years. It can be argued that one reason why there were fewer flamboyant demonstrations than before the war was that women's groups had become 'political insiders rather than outsiders' [90], seeking to achieve their goals by lobbying and negotiating in the corridors of power, successfully enough not to require resort to violence. Demonstrations, however, still occurred when it was judged necessary to make a public display of the united strength of women. The main focus of demonstrations in the 1920s was the extension of the franchise, though they occurred also on other issues, for example against the 'marriage bar', which excluded women from many occupations on marriage [91].

Fifty women's groups supported a demonstration in London in 1923 for the equal franchise. There were three major rallies on the issue in 1924 and public campaigning continued until the franchise law was changed in 1928, accompanied by some revival of talk about the need for a return to suffragette militancy [92]. In a great march to Hyde Park in 1926 3,500 women walked, many of them in professional groups (as teachers, journalists etc) to emphasize the contribution women were making to society. The march included groups of women too young to vote, such as the Guild of Girl Citizens, representatives of American suffrage societies, female parliamentary candidates, mayors and magistrates, and veteran suffragettes wearing their prison badges. Millicent Fawcett and Annie Besant, both aged 79, Charlotte Despard, leader of the WFL, aged 83 and still politically active, and

Emmeline Pankhurst, a mere 70 years old and by now a parliamentary candidate for the Conservative Party, walked the whole route; whilst the pioneer aviator, and member of the Women's Engineering Society, Mrs Elliott-Lynn, flew her plane above the marchers in salute. On fifteen platforms in Hyde Park the array of women's causes was promoted. Visually, also, the march was striking. The *Woman Teacher* reported:

> One after another, each with its distinctive colours, the contingents swept across the park; green, white and gold; blue and silver; green and rose; blue, white and silver; red, white and green; purple, green and white... in one section the members wore pink dresses with wreathes of green leaves, or green dresses trimmed with roses; in another section a group of 'Under-Thirties' very appropriately wore bright green dresses, the colour symbolical of spring and hope [93].

This procession, like many others 'was a reminder of the underlying unity of the extraordinary network which the women's movement had created in less than fifty years' [94]. But it also showed how the movement had changed, in the very variety of different interests it expressed. Another occasion for a public demonstration of the extent of support for the women's cause was the funeral of Emmeline Pankhurst in London in June 1928. She lived until the equal franchise was assured of parliamentary success. Representatives of the range of women's associations attended the service and thousands of people lined the streets.

At least as impressive as the public demonstrations was the quieter work behind the scenes of Whitehall. NUSEC in particular took on the role of developing the expertise which enabled it to achieve some of its own legislative goals and to help other groups to do so. It believed that it could "act for the whole women's movement as a kind of Corps of Royal Engineers, engineering its Bills on already prepared territory and continually exploring and pushing forward into fresh areas" [95]. Its objectives were democratically decided at its annual conferences. NUSEC activists, such as Eva Hubback [96] and Chrystal Macmillan gained expertise in drafting Bills, which were introduced in parliament by sympathetic supporters, usually male. These techniques were credited with securing in particular the 1925 Summary Jurisdiction (Separation and Maintenance) Act and the 1929 Age of Marriage Act. NUSEC worked jointly with the National Council of Women and the Consultative Committee of Women's Organizations (to which 49 organizations were affiliated) [97] and a range of other organizations (including the YWCA) to achieve these legal changes. NUSEC was too realistic politically to expect to achieve its complete objectives, believing rather in gradualism and in securing the best achievable instalment of reform. It recognized the inevitability of compromise. It was criticized by *Time and Tide* for placing too much faith in minor legislative changes and came to recognize the limitations of its approach, important though the outcomes had been for women. Larger changes, it was decided, such as major reform of the divorce law, or the achievement of equal pay, required involvement and pressure from women on a larger scale, hence the formation of Townswomen's Guilds, designed to politicize a wider range of women. Different objectives indeed required different tactics.

Another important, and effective, level of political activity was that of pressurizing local authorities to implement national legislation, as described above in connection with maternal and child welfare legislation. Women in party and non-party organizations were active in pressing for, among other things, implementation of the succession of Housing Acts of the inter-war years and the improvement of education. It can be argued that women voters played an important role in placing social welfare centrally on to the national political agenda, especially in forms responsive to the needs of poorer women [98].

A NEGATIVE ACHIEVEMENT?

It has been argued that the impact of the new women voters was limited and ambiguous, because they did not achieve all of their ambitions since much of the legislation outlined above was the outcome of compromise and such achievement as can be detected came about only with the support other political groups with different motives.[99] Compromise, however, as NUSEC and other women's associations recognized, is the nature of politics and they were realistic enough to recognize that they would not sweep all before them. Once more, it is important not to judge by impossible standards. The Labour Party was incomparably stronger in the 1920s than before 1914 and more securely established in the political system than the women's organizations, but it also fell far short of achieving its full goals and indeed such achievement is rare in parliamentary democracies.

Since most of the legislation was the outcome of compromise it is difficult to assess the precise impact of women as voters, demonstrators and political organisers or to answer the counterfactual question: would British politics between the wars, or later, have been different if women had not obtained the vote? Certainly there had been legislation before 1918 which favoured women, and women as political activists had helped to bring about these and also other changes affecting men as well as women. But, as Millicent Garrett Fawcett pointed out, there was strikingly more such legislation, after 1918 than before. It would be surprising if this flow of legislation was unconnected with the fact that women had, and used, the vote.

Some commentators minimize the impact of the women on the grounds that some of the changes they claimed as victories, such as the 1923 Intoxicating Liquors Act and the 1926 Legitimacy Act, are not perceived as 'feminist', in the sense that they did not promote gender equality.[100] There is no reason why women as voters, even those who identify as feminists, should concern themselves only with the promotion of gender equality. Feminists in the 1920s did, however, give high priority to these issues. They regarded legislation which promoted the equal moral standard and civilized, non-violent and non-exploitative, relations between the sexes, as protective of women and designed to civilise those men who required it, and hence as contributing to gender equality.

It has rightly been pointed out that women's associations came closer to achieving their goals in the sphere of personal life and social welfare than in that of the labour market and economic activity. Less convincingly, changes in family and welfare law are described, not as advancing the cause of women but rather as serving to reinforce traditional gender roles, being concerned primarily with women in their maternal and domestic capacities, expressions of the reimposition of domesticity rather than of progressive advance.[101] This is too simple a view of the legislation and of the motivation for it. Firstly, the roles which it aimed to influence were by no means traditional. Reforms of the procedures for divorce, separa-tion and maintenance were designed to support rather than to undermine marriage as an institution ; but they were expected to do so by demonstrating to men that the sexual dou-ble standard was crumbling, by creating sanctions against abuse of wives, and by enabling women to escape from oppressive and unhappy marriages and to enter more satisfactory partnerships or to live independently, if by no means always prosperously, as had not been possible before. Measures for which women campaigned which improved conditions of child-care and child-birth, housing conditions and health-care began dramatically to improve the appalling conditions in which many thousands of women and men lived their lives in the 1920s, as they had throughout history. Women's groups advocated these partly as being good in themselves. Many women had wanted the vote precisely because they believed that women's influence in politics would bring about improvements in social con-ditions which male politicians had allowed to fester for far too long. Prominent feminists, such as Vera Brittain, believed that women played an important role in bringing about the major extensions of state welfare which followed the second world war. The relative impor-tance of this role is difficult to estimate, but if women voters and campaigners helped to bring modern welfare states into being it was no small achievement. Whilst not ambigu-ously beneficent, the modern British welfare state has done a great more for women and for men than simply to reinforce gender roles.

But welfare improvements were not always seen by their supporters just as goods in them-selves, but also as essential preconditions for the mass of women to play a larger part in the world outside the home; they were designed to liberate women from entrapment in domes-ticity, not to constrain them within it. It was believed that if women became physically fit-ter and less burdened with the care of decrepit housing they would have more time for and would be better able to engage in other pursuits. This view was propounded especially vig-orously by the women of the Labour Party. An editorial in their journal *Labour Woman* in September 1922 asserted:

> As soon as married women organize themselves strongly and make use of their political power in local and national elections, so soon will they be able to make such improvement in hous-ing and the care of homes as will reduce their labour and give them more fruitful leisure... They must raise themselves out of the overwork and drudgery of their lives and insist on conditions which give them opportunities for
> FREEDOM
> HEALTH
> REASONABLE LEISURE
> and USEFUL PUBLIC SERVICE.

This view was shared by other women's organizations. It was not an appeal for further imprisonment in domesticity.

Welfare goals were not perceived by their female advocates in isolation from other goals nor in terms of domesticity being women's all-consuming role. Rather they took as their starting point the assumption that a very high proportion of women were likely to marry (and it was assumed that they *would* marry rather than that they *should*) and have children and that they should do so in conditions which ensured that domesticity did not control their lives and which allowed them choices as to how to spend their non-domestic time. Improvements in women's domestic lives were to be complemented by wider access to employment and training and to equal pay with men for work of equal worth once they were in paid employment. The aim was to give women a genuine choice between work in or out of the home. Again, this was well expressed by the leader of the Labour party women:

> The right of a married woman to earn outside the home must be insisted upon; and equally her right not to be forced to work outside the home through economic necessity if she wants to make home and children her work. (In the past outside employment for married women has meant the burden of two full-time jobs instead of one) [102].

It was an approach to social policy and labour market policy, which saw these two areas as complementary rather than opposed, and which was designed to liberate rather than to constrain women. It gained wide agreement among women's associations in the 1920s and 1930s.

There is no doubt that alongside those who strove to ease the domestic roles of women in inter-war Britain were those who wished to lock women into lives dominated by domesticity and child-bearing, at this as at other times. But as at other times it is important to not to read prescriptive polemic, of which there was much, as transparent description of the lives of many women, or to assume that women were passive receptors of contemporary domestic imagery conveyed by the spreading new media of communications, such as women's magazines and films. The polemics were perhaps all the more strident precisely because many women were not embracing domesticity as their sole role. There was during the 1920s and 1930s an active contest between those who wanted to impose domesticity firmly upon women – all previous attempts having been less than wholly successful – and those who wished to enable women to control domesticity and to enable it to serve their own interests.

The outcome of the contest in the inter-war years was mixed: the marriage bar spread and excluded many married women from paid employment, mainly in the public service and professions and some industries. But increasing numbers of women, including married women, were recorded as being in paid employment in the 1930s, though not at the higher levels; they were concentrated especially in the expanding factory areas and in 'white blouse' occupations. Demands for equal pay were less successful in the short run than welfare demands, but the campaign continued through the Second World War, was successful in the public service by 1954 [103], was actively taken up by women in the trade unions from the early 1960s, leading to the Equal Pay legislation of 1970 – which has had mixed but not wholly negative results. There is a danger of underestimating the continuity between the campaigns and aspirations of the inter-war years and the poorly researched post-second World War situation. The environment of the inter-war years, of heavy, sustained unemployment and of government non-intervention in the economy was not favourable for any group, male or female, seeking improved conditions in the labour market. The full-employment era from 1945 to the early 1970s was somewhat more hospitable to demands for certain types of change, though the outcome was limited.

Also in the 1930s many women were diverted from the issues which had preoccupied them in the 1920s by concern with the increasingly threatening world situation [104]. They could be forgiven for believing that nazism was a greater threat at this time than sex discrimination.

Also, a higher proportion of women, and men, were married by the 1930s than before world war one, and more of them had children, which might seem confirmation that a domestic ideology was triumphant. But family life was changing. The birth-rate and family size fell to an historically low level in the early 1930s, to an average of around two per family, born earlier in the mother's life than had previously been normal. At the same time, life expectancy rose. A smaller proportion of a woman's life was encompassed by child-rearing and childbearing. This took place against the frequent and sometimes hysterical expressions of concern by public figures about the danger to the nation posed by the dwindling birth-rate and the need to encourage women to have more children. Women were wholly unresponsive to such pressure, indeed were hostile to and suspicious of it when their opinions were surveyed. They made such comments as: 'They only want more cannon-fodder for the next war' [105].

For these women and their husbands having fewer children was the key to improved living standards, to escape from the poverty and misery of the large families they had known when they were young. They did not simply absorb official ideology. Official publications in the 1940s recognized that women were not to be so easily manipulated. The Report of the Royal Commission on Population, set up in 1943, in response to concern about the declining birth-rate, reported in 1948, when the birth-rate was rising but not to previous levels, and commented:

> it is clear that women today are not prepared to accept, as most women in Victorian times accepted, a married life of continuous preoccupation with housework and care of children and that the more independent status and wider interests of women today, which are part of the ideals of the community as a whole, are not compatible with repeated and excessive childbearing...

> Concern over the trend of population has led to attempts in some countries, e.g. Germany and Italy, in recent times to narrow the range of women's interests and to 'bring women back into the home'. Such a policy not only runs against the democratic conception of individual freedom, but in Great Britain it would be a rebuking of the tide. It ignores the repercussions which the fall in the size of the family itself has had on the place of women in modern society... The modern woman is not only more conscious of the need for outside interests but has more freedom to engage them; and it would be harmful all round, to the women, the family and the community, to attempt any restriction of the contribution women can make to the cultural and economic life of the nation. It is true that there is often a real conflict between motherhood and a whole-time 'career'. Part of this conflict is inherent in the biological function of women, but part of it is artificial... we therefore welcome the removal of the marriage bar in such employments as teaching and the civil service and we think that a deliberate effort should be made to devise adjustments that would render it easier for women to combine motherhood and the care of the home with outside activities [106].

That such comments could appear, apparently unchallenged, in an official document suggests that there had been some shifts in gender roles and in influential perceptions of them since the end of the previous war.

Conclusion

There is reason to question the assumption that a reasserted ideology of domesticity was successfully imposed upon women in the 1930s and again, after a brief respite, after the war, with, among other results, conservative effects upon their place in the political culture. More generally this chapter has sought to examine what difference votes for women made to the first generations of women to cast votes, and to British politics, and to challenge the view that the change was insignificant. After 1918 women sought to assert their citizenship within the profoundly inhospitable political culture to which they had been reluctantly admitted. What is surprising is not that so few but that so many voted, agitated, campaigned and made some indentations in the political order. Fully to assess the changes brought about by full democratisation of the British franchise would require equally detailed study of the roles of women in politics in the second half of the 20th century, a study which is urgently needed, but for which there is no space here.

Clearly there had been no revolution in gender roles between 1918 and 1939, or 1945 or 2000. Equally clearly the roles of men and women are not the same in the 1990s as in the 1920s and the differences help to shape the political culture and political decisions. There was change in the ways in which women lived their lives, which enabled successive generations to imagine a wider range of possibilities and a greater sense of their capacity to control their own lives. The feminists of the 1960s, after all, were the daughters of the first generation of women to grow up knowing that they could control the size of their families, that they had the vote on equal terms with men, and had effective equality before the law.

 Notes

[1] Caine B., *English Feminism, 1780-1980*, Oxford 1997, pp. 173-255; Smith H.L., *British Feminism in the 1920s*, in H.L. Smith H.L. (ed), *British Feminism in the Twentieth Century*, Aldershot 1990; Pugh M., *Women and the Women's Movement in Britain 1914-1959*, London 1992, presents a rather more complex picture.

[2] Pugh, *Women's Movement*, p. 312.

[3] Caine, *English Feminism*; Smith, *British Feminism*; Pugh, *Women's Movement*.

[4] Quoted in Caine, *English Feminism*, p. 183.

[5] Eoff M.S., *Viscountess Rhondda. Equalitarian Feminist*, Columbus 1991, p. 64.

[6] Ibid., p. 132, quoted from *Time and Tide*.

[7] e.g. Banks O., *Faces of Feminism*, Oxford 1981.

[8] Eoff, *Rhondda*, p. 174.

[9] Pankhurst S., *The Suffrage Movement* (1931; reprinted: London 1977).

[10] Pugh, *Women's Movement*.

[11] Pankhurst, *Suffrage*, pp. 607-8.

[12] Kingsley Kent S., *Making Peace. The Reconstruction of Gender in Interwar Britain*, Princeton 1993; Gilbert S.M., *Soldier's Heart: Literary men, Literary Women and the Great War*, in Margaret R. Higonnet M.R. et al., *Behind the Lines. Gender and the two World Wars*, New Haven 1987, pp. 197-226. This interpretation has been ably criticized by Cullen S., *Gender and the Great War. British Combatants, Masculinity and Perceptions of Women, 1918-39*, unpublished D. Phil thesis, Oxford University 1999.

[13] Eoff, *Rhondda*, p. 149.

[14] Linklater A., *An Unhusbanded Life. Charlotte Despard: Suffragette, Socialist and Sinn Feiner*, London 1980, p. 249.

[15] *The Vote*, 6 July 1928, 212 quoted in Law C., *Suffrage and Power. The Women's Movement, 1918-28*, London 1997, p. 224.

[16] Holton S., *Feminism and Democracy*, Cambridge 1986.

[17] Garrett Fawcett M., *The Women's Victory- and After: Personal Reminiscences, 1911-1918*, London 1920.

[18] e.g. Caine, *English Feminism*, p. 173.

[19] *Times*, Oct. 30 1924.

[20] Quoted in Law, *Suffrage*, p. 227.

[21] Strachey R., *The Cause. A Short History of the Women's Movement in Great Britain* (1928; reprinted: London 1978).

[22] Caine, *English Feminism*, p. 197.

[23] Strachey, *Cause*, p. 367.

[24] Butler D. and G., *British Political Facts, 1900-1994*, London 1994, pp. 213-19.

[25] *Times*, Nov. 16 1922.

[26] *Times*, Dec 7 1923.

[27] *Times*, Dec. 8 1923.

[28] *Times*, Oct. 30 1924.

[29] *Times*, May 30 1929.

[30] Ibid., *Election Day Report from the North-East.*

[31] Ibid., *Report from Greater London.*

[32] Ibid., *Report from the Midlands.*

[33] Ibid.,. *Report from Scotland.*

[34] *Times*, May 31 1929.

[35] Davies S., *Liverpool Labour. Social and Political Influences on the Development of the Labour Party in Liverpool, 1900-1939*, Liverpool 1996, p. 190.

[36] e.g. Blondel J., *Voters, Parties and Leaders*, London 1965.

[37] Randall V., *Women and Politics. An International Perspective*, London 1987.

[38] Ibid., pp. 69-70.

[39] Among others, Butler D., Stokes D., *Political Change in Britain: the Evolution of Political Choice*, (second edition, London 1974), p. 160; Crewe I., Day N., Fox A., *The British Electorate, 1963-87: A Compendium of Data from the British Election Studies*, Cambridge 1991, p. 6.

[40] Lovenduski J. et al., *The Party and Women*, in Seldon A., Ball S., *Conservative Century. The Conservative Party since 1900*, Oxford 1994, pp. 611-35.

[41] Turner J., *The Labour Vote and the Franchise after 1918: an Investigation of the English Evidence*, in Denley P., Hopkin D. (eds), *History and Computing*, Manchester, 1987; Rasmussen J., *Women in Labour: the flapper vote and party system transformation in Britain*, "Electoral Studies", 3, 1984. For a critique see Tanner D., *Political Change and the Labour Party, 1900-1918*, Cambridge 1990, p. 308.

[42] Ibid.

[43] Randall, *Women and Politics*, pp. 70-6.

[44] Thane P., *The women of the British Labour Party and Feminism, 1906-1945*, in Smith, *British Feminism*, p. 124.

[45] Mark-Lawson J. et al., *Gender and local politics: struggles over welfare policies, 1918-1939*, in Murgatroyd L. et al. (eds), *Localities, Class and Gender*, London 1985.

[46] Hollis P., *Ladies Elect.Women in English Local Government, 1865-1914*, Oxford 1987.

[47] Savage M., *The dynamics of working class politics: the Labour Movement in Preston, 1880-1940*, Cambridge 1987.

[48] Davies, *Liverpool Labour,* pp. 186-8.

[49] Graves P.M., *Labour Women. Women in British Working Class Politics, 1918-1939,* Cambridge 1994.

[50] Pugh, *Women,* p. 125.

[51] Ibid.

[52] Thane P., *Women, Liberalism and Citizenship, 1918-1930,* in Biagini E. (ed), *Citizenship and Community. Liberals, Radicals and Collective Identities in the British Isles 1865-1931,* Cambridge 1996, p. 68.

[53] Ibid., *Liberal Women's News,* April 1925.

[54] For details see Thane, *Women in the Labour Party.* Graves, *Labour Women.*

[55] And see Pugh, *Women's Movement,* pp. 124-9.

[56] *Labour Woman, Liberal Women's News;* Graves, *Labour Women,* pp. 22-40, 154-180; Thane, *Women, Liberalism and Citizenship.*

[57] Law, *Suffrage,* p. 113.

[58] Harrison B., *Separate Spheres. The Opposition to Women's Suffrage in Britain,* London 1978, p. 229.

[59] Graduates, male and female, could vote both in their constituencies and for a separate list of university candidates. This practice was abolished in 1948.

[60] Butler and Butler, *Facts,* pp. 167-8.

[61] I am grateful to my research student, Janet Howes, for this information.

[62] Davies, *Liverpool Labour,* pp. 247-361.

[63] In *Liverpool Labour* women and the local WCA drew increasingly apart in the 1920s. Ibid., p. 176.

[64] Pugh, *Women's Movement,* pp. 70-1.

[65] Andrews M., *The Acceptable Face of Feminism. The Women's Institute as a Social Movement,* London 1997.

[66] Pugh, *Women's Movement,* pp. 240-1.

[67] Law, *Suffrage,* pp. 232-7.

[68] Also Andrews, *Womens Institutes;* C. Beaumont (Warwick University Ph.D.).

[69] de Vries J.R., *Challenging Traditions: Denominational Feminism in Britain, 1910-1920,* in Melman B. (ed), *Borderlines. Genders and Identities in War and Peace, 1870-1930,* London-New York 1998, pp. 265-284; Fletcher S., Maude Royden A., *A Life,* Oxford 1989.

[70] I am grateful to Sue Innes for this information.

[71] Pugh, *Women's Movement,* pp. 241-2.

[72] Caine, *English Feminism,* p. 200.

[73] Ibid., p. 176.

[74] These extended the rights of women to sit on municipal and county councils. Hollis, *Ladies in Council,* p. 491.

[75] Fawcett, *Women's Victory,* p. 165.

[76] Nurses Registration Act, 1919

[77] Peretz E., *Maternal and Child Welfare in England and Wales between the wars: a comparative regional study,* unpublished Ph. D. dissertation Middlesex University, 1992. Davies, *Liverpool,* pp. 173-181. Mark-Lawson, *Gender and local politics.*

[78] Thane, *Women, Liberalism,* p. 68.

[79] Caine. *English Feminism,* p. 200.

[80] Ibid., p. 176.

[81] Peretz, *Maternal Welfare.*

[82] Leathard A., *The Fight for Family Planning,* London 1980. Grier J., *Eugenics and Birth Control: Contraceptive Provision in North Wales, 1918-1939,* "Social History of Medicine", 11(3), 1998, pp. 443-459.

[83] Law, *Suffrage*, pp. 82-4. Dyhouse C., *Women Students and the London Medical Schools, 1914-39: The Anatomy of a Masculine Culture*, "Gender and History", 10(1), 1998, pp. 110-132.

[84] Fawcett, *Women's Victory*, pp. 162-5.

[85] Ibid., p. 161.

[86] Moyse C., *The Reform of Marriage and Divorce Law in England and Wales, 1909-1937* (Ph.D. dissertation, University of Cambridge, 1996), pp. 201-4.

[87] Ibid., pp. 211-20.

[88] Ibid., p. 264 n. 1.

[89] Ibid., p. 389.

[90] Pedersen S., *Family, Dependence and the Origins of the Welfare State. Britain and France, 1914-1945*, Cambridge 1993.

[91] Banks O., *Faces of Feminism*, Oxford 1981, pp. 169-171. Smith H.L., *British Feminism in the 1920s*, in Smith, *British Feminism*, pp. 124-143.

[92] This had occurred at Oxford in 1921.

[93] Law, *Suffrage*, p. 143.

[94] Moyse C., *Reform of Marriage and Divorce Law in England and Wales, 1909-1937*, Ph. D. thesis (Cambridge University, 1996), p. 111.

[95] Law, *Suffrage*, p. 85.

[96] Ibid., pp. 193-218.

[97] *The Woman Teacher*, 9 July, 1926, 305, quoted Law, ibid., pp. 212-3.

[98] Ibid., p. 213.

[99] Moyse, *Marriage and Divorce Law*, pp. 111.

[100] Harrison B., *Prudent Revolutionaries*, Oxford 1987, pp. 273-300. Banks O. (ed), *The Biographical directory of British Feminists, Vol. 1 1800-1930*, Brighton 1985, pp. 95-9.

[101] Pugh, *Women' Movement*, pp. 70-1.

[102] For further examples see Thane P., *Women in the British Labour Party and the Construction of State Welfare, 1906-1939*, in: Koven S., Michel S., *Mothers of a New World. Maternalist Politics and the Origins of Welfare States*, London-New York 1993, pp. 343-377. Peretz, *Maternal Welfare*.

[103] Smith, *British Feminism*.

[104] Pugh, *Women's Movement*, p. 109.

[105] Caine, *English Feminism*; Smith, *British Feminism*.

[106] *Labour Woman*, February 1944.

[107] Smith, *British Feminism*.

[108] Alberti J., *Beyond Suffrage:Feminists in War and Peace, 1914-28*, London 1989.

[109] Mass Observation Archive, University of Sussex.

[110] Report, *Royal Commission on Population*, 1946, p. 156.

Women in Bulgarian Society:
History and recent changes

Roumen L. Genov

Sofia University St. Kliment Ohridski

 Българските жени бавно и мъчително излизат от "сянката на историята". Може да се проследи изминатия исторически път от пълна анонимност и подчиненост към признаване на техните права и участието им в различните области на обществения живот. Ние знаем много малко или почти нищо за живота и мислите на безчислените поколения жени през десетте хилядолетия на човешко обитаване на Балканите

Можем да допуснем на основата на изворовите данни след създаването на българската държава през втората половина на VII век, че на двата пола в ранносредновековното общество се е гледало повече или по-малко като на равни. След християнизацията в средата на IX век, държавата е защитавала статуса на жените като майки и правото им на собственост, макар че те са били лишени от право на участие в обществения и икономическия живот. Положението им се влошава след османското завоевание в края на XIV век, доколкото ислямът и религиозното право гледат на жените като на низши и те са затворени в стените на дома. По време на българското национално Възраждане (средата на XVIII век до средата на 70-те години на XIX век), под влияние на европейските идеи отношението към жените започва да се променя. Те могат да получават начално образование, биват допускани в някои обществени институции, самите те създават свои дружества.

След Освобождението през 1878 г. Българското общество претърпява значителна модернизация, запазвайки своя, в основата си аграрен и патриархален, характер. Традиционният буржоазен феминизъм е твърде умерен и набляга върху самопомощта и самоусъвършенстването, а радикалният социалистически феминизъм обещава на жените освобождаване от веригите на капитала в резултат на социалната революция.

Но макар че тази революция започнала от 1944 г. дава на жените пълно избирателно право и равноправие по конституция, тяхното фактическо неравно положение не може да бъде прикрито от официалната пропаганда. Увеличава се многократно заетостта на жените в държавната икономика, но обстоятелството, че 90 % от жените работят, е не толкова резултат на осъществяване на конституционното право на труд, колкото на икономическата принуда. Социалистическото общество си остава патриархално и доминирано от мъжете. Макар че управляващата комунистическа партия определя квоти за представителство на жените в изборните органи на управление (парламент, местни органи), едва 2 % от жените заемат важни управленски постове. В едно общество на нисък стандарт на живота, на планов дефицит на важни стоки, на липса на достатъчно спестяващи труда уреди, жените трябва да носят двойно бреме: като съпруги, майки и домакини, от една страна, и като работещи жени, от друга.

Въпреки пълното спокойствие на повърхността на живота, строго контролиран от управляващите, обществото през 80-те години беше в състояние на икономическа и морална криза. Сгромолясването на комунистическия режим през 1989 г. беше колкото неочаквано, толкова и неизбежно. За разлика от другите източноевропейски страни, промените в България започнаха не с "нежна революция", а с дворцов преврат. Независимо от това, беше сложено началото на процес на демократизация, на икономическа и съответно социална трансформация. Свръхочакванията на на българите, които отъждествяваха демокрацията с високия жизнен стандарт и благоденствие на Запада не се оправдаваха. Промените, за необходимостта, от които има широк консенсус, донесоха и масова безработица, и обедняване на голяма част от населението, и социална поляризация, и масово разграбване на държавната доскоро икономика. Жените са социалната група, която е най-силно засегната от от негативните страни на промените. Те страдат от безработицата, подложени са на полова и възрастова дискриминация при наемането на работа, на сексуален тормоз на работното място. Те са и по-голямата част от "новите бедни", особено самотните майки (2/3 от домакинствата оглавявани от жени живеят в абсолютна бедност).

Не се промени неравноправието в семейството, домашното насилие и тормоз, разводите са една от важните причини за обедняване на жените. Те са жертва и на други негативни явления, ръста на престъпността, превръщането на сексиндустрията в нов клон на бизнеса. Намаля делът на жените в изборните органи на властта на централно и местно ниво (до 5-10 %).

Все пак, има и положителни тенденции, жените могат да изразяват и защитават своите специфически интереси чрез новите синдикати и съсловни организации, чрез женските и неправителствени организации. Времето на еуфория и свръхочаквания принадлежи вече на историята, дойде времето на реализма, на практическото отстояване на достойно място на жените в новото българско общество.

Roumen Genov was born in Yambol (Bulgaria) in 1948. He graduated from the Sofia University St. Kliment Ohridski in 1972 and completed his Ph. D. dissertation at the same institution in 1979. From 1980 onwards Dr. Genov has taught Modern and Contemporary History at Sofia University, and as visiting professor at the New Bulgarian University (Sofia), the National Academy of Art, and the South-Western University (Blagoevgrad). His scholarly interests are in the field of European, British and American history. He is author of books and scholarly articles on British and American political and social history, and of biographies of political figures (W. E. Gladstone).

 Bulgarian women, as the title of a recently published book suggests, are coming "out of the shadow of history". It is a slow, gradual and painful process. Still, historically speaking, there is advancement from the state of complete anonymity and subjection towards recognition of the rights of women, and their full participation in different spheres of public life. To understand the present position of women in Bulgarian society, their status and the problems they are confronted with, we have to examine briefly the historical legacy.

For centuries Bulgarian women were, if not "excluded" from history, present in it as a faceless and voiceless mass. There are drawings of women on the walls of caves in Bulgarian lands (late Paleolithic to the late Bronze periods), clay figurines from mounds of the Neolithic, Eneolithic and Bronze ages that show that the population had a cult of the mother-goddess. We know too little of the status of women in the ancient Thracian society, [1] but we can make a guess that they had few rights from the fact that kings and aristocrats had their wives and concubines buried with them, along with their favorite horses. For the entire medieval period – the First (681-1018) and Second Bulgarian Kingdom (1186-1396) – we know the only the names of few czarinas, and a couple of names of wives of feudal lords, who happened to be donors for building churches and had their portraits painted in them (as in the Boyana church, near Sofia, or the church of Zemen, near Kyustendil, in south-west Bulgaria). We know only some details about the life of few czarinas, for instance about Theodora, wife of Ivan Alexander (1331-1371), mostly because of the great love story of the couple which reads like a folk tale. The czar fell hopelessly in love with Sarah, daughter of a Jewish goldsmith from Turnoff (the ancient capital of the Second Kingdom), he divorced his first wife, daughter of a Walachian voivode (prince), and married the beautiful Jewess (converted to Christianity with the name Theodora). She became mother of the last czar of Bulgaria, Ivan Shishman. But these are only a few exceptions in a long history.

The Bulgarian nation was formed as a result of the assimilation of three ethnic elements, the Slavs who invaded and settled in the Balkan Peninsula in the 6th and 7th century A. D., the Bulgarians or Proto-Bulgarians [2], who came in the mid 7th century, and the Romanised Thracians who survived the ravages of the Great Migration of Peoples. It seems that women in their otherwise patriarchal society enjoyed certain traditional freedoms at least before marriage, unlike their sisters in the Mediterranean countries in classical antiquity. The traditional culture did not emphasize sexual differences and it seems both sexes were regarded as more or less equal. At the beginning of the 9th century Bulgaria was already one largest mediaeval states in Europe matching in territorial extension the Byzantine Empire and the empire of Charlemagne. In 864 A.D. Bulgarians were converted to Christianity in the Eastern Orthodox rite and thus became involved in the cultural perimeter of Byzantine culture. Christianisation did not change the structures of social life and roles deeply, despite the fact that blame for original sin was now placed on womankind. The legal status of women in mediaeval Bulgaria was determined by the political system of Caesaro-Papism characteristic of Byzantium, the predominance of strong lay power over the church's authority. Through its laws the state put women in a subject and inferior position (they were not able to testify before courts, or to engage in any form of economic activity in trade or crafts guilds). At the same time the state upheld the position of women as mothers (they could dispose of their dowry, inherit from their deceased husbands – especially if they had children –, widows paid lower taxes, etc.) The church, of course, played a major role in the regulation of social functions and the gender stereotype of women. Abortion was regarded as a sin equal to infanticide; divorce was obtained only with great difficulty from the church courts.

The situation of Bulgarian women grew worse under the long period of Ottoman domination (1396-1878), as they belonged to a community which was contemptuously treated as *rayah* (literally flock – general name of the tax paying non-Moslem population), and discriminated as *giaours* (infidels) for the most part of the period, despite of the relative religious tolerance of their Ottoman masters.

After the Ottoman conquest in the late 14th century, the new religion, though adopted by a relatively small minority of Bulgarians, influenced deeply gender roles and relations. Women were regarded by Islam as inferior, were subject to numerous restrictions and were confined to the family house. Women did not dare leave the neighbourhood unattended; the only public place they were permitted to visit was church but even there sexes were rigidly separated. The life and activities of peasant women were, of course, less restricted because the agricultural economy largely depended on them. As the Bulgarian pioneer-sociologist Ivan Hadjiyski claims, women could play a crucial role within the family circle, even in business matters, however, this was not to be shown out of the home. There were exceptions to the rule, like women's involvement in the bands of the haiduts, the Balkan Robin Hoods, avengers and heroes of the oppressed people [3]. There were cases when women became even band leaders or voivode, but they had to give up their identity, dressing like men and acting like men.

The period of National Revival (from the late 18th century to the 1870s) was marked by certain changes and new attitudes towards women, greater openness towards new trends and ideas. A wealthy Bulgarian bourgeoisie appeared, enriched through trade, large scale stockbreeding and import-export operations, together with considerable stratum of town craftsmen and traders. They aspired to a new social position, to European culture and education, and to political freedoms. Modern schools were established; a long campaign for religious independence which was tantamount to asserting national autonomy began [4]. European culture was accepted axiomatically as higher and more advanced; western European societies were regarded as models for development and reform in Bulgaria. Of course, there was a critical reaction against superficial or apish copying of European (or "frank") dress and ways, and false "Europeanization". Advanced political leaders and writers, like Konstantin Fotinov (a teacher, merchant and the first Bulgarian journalist) and Petko Slaveikov (an educator, journalist, poet and politician) began to speak of the equality of women, of the necessity of women's education and of the "women's question". Primary education was comparatively widespread, and in the mid 19th century establishment of girls' schools began. Women were admitted to certain public institutions, reading rooms (a peculiar cultural institution with various functions), women's cultural and philanthropic associations. Yet women were not admitted to the board of any public or governing body. Expressions of opinion, public appearances and activities of women were regarded as inappropriate. The few professional women and schoolmistresses were to quit their occupation upon marriage.

The Liberation of Bulgaria (or rather part of it) from Ottoman domination in 1878 resulted in changes not only in political structure, but also in social life and culture. The influx of Western ideas became unhampered; primary education for both sexes was free and compulsory; many young Bulgarians, including women, were getting higher education in the universities of central and western Europe. Industrialization and urbanization had changed considerably the structure of Bulgarian society, although it retained its predominantly agricultural and patriarchal character. Women's societies established before the Liberation continued their activities to promote self-improvement and self-help of women. The forms of modern feminist thought and organization in Bulgaria were, however, rather moderate and timid. They did not offer a breakthrough in the traditional role of women, and were confined to the thin layer of educated professional women and intellectuals. Women were confronted with traditional views of their gender role and with male chauvinism. (For instance, male students of the University of Sofia, established at the end of the 19th century, vigorously protested against admission of female students). The number of employed women (schoolteachers, clerical employees, nurses), especially after World War I, increased considerably, but still the great majority were housewives.

There was at the same time a certain presence of women in the Social-Democratic party formed in the 1890s, whose ideology promised them, and the other oppressed and exploited workers, liberation from the chains of capitalism. But even this form of radical socialist feminism did not uphold the demand for immediate political rights. Women in Bulgaria were admitted to the ballot box in municipal elections only in 1936, and could cast their vote in general elections after 1945.

The latter date coincided with the beginning of the "socialist revolution" and establishment of Communist dictatorship, though during the first years non-Communist parties were tolerated. By the end of the 1940s Communist hold over every aspect of economic, political and cultural life was complete, and construction of new "socialist" society began in earnest. The Communist project included not only complete control of economy and society, but their radical change and modernization. The Soviet model of centralized bureaucratic planning, of rapid industrialization, with an emphasis on heavy industry and gigantic projects, of "collectivisation" of agriculture, that is, taking the land from the peasants and turning them into wage workers, of migration of great masses of people, of regimentation of every form of cultural life, was faithfully followed. As a result there was a great increase in the number of women in state owned industrial plants and agricultural farms. Formally, both sexes were getting equal pay for equal work and were enjoying equal job opportunity. In practice, however, women were rarely admitted to higher and better-paid administrative posts, and were largely discriminated in terms of promotion and career. The ruling party had set up quotas of women's representation in parliament and in local government of 18-20% of their members. By the 1980s under 2% of women were engaged in management, administrative and decision-making spheres. This system could hardly conceal the fact of institutionalised inequality. In fact, the promise of women's liberation in communist society was betrayed. In a society of low living standards, of planned deficits of essential goods and labour saving appliances, "emancipated" women were trapped in a double slavery of both their traditional role as wives and mothers, and the new one as members of the labour force. It is true that under socialism there was full employment and even a deficit of labour force in certain sections of the economy. Up to 90% of women worked outside the family, but most of them had to do it out of necessity, for low paid men could not earn enough money to support family. Nine-tenths of employed women were manual workers, sales attendants, and clerical staff, nurses, primary and day care school teachers [5].

Despite of the firm control of the ruling party over the society as a whole, and dead calm on the surface, the system was affected by a number of moral crises, following de-Stalinization, the events in 1957 and 1968, re-Stalinization and finally, Gorbachev's *perestroika*. For over thirty years the country was autocratically ruled by Todor Zhivkov, a shrewd politician of little formal education, who depended entirely on personal loyalty to Soviet leaders (and managed to survive four General Secretaries of the CPSU). At the end of the 1950s he proclaimed the "complete victory" of socialism, and in the 1970s he followed the ideological instructions from Moscow to start building "mature" or "real" socialism and an "all-people" state. By the mid 1980s the country, as well as the Soviet block, was in state of economic and moral crisis.

The final collapse of Communist regimes in Europe was as unexpected as inevitable. The political change in Bulgaria, however, differed from the "velvet" revolution in central-eastern Europe. By that time the octogenarian Zhivkov had become a mock figure, but his party colleagues decided to depose him, in November 1989, only after indications appeared that he had lost the favour of Moscow. Anyway, the palace coup of "November 11" marked the beginning of rapid political and economic changes, of democratisation and transition to a liberal market system. These changes were not so much a "return to history", as seen by some Western observers, but a new and unparalleled phenomenon in European history. The "surge to freedom" and complete restructuring of economy through massive privatisation, were, however, most fully exploited by the former "new class" of Djilas, the members of the *nomenklatura* who used the opportunity to turn their collective ownership of the economy into individual ownership, and to maintain their grip on society. In terms of political life the country passed to a multiparty system, free elections, freedom of media, and all other attributes of modern democracy.

The reformist drive during the last decade has achieved a certain success: most of the industrial enterprises were privatised, land was given back to peasants, the larger part of the [GDP] is now produced in the private sector; the export directed mostly to the former Soviet Union and Comecon countries is now redirected to the European Union countries. Bulgaria has joined the CEFTA and started negotiations to join the European Union. After the collapse of almost half of the banks and hyperinflation in 1996-97 a monetary board was introduced and the financial system was stabilized, but the possibilities of government to spend, especially for social programs, have been strictly limited. Bulgarian governments during the last decade have had to act under harsh economic conditions, industrial decay and low productivity, ecological problems, a foreign debt of $11 billion (a gigantic sum by Bulgarian standards), loss of the traditional markets in Russia and former Comecon countries, as well as in the Arab world.

There is a broad consensus in Bulgarian society, and among political parties as to the necessity of reforms, as to the priority of joining the Euro-Atlantic community (the European

Union and the NATO). Disagreement and discontent concern the price of the changes and the equal place of the social groups in bearing the burden of transformation. The mass of the people enthusiastically greeted the new freedom and the beginning of reforms, however, they brought with them high unemployment (up to 16-17% of the working force according to official figures or even more according to the trade unions; 33% among young people are unemployed; and unemployment is especially high in certain agricultural regions dependent on tobacco growing, with compact masses of ethnic Turks, and among the Rom population reaching up to 70-90%), a sharp rise of prices after deregulation, a process of dismantling of most of the inefficient industries, sharp social polarization, and generally, a severe economic crisis and a sharp fall even in the modest living standards enjoyed by the population in the 1980s. The results were intensive emigration, especially of younger and better-educated people (about 530,000 for the period 1989-99), a negative birth rate, and an aging nation.

Under the new conditions women are the social group that fares worst. Democratic transformation has not changed the basic character of patriarchy and male domination. There is a vertical segregation in economy (industry is a predominantly male sphere, while in services, including education, health service, and so forth, the share of women is about 70%). Horizontal segregation is a general characteristic of economy and decision making, top management and decision making positions, both appointed and elected positions are prevailingly male spheres (76% of employers are men, 80% of elected offices are occupied by men). Wages and salaries are all very low (median monthly income was about 200 levs or 100 Euros in 1999), and tend to be even lower among women [6]. As a result the income gap is widening. Women are the larger part of the "new poor", especially in woman-headed households (64% of these live in absolute poverty). During the last decade the consumption of basic foodstuffs decreased significantly, as well as access to medicine. As a result there are inequalities in self-evaluated health status, 39% of women report serious health problems in 2000 (compared to 28% of males). The relative share of women among all unemployed persons is about 60% (1997), and they are largely subject to sex and age discrimination in getting employment.

There are gross inequalities in family life, less women's mobility; there is domestic violence and harassment; divorce is single main reason for impoverishment in woman-headed households, 70% of the housework is done by women.

In fact, women's representation in politics has decreased during the last decade, their share in elective bodies of government both central and local has decreased. In 2000 only 11% of members of parliament, 5% of mayors and 23% of municipal councillors were women. That is why some women's organizations now insist that political parties should include a certain quota of women in their list of parliamentary and local election candidates [7].

There are other negative factors affecting mostly women, such as the sharp rise of criminality rates, violence in the streets and domestic violence, sexual harassment at the work place. The sex industry and traffic in women have become new sectors of business.

Still, there are certain positive elements in recent developments. Old state controlled trade unions have been replaced by new democratic ones, a number of nongovernmental organizations have sprung up, including ones defending specific women's interests and causes.

They work in conjunction with their European counterparts and in some cases, governmental agencies seek their collaboration in preparing legislative measures (as is the case with the Equal Opportunities Bill of 2000). Euphoria and great expectations that followed the beginning of the changes in 1989 belong already to history, it is time now for realism, for painstaking work and relentless efforts in defence of practical demands, of human and social rights of women, their dignity and their due and deserved place in society.

 NOTES

[1] The Tracians, a large group of Indo-European tribes, inhabiting from the second half of the 4th millenium B.C. the area from the Carpathian Mountains to the Aegean Sea, as well as the northern shores of the Black Sea, and parts of Asia Minor, were the first population of the region which we know by its name.

[2] Bulgarians or Proto-Bulgarians – a group of tribes of Turcic-Altaic origin, who had formed a large state in the lands north of the Black Sea in early 7th century B.C. – were dispersed under the attacks of the Khazars. They migrated reaching as far as the Middle Volga basin, Pannonia, southern Italy, Macedonia. A group of Bulgarians under Khan Asparuch founded the state of (Danubian) Bulgaria in the North-Eastern Balkans in 681, the precursor of modern Bulgaria.

[3] Haidut (haiduk) – members of brigands or social bandits in the Balkans under Ottoman domination from the 15th to the 19th century. See Hobsbawm E.J., *Bandits.*, Rev. edn. New York 1981.

[4] After the fall of the Byzantine Empire in 1453, all Eastern Orthodox Christians were organized along religious lines in the "Rum millet" ("Romaic people"), headed by the Greek Patriarch of Constantinople.

[5] According to national statistics for the late 1980s about 35% of working women were engaged in industry, 18% in agriculture, 12% in services, 10% in education, 8% in health service.

[6] Median monthly salaries and wages of women were 68.9% of those of men (in 1996-68), and rose by 3.9 points in 1998.

[7] As a result of the last general elections of 17 June 2001 the share of women MPs was increased to 20%.

 SELECTED BIBLIOGRAPHY

Conrad J.L., *Metaphorical Images of Women in South Slavic Proverbs*, "Balkanistica", Bd. VI, 1980, pp. 147-160

Corin C. (ed), *Superwoman and the Double Burden: Women's Experience of Change in Central and Eastern Europe and Former Soviet Union*, London 1992.

Crampto R.J., *A Concise History of Bulgaria*, Cambridge 1997.

Corin C. (ed), *Superwoman and the Double Burden: Women's Experience of Change in Central and Eastern Europe and Former Soviet Union*, London 1992.

Koch S.J., Koch K.L., Moneva Z., *In Their Own Words: An Ethnographic Analysis of the Quality of Life of Bulgarian Women and Their Children*, Paper presented to: Transitions and Transcendence. Mutual Perspectives of East and West, Conference on Women's Issues. American University in Bulgaria. Blagoevgrad may 1994, pp. 21-23.

Kostova D., *Similar or Different? Women in Postcommunist Bulgaria*, in Rueschemeyer M. (ed), *Women in the Politics of Postcommunist Eastern Europe*, New York 1994, pp. 116-128.

Kostova D., *The Transition to Democracy in Bulgaria: Challenges and Resks for Women*, in Moghadam V.M. (ed), *Democratic Reform and the Position of Women in Transitional Economies*, Oxford 1993, pp. 92-109.

Merdjanska K., Panova R., *The Family Enclosure in the Bulgarian Context. From Herodotus to the End of the Twentieth Century*, "The European Journal of Women's Studies", 2(1), 1995, pp. 21-32.

Merdjanska K., Panova R., *The Family Enclosure in the Bulgarian Context. From Herodotus to the End of the Twentieth Century*, "The European Journal of Women's Studies", 2(1), 1995, pp. 21-32.

Stoev V., *The Ghetto. The Bulgarian Woman and the Iron Regime*, "Women's Studies International Forum", 17(2-3), 1994.

Petrova D., *What can Women do to Change the Totalitarian Cultural Context?*, "Women's Studies International Forum", 17(2-3) 1994, pp. 267-271.

Sokolova B., *Bulgarian Women: Problems Past, Problems Present*, "Women a cultural review", 3(3), 1992, pp. 261-270.

Staikova R., Gadeleva S., *Die Frauen in Bulgarien - ihre Bestimmung heute und in Zukunft*, "Feministische Studien", 2, 1992.

Todorova M., *Balkan Family Structure and the European Pattern Demographic Developments in Ottoman Bulgaria*, Washington D.C. 1993.

Todorova M., *Historical Tradition and Transformation In Bulgaria: Women's Issues or Feminist Issues?*, "Journal of Women's History", 5(3), 1994 (Special Issue), pp. 129-143.

Vitanova I., The Establishing of Women's Studies in Bulgaria - or How Far Can You Go, "Women's History Review", 2(1), 1993, pp. 143-148.

 **SOURCES**

Women's social position and rights according to the Bulgarian constitutions

There are not any specific texts in the first Bulgarian constitution of 1879 (the "Turnovo Constitution", called so after the name of the city where it was adopted), relating to the position of women.

The second republican constitution was adopted in 1947 (the so-called "Dimitrov's Constitution", after the name of the Communist leader and prime minister Georgi Dimitrov, 1882-1949, contained several relevant articles.

From the Constitution of People's Republic of Bulgaria (1947):

Art. 3. All citizen of the age of 18 years and over, can elect and be elected (members of any body of government), irrespective of their sex, nationality, race, creed, education, occupation, social and economic standing, except for mentally disabled persons and those stripped of civil and political rights by judgment-at-law...

Art. 72. Women are equal with men in all spheres of public, private, economic, social, cultural and political life.

Equality of women is realized by guaranteeing equal right to work, equal pay, right of annual holidays, right of social security, old age pensions and right to education.

Women-mothers enjoy a special protection in terms of conditions of work. The state takes special care of mothers and children by setting up of maternity hospitals, day care centers and dispensaries, women are guaranteed paid leaves from work both before and after giving birth, and free obstetrical and medical service...

Art. 76. Marriage and family are under the special protection of state.

Only the civil marriage contracted before respective authorities has legal value.

Children born out of wedlock enjoy the same rights as those born in wedlock ...

From the Constitution of People's Republic of Bulgaria (1971):

(This one was called "Zhivkov's Constitution" after the name of the then Communist leader and President of the State Council, Todor Zhivkov (1911-1998).

Art. 36. Women and men in People's Republic of Bulgaria enjoy equal rights.

Art. 37. Women-mothers enjoy a special protection by the state, the economic and public organizations, which guarantee them leave before and after giving birth while retaining their pay, free obstetrical and medical care, maternity clinics, alleviation of the conditions of work, extension of the system of children's care centers, of the public utilities and catering estalishments.

Art. 38. (1) Marriage and family are under the protection of the state.

(2) Only the civil marriage has legal value.

(3) Spouses have equal rights and obligations in marriage and family. Parents have the right and obligation to bring up their children and educate them in the spirit of Communism.

(4) Children born out of wedlock enjoy the same rights as those born in wedlock …

In 1991, after the end of the one-party Communist regime, a new democratic constitution was adopted by the 7th Grand National Assembly.

From the Constitution of Republic of Bulgaria (1991):

Art. 46. (1). Marriage is a free union between man and woman. Only the civil marriage is legal.

(2) Spouses have equal rights and obligations in marriage and family.

(3) The form of marriage, the conditions and ways of contracting or dissolving it, and personal and property relations between spouses, are regulated by law.

Art. 47. (1) Bringing up and education of the children until their coming to age is obligation of their parents and is supported by the state.

(2) Women-mothers enjoy the special protection of the state, which guarantees them paid leave before and after giving birth, alleviation of the conditions of work and other forms of social support.

(3) Children born out of wedlock enjoy the same rights as those born in wedlock.

(4) Conditions and the form of limitation or deprivation of parental rights are regulated by law …

Art. 48. (1) Citizens entitled to the right to work. The state is setting up the framework guaranteeing this right …

Art. 52. (1) Citizens are entitled to the right of health insurance, which guarantees them access to medical service and to free health service under conditions and form regulated by law ….

Literacy and social order: writing and reading in Lisbon in the 18th century

Ana Cristina Araújo

Universidade de Coimbra

Em Lisboa, como na maior parte dos países europeus no século XVIII, o acesso às práticas da escrita delimita uma importante fronteira cultural e social.

A fonte que elegemos para esta sondagem adequa-se ao carácter selectivo da norma escriturária na sociedade de Antigo Regime. Como veremos, a formalidade jurídica que impõe a validação do acto testamentário explora, eficazmente, as justificações de incapacidade dos outorgantes que não subscrevem, de motu próprio, as suas declarações de última vontade. Portanto, neste caso, é pelo viés da exclusão que a lógica de subordinação à cultura da escrita se faz sentir.

A frequência de assinaturas nos testamentos da população de Lisboa, escritos ao longo do século XVIII e durante o primeiro quartel do século XVIII, permite-nos, todavia, verificar ganhos significativos, no processo de alfabetização das mulheres e dos grupos sociais inferiores. Contextualizando os resultados obtidos, procuraremos analisar as razões do dimormismo e da desigualdade de oportunidades que a sociedade portuguesa acentua neste período crucial de transição.

O analfabetismo, invariavelmente sentido como factor de discriminação social, aflora ao nível da consciência individual como uma marca imperecível de inferioridade. Para sempre, ficaram guardadas em segredo, amortecidas pelo alheamento e sem qualquer impacte colectivo, palavras como estas: – "Em virtude de não saber escrever e ser pobre", "por ser mulher e não saber escrever". Por isso, não espanta que, em 1746, o pedagogo das Luzes Luís António de Verney escreva, a propósito da aprendizagem da escrita e da leitura: – "Isto é o que rara mulher sabe fazer em Portugal. Não digo eu escrever correctamente, pois ainda não achei alguma que o fizesse; mas digo que pouquísssimas sabem ler e escrever; e, muito menos, fazer ambas as coisas correntemente. A ortografia e pontuação, nenhuma as conhece".

Na charneira da alfabetização, o mercado de trabalho ocupa um papel de relevo, estimula a aprendizagem básica, incita ao autodictadismo e fornece as bases para a procura do ensino de "Primeiras Letras". As competências básicas e necessárias ao desenvolvimento económico parecem desenhar-se no quadro de uma nova cultura urbana. É neste ambiente que devemos inserir os progressos tardiamente realizados pelas mulheres e pelas camadas populares menos qualificadas, trabalhadores, servis, marítimos, pescadores e tantos outros de profissão incerta. Mesmo assim, no termo desta evolução, é fácil verificar que as bolsas mais persistentes de analfabetismo se encontram no campo, em redor da capital, no seio das classes laboriosas e entre a população feminina.

Entre os alfabetizados não são muitos os que, nos seus testamentos, declaram possuir livros. A nomeação destes objectos de prestígio e de fruição cultural escapa, normalmente, à estratégia de transmissão de bens no interior da família. O nosso ângulo de observação permite portanto verificar que o escrito nem sempre estava presente na forma escrita e que, de um modo geral, a literacia não era sinónimo de acesso directo à leitura.

A alfabetização rudimentar acaba, em suma, por encobrir o peso e a enorme importância que as práticas da oralidade tinham nos sistemas básicos de comunicação, à escala da família, da confraria, da paróquia e da oficina.

Ana Cristina Araújo was born in Angola in 1957, and completed her studies at the University of Coimbra (Ph.D in Modern History). She is professor of Cultural History and Religious Studies at the University of Coimbra. She has published many studies in Portugal and abroad and she is the author of *A Morte em Lisboa. Atitudes e Representações (1700-1830)*, Lisbon 1997 and the coordinator of *O Marquês de Pombal e a Universidade*, Coimbra 2000.

 In modern society, those unable or unused to writing make up a silent majority that sanctions, by absence or ommission, the prestige and cultural supremacy of those who are identified with codified orthographic rules and reading practices. The use of writing has developed far beyond the well defined and restricted circles which once practiced it, but, in enlarging its domain, it has encountered reservations and important resistances.

Strictly speaking, that one could read did not mean that he could also write. The two acts involved rather different and not always related assimilation and training processes. In fact, it is well known that – in the words of Chartier – in "Ancien Regime societies, where the learning of writing followed the learning of reading and only touched part of the children, it is obvious that if everybody who could sign his or her name was also able to read, not all who could read knew how to sign their name. And it is also clear that among those who could sign, not all were able to write more extensive texts, either because the signature was the last stage of their cultural learning or because, by lack of practice, they had lost the writing ability, so that the signature was only a relic of the past" (Chartier, 1990, 114).

As these considerations show, it is generally accepted that the ability to sign one's name can not be taken simply as an indicator of the existence of a specific cultural competence: being able to write.

CRITERIA, SOURCES AND METHODS

In any case it must be admitted that the graphic self-representation of one's name, aside from its intrinsic meaning, demonstrates the existence of some level of alphabetical ability that cannot be ignored. Even that fragile trace, because it is the result of the individual's participation in the community, even that elementary indicator of literacy behavior, clearly links those who can sign to the cultural universe of writing. So, it can be said perhaps that a signature shows, at the same time, an ambition and a competence. In both cases it has in itself an irreplacable historical and anthropological value. By appropriation or even limited use of alphabetical signs, the individual tests his singularity and widens his memory. In other words, he affirms his position respect to others and, at the same time, creates the conditions for the future recognition of his existence.

These issues gain further dimensions when the new historical figures appear. Wills are full of expressions revealing the relationship that the common citizen has with writing. Obliged to justify the absence of a signature in his will, the testator presents two kinds of explanation. He confesses his inability to write or, even more important, "the inability to write in a capable way", or, as an alternative, he states that he "can't write". The first attitude is much more common. The close relationship between writing in its more basic expression – signature – and the absence of a specific cultural competence – the ability to write – is confirmed in wills much more clearly than is common in other kinds of sources.

Beyond all the doubts and perplexities we have mentioned, the signature, particularly when made under strict control (i.e., of others who are competent writers), remains an important element in the process of access to writing practices. Several documents produced in common formal situations point out how frequently signatures were required. Apart from internal and external cautions imposed by a certain kind of source, and even knowing that a signature means, in Ancient Regime societies, that an obligation has been performed, most often because of a request and on delegation, more consistent historiographical studies on alphabetisation have shown, in different ways, the potentialities that conventional and repeated writing formulas have in giving us information. In studying pre-statistical societies, the sources most used to describe alphabetised areas, on an intergroupal and regional scale, have been parish record books, wills and other notarial acts, inquisitorial trial records and documents, town council minutes, other town council documents, fraternity members' admission records and military recruitment books. Research on more recent societies instead has given a privileged place to census records, general surveys and inquiries. The choice of such kinds of sources, which have the merit of giving clear overall results, does not exclude making graphological analyses of signatures, thus adding richer dimensions to the evaluation of writing performance.

The stress put on research based on signatures, even when the researchers themselves express doubts about its relevance for understanding the signers' writing competencies and habits, divides historians. Three different hermeneutical tendencies stand out clearly. Some hold that the signature marks the border (which is of course not a totally impenetrable border, but rather a border area) between oral and written culture in Ancien Régime societies. So the signature is both a "false friend" and a good revealer, a kind of universal key for mapping a kind of minimal alphabetisation rate of a particular society. To others the signature is an element for understanding more subtle differences, which gives much solid information about the signer's ability and his familiarity with orthographic formal proceedings. Finally, for those who ask more from them, signatures have even a greater value insofar as they are seen as a distinctive measure of social affirmation within the so-called alphabetical cultures. This last assumption does not minimize the shadow effect caused by early or late use of the pen, although this has to be contextualised with the relationships established by the individual with his family, his social group, his job, his school, his church and, eventually, with the circulation of printed works.

By imposing a multilateral perspective on the study of alphabetisation, contextualising the rules of writing has brought about not only a reduction of the initial quantitative and sociological enthusiasms but also new phase of investigation within the history of culture and the study of the circulation of behavioral patterns, mediated by more abstract and complex communication symbols. Respect to this broader field of research, one can agree that alphabetisation is no longer just a parameter of progress or backwardness; it now "begins to be understood as a *way of life*: a certain relationship with literate culture" (Ramos, 1988, 1079).

In Portuguese historiography, the largest study of alphabetisation has been carried out by Justino de Magalhães. However, other sectorial investigations show similar concerns for context, specially those published in the 1980s by Francisco Ribeiro da Silva, Jaime Reis and Rui Ramos. Going beyond the strict and narrow conception of relating alphabetisation to progress and to the modernization of society, these authors have been trying to define, within certain parameters, the behavior of the literate rural and the urban populations in particular social and professional circles and their formal relationships with local powers and the church. There have also been case studies focused on in the evaluation of a certain number of alphabetisation strategies.

The source we have chosen to use for this study is suitable for investigating Ancient Regime families and illuminates the selective character of their writing rules. As we have already seen, one of the legal formalities required for the validation of a will actually permits us to explore the reasons for the testators' inability to write *de motu proprio* their last will and testament. Thus it is those that are excluded from writing culture that show us their subordination to it.

In any case, we must ask whether the sample of 1273 wills, randomly distributed in periods of 31 years (with the exception of the final period in which the period examined is limited to eleven years) is truly representative of Lisbon's population.

To an extent, the analysis of wills stresses the vertical character of the social structure, by giving more space to the representation of aristocratic and bourgeois worries, strategies and compromises. Yet, it at the same time it includes all social groups, except captive slaves. So, although it does not give us a complete and statistically correct portrait of Lisbon's society, we have not discarded the results, but rather grouped them in such a way as to establish comparisons and connections with other parametres and validate general and specific frequency indexes. If the strength and weakness of this study lie in the high representation of the élite, it cannot be ignored that it also gives us a knowledge about other important social actors. The data overall show the many opportunities that the city offers to its inhabitants in the crucial turning period that is about to open the way to the contemporary age.

Some previous data help to clarify the characteristics and sociological morphology of the sample. In this universe of 1273 wills, men represent 59% of the testators and women 41%. Along the time intervals considered, the variation in the representation of the two sexes never changes the fact that men's wills are more frequent in the city of Lisbon. On the other hand, it should be stated the marks of urban life are clearly perceived in all the population studied. Globally, the middle class of the smaller shops and enterprises is represented by more than 25% of the wills. All social groups, proprierty owners and farmers – mainly from the city rural limits – represent 9,1% in this universe, practically the same as the great number of workers and servants, here represented by only 9,2% of the testators. The representation of the fishermen and sailors is lower, only 3%. Within the individuals classified as indeterminate are the many abandoned by fortune who, because of their humble condition, ended up without any indication of their social classification. Together these are 7,4%.

From the point of view of its dynamics, the sociological sample reveals little significant evolution but, in any case, it does shows two trends. One, of slight progressive contraction, affects the percentages represented by wills of the aristocracy and the clergy, which descend, respectively, from 19,6% and 8% in 1700, to 11,8% and 5% in 1830. Another one, more irregular, emphasizes the growing power of literate persons and middle classes in initiating procedures concerning wills. Successorial law seems to serve these groups' interests particularly; at the same time they use their wills as a privileged way of stressing their familiar living patterns, as well as dealing with other concerns, mainly religious ones.

With the passage of time, the importance of will making becomes greater and greater for the middle and upper bourgeoisie. In the 1830s it is this group that tends to replace the space previously occupied by aristocracy and the clergy. In 1700 the wills made by merchants are 12,5%, whereas this figure goes up to 18,4% in 1830. In the tertiary or service sector something identical happens. In the beginning of the 18th century, the group constituted by the lower officership and by the liberal professions comes to a modest 6%, while in 1830 it is close to 10%. The aristocracy's share progressively descends, although it maintains a certain stability between 1790 and 1830. The growth of the percentage of wills made by traders, officers and liberal professions is less regular; however both groups show similar changes. They reach a high level during the first decades of the 18th century, they remain constant during that century and increase, at different rates, between 1790 and 1830. Finally, we should note that the sample includes betwen 8% and 10% of the total of adults who actually died in Lisbon.

SIGNATURES: AN UNEQUAL AND DIFFERENTLY SHARED DOMAIN

After all that has been said, the value of the testators' autographs is still open to discussion. Drawn or scribbled, easily written or rudely abbreviated, the name inscribed by its owner in a document has a very strong meaning. More than a gesture to give authenticity, it is an performance which illustrates individuality.

Without forgetting the fundamental ambiguity of this sign and knowing that it is a key that allows us to proceed from a detailed sectorial analysis to the study of large numbers, we think that signatures, as alternatives are lacking, should be used as a first approach to the universe of alphabetised people.

In the declaration that precedes the approval of the act, the warning that the testator cannot sign must be taken into consideration. Only few say they have not signed for a particular reason, normally because of being ill, having their right arm wounded, being sickly or weak, etc. Most of them leave their inability to sign in a misterious silence. That strategy has a double effect. On one side, it shows an ability that, for some reason, cannot be exercised in practise and, on another side, it may really hide an ability. The assumption that the testator possesses this ability even if he or she does not use it is implicit, until the middle of the 18th century, within the aristocracy; those who strongly benefit from it are aristocratic women. It seems reasonable that it might have actually been that way. The aristocracy, for convenience and because of its social position, is closer to written culture. Nevertheless, noble women who write wills and then do not sign them personally seem at times not so much to act on the basis of an assumption that they have or do not have writing abilties, as on a desire to conceal their abilities or the lack of them. This is only a suspicion which is difficult to confirm and which only applies to the female component of the lower aristocracy.

Some of the reasons for the testators' cultural differences can still be found in the expression of the gesture which they have not performed. Analphabetism is normally felt as a factor of social discrimination; it appears at the level of individual conscience as an sign of an everlasting inferiority. The inability to write appears as a secret, a personal rather than a general problem or deficiency, without any collective impact and due to some kind of alienation, as in words like this: – "Due to the fact of not being able to write and being poor", "because she is a woman and not able to write". Such words are normally placed by the testator at the end of the last will and testament. In this context, the words go beyond mere conventional formality. Rather than an excuse or a justification, here we find that the testator dares to admit to a fundamental difference.

Overall there are few who end their wills in such a way, but in this respect numbers have a relative importance. That these words show the feelings of inadequacy of those who feel ignorant and inferior remains a fact. By assuming that their status as women explains their inability to sign, these testatrices are prisoners of a strange culture that both includes them and identifies them as not being part of it. Badly equiped culturally and without hope of ever being literate they finish their wills with a final declaration, gaining awareness of their own cultural and social status. This reality is perceived, in 1746, by Luís António de Verney who, referring to learning reading and writing, says: "This is what few women can do in Portugal. And I don't mean to write correctly because I still haven't found one that did it; but I'm referring to those few who know how to read and write; and, even fewer, those able to do both fluently". (Verney, 1952, V, 127)

In the Lisbon wills we have privileged the testators' signature and, because they were not so rigorously controlled, not considered those of the witnesses. Within the alphabetised category we have included those who appear to know how to sign despite being kept from doing it. Given that there are very few uncertain cases, we have decided that it is best to describe both the evolution of the curves of those who actually sign, as well as of those who are presumed able to do it in other circumstances.

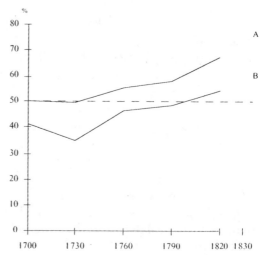

Fig. 1
Percentage of signatures in Lisbon wills.

Ana Cristina Araújo

Between the 18th and the 19th centuries, the low level of alphabetisation as measured through testamentary writings expands in very slowly. During the first thirty years of the 18th century, a reasonable growth the percentage of signatures can be registered. From the 1760s there is an increase and approximately half of those who make wills sign or declare that they are able to do so. It will be only in the 19th century that the limit of 60% will be exceeded. Progress until the end of the 1830s suggests that about two thirds of the population was alphabetised.

Given the composition of the sample, these values never applied to the popoulation of Lisbon, even if they prove that wills are made by the illiterate as well as the literate population. Anyway, the uniform movement of the two curves shows some moments of stability in the unceasing recession and progression of alphabetisation, and makes comparison with data of other European cities of the same period possible.

In the beginning of the 18th century, Lisbon, Toledo and Marseille present very similar values. In absolute terms, the percentage of signatures, selected by the same method, is slightly higher in Lisbon than in Madrid, 41,2% against 37%. On the other hand, as was noticed in Madrid and in the south of France, alphabetisation also declines in the first years of the 18th century in Lisbon.

Going a little farther in our inquiry, we notice that in Avignon and Marseille the percentage of alphabetisation, measured using signatures on wills, is close to 50% in 1680, slightly declining until 1740. Even if these examples prove that in southern Europe access to writing did not follow a linear and continuous progression, we have to think about each society's social-cultural conjunctures, as well as the existence of a more complex context of social differentiation on an urban scale.

Seville, for example, presents, during the 17th century, far more regular alphabetisation percentages as detected in wills. The level of signatures keeps slowly growing, from 52,4% in 1701 to 75,7% at the end of the century. Higher than these values are those for Paris presented by Pierre Chaunu. In the city of the 'lumières' in the 18th century, 90% of the men and 80% of the women are close to the minimum level of alphabetisation.

MEN, WOMEN AND WRITING

In Lisbon, as elsewhere, familiarity with writing is unequally shared by men and women and differs according to social groups. Therefore, the suspicions towards wills as a source because of the different degree to which they are representative of the various sectors of society can

Table 1 - Distribution of signers according to sex (% respect to all testators of the same sex)

	1700	1730	1760	1790	1820	1830
Men	69	64	68	71	77	83
Women	23	17	24	36	39	46

occasionally be alleviated. To do so it is necessary to put aside the very general curves which tend to obscure the results and analyse instead well defined groups and sectors.

According to unquestionable evidence, in Lisbon, and until the middle of the 18th century, two thirds of the signers are men. Only a few women are alphabetised. Men have a much higher participation in the writing universe, but their relative importance in this area diminishes considerably in the 19th century. Beginning in 1790 the relationship between alphabetised men and women is two to one; this tendency remains stable until the end of our study.

After the general unheaval that came about in the first third of the 18th century, a recovery period occurred. A new increase in male alphabetisation takes place at the turn of the century and, in 1830, 83% of all the men who make a will are alphabetised. Surprisingly, in the same period, alphabetised women are double the percentage that they were before. In 1820 they represent almost 40% of the total of female will makers and, in 1830, almost half.

Until the middle of the 18th century most of the alphabetised women can be found within the aristocracy (56%), the upper merchant bourgeoisie (24%) and the strata of public functionaries and liberal professions (10%). Nevertheless, not all of the wives of important men repeat the gesture of signing. Alphabetisation remains a solidly established characteristic among the male élite. In the following years, wives from these groups show more confidence and trust in writing but, at the same time, they tend to lose their social pre-eminence. Respect to the whole of feminine wills, their number is reduced to 44% in 1790 and is limited to 33,7% in 1830. This break in upper and upper middle class hegemony is compensated by the presence of women coming from other social groups.

Over and above what is shown by these simple numbers, this movement is something new. The working women's social relevance is now much greater. From 1820, over a fourth of the women who sign their wills are working women. Female work is social demanding and its context in areas that are close to writing culture surely help to weaken the sexual inequality in the area of alphabetisation. The numerical incidence of this particular social phenomenon however, despite its undeniable importance, is limited. We can balance our analysis by focussing on couples. In order to do so, we have used wills made in common by a man and a woman. These documents help to reveal the relationship with writing established inside families, that is, between husband and wife and, less important, between father and daughter. From the sample we have selected such double wills and studied the 158 testators' behavior, dividing them into three groups:

– In the first we have included 38 couples where neither the husband nor the wife signed the will. Among these, there are about 60% after 1760. We definitely find such illiterate couples within low manual professions.

– 12 couples are part of a second group in which only one of the members sign. Their wills are equally distributed along the analysed period and have the advantage of being more intergroupal than the previous ones. Those who sign are only men, which proves that in Lisbon, as in Madrid, an alphabetised woman would never marry an illiterate man.

– At last, we have 29 couples in which both members can sign. Only fishermen, farmers or rural holders are not included in this category. The sample is not very representative of the first half of the 18th century (17 wills) but is very indicative of the following period, after 1760. The importance of commerce is very evident. Half of these couples come from trading and shopholding families. This leads us to think that, in these environments, marriage could have had an important role in women's cultural adaptation.

SOCIAL CONTRASTS

In the town, contrary to what happened in the country, reading and writing was a skill necessary for qualification for the working world and, thus, is a less unequally shared competence. The comparison made between farmers and landholders selected from Lisbon's rural limits, mostly not alphabetised, with urban workers and craftsmen, more and more alphabetised, is undeniable proof of the differences between the town and the country.

In Lisbon, as we suspected, the hierarchy of signatures closely follows the professional and social hierarchy. The strong signs of social alphabetisation in the capital are not substantially different from those detected in Porto a hundred years earlier. The evolution of social groups' behavior towards writing – in its most basic expression – allows us to distinguish precisely between several cultural universes in urban daily life and consider the gains made through the years by each one of them. The beneficiaries of the change that occurred in these hundred and thirty years are not the élite, but the anonymous many that live by their own initiative and businesses.

The differences are quite clear and indicate the existence of two stable universes. One of the two was that of the notables, which already shows a high level of writing quite early; on the other hand we find the rural world, characterized by slow modifications over long periods of time, ignoring the great cultural changes that affect even lower urban social groups. Not even the fact of being close to a big city like Lisbon can change the persistent and deep-rooted analphabetism of the people connected to the land.

The clergy's absolute dominion in the field of alphabetisation is not surprising. We must not forget that the culture of literacy was maintained for a long time in connection with ecclesiastical teaching. Along with the clergy, aristocracy, traders, public functionaries and officers present strong signs of alphabetisation. The breaks that appear in the data regarding each one of these social groups are, in most of the cases, related to the appearance of non-alphabetised female elements. Major breaks occur in 1730 when 5 out of 8 traders' wives confess their inability to sign, and among 17 noble women 6 claim to be in the same condition. This situation occurs even more frequently when women coming from public functionaries' or officers' families are involved.

This small but shifting margin of analphabetisation is not enough to blur important people's reputation but, even so, it can be a useful key for understanding the dominant culture and its inner forms of communication.

Going back to the 18th century, we notice that the non-alphabetised area includes all fishermen and sailors, almost all the anonymous population that appears professionally undetermined in the sample and extends with the same intensity to workers and servants and then spreads across the craftsmen's and shopholders' world. After a while these groups end up by showing substantial gains.

Craftsmen have a difficult route towards alphabetisation. Writing does not attract all urban craftsmen in the same manner. For example, at the end of the 18th century, watchmakers, jewelers, tailors, coach carpenters and sword makers usually can sign their name. But the same doesn't apply, among others, to shoemakers, tanners, smiths, esparto makers, needle-makers, mat makers, knife makers, weavers and glaziers. So, in Lisbon, as happens in Porto in the 17th century, some mechanical professions reveal similar behaviors towards writing. But it has to be pointed out that, for the same profession, a contrast between those who can sign and those who cannot is also common. In this different universe, with shifting bright and dark areas, progress in alphabetisation is slow. Nevertheless, during the century, a doubling of the volume of mechanical workers' signatures can be detected. In practical terms, in 1830, one in two craftsmen reaches the writing threshold. But, respect to other social groups, mechanical workers' behavior is disappointing. In this regard, the best term of comparison term is furnished by the shopholders.

With a more solid alphabetisation base, people connected to small-scale trade do not show any significant evolution until the middle of the 18th century. Strangely, writing demand seems to be outside the range of these men's professional activity. It is clear that the volume of shopholders' signatures rises in the second half of the 18th century, and the increase is to be confirmed in the following decades.

In 19th-century Lisbon, the retail trade belongs more and more to those who can sign and probably write. Basic and necessary competences for economic growth seem to be designed within a new urban culture environment. In a way, it is in this more demanding context, in terms of alphabetisation, that we must insert the late advances accomplished by the popular and less qualified groups: workers, servants, sailors, fishermen and many others with uncertain occupations. Nevertheless, at the end of this evolutionary process it is easy to verify that the most persistent analphabetised areas are located in the country, and, in the capital, within the labouring classes and the female population.

One can object that the view presented is too optimistic, claiming that a sample based on wills leaves out a substantial part of Lisbon's population. By connecting alphabetisation levels to social groups however we end up with a picture of a strong unbalance necessary reflected in the population.

Observing the whole process we have never lost track of analphabetisation, estimated at 80% in the middle of the 19th century in Portugal. Yet, it has to be considered that by that time Lisbon presented a quite high percentage of alphabetised members of its population. In the 1878 census, the alphabetisation line almost divides the city in half. It is true that a little later, in 1890, the age groups from 64 to 84 years old are not the ones that show the highest percentages of unalphabetised population. About 58% of those men and women, descending from the testators we have mentioned, arrive at the end of the 19th century already alphabetised. If we observe the frequency with which Lisbon's popular groups sign in 1830 (37,6%), we notice that the values fit in with the overall evolution described. More than those regarding the other social groups, these are the values that dominate the capital population's behavior pattern at the end of the first quarter of the 19th century.

In the evolution of alphabetisation, the work market has an important role because it stimulates basic learning, encourages self-learning and provides the basis for the search for ways of acquiring elementary reading and writing abilities. These principles are linked to the set of elements shown in the study of alphabetisation indicators based on the population who made wills. If we wanted to take our inquiry a little farther, we would have to investigate other factors, including institutional ones, in the context of the time. We would inevitably raise the problem of the school system, the educational institutions and the frequency of school attendance, all important elements but that are beyond the objectives of this study, at least for now. Despite this limit, it has to be admitted that, even in the second half of the 19th century – a strong period of expansion of the public education system – a great number of alphabetised people had not gone to school to learn to read and write. As in the traditional model, many of them only accede to the benefits of written culture during their professional life.

SELECTED BIBLIOGRAPHY

Araújo A.C., *A Morte em Lisboa. Atitudes e representações (1700-1830)*, Lisbon 1997.

Araújo A.C., *Livros de uma vida: critérios e modalidades de constituição de uma livraria particular no século XVIII*, "Revista de História das Ideias", Coimbra, 20, 1999, pp. 149-185.

Chartier R., *As práticas da escrita*, in *História da Vida Privada*, vol. 3, *Do Renascimento ao Século das Luzes* (dir. P. Ariès e G. Duby), Lisbon 1990.

Fernandes R., *Os Caminhos do ABC. Sociedade Portuguesa e Ensino das Primeiras Letras*, Porto 1994.

Frago A.V., *Del analfabetismo a la alfabetizacion: analisis de una mutacion antropologica e historiografica*, "Historia de la Educación", 3, 1984, pp. 151-189.

Furet F., Ozouf O., *Lire et Écrire. L'alphabétisation des Français de Calvin à Jules Ferry*, 2 vols., Paris 1977.

Graff H., *Literacy and Social Development in the West: A Reader*, Cambridge, Cambridge 1981.

Larquié C., *L'alphabétisation à Madrid en 1650*, "Revue d'histoire moderne et contemporaine", 28, janv.-mars, 1981, pp. 132-157.

Magalhães J.P., *Ler e escrever no mundo rural no Antigo Regime: um contributo para a história da alfabetização e da escolarização em Portugal*. Braga 1994.

Marquilhas R.M., *A Faculdade das Letras. Leitura e escrita em Portugal no século XVII*, Lisbon 2000, pp. 117-134.

Ramos R., *Culturas da alfabetização e culturas do analfabetismo em Portugal: uma introdução à história da alfabetização no Portugal contemporâneo*, "Análise Social", Lisbon, 3ª série, 24 (103-104), 1988, pp. 1067-1145.

Reis J., *O analfabetismo em Portugal no século XIX: algumas reflexões em perspectiva comparada*, in *1° Encontro de História da Educação em Portugal*, Lisbon 1988, pp. 75-79.

Rodriguez M.-C. Rodriguez et Benassar B., *Signatures et niveau culturel des témoins et accusés dans les procès d'Inquisition du ressort du tribunal de Tolède (1525-1817) et du ressort du tribunal de Cordue (1595-1632)*, "Caravelle. Cahiers du Monde Hispanique et Luso-Brésilien", Toulouse 1978.

Silva F.R. da, *Alfabetização no Antigo Regime: o caso do Porto e da sua região (1580-1650)*, "Revista da Faculdade de Letras. História", Porto, 2ª série, 3, 1986, pp. 101-163.

Silva F.R. da, *Níveis de alfabetização de oficiais administrativos e judiciais dos concelhos de Refojos de Riba d'Ave e da Maia na 1ª metade do séc. XVII: instituições e níveia de alfabetização dos funcionários*, "Gaya", Vila Nova de Gaia, 2, 1984, pp. 187-212.

Stone L., *Literacy and education in England, 1640-1900*, "Past and Present", 42, 1969, pp. 69-139.

Soubeyroux J., *L'alphabétisation à Madrid aux XVIIIe et XIXe siècles*, "Bulletin Hispanique", Madrid, 1-4, 1987, pp. 227-265.

SOURCE

Luís António Verney, *Verdadeiro Método de Estudar*, Lisbon, 1952, Vol. V, pp. 123-127.(first edition 1746)

Sobre o estudo das Mulheres

Mas, antes que acabe, tocarei um ponto que se deve unir aos estudos que apontámos; e vem a ser o estudo das Mulheres. Parecerá paradoxo a estes Catões Portugueses ouvir dizer que as mulheres devem estudar; contudo, se examinarem o caso, conhecerão que não é nenhuma parvoíce ou coisa nova, mas bem usual e racionável. Pelo que toca à capacidade, é loucura persuadir-se que as Mulheres tenham menos que os Homens. Elas não são de outra espécie no que toca a alma; e a diferença do sexo não tem parentesco com a diferença do entendimento. A experiência podia e devia desenganar estes homens. Nós ouvimos todos os dias mulheres que discorrem tão bem como os homens; e achamos nas histórias mulheres que souberam as Ciências muito melhor que alguns grandes Leitores que nós ambos conhecemos. Se o acharem-se muitas que discorrem mal fosse argumento bastante para dizer que não são capazes, com mais razão o podíamos dizer de muitos homens. Compare V. P. uma freira moça da Corte com um Galego de meses, e verá quem leva vantagem. De que nasce esta diferença? Da aplicação e exercício, que um tem e outro não tem. Se das mulheres se aplicassem aos estudos tantas quantas entre os homens, então veríamos quem reinava.

Quanto à necessidade, eu acho-a grande que as mulheres estudem. Elas, principalmente as mães de família, são as nossas mestras nos primeiros anos da nossa vida: elas nos ensinam a língua; ela nos hão-de ensinar as primeiras ideias das coisas. E que coisa boa nos hão-de ensinar, se elas não sabem o que dizem? Certamente que os prejuízos que nos metem na cabeça na nossa primeira meninice são sumamente prejudiciais em todos os estados da vida; e quer-se um grande estudo e reflexão para se despir deles. Além disso, elas governam a casa, e a direcção do económico fica na esfera da sua jurisdição. E que coisa boa pode fazer uma mulher que não tem alguma ideia da economia? Além disso, o estudo pode formar os costumes, dando belíssimos ditames para a vida; e uma mulher que tem alguma notícia deles pode, nas horas ociosas, empregar-se em coisa útil e honesta, no mesmo tempo que outras se empregam em leviandades repreensíveis. Muito mais, porque não acho texto algum da Lei, ou Sagrada, ou Profana, que obrigue as Mulheres a serem tolas, e não saberem falar. As Freiras já se sabe que devem saber mais alguma coisa, porque hão-de ler livros latinos. Mas eu digo que ainda as casadas e donzelas podem achar grande utilidade na notícia dos livros. Persuado-me que a maior parte dos homens casados que não fazem gosto de conversar com as suas mulheres, e vão a outras partes procurar divertimentos pouco inocentes, é porque as acham tolas no trato; e este é o motivo que aumenta aquele desgosto que naturalmente se acha no contínuo trato de marido com mulher. Certo é que uma mulher de juízo exercitado saberá adoçar o ânimo agreste de um marido áspero e ignorante, ou saberá entreter melhor a disposição de ânimo de um marido erudito, do que outra que não tem estas qualidades; e, desta sorte, reinará melhor a paz nas famílias. O mesmo digo das donzelas a respeito dos parentes. Enfim, esta matéria é de tanta consideração para a República, que um homem tão pio e douto M. de Fénelon, Arcebispo de Cambrai, compôs um belíssimo tratado sobre esta matéria (e depois dele alguns Autores Franceses e Italianos que eu li), em que ensina como se deve regular este estudo, e as utilidades que dele se podem tirar. Ao que eu podia acrescentar algumas experiências e reflexões minhas, feitas sobre as aplicações que observei em algumas mulheres.

Reduzindo, pois, em pouco o que se pode dizer nesta matéria, principalmente acomodando-se ao estilo de Portugal, digo que com as mulheres se deve praticar o mesmo que apontei dos rapazes. O primeiro estudo das mães deve ser ensinar-lhe, por si, ou, tendo possibilidade, por meio de outra pessoa capaz, os primeiros elementos da Fé, etc., explicando-lhe bem todas estas coisas, o que podem fazer desde a idade de cinco anos até aos sete. Depois, ler e escrever Português correctamente. E isto é o que rara mulher sabe fazer em Portugal. Não digo eu escrever correctamente, pois ainda não achei alguma que o fizesse; mas digo que pouquíssimas sabem ler e escrever; e, muito menos, fazer ambas as coisas correctamente.

On Women studying

Before concluding, I shall touch on a point which should be associated with the studies we have referred to: Women studying. The statement that women should study will seem paradoxical to these Portuguese Catos. However, taking the case under examination, they will appreciate that such is neither foolish nor novel, but rather common and reasonable. As far as Women's capabilities are concerned, it would be insane to convince ourselves that they are less capable than Men. They are not a different species regarding soul, and the difference in sex has no bearing on the difference in understanding. Experience could and should discourage these men from thinking the way they do. Women can reason as soundly as men, and we are all familiar with this common occurrence. History teaches us that there existed women who knew more about Sciences than many of our great Lecturers. If the poor reasoning of some women is used as an argument against their being capable of reasoning, we may claim it equally true of many men. Let us compare a young novice at Court with an errand boy who has recently arrived from Galicia, and we shall have no doubts about who reasons best. Where does the difference stem from? From regular practice, which the former has and the latter has not. If the number of women who study equalled that of men, nations would be run by different people.

As regards the utility of women studying, I deem it important. Women, especially those who are mothers, are the persons who transmit to us the very first notions of life in childhood, including our mother tongue. And what good things will they be able to teach us, if they do not know how to express those things? It seems obvious that the damage caused to our minds by the conveyance of wrong ideas in our very young years will prove devastating in its effects throughout the various stages of our lives. It will also require long and hard hours of study and reflection to repair. Moreover, women have to run their households and thus the economic aspects involved in that belong to them. How may they successfully fulfil that duty if they do not know the first thing about economic matters? It is also true that studying may shape customs, providing us with magnificent principles to live by; and women who have some knowledge of them may, in their leisure time, employ themselves in doing something useful and honest. Those who do not have that knowledge will waste their time on futile and reprehensible things. I will go even further and state that I have never come across any legal, religious or profane text conveying the idea that women should be foolish and inarticulate. Nuns are known to have some form of knowledge as they read Latin books. I believe that both maidens and wives might find books very useful. In my mind, if the majority of married men derive no pleasure from talking to their wives, and seek far less innocent ways to amuse themselves elsewhere, it is because they think they are shallow. This situation is only aggravated between husband and wife with the passage of time. It is certainly true that a sensible and experienced wife will know how to soothe the mood of a harsh and ignorant husband or entertain an erudite one better than the wife who does not possess those qualities. And all of this will be to the advantage of family harmony. The same may be said of maidens in relation to their family members. This is such an important issue for the Republic that M. de Fénelon, the most wise and pious Archbishop of Cambrai, wrote an excellent treatise on the subject (and also other French and Italian authors whose works I am familiar with). In his book, the Archbishop teaches us how this study should be regulated and speaks about the benefits to be derived from it.

I might add some of my personal experiences and some reflections on what I have observed about women studying.

Summarising what may be said on this subject and adjusting it to the Portuguese manner of doing things, I believe that we should put into practice with women what I have referred to about boys. The first thing which mothers, or somebody competent in their place if such is possible, should teach their daughters are the essential elements of Faith, taking care to explain everything in detail. This may be accomplished between the ages of five and seven years. Being able to read and write Portuguese correctly comes next, but this is a rare case in Portugal among women. And by rare I mean being able to read and write, for so far I have never met any woman who could do both correctly.

Ana Cristina Araújo

Women and the writing of national history. Italy, 1860-1914

Ilaria Porciani
Università di Bologna

Si analizzano, nel loro rapporto con il tema della costruzione della nazione, i lavori storici scritti da donne in Italia tra il 1860 e la prima guerra mondiale. In questo modo si desidera contribuire ad aumentare le conoscenze della scrittura della storia da parte delle donne, ma non solo. Scrivere la storia di genere non vuol dire semplicemente osservare il mondo delle donne. Si tratta invece di sottoporre ad un nuovo livello di analisi, più complesso ed illuminante, tutti i temi che vengono esaminati. Qui si mira ad analizzare brevemente quattro punti: la teoria delle sfere separate; la struttura della professione degli storici; il sistema famiglia-nazione nel canone del Risorgimento; e la struttura retorica della storiografia sul Risorgimento. I lavori di storia nazionale prodotti da donne italiane durante il periodo esaminato sono significativi; trattano eventi e temi politici e dimostrano che le attività delle donne non erano limitate alla sfera privata. Nella prima generazione, molte donne scrivevano come testimoni di eventi cui avevano preso parte. Inoltre sostenevano le guerre patriottiche non solo con i mezzi tradizionali di raccolta di fondi per scopi caritatevoli, ma anche scrivendo e vendendo i loro libri, nel contempo negoziando il loro diritto ad entrare nella vita politica del paese. Dopo l'unificazione nazionale, le donne continuarono a scrivere libri di storia, soprattutto del periodo recente. Ciò è dovuto fra l'altro anche alla struttura degli studi accademici dell'epoca, sul modello, fortemente connotato in termini di genere, del seminario. Le donne con maggiore frequenza accedevano a società storiche non professionali o lavoravano isolatamente. Tendevano infatti ad indirizzare i loro sforzi verso settori meno codificati accademicamente, dove le loro conoscenze ed esperienze dirette potessero essere utilizzate. Complessivamente, l'opera di questa generazione di storiche venne ignorata o trascurata dagli storici 'ufficiali'. Man mano che il campo della storia del Risorgimento veniva strutturandosi accademicamente, i posti furono occupati quasi esclusivamente da uomini. E' paradossale che una delle prime professoresse di storia sia stata chiamata ad occupare una cattedra di Storia del Risorgimento. In genere le donne lavoravano in scuole e biblioteche, senza accedere all'apice dell'organizzazione dell'istruzione. Oltre a scrivere, le donne entrarono nel dibattito politico pubblico. Il loro contributo alla definizione del rapporto fra famiglia e nazione fu grande. Si trattava di produrre un modello di rapporti personali e di domesticità che potesse in qualche misura proporsi come modello nazionale. Oggi si dispone, grazie a Maria Pia Casalena, di un inventario di tutti gli scritti storici prodotti da donne italiane. E' quindi possibile approfondire ulteriormente le ricerche.

Born in Rome in 1952, Ilaria Porciani is professor of History of the Age of the Risorgimento at the University of Bologna. Her interests are in the area of European and Italian cultural and intellectual history. She has published numerous volumes and essays including *L'Archivio storico italiano* (1979) and *La festa della nazione. Rappresentazione dello Stato e spazi sociali nell'Italia unita* (1997).

Here we wish to analyse women's historical work between 1860 and the First World War in relation to the theme of nation building. We thus aim to contribute towards improving knowledge of women's historical writing, but this is not all. The writing of gender history does not just mean concentrating on the world of women, but above all subjecting themes not exclusively limited to women to a new and more complex analysis. I believe that this study will enable us to take a fresh look at a number of questions, at least with respect to four points: 1) the theory of separate spheres; 2) the general structure of the historian's profession as a whole; 3) the family-nation system within the canon of the *Risorgimento* in which the work of women historians plays an important role; 4) the rhetorical structure of the historiography on the *Risorgimento*.

Works of national history produced by Italian women during the period considered are important for their number, the sources used and – sometimes – the quality of writing. They tackle events and themes with considerable political content and above all, their study enables us to put the theory of separate spheres up for debate once again; and then demonstrate that not all the women were relegated to the private sphere. A number of them, in fact, entered (sometimes to play a leading role) the highly political arena of building the nation's history.

The preparation of a number of the women whose writings we will consider consisted of reading the patriotic novels which, during the first half of the 1800s, represented one of the strong points (and perhaps the core) of the debate on nationhood, a debate which would persuade many to give up the comforts of their upperclass lives and venture out on the great gamble of independence. Others were influenced by the charisma of heroic characters such Garibaldi. For the "emancipated" Bianca Milesi, the Lombard princess Cristina Trivulzio di Belgiojoso and the democrat Jessie White, wife of patriot Alberto Mario, the writing of history (I hesitate to use the more pompous and specialised term of historiography) represented a way of continuing their conspiratorial work within secret societies or battles fought at first hand in the Milan of the *Cinque Giornate* or in Rome following Garibaldi.

The first fact to emerge is that the first generation of women took a direct part in political (and sometimes even military) action towards the conquest of national independence. They write as witnesses. Most of these women were on the side of democrats and experienced partial defeat, given that the unification of Italy occurred under the leadership of the moderates. Both the concept of *pariah*, according to Bonnie Smith's definition, and that of *traumatic history* can be applied to these women and their writings.

Studying them implies a link with a whole series of recent studies focussing on women's participation in the 1848 revolution wars (Soldani) or the conspiratorial activities of patriotic women in southern Italy (Guidi).

For many of these women, writing history was also a way of constructing their own identity as women in relation to nation building. The limits placed on access of women to the public sphere – the most evident being their exclusion from the right to vote – are obvious considerable. However, on the terrain of the nation, these women negotiated their right to

Ilaria Porciani

enter the public sphere, sometimes taking their inspiration from traditional women's charitable activities such as the collection of funds through charity sales. But they transformed this ancient practice by acting as protagonists and authors. Instead of selling embroidery or the other products of activities traditionally define as "women's", they sold books they had written themselves. An example of this can be seen in the group of women consisting of Gualberta Alaide Beccari, editor of the Veneto magazine "La Donna", Caterina Croatto Caprin, Adele Butti, Giulia Ballio, Cesia Airoldi, Matilde Ferluga Fenter, Ernesta Margarita, Elisa Panizza Scari, Adele Pelliccia, Rosa Piazza, Felicita Bozzoli, Caterina Tetamanzi Boldrin and Anna Vertua Gentile. These wrote biographies of Italian patriots for a volume entitled *Martiri Italiani. Scritti storici e raccolti da alcune donne dei danneggiati poveri dell'inondazione di Roma* (1871). I would like to discover the correspondence leading up to this work to understand what arguments were used to obtain the participation of each of these women.

For some of theme, publication was not a novelty. These were women used to writing, who considered themselves authors and were recognised as such. This is the case of Anna Vertua Gentile, author of, amongst other works, a famous *Galateo* and editor of a volume entitled *L'istruzione in famiglia* containing educational texts for young women with a marked conservative tone, particularly evident when talking of the French Revolution. Or of Felicita Pozzoli who made her debut with this text, to then go on three years later to write *Le donne nelle lotte italiane* (1874); a children's book, *Le vicende più memorabilia d'Italia narrate alla gioventù* (1889); and *Eroi ed eroine del Risorgimento italiano* (1896). It would be interesting to follow the "gender" typification of these "heroes" and "heroines" and the two currents of model biographies of men and women, sometimes moving apart, sometimes coming together. For some of these women, contributing to this volume had a great significance. It mean that their writing for the first and maybe for the only time did not stop at that "pleasing and agreeable gift" of private letters or at the diary, but came out into the open becoming public. Probably this meant a lot to their self-awareness.

The study of the subsequent generation, in other words, of the daughters of the protagonists, those who were children at the moment of unification, enables our prospective to be extended further.

From 1861 onwards, in other words, at the time when history – but only ancient, medieval and modern history – acquired the right of citizenship in the universities of the new nation state, women's history writing was clearly focussed towards contemporary history, namely the history of what was already starting to be known as the Risorgimento, or more generally, the history of the present. Compared with the small minority of studies on ancient, medieval and modern history, studies on history of the Risorgimento and contemporary period were heavily predominant. One endogenous reason can probably be found in the organisation of university teaching and research, its paradigms and its hierarchies.

Bonnie Smith has shown how the seminar, archive research and, more generally, all practices associated with the emergence of the professional historian have given a highly pronounced gender character to history. This is above all true in Germany where the seminar model was defined, but also in the United States which closely follows the German model. There, women historians worked mainly in isolation or in the context of local historical societies more open to "amateurs". In these two countries, women were kept outside the spaces reserved for professional history – in other words, the universities – and oriented towards other less precise and less professionalised spaces. Spaces which, to use a term dear to historians, I would define as "genre" (as in a genre picture, for example). Women were therefore pushed towards more "feminine" contexts: the historical tale for children, the teaching of history and the "genre" aspects more associated with everyday life. In Italy, a number of women were active in these sectors, but I believe the situation to be largely different. Rather than enter into strongly codified disciplines such as ancient and medieval history, women wanting to carry out the research (and in this sense differing from the first generation women historian-patriots or popular historians) concentrated on a new and academically weaker sector, that of recent history, which from the 1880s was known as the history of the Risorgimento. This sector was considered as less important by academic historians because it was too recent and thus based on a corpus of unstable sources, letters and memoirs rather than archive documents. For this sector the knowledge of basic tools (Latin, Paleography, Diplomatics) was not required. More useful, on the other hand, could be direct contact with the protagonists, the possession of memoirs and documents in the family, an association with milieus directly linked to situations of exile and the battles of the Risorgimento. The fact of having lived in environments where such matters were learned not didactically, but through conversations, direct participation through family stories, through the discovery of letters kept within one's own family, through the receipt of bundles of documents from one's lover and companion or simply from a friend

Knowledge of these events was thus limited to highly protected circles of friends where the historical event was lived in a dimension of passion and moral commitment. In this context, it is not hard to understand the writing of Anna Filippini Poma, Zellide Fattiboni and Marietta Campo.

These women, however, are absent from the traditional histories of historiography (Croce does not name even one in his history of 19th-century Italian historiography) and from histories of Risorgimento historiography. In his *Interpretazioni del Rinascimento* from 1945-47, Walter Maturi names Zellide Fattiboni just once and not for her work, but for a letter that she had given to a better-known male historian, Carlo Tivaroni. Belgiojoso is absent; Campo is absent; White Mario is mentioned just three times on the basis of writings of Tivaroni or to express highly misogynous judgements. It would seem that Maturi, who quotes many minor historians, had not even read her works. On the other hand, Maturi does not even define her as a "historian", but as an "ardent writer on Mazzini's side" – *writer* and not historian, *ardent* and not impartial.

However, the production of these women is of a relatively high level. Sometimes it even appears as remarkable for the originality of the research and use of documents and the high quality of the writing, repaid by a far from indifferent editorial success. It is, therefore, in no way inferior to the work of those memorialists and historian who, after unification, started writing history of the nation and defining the concept of Risorgimento. Furthermore, many if not all of these writers rather than professional historians had been directly politicised by the Risorgimento battles or in the liberal movement.

We are left, therefore, looking for the reasons for this absence, trying to understand when it began and to identify any possible breaches in this sort of "choice of silence". There are, in fact, exceptions. Carducci (who had been a democrat and therefore had belonged to the same milieus as some of these women) includes at least Fattiboni in his *Letture del Risorgimento Italiano*.

The erasure seem rather to have been introduced by academic historians as the history of the Risorgimento began gradually to take the shape of well-defined discipline through the foundation of periodicals and, later, in the 1930s, the first university chairs.

To sum up, during the first phase of historical studies of the Risorgimento, still closely linked to memoirs and the direct memory of political battles, we have works located within a canon not yet clearly defined, written by women who were in one way or another exceptional and who could be define as *pariahs*. This is the case of Cristina Belgiojoso who abandoned society conventions and spent a large part of her wealth to arm troops against Austria, who fled in exile, who frequented all the great French historians and travelled at length, sometimes alone, in the Orient, who bore arms, inflicted wounds and was in turn wounded. This is the case of Jessie White Mario who earned her living as a newspaper correspondent, who sorted the archive of Cattaneo with and for Bertani, and who never forgot that she had left her country determined to serve the cause of Italian revolution as a field nurse, following Garibaldi. Or the case of certain daughters of patriots such as Zellide Fattiboni or Marietta Campo, all women who, in one way or another, were proudly aware of their uniqueness, with a strong sense of identity, a predisposition for looking within themselves in search of truth, who, rejected by the majority, learned to rely on the support of a limited circle of friends, and finally, sharing a passionate relationship with writing, which represented an opportunity for vindicating and, sometimes, constructing their own identity. As a whole, I would define their writing as exceptional, a writing of witnessing and compensation.

Later however, things changed. The *pariah* of sometimes original and vehement, sometimes transgressive writing, gave way to academics, researchers, the first women graduates: scholars, in clearly subordinate positions, who held posts as librarians or secondary school teachers, who mastered a method and worked in a more or less philological manner while continuing to review the subject of their study from the point of view of nation and often Irredentism. But they were characteristics of neutral specialists, cancelling or considerably weakening gender aspects and their own individuality. The "*I Narrator*" so strongly present in, for example, the writing of Marietta Campo, begins to vanish. The personality of the writer, her passionate participation, disappears.

As the profession gradually became organised within a nation state which increased the number of its school and libraries, women on one hand started to work in these institutions, while on the other they remained consistently at the margins of the academic profession. The number of post increased, a growing number of men occupied university chairs. Women lagged behind, with one exception which can be taken in various ways, that of Emilia Morelli. Paradoxically, it was precisely a recently founded lecturer's post of history of the Risorgimento that we find occupied by one of the first woman history professors.

However, there are other elements of interest to a study of women's contemporary and national history writing. Firstly, their ability to stand out in public commemorative debate. At first, it was difficult. In 1847, Cristina di Belgiojoso, the albeit eccentric Lombard aristocrat, friend of all the most famous French historians, extremely wealthy, brave and transgressive, wrote:

> In Florence I received an invitation to go into the midst of a popular assembly, and having arrived there, I was received with cheers and shouts of 'viva', and they had me sit on a high chair...Do you see me in the midst of five or six hundred men, all of whose eyes were fixed on me, in the middle of a formidable silence, ready to say I don't know what? The sound of one's own voice in such a case is the most imposing thing that there is in the world. Never has a woman found herself placed as I was; and emotions similar to those which I felt are such as to throw female nerves out of balance. What is the emotion of an actress compared to mine? Mademoiselle Rachel presents to the public the looks or the feelings of Camille or Phèdre: I, it is my face and my person which I bring to it. [*See Source 1*].

Women of subsequent generations lived in situations which were certainly less dramatic and less directly political. They did not take part in the actual Risorgimento struggles but in its commemoration, and spoke often in public, talking of subjects such as war, the constitution and Italian history. And they did not always talk in segregated environments such as girls' schools.

More often, however, the work of women historians remained linked to terrain which brought the public and private sectors together, focussing on the theme of the family-nation complex, highly relevant both before and after Unity in light of the nation building project. Previously, the church had considered the family as a private matter. The liberal movement, with its public debate, narrative and historiography, gave ever more importance to the theme.

Construction of the family-nation association was not limited to women alone, but women's writing made a significant contribution.

A passage by the Sicilian Marietta Campo provides example.

This is how Campo presents her work *Francesco Riso. Cenni storico-biografici* (1886):

> I am driven to dedicate these pages – 26 years after the period during which the glorious actions of the man to whose memory I pay tribute today took place – by a sentiment of friendship and deep admiration for that generous martyr who, on April 4, 1860, courageous and proud with a few bold and generous folk at his side, began that momentous revolution during which freedom of the island and the unity of Italy triumphed.
> Still young, during that time of conspiracy when my family met and became intimate with Francesco Riso, I was able to admire the noble and generous sentiments which distinguished him and led him to perform his great deed. His thoughts and his words expressed an ardent and enthusiastic soul, capable of the highest and most sacred of sacrifices in order to redeem his homeland. [...] In my family, his noble self-denial and heroic sacrifice always inspired sentiments of genuine and profound respect for the memory of that generous son of the people and today, in repaying this debt of friendship which I feel in my heart, I am also expressing that of my family.

Women's history writing seems to me to be central – although not exclusive – in elaboration of a phase of the family and nation debate. It was neither new nor the sole prerogative of women. Neither was limited to the context of historiography. It starts a long way back and during the post-unification period already had an important preparatory phase behind it, consisting of input dictated by the new pedagogy; examples contained in Sismondi's *Storia delle repubbliche*, models spread directly or indirectly by the historical novel end iconography (the theme of Hayez's *Sicilian Vespers* for example), but above all from the lives of patriot. This model was formed in a climate of conspiracy and insurrection, exile and political struggle in which it was necessary to rely on a circle of private friends, when for patriots the bonds of family and friends became essential to feel, to be hidden and to be protected.

Yet debate on family and nation took a considerable leap forward both in size and in quality after Unification. At this time, alongside the construction of models of exemplary lives (*Plutarchs* in male and female version; *Martyrologies* of the Risorgimento; a series of heroines and heroes, divided or otherwise by gender), there was also the much more extensive construction of family models. In the political construction of the nation, re-appropriation of the domestic sphere – the sphere of emotions and sentiments, of building relationship between husbands and wives, of maternal and (to a lesser extent) paternal responsibilities – also played an important role. Within the great metaphor of the family, inclusive and exclusive, the difficult building of the nation took shape at various levels – a nation which still had to be "invented". It consisted of a model of uniform "domesticity" to which different social and cultural realities could conform. And it was on this basis that a model could be offered to "civilise" the south, constructing a sense of national sentiment there as well. We could, perhaps, compare this with the situation in the United States in relation to the role played by domesticity in imposing an American model against all those outside the dimension of the national family (Indians, enemies).

In Italy, the domestic sphere also acquired an important role in building a national identity consisting of numerous regional identities. In the first national exhibition the variety of regional identities which makes up the framework of the nation is represented by the women, their traditional costumes and works (Villari): ethnology grows up gendered.

However, the women's narrative about nation building is also about suffering, pain and war endured. Is this the narrative coming from the *zoè* or the zone of the *bios*? Is it a truly all-women's narrative? in constructing this discourse, drawing on memoirs which often draw on letter, it sometimes seems to me to be rather a play of cross mirrors.

Let me give an example.

Evelyn Carrington Martinengo, a British aristocrat who married an Italian aristocrat and identified herself with her family, wrote a series of profiles of Italian patriots – a work which became enormously popular just before and during the First World War. One of these figures was Settembrini. To write this portrait, Martinengo makes ample use of Settembrini's *Mie Memorie*, which in turn uses the writing of his wife Raffaella Faucitano Settembrini.

This play of reciprocal use can sometimes be traced in detail. Settembrini's wife, a strong character playing a decisive role in the patriotic conspiracy, disappears as an individual in Settembrini's memoirs where she is referred to exclusively by the name Gigia. In his

Memorie, Settembrini uses her writing containing not just a description of exile and imprisonment, but also domestic aspects (the children, the family, their hardships). These same elements, filtered through the account of Settembrini, who uses his wife's writing without giving her an independent voice, then pass into Martinengo's account. In this narrative, is thus difficult to decide what belongs to whom, what is "masculine" and what is "feminine".

What is the overall significance of women's historical writing for the history of the nation? The question seems an important one to me, but I am not sure that I can provide a definitive and exhaustive answer at this stage. As is often the case where the overall picture is complicated by the accumulation of information of greater or lesser importance, one tends to make gains in detail but to lose in clarity. There are joints in the mosaics which make the overall design less easy to discern.

Individual fragments are evident but the composition eludes us. The data brought to light by Maria Pia Casalena's survey has enlarged the context and multiplied the available evidence. Now that we have her inventory of all historical texts published by Italian women we can begin to identify specific characteristics, and to make those comparisons which seem to me ever more necessary for successful research. We can and we must begin to compare female writing in relation to the various genres. It will thus become possible to understand whether the structure of discourse and the narrative programme, the rhetoric and the relation with the women writers' subjectively or the dialogue with the reader are the same within the context of Risorgimento history and – let us say – medieval and ancient history. This will also allow us to understand better how any specificity in women's writing is to be defined in relation to the historiographic sources and paradigms of a different type. So the situation becomes more complicated and the paradigms of individual disciplines have to be taken into consideration.

On other hand the advantage of a very thorough survey (such as Maria Casalena's) is that it brings to light many "uncomfortable" elements that complicate and contradict overhasty hypotheses. Thus it will be necessary to identify and investigate more carefully the various typologies which are found one after another. To consider only the Risorgimento, we have texts dealing with very varied subjects, from foreign policy and treaties to institutional history, from the history of war to that of secret societies , from portraits of patriots and martyrs to edition of documents.

Among historical publications by women there are many biographical studies (not all the same type), many of which powerfully reveal the individuality of their authors and which bring to the fore everyday details, domestic comfort, the family, the sufferings caused to women and children by war and by the absence of imprisoned dear ones. These elements dominate the early phase but sometimes return in the early years of the 20th century in the guise of editions of memoirs and correspondence, in which female (and male) scholars have taken the place of family members. But it is not easy to generalise. Alongside the more "warm" and "gendered" approaches we find among women's historical writings also "cool" and "neutral" ones. On the other hand we should be aware that representation of feeling, of the private, is not an exclusively feminine domain, especially in the 19th century. Emotion, individuality and subjectivity emerge very strongly in letters, but also in memoirs and biographical writings on patriots, whether they be written by women or by men.

Furthermore, we notice a number of regional variables in the approach to memoir writing. The historian Ernesto Sestan has emphasised the fact that Tuscan 19th-century memoirs are much more attuned to the figure of the mother than are those of Lombardy or Piedmont. This too is a subject to explore, building on these indications and complementing them by a gender-based approach.

On the other hand the situation becomes more complicated also as regards methodology, especially if we intend to take into account the findings which are emerging as the result of research in other countries. Many of the questions posed by Bonnie Smith seem to me to be relevant to my topic. What place does "traumatic narrative" have in the writings of women about the Italian Risorgimento? What is the role of biography?

In my opinion history cannot be considered on the same level as fiction. It is constructed using documents, it is tied to its sources. Nevertheless even history is subject to the rules of narrative, which for this reason are worthy of investigation. We should therefore begin to ask ourselves what was the narrative programme of these women historians and what was their understanding of it; what were the models they followed, and whether they adhered spontaneously to them or whether they were constrained to adhere to them by academic conventions, by the standards of the journals, and so on. In particular, it would be interesting to compare the various genres: that of the "first generation" based on direct experience, on direct memories and on correspondence, without particular reference to external models; that of the generation of female scholars, ever more restricted by their models, and lastly that of the "parliamentary" historical novel such as that for Dora Melegari, which constitutes a genre in its own right and leaves more space for an autonomous narrative programme. At this point we shall have to look once more beyond the confines of disciplines to try to understand whether the sociology of literature and the history of reading habits and practices can give us further indication on female reading in 19th century, especially the reading works of history. But this too is so far only an idea for research.

In conclusion I should like to draw attention to something that seems to me to be of great importance. In the area of textual investigation Italian historiography is undoubtedly very much behind, on account of the undue influence exercised by the historiographical paradigms first of historicism and then of Marxism. Beginning with a reflection on the historical texts written by women, possibly a gender history may help us to introduce a salutary innovation into the discussion of 19th century historiography.

 **SELECTED BIBLIOGRAPHY**

Banti A.M., *La nazione del Risorgimento. Parentela, santità e onore alle origini dell'Italia unita*, Turin 2000.

Biagianti I. (ed.), *La "Nuova Italia" nelle corrispondenze americane di Jessie White Mario (1866 - 1906)*, Florence 1999.

Daniels E.A., White Mario J., *Risorgimento revolutionary*, Athens (USA) 1972.

Davidson C.N., *Preface: No more separate spheres!*, "American Literature", 70, 1998, pp. 443 ff.

Kerber L., *Separate spheres, female worlds, woman's place: the rhetoric of women's history*, "The Journal of American History", 1988 (repr. in Kerber L., *Toward an intellectual history of women*, Chapel Hill 1997, pp. 159-199).

Porciani I. (ed.), *Le donne a scuola*, Florence 1987.

Porciani I., Soldani S. (eds.), *Donne, ricerche e scrittura di storia in Italia tra Otto e Novecento. Un quadro d'insieme*, "Annali dell'Istituto storico italo-germanico in Trento" - *Jahrbuch des italienisch-deutschen Instituts in Trent*, 23, 1997, pp. 265-299.

Porciani I., *Les historiennes et le Risorgimento*, "Mélanges de l'École Française de Rome. Italie et Méditerranée", 112, 2000-1.

Smith B.G, *The gender of history. Men and women and historical practice*, Cambridge (Mass.) - London 1998.

Soldani S. (ed.), *L'educazione delle donne. Scuole e modelli di vita femminile nell'Italia dell'Ottocento*, Milan 1989.

Whitehouse H.R., *Une princesse révolutionnaire. Christine Trivulzio-Belgiojoso*, Paris 1907.

 SOURCES

1. *A Florence j'ai re(u une invitation pour me rendre au milieu d'une assemblée populaire et, m'y étent rendue, j'ai été re(ue par des cheers et des vivats, on ma fait asseoir sur un siège élévé... Me voyez vous au milieu de 5 à 600 hommes, dont tous les yeux sont fixés sur moi, au milieu d'un silence formidable, prete à prononcer je ne sais quoi? Le son de sa propre voix est dans ces cas le plus imposant qu'il y ait au monde.. Jamais femme ne s'est trouvée placée comme moi; et les émotions pareilles à celles que je prouve devant le public sont de nature à détraquer des nerfs feminins. Qu'est-ce que l'emotion d'un actrice comparée à la mienne? Mlle Rachel présente au public les traits ou le coeur de Camille ou Phèdre; moi, c'est bien mon visage et ma personne que je lui apporte"* (Thierry p 123-5)

2. The reaction of the Marquess of Florange to Christine Trivulzio-Belgioioso's historiographical works (quoted by H.R. *Whitehouse, Une princesse révolutionnaire. Christine Trivulzio-Belgiojoso*, Paris, 1907, p. 70).

La princesse de Belgiosioso faisait donc des livres, de grands et lourds livres; non contente de conspirer, d'être belle, de savoir jouer de la guitare et du couteau, de peindre des éventails, de laisser connaître à tout Paris que l'Autriche la persécutait, voici qu'elle lisait l'hébreu et composait des livres, et quels livres! Des amas gigantesques, vous-dis-je, des pyramides de pages! Pensant que ce fussent des romans – une femme, que conterait-elle, sinon son cœur et celui du prochain? – j'osai jeter les yeux sur un feuillet. Grand Dieu! Mon chapeau m'en tomba des mains! C'était de la théologie.

The Princess of Belgioioso wrote then some books, big and heavy books; not content with conspiracy, with being beautiful, knowing how to play the guitar and use the knife, painting fans, letting all Paris know that Austria was persecuting her, here she is reading Hebrew and composing books, and what books! Gigantic heaps, I would say, pyramids of pages! Thinking that they were novels — a woman, what will she recount, if not her heart and that of her neighbour? – I dared to cast a glance on a page. Great God! My hat fell from my hands. It was Theology.

Women Artists of the 1920s in the Hannover Region

Ines Katenhusen

Universität Hannover

Seit Mitte des 19. Jahrhunderts und im Zusammenhang mit der Industrialisierung drängten in Deutschland zunehmend bildende Künstlerinnen auf den Kunstmarkt. Einmal wegen der ihnen anerzogenen Wertschätzung für Ästhetik und Schönheit, zum zweiten aufgrund der Tatsache, dass diese Tätigkeit von einer breiten Öffentlichkeit als weniger „unschicklich" wahrgenommen wurde als andere Formen des Broterwerbs, waren es zumeist Angehörige des gehobenen Bürgertums, die sich zu einer Künstlerinnenexistenz entschlossen.

Trotz vielfältiger Abwehrtendenzen seitens männlicher Kunsthistoriker, Sammler, Kunstfunktionäre und Künstler konnten sich einzelne Malerinnen durchsetzen. Allerdings wurde ihre Arbeit erschwert durch das Verbot, an staatlichen Kunstakademien und Universitäten zu studieren. Vor allem Gründungen von eigens auf die Interessen von Künstlerinnen ausgerichteten Vereinigungen von Frauen für Frauen sorgten für Verbesserungen auch in der Ausbildungssituation.

Mit dem Frauenwahlrecht ging in den Jahren nach dem Zusammenbruch der Monarchie 1918/ 19 der Schritt einher, nun auch Künstlerinnen für das Studium an den staatlichen Institutionen zuzulassen. Freilich zeigte sich bald, dass viele von ihnen auch in den so genannten 'Goldenen Zwanzigern' angesichts Beschränkungen und Diskriminierungen Schwierigkeiten hatten, ausschließlich von ihrer Kunst zu leben. Weiterhin bedurfte es der Unterstützung einflussreicher Frauenorganisationen. Eine von ihnen war die 1926 in Hamburg gegründete GEDOK (Gemeinschaft Deutscher und Österreichischer Künstlerinnenverbände aller Kunstgattungen), die Dank ihrer prägnanten Struktur – hier Künstlerinnen, dort Kunstfreundinnen oder – förderinnen – in den folgenden Jahren und Jahrzehnten vielen Künstlerinnen wertvolle Hilfe zum selbständigen Arbeiten bot. Es folgten Gründungen in vielen deutschen Großstädten. Heute vereinigt die GEDOK ca. 4.5000 Mitglieder in 23 deutschen und österreichischen Gruppen.

1927 wurde die hannoverschen GEDOK mit zunächst 150 Mitgliedern gegründet, später wurden es zeitweilig über 300. Künstlerinnen und Kunstfreundinnen hielten sich auch hier zahlenmäßig die Waage, Männern war die Mitgliedschaft verwehrt. In der hannoverschen GEDOK waren von Beginn an neben den Förderinnen Architektinnen, Bildhauerinnen, Fotografinnen, Gymnastikerinnen, Journalistinnen, Kunsthandwerkerinnen, Malerinnen, Musikerinnen, Schauspielerinnen, Schriftstellerinnen und Tänzerinnen zur Mitarbeit eingeladen.

Ein großer Teil der GEDOK-Angehörigen unterhielt sehr gute Kontakte zur lokalen bürgerlichen Frauenbewegung und unterstützte wie diese Maßnahmen zur politischen Schulung von Frauen in der Weimarer Demokratie. Doch war auch die GEDOK letztlich um eine neutrale und ‚unpolitische' Haltung zum Zeitgeschehen bestrebt, was sie für viele politisch interessierte Zeitgenossinnen als langweilig erscheinen ließ. Ebenso stieß die diffuse Haltung zur weiblichen Erwerbstätigkeit auf Kritik. Neben Stimmen, die einer generellen weiblichen Unterlegenheit und mangelnden Befähigung für viele Berufsfelder das Wort redeten, standen andere in der GEDOK für eine Position ein, die qualitativ gleichwertige Fähigkeiten von Frauen und Männern betonten.

Wenn sich in der GEDOK auch Künstlerinnen fanden, die von der wirtschaftlichen Krisenzeit Ende der zwanziger, Anfang der dreissiger Jahre in ihrer Existenz bedroht waren, so gilt doch, dass viele Vereinsmitglieder angesehenen und wohlhabenden bürgerlichen Gesellschaftsschichten entstammten – vor allem unter den Kunstfreundinnen fanden sich Ehefrauen von Lokalpolitikern, Beamten, Kunst- und Kulturfunktionären, Künstlern sowie Industriellen und Mäzenen. Doch Hilfsaufrufe für bedürftige Frauen in- und ausserhalb des Vereins blieben vielfach ohne Nachhall. Mangelnde Fähigkeit und wohl auch Bereitschaft, sich die Not jenseits der eigenen Lebenswelt bewusst zu machen, trugen dazu bei, dass das karitative Element bei vielen wohlhabenden GEDOK-Mitgliedern keine nennenswerte Rolle spielte.

Freilich waren ihnen auch in dieser Hinsicht die Hände gebunden: Einerseits profitierten diese GEDOK-Frauen in der Vereinsarbeit von ihren persönlichen, familiären und gesellschaftlichen Kontakten. Andererseits konnten sie sich, fest eingebunden in die soziale, politische und kulturelle Hierarchie der Zeit, nicht über den von ihren männlichen Ehemännern und Verwandten gesteckten Rahmen hinwegsetzen, wollten sie nicht ihre eigene Positionen in diesen Strukturen riskieren. Nicht das Sprengen von gesellschaftlichen, kulturellen und politischen Konventionen und Traditionen war das Ziel von GEDOK-Arbeit auch in Hannover, sondern allenfalls das Ausloten der eigenen Grenzen und die Nutzung der sich in dem vorgegebenen Rahmen bietenden Möglichkeiten.

Born in Gifhorn, Germany, in 1966, Ines Katenhusen completed her studies in literature, lingustics and history in 1992. In 1997 she completed her doctoral thesis about art and politics in the Weimar republic, with particular reference to Hannover. After teaching at the University of Fine Arts, Braunschweig, she now teaches History of European Integration, especially in the 20th century, at the University of Hannover. She is the coordinator of the Hannover Masters Programme in Europäische Integration/ European Studies. In addition to her work in the field of European integration, she is particularly interested in the connection between politics and art, especially in German society in the 20th century.

"PROFESSION WITHOUT TRADITION" - THE PIONEER WORK OF WOMEN ARTISTS SINCE 1850 IN GERMANY [1]

During the mid 1930s a Berlin art dealer offered a painting of a local woman artist to the Director of the Hannover art museum [2]. Because the museum's director did not know her name, he began to enquire after both the artist and her painting. In the *Allgemeine Deutsche Biographie* (*General German Biography*), the following is said about the painter: "Margarethe Jonas has become an artist of great significance through her hard work, although she never enjoyed any formal training. Her exceptional portraits are outstanding in their execution, as well as their resemblance to the subject. She was living rather comfortably and was able to work for pleasure only. Several of her best paintings are owned by her home town museum and several are with the local Deaf-Mute Institute" [3]. Apparently the museum's director was not very interested. He never replied to the letter and never purchased the painting.

His decision might not be too surprising, given that the 1930s were a time of great economic despair when Jonas' painting was offered to the museum's director with a description that suggested mediocre work. There is mention of "much diligence" and that the painting is of "significant value", which leads one to conclude that there was not much to it. The main talent of Jonas was said to be to produce photograph-like portraits more or less for pure fun since she had not studied art and did not need to make a living out of it. Mentioning the Deaf-Mute Institute did not help either to convince a prospective buyer that this was a rare painting that one absolutely had to have. Since the turn of the century – at that time more than 30 years before – a broad range of new artistic styles had been developed in many European countries: Futurism in Italy, Expressionism mostly in Germany and in France the influence of the late Impressionism had then been significant. Also, in Switzerland, France and Germany Dadaism had been prevalent, while in England there had been Symbolism. Why then would anyone buy a painting from a mere craftsperson, who had absolutely nothing in common with what you would call an artistic genius?

This example was chosen to illustrate how working conditions and life's circumstances affected women artists at the beginning of the 20th century and far into the 1920s in Germany. I will introduce the topic by first speaking of the social strata of female artists, especially those in fine arts, before I specifically discuss Hannover. Hannover is not chosen because its developments were exceptional. On the contrary, the circumstances of this city – with 430,000 inhabitants in the 1920s the ninth largest in Germany – were rather typical and can be considered generally similar, with slight variations, to other cities, such as Frankfurt, Stuttgart, Düsseldorf, Munich or Dresden [4].

One consequence of industrialization in Germany was a rising number of female artists pushing themselves into the art market during the mid 19th century. Many of them belonged to the upper middle-class. The desire to be employed and to achieve greater self-esteem coincided with the slowly developing necessity of contributing to the family income or to securing one's own existence [5]. These women risked a lot. Depending on their social class, working women were stigmatized as "incapable" and, hence, it demanded courage and conviction. If a middle-class woman earned money, she conveyed the idea that she needed it and reduced, by this, her chances of a personally desired or socially expected marriage fitting her status.

Not without reason many women pursued a career in the fine arts. They had been raised to enjoy and value what was aesthetically pleasing, they had been taught needlework, drawing and painting and they had received piano lessons. However, it soon became obvious that the knowledge acquired did not further one's own career with respect to the arts. In a critical commentary in 1929 one could read the following: "When you see these young women painting porcelain, dying ties, sewing ribbons, or occupying themselves with designing things for every day life, one has to conclude without hesitation that women are trained to be societal dilettantes" [6]. Weighing even heavier than the societal risks that employment brought with it was the fact that the first female painters, musicians, artisans, poets or writers did not have their own role models to turn to. Instead of developing their own style, the focus of many female artists of the 19th century was on the achievements of their male counterparts of the past and present. Nonetheless, in this way many were quite successful [7].

It comes as no surprise that the majority of male artists viewed their female competitors as inconsequential and distracting. It might be of interest that the art market at the time was

Fig. 1
Gathering in the Hamburg Women's Club, 1909.

rather unpredictable as a result of the movement away from the conventional, feudal art by demand toward art for more widespread consumption [8]. Art historians and critics as well as the male-dominated art scene reacted often in an equally negative way with respect to interested women. In 1908, for instance, the influential Berlin art critic Karl Scheffler wrote: "The creativity of a woman is limited to childbearing. She is not able to excell in any of the fine arts, let alone architecture and music. At best she is capable of dancing. Women are inferior to men, and foolish as men say them to be" [9].

Until the fall of the last German Kaiser, women, with the exception of a few, were prohibited from attending state art academies. While they have always been accepted as models, subjects, or muses, women have been neglected or entirely forgotten as artists [10]. Their works often were lost. It is therefore not surprising that the search for Margarethe Jonas' painting, which had been offered to the museum's director in Hannover during the 1930s and which also was produced by an upper-class woman "without professional training", has been unsuccessful so far.

The quality of training at private art schools or acquired through private tutors was not comparable to that of official academies, especially since the central and essential studies of the (naked) human body was often perceived as "inappropriate for ladies" and therefore not permitted [11]. Around the turn of the century there were only three state-subsidized art institutes that German women were able to attend. However, given the high admission fees only privileged daughters from good homes could attend [12]. As a result the spectrum of women artists comprised professionals at one end and dilettantes at the other, with the emphasis being on the latter [13]. For the longest time, women were accepted as hobby artists who eagerly painted and stitched, composed and wrote poetry – as long as they did not directly threaten the existence of their male counterparts. At the moment, however, when women began to actively dispute preconceptions of female incompetence, and simultaneously began to associate a paycheck with their artistic endeavour, they no longer could expect any sympathy from most men.

Ines Katenhusen

The female protagonists of the 19th century were not lacking in self-esteem. Due to their upper middle-class upbringing, they brought with them two further prerequisites for artistic success: first, their names enabled them to enter the artistic world and market – and second, their financial situations permitted the establishment of professional associations to enhance the vocational situation of female artists [14]. The founding of the Association for Female Artists of Berlin in 1867 marked the first step in women helping women. A series of similar groups followed in the beginning of the next century. The involvement of influential and wealthy friends of the arts in the Berlin Association enabled less financially fortunate women to receive an art education. In addition, there were scholarships, health and pension plans as well as networking opportunities with art collectors and museum people [15]. A group of female artists, supported by the Berlin Association, was able to venture their first successful steps into female art production as a "profession without tradition" and from dilettantism to professionalism.

More than half a century later, in March 1919, German women were granted the right to receive an education at state academies, thanks to the Equal Rights Act of the Weimar Constitution. One might expect that circumstances thereafter improved dramatically, and the number of females at universities did indeed increase. However, studies alone did not bring the much desired prestige and financial success. What good was the Equal Rights Act for when museum directors and gallery owners refused to display women's work, when art historians questioned their validity and talent, their male counterparts belittled them, and exhibitions and support programs targeted male artists only? [16] What was the tolerant climate of the so-called golden 1920s worth to women at a time of permanent economic crises and uncertainty? [17]

Female artists continued to be daughters, sisters-in-law, wives and mothers, hence, an act of law did not simply change the expectations that their parents, relatives, husbands and children had of them [18]. If women *did* have success, despite these traditional role expectations, it was largely due to their courage, conviction, creativity – and a ton of talent! Therefore, every critical discussion of the prevalent female image during the 1920s points to the contradictions inherent in this time and to the clashing of tradition with modernity, of progressive-liberal views with traditional values of past eras, which were not really past [19].

The founding of the first Association of German and Austrian Women Artists and Patrons (GEDOK) [20] in Hamburg in 1926 was marked by contradiction and diversity. With its two-tiered structure (on the one side artists, on the other patrons) GEDOK took on a leadership role. It was crucial for local women's groups especially with respect to its exceptional position on social-political and charity issues, but also in making clear the significance of the women's movement, in general, and the work of women artists and their identity, in particular [21].

"WE ARE ON A JOURNEY OF DISCOVERY. WE WORK AND WE WANT TO GO AHEAD" – THE GEDOK IN HANNOVER [22]

In 1927, one year after the founding of the Hamburg GEDOK, the local chapter of the Hannoverian GEDOK was established. Apart from socializing, the goals of the association included an exchange of ideas and experiences among women artists. With the patrons, these women artists were supposed to create a community and be part of "a nice coming together" [23]. If one can believe the stories of the founding members, this event received very little attention from the general public of Hannover. A newspaper reported fairly bluntly that this community now gave women a greater chance to meet for coffee while keeping up with the latest gossip.

The Hannoverian GEDOK started out with 150 members, of whom 75 were artists and 75 were patrons. In the following years, the balance between these two groups seems to have been of equal importance in the planning by the board of directors. Until the 1940s the artists always comprised the majority, however, never exceeding more than 60% [24]. Although men were excluded from membership, their presence at social gatherings was strongly encouraged. Working with male artists was accepted, but not financially subsidized, something which holds true up until today.

Apart from bigger festivities, GEDOK, partly in association with other institutions, organized dance matinees, house concerts featuring both works from past eras as well as timely avant-garde pieces. There were also exhibitions and readings. In addition to courses in painting, GEDOK offered book-keeping seminars and an introduction to associate law. Conversation courses in French, English and Italian, as well as afternoon tea parties and discussion circles completed the extensive program [25].

GEDOK grew quickly. Within two years after its establishment, the membership had increased to 340; it reached its peak in 1932 with 409 members. During the Nazi regime the numbers dwindled drastically. However, at the end of World War II, the GEDOK Hannover still had 118 members. After the Nazis had taken over, the GEDOK underwent the same incorporation into the National Socialist political system as other organizations. During World War II, the board gave consideration to dissolving the association, but later decided against it due to the "sense of duty its members felt towards the community and cultural circle" [26]. Shortly after the war, the association was actually dissolved but permitted to continue under the British Occupation [27]. Today the German GEDOK counts about 4500 members in 23 local groups in Germany and Austria; there are 170 members in Hannover.

Varying membership requirements for artists or patrons became evident during the 1920s and early 1930s. A female artist could join after showing her work to an appointed advisory board. This board consisted of 2-4 actual members. According to the nine different areas of competence of GEDOK, there were boards for architecture, sculpture, theatre, gymnastics, arts and crafts, painting, music, writing, and dance. In order for an applicant to be accepted as a patron, two GEDOK members were needed to sponsor her. Ultimate acceptance or refusal was determined by the 6 members of the Association's Board of Directors.

Right from the beginning until World War II, the largest group was comprised of musicians. Every fourth GEDOK artist was either a music or singing instructor, pianist or violinist. If we include the dancers and gymnasts, these add up to almost half of the entire artist membership. Second in size was the group involved in arts and crafts (20% of the members). This group comprised a broad spectrum of clothing and ceramic designers. 15% of the

Fig. 2
The first women voters in Berlin, 1919.

members were painters and graphic artists; another 15% were authors, poets, and journalists. The latter group showed the greatest reduction in number during the Nazi regime. Approximately 10% of the GEDOK members were either actresses or opera singers. Women photographers, architects and sculptresses were rare in the GEDOK.

Regarding the Hannoverian artists, it is interesting to note that many of them had hyphenated last names (approximately 15% of the artists and 4% of the patrons). Unfortunately, most of the documents found from the late 1930's give us little insight into the family status of most of the members. Nonetheless the homogeneous structure of the membership leads one to suspect that prior to the 1930s 60% of the women artists were single. On the contrary, most of the patrons were married women. One can even go so far as to say that most of the married, divorced, or widowed women put such emphasis on keeping their identities that throughout their professional lives they carried their maiden names along with the last name of their husbands. Does this show a growing self-esteem or does it just reflect a trend of the time? Unfortunately very little can be said about the extent of actual employment of either group. It is uncertain whether the first group – single, married and/or with family – was actually able to support themselves – or if indeed they even wanted to!

"THE WOMAN AS BEARER OF SOCIETAL THINKING" – GEDOK AND THE CIVIL WOMEN'S MOVEMENT [28]

Immediately after its establishment, the GEDOK became a member of the Women's Organization of Hannover. In the 1920s, this association acted as an umbrella organization for all civil women's groups. Its main interest lay in coordinating social networking and in working towards an improved educational system for women [29]. Close personal ties existed between the GEDOK and other groups belonging to this organization. Strengthening women's position as a citizens was a characteristic goal of the organization. During the world economic crisis and the political radicalisation of the 1930s, it offered courses helping women to vote, which was actually an important political move [30]. In the end, however, GEDOK had to distance itself from any political and religious affiliation. In a proclamation in February 1929 it stated: "The dispute of the parties may be fought in parliament, but there is no room for it within women's groups. There is one personal outlook shared by all women – and rightly so. These are the morals in one's bosom" [31]. For this reason, some members saw the GEDOK politically as "too conservative, too tame" [32]. Maybe this explains why during such a tumultuous time as the late 1920s and early 1930s, the GEDOK's program with respect to political and social matters remained largely the same, even though its membership comprised women of rather different political colours: at several events members of the Communist Party were found sitting next to Nazis, Social Democrats next to nationalists.

"FEELING AND EMOTION IS EVERYTHING!" – GEDOK's ATTITUDE TOWARDS FAMILY AND WORK [33]

When looking both at the yearbooks of the late 1920s and early 1930s as well as at the correspondence and other documents of that time, one might be surprised by contradictory views with respect to women's employment and the family. Some female authors stressed the importance of motherhood, which allowed women to behave more "naturally" [34] than men and enabled them to judge matters in a more "passionate" rather than "rational" manner, both qualities which rendered women ill-suited for a number of art professions [35]. Other GEDOK members denied an essential male superiority in these fields. In an article entitled: "Courage toward Architecture" it is stated in 1928 that female architects were by no means worse than their male colleagues, they only were trained worse: "Talent was not a matter of one's sex, but rather tied to that which is thus far not understood, i.e. heredity" [36]. If GEDOK female artists had something in common despite all their differences regarding the image of women and women's employment, it was the effort to present only work of exceptional quality to the public. The sometimes very critical reviews by male journalists in the local papers made it evident that keeping up standards was vital.

"LADIES WITH INFLUENTIAL NAMES" – WOMAN ARTISTS AND PATRONS IN HANNOVER [37]

It was common for the Hannoverian GEDOK group to meet at a person's home, since in the first years there were no official meeting rooms available. Striking is the fact that many of the members – artists as well as patrons – lived in generous apartments or homes in the best areas of the city, often with large properties. Rightly so, a newspaper in 1930 stated that GEDOK was comprised of "ladies with influential names" [38]. Based on birth or marriage, both artists and patrons counted between 6 and 10% aristocrats within their ranks. Among the patrons were wives of representatives of art and culture at the local and provincial levels, the wife of the director of the Hannover general museum, the former city director, and the wives of high-ranking civil servants and well-known industrialists.

Among the GEDOK artists – especially among the painters and graphic designers – it is apparent that followers of more conventional styles coexisted with the (few) women who are named in connection with Hannover's pronounced avant-garde blossoming during the

Fig. 3
The "new woman": a secretary in a Berlin broadcasting company, 1931.

1920s [39]. Generally, however, one can say that not all GEDOK members were financially as well off as the records might suggest. Testimonies of hard times are known. For instance, a GEDOK painter described the ice flowers on the windows of her small bachelor apartment in a loving manner: Previously she had resided in a modified dog house [40]. One of her colleagues, also single at the time, tells of her life in an attic with a view of rats dancing and garbage piling up [41].

Especially in the 30's, several GEDOK artists asked for financial aid from the city. When these women actually did receive assistance, it was not only from the city and provincial offices, but also from the GEDOK itself. But this was more of a moral gesture than a recognition of financial needs. Other GEDOKs in other cities pursued direct methods to support the needy artists during the economic crisis, among them fund raising, bridge competitions, food banks and the distribution of painting supplies [42]. The Hannover GEDOK rejected such methods and was convinced that direct material support would be "demeaning" [43]. Instead, a financial aid fund was established. This fund, however, did not receive much member support despite permanent appeals from the board. If one takes a look at the social events organized by the GEDOK, one can conclude that financial problems were not responsible for lack of support for the fund. For instance, the ticket for an cabaret evening in the GEDOK cost 8 RM – the equivalent of a worker's daily income or 20 kg of bread [44]. So, the lack of empathy for other people's poverty rather than one's own material circumstances seem to be responsible for the fact that the charitable element did not play much of a role among Hannover's ladies with influential names.

CONCLUSION

GEDOK's character was determined by its members' social status. The important names allowed the GEDOK to develop a healthy self-esteem. If an event ended in the red, municipal or provincial authorities picked up the tab. This was even the case after the Nazis came into power – protection from the highest level was also guaranteed [45]. During World War II too the institution was safe due to its non-political partisanship and its patronage by influential persons. But this also forced the GEDOK to conform – and here lies the key to another aspect of GEDOK's work and, beyond this, to civil women's associations in general: these women profited from their personal, family, and social networks in many ways by being related or acquainted with influential figures in society. These contacts emgendered self-esteem and a certain financial security, while still maintaining boundaries. The relationships worked as long as these influential men were not undermined in their authority. Rules and laws of their social class had to be respected, should the female artists or patrons not want to risk their positions in society. This especially is true for the rules governing women in the arts and the art market [46]. Women artists and women patrons – not only in the GEDOK, not only in Hannover, and not at all only in Germany – in the 1920s and 1930s were still ruled by traditional rules and traditional role expectations.

 NOTES

[1] This is the title of an exhibition catalogue: *Profession ohne Tradition. 125 Jahre Verein der Berliner Künstlerinnen*, ed. by the Berlinische Galerie, Berlin 1992.

[2] Letter of the art dealer Hermann Gotter to the Art Gallery of the Landesmuseum Hannover, 11.09.1936 (Landesmuseum Hannover, file II.2.1.a/ II.2.2.a: Ankauf alte und neue Meister 1936-37).

[3] *Allgemeine Deutsche Biographie*, Bd. 14, 1881, pp. 498-499.

[4] See Ines Katenhusen, "... *das bedürfnis nach geistiger anregung*". *GEDOK-Künstlerinnen und Kunstfreundinnen im Hannover der zwanziger und dreissiger Jahre*, in Schröder K.E.C. (ed), *Adlige, Arbeiterinnen und... Frauenleben in Stadt und Region Hannover*, Bielefeld 1999, pp. 211-239.

[5] See Berger R., *Malerinnen auf dem Weg ins 20. Jahrhundert. Kunstgeschichte als Sozialgeschichte*, Cologne 1982, pp. 78 ff. Nobs-Greter R., *Die Künstlerin und ihr Werk in der deutschsprachigen Kunstgeschichtsschreibung*, Zurich 1984, pp. 60 ff. Stelzl U., '*Die Zweite Stimme im Orchester*'. *Aspekte zum Bild der Künstlerin in der Kunstgeschichtsschreibung*, in Frandsen D., Huffmann U. (eds), *Frauen in Forschung und Lehre*, Bonn 1982, pp. 39-54. Muysers C., '*In der Hand der Künstlerinnen fast allein liegt es fortan...*' *Zur Geschichte und Rezeption bildender Künstlerinnen von der Gründerzeit bis zur Weimarer Republik*, "Feministische Studien", 14. Jhg., 1996, pp. 50-65. Schulz I., *Die Frau als Künstlerin. Über das Leben und Werk von Künstlerinnen früher und heute*, Hamburg 1986.

Ines Katenhusen

6 Buddemann Dr., *Warum Kunstgewerblerin?* in: *Frau und Gegenwart, vereinigt mit Neue Frauenkleidung und Frauenkultur*, H. 10, Karlsruhe 1929/1930, p. 364.

7 See Muysers.

8 See Nipperdey T., *Wie das Bürgertum die Moderne fand*, Berlin 1988, pp. 10f. Vgl. Lenman R., *Painters, Patronage, and the Art Market in Germany, 1850-1914*, "Past and Present",123, 1989, pp. 109-144, pp. 132-133.

9 Scheffler K., *Die Frau und die Kunst*, Berlin 1908, p. 17.

10 Schulz, pp. 3-4.

11 See Berger, p. 144, and on pp. 87-93 further information on the vocational situation. Schulz, pp. 18-19. Germaine Greer, *Das unterdrückte Talent. Die Rolle der Frauen in der bildenden Kunst*, Berlin-Frankfurt-Vienna 1980, p. 325.

12 Sauer M., *Diletantinnen und Malweiber. Künstlerinnen im 19. und 20. Jahrhundert*, in Neue Gesellschaft für Bildende Kunst e.V., Berlin (ed), *Das verborgene Museum I. Dokumentation der Kunst von Frauen in Berliner öffentlichen Sammlungen*, Berlin 1987, pp. 25 ff.

13 See Sauer, pp. 21 ff.; Nobs-Greter, pp. 61-62.; Berger, pp. 78-86.

14 Muysers, pp. 52 ff.

15 Jestaedt K., Fuhrmann D., '*Alles das zu erlernen, was für eine erfolgreiche Ausübung eines Berufs von ihnen gefordert wird*'. *Die Zeichen- und Malschule des Vereins der Berliner Künstlerinnen*, in Ausstellungskatalog Profession ohne Tradition. *125 Jahre Verein der Berliner Künstlerinnen*, Berlin 1992, pp. 353-367.

16 See Gatermann B., '*Malweiber*'. *Bildende Künstlerinnen in den zwanziger Jahren*, in Ausstellungskatalog Hart und Zart. *Frauenleben 1920-1970*, Berlin 1990, pp. 99-105.

17 See Frevert U., *Frauen-Geschichte. Zwischen Bürgerlicher Verbesserung und Neuer Weiblichkeit*, Frankfurt 1986, esp. pp. 171-172.

18 Sauer, pp. 22 ff.

19 Frevert, pp. 171 ff.

20 GEDOK is the acronym of *Gemeinschaft Deutscher und Österreichischer Künstlerinnenvereine aller Kunstgattungen*.

21 Weber A.-K., *Die Geschichte des Verbandes der Künstlerinnen und Kunstfreunde e.V. (GEDOK)*, thesis, University of Oldenburg, pp. 57 ff., unpublished, GEDOK Archives Hannover.

22 Froelich E., *Jahresbericht*, "GEDOK – Jahrbuch", 2, 1929, p. 1.

23 Froelich E., *Jahresbericht*, "GEDOK – Jahrbuch", 1, 1928/29, p. 3.

24 Membership lists as indicated in the yearbooks; see also GEDOK Archives Hannover, file 1929-1944.

25 See GEDOK Archives Hannover, file 1929-1944. See also the GEDOK Hannover news in the journal of the Frauenstadtbund Hannover, *Frauenstadtbund* (FSB), (January 1929 - June 1933).

26 GEDOK Hannover news, October 1941 (typed copy, GEDOK Archives Hannover). See Dietzler A., '*Gleichschaltung' des Kulturlebens in Hannover. Ein vielschichtiger Prozeß*, unpublished copy (Archives of the City of Hannover), (1994), p. 37 f. Bremer I., *Zur Geschichte der GEDOK. 1929. Ein Jahr von Bedeutung*, in 50 Jahre GEDOK. *1927-1977*, Hannover 1977, p. 33.

27 *Hannoverische Frauenvereine III. GEDOK*, Hannoverscher Kurier, December 16, 1931.

28 GEDOK Archives Hannover, letter of Else Froelich to the Board of Directors, June 17, 1932.

29 FSB, vol. 1/1, January 1929. As concerns the history see FSB, vol. 5/ 6, June 1933. See Reagin N.R., *Die bürgerliche Frauenbewegung vor 1933*, in Schröder C., Sonneck M. (ed), *Ausser Haus. Frauengeschichte in Hannover*, Hannover 1994, pp. 137-145, esp. p. 145.

30 See FSB, vol. 1/3, March 1929 and 7/8, August 1930.

31 FSB, vol. 1/2, February 1929. Hildebrandt I., *Die GEDOK. Eine Idee im Dauertest*, in 60 Jahre GEDOK. *Festschrift 1927-1987*, Hannover 1988, pp. 7-10, p. 8.

32 Interview with Kläre Spengemann-Morf, August 27, 1992.

33 Dorner von Broich C., *Gefühl und Herz ist alles*, in "GEDOK – Jahrbuch", 2, 1929, p. 13 f.

[34] Drechsler-Hohlt M., *Vom Wesen und 'Beruf' der Frau*, in "GEDOK – Jahrbuch", 2, 1929, p. 24 f.

[35] Eilers R.-S., *Frau und Journalismus*, in "GEDOK – Jahrbuch", 1, 1928-29, p. 19.

[36] Trost K., *Der Mut zur Architektur*, in "GEDOK – Jahrbuch", 1, 1928-29, p. 37.

[37] *Kabarett und so. Künstlerfest der GEDOK*, "Hannoversches Tageblatt", February 16, 1930.

[38] Ibid.

[39] See Katenhusen I., *Kunst und Politik. Hannovers Auseinandersetzungen mit der Moderne in der Weimarer Republik*, Hannover 1998.

[40] Reinhardt, p. 11. As concerns Grethe Jürgens: Seiler H., *Grethe Jürgens*, Göttingen 1976. Katenhusen, *Kunst und Politik*, pp. 262 ff.

[41] Overbeck G., *Es liegt in der Luft mit der Sachlichkeit*, in Kunstverein Hannover (ed.), *Neue Sachlichkeit in Hannover*, Hannover 1974, p. 89.

[42] See Else Froelich's talk on the occasion of the female patrons on December 3, 1931 (typescript, GEDOK Archives Hannover).

[43] Ibid.

[44] Mlynek K., *Hannover in der Weimarer Republik und unter dem Nationalsozialismus 1918-1945*, in Röhrbein W.R. (ed), *Geschichte der Stadt Hannover*, vol. 2, Hannover 1994, p. 450.

[45] See GEDOK's letter to the City Administration, January 3, 1936, also the letter of the local head of the Reichskammer der bildenden Künste to the City Administration, January 21, 1936 (Archives of the City of Hannover, HR 15, No. 818).

[46] See Reagin, *Bürgerliche Frauenbewegung*, pp. 141 f.

 **SELECTED BIBLIOGRAPHY**

On Hannover

Ehrich K., Schröder C. (ed.), *Adlige, Arbeiterinnen und… Frauenleben in Stadt und Region Hannover*, Bielefeld 1999.

Katenhusen Ines,... *das bedürfnis nach geistiger Anregung…'.GEDOK-Künstlerinnen und- Kunstfreundinnen im Hannover der zwanziger und dreissiger Jahre*, in Ehrich K., Schröder C. (ed.), *Adlige, Arbeiterinnen und… Frauenleben in Stadt und Region Hannover*, Bielefeld 1999.

Katenhusen I., *Kunst und Politik. Hannovers Auseinandersetzungen mit der Moderne in der Weimarer Republik*, Hannover 1998.

Reagin N.R., *A German Women's Movement. Class and Gender in Hanover. 1880-1933*, Chapel Hill-London 1995.

Schröder C., Sonneck M. (ed.), *Ausser Haus. Frauengeschichte in Hannover*, Hannover 1994

On Germany

Berger R., *Malerinnen auf dem Weg ins 20. Jahrhundert. Kunstgeschichte als Sozialgeschichte*, Köln 1982.

Frandsen D., Huffmann U. (ed.), *Frauen in Forschung und Lehre*, Bonn 1982.

Frevert U., *Frauen-Geschichte. Zwischen Bürgerlicher Verbesserung und Neuer Weiblichkeit*, Frankfurt/M. 1986.

Gatermann B., *'Malweiber'. Bildende Künstlerinnen in den zwanziger Jahren*, in *Hart und Zart. Frauenleben 1920-1970*, Berlin 1990 (exhibition catalogue).

GEDOK Hamburg (ed.), *Die GEDOK 1926-2001*, Hamburg 2001 (exhibition catalogue).

Meyer-Büser S. (ed.), *Bubikopf und Gretchenzopf. Die Frau der Zwanziger Jahre*, Hamburg 1995 (exhibition catalogue).

Muysers C., *"In der Hand der Künstlerinnen fast allein liegt es fortan". Zur Geschichte und Rezeption bildender Künstlerinnen*

Ines Katenhusen

von der Gründerzeit bis zur Weimarer Republik, in Feministische Studien, vol. 14/ 1, 1996.

Nobs-Greter R., *Die Künstlerin und ihr Werk in der deutschsprachigen Kunstgeschichtsschreibung*, Zürich 1984.

Profession ohne Tradition. 125 Jahre Verein der Berliner Künstlerinnen, ed. by the Berlinische Galerie, Berlin 1992 (exhibition catalogue).

Sauer M., *Diletantinnen und Malweiber. Künstlerinnen im 19. und 20 Jahrhundert*, in Neue Gesellschaft für Bildende Kunst e.V. Berlin (ed.), *Das verborgene Museum I. Dokumentation der Kunst von Frauen in Berliner öffentlichen Sammlungen*, Berlin 1987.

Schulz I., *Die Frau als Künstlerin. Über das Leben und Werk von Künstlerinnen früher und heute*, Hamburg 1986.

General

Deepwell K. (ed.), *Women Artists and Modernism*, Manchester 1998.

Issak J.A., *Feminism and Contemporary Art*, London 1996.

Johnson S.P., *Boundaries of acceptability*, New York 2000.

Lesser W., *His Other Half. Men looking at Women through Art*, Cambridge 1991.

Nochlin L., *Representing Women*, London 1999.

Nunn P.G., *Victorian Women Artists*, London 1987.

Piland S. (ed), *Women Artists. An Historical, Contemporary and Feminist Bibliography*, Lanham 1994.

Pollock G., *Differencing the Canon*, London 1999.

Suleiman S.R., *The Female Body in Western Culture*, Cambridge 1986.

 **SOURCES**

Margarethe Jonas wurde durch eigenen Fleiss, ohne eigentlichen Unterricht eine Künstlerin von nicht geringer Bedeutung, deren vortrefflich ausgeführte Porträts hinsichtlich der Ausführung wie der Ähnlichkeit nichts zu wünschen übrig lassen. Sie lebte in günstigen Verhältnissen und arbeitete zu ihrem Vergnügen. Mehrere ihrer vorzüglichsten Arbeiten besitzt das Städtische Museum ihrer Vaterstadt und einige ausgezeichnete Porträts das Taubstummeninstitut daselbst.

Margarethe Jonas has become an artist of great significance through her hard work, although she never enjoyed any formal training. Her exceptional portraits are outstanding in their execution, as well as their resemblance to the subject. She was well off, and able to work for pleasure only. Several of her best paintings are owned by her home town museum and several are with the local Deaf-Mute Institute.

(Allgemeine Deutsche Biographie/ General German Biography, 1936)

Die Kreativität der Frau erschöpft sich im Gebärakt, keine der Künste kann sie ausüben, am wenigsten die Architektur und die Musik, gerade der Körpersprache des Tanzes ist sie noch befähigt; Frauen sind so mittelmäßig und dilettantisch wie die Männer berufen.

The creativity of a woman is limited to childbearing. She is not able to excell in any of the fine arts, let alone architecture and music. At best she is capable of dancing. Women are inferior to men, and foolish as men say them to be.

(Karl Scheffler, Art Historian, 1908)

---

*Der Streit der Parteien soll in den Parlamenten mit aller Deutlichkeit und Schärfe ausgefocht-
en werden, aber in den Frauenorganisationen darf dieser Streit keinen Platz finden. Es gibt eine
Weltanschauung, die alle Frauen und alle Frauen binden sollte, das ist das Sittengesetz in der
Brust.*

The dispute of the parties may be fought in parliament, but there is no room for it within
women's groups. There is one personal outlook shared by all women - and rightly so. These
are the morals in one's bosom.

(Civil Women's Group, Hannover, 1929)

*Architektinnen waren in der Vergangenheit nicht schlechter als ihre männlichen Kollegen, son-
dern nur schlechter ausgebildet. Talent ist nicht an das Geschlecht, wohl aber an die uns
unfasslichen Begriffe der Vererbung gebunden.*

Female architects were by no means worse than their male colleagues, they only were trained
worse. Talent was not a matter of one's sex, but rather tied to that which is thus far not understood, i.e. heritage.

(GEDOK Hannover, 1928/ 29)

Ines Katenhusen

The Post-Soviet Body of Latvian Literature: Gender and *genre*

Ausma Cimdiņa

Latvijas Universitate, Riga

Ievadlekcijas "Latviešu postpadomju literatūra: dzimums un žanrs" nolūks ir sniegt pamatzināšanas Eiropas cittautu studentiem par mūsdienu latviešu literatūras vēsturiskās attīstības īpatnībām, akcentējot dzimumdiferences un žanra aspektus literatūras procesā. Lekcija ir strukturēta trīs daļās. Sākumā ir dots atskats senākajā vēsturē (informācijas minimums par latviešu literatūras sākotni, atgādinot ne tikai par sociālistiskā reālisma normatīvās estētikas periodu latviešu rakstniecībā, bet arī par latviešu literatūras un kultūras dziļākajiem slāņiem- sakņojumu trīs Eiropas tautām kopīgos kultūras avotos: antīkās kultūras mantojumā, kristietībā un nacionālajā folklorā). Seko19.gs.nogales un 20.gs. pirmās puses literārās situācijas, kam ir bijusi izšķiroša nozīme visā tālākajā latviešu literatūras un kultūras attīstībā, apskats.

Lekcijas otrā daļa ir veltīta nacionālās Atmodas un potspadomju pārmaiņu laikam (20.gs.90.gadi) Latvijā un tā radītās "jaunās realitātes" atspoguļojumam latviešu rakstniecībā. Trešā daļa ir veltīta tieši sievietes rakstītās literatūras savdabībai žanriskā un tematiskā aspektā, vietai un nozīmei, kā arī recepcijas īpatnībām kopējā latviešu literartūras un kultūras mantojumā, akcentējot dzimumidentitates kā nacionālās kultūridentitates aspektus. Lai iezīmētu izcilāko mūsdienu latviešu rakstnieču (R. Ezeras, V. Belševicas, A. Nesaules u.c.) daiļrades vadlīnijas, literārās tradīcijas, žanra un kanona problēmas kontekstā ir sniegts ieskats arī starptautiski pazīstamāko latviešu rakstnieču, piemēram, Aspazijas un Z.Mauriņas literārajā mantojumā.

Divdesmita gadsimta deviņdesmitie gadi ir raksturoti kā būtisku pārmaiņu laiks visās dzīves sfērās, arī literatūrā un kultūrā. Literatūrā tas izpaužas, pirmkārt, tematiskās un žanriskās paplašināšināšanās un atjaunotnes veidā. Abu dzimumu un visu paaudžu reālisma tradīcijai uzticīgo autoru darbos nozīmīgu vietu ieņem politisku un ideoloģisku motīvu dēļ agrāk noklusēti vēsturiskās pieredzes slāņi: Otrais pasaules karš, deportācijas un dzīve Sibīrijas nāves nometnēs, emigrācija un latviešu tautas dzīve svešumā. Poētikas un arī pasaules izjūtas ziņā šis laiks latviešu rakstniecībā sevi piesaka kā spilgtu galējību laiks. No vienas puses, tas parādās kā literāri izsmalcināta postmodernisma apokalipse (tā mākslinieciski pārliecinošākā izpausme ir prozas darbs "Dukts", kas strikti šķir tekstualitātes un dzīves realitātes nojēgums), no otras-kā droša uzticēšanās reālismam, proti, postmodernisma apziņas pieredzes nesatricināta, patiesa un objektīva cilvēka dzīves gājuma un vēsturiskās pieredzes atspoguļojuma iespejamībai literatūrā. Reālistiskās literatūras jomā liels īpatsvars ir bijis arī tā saukto neprofesionālo autoru dzīves stāstiem, kas popularitātes (tirgus noieta un lasāmības) ziņā ir pārspējuši tā saukto profesionālo rakstnieku piedāvājumu.

Feminisma literatūrteorijas un kritikas perspektīvā kā mākslinieciski spilgtākie un koncptuāli nozīmīgākie darbi latviešu (post)padomju literatūras klāstā ir raksturoti R. Ezeras romāns "Nodevība" un V. Belševicas dzeja. Kā izteiksmīgs piemērs latviešu sievietei specifiskās vēsturiskās pieredzes un pārdzīvojumu Otrā pasaules kara laikā, kā arī trimdas un svešatnes atspoguļojumam literatūrā, ir raksturots A. Nesaules romāns "Sieviete dzintarā".

Ausma Cimdiņa was born in Latvia in the village of Jaunpiebalga in 1950. She completed her studies at the University of Latvia, Riga, in 1974. She defended her doctoral thesis, *The essay in Latvian literature: poetics and philosophy*, in 1992. Now she teaches History of Latvian Literature at the University of Latvia. She is particulary interested in the history of modern and contemporary literary criticism and theory, sociology of literature and feminist epistemology. She has published two books and more than 100 articles; she directs the review "Feministica Lettica".

BRIEF HISTORICAL FLASH-BACK

The aim of this introduction to "The Post-Soviet Body of Latvian Literature: gender and genre" is to provide the student with a certain amount of information about the most important processes in Latvian literature in the latter half of the 20th century. If one is to understand the emergence of contemporary Latvian literature, it is necessary to have at least a minimal understanding of the origins of the genre and the specifics of the way in which it developed over the course of history. The word "specifics" in this case refers first and foremost to the fact that Latvian literature belongs to one of the smaller nations in Europe. There are fewer than two million people who speak Latvian today. The language comes from the Baltic branch of Indo-European languages and is only one of two surviving languages from the branch (Lithuanian is the other; Galindian, Jatvingian and Ancient Prussian are all extinct). Second, the Baltic States, including Latvia, are in a part of the world which has always been subject to powerful linguistic and cultural influences from other nations. Third, Latvian literature and culture, just like the overall economic and political situation of the Baltic countries, are perceived in the world today mostly as a post-Soviet phenomenon. This is not an entirely incorrect concept, but it must be said for the sake of clarity that it is an incomplete one. The fact is that Latvian literature is rooted in far deeper and wider strata of human cultural experience than just the Soviet period. In fact, Soviet-era works make up only one-tenth of the whole bibliography of printed Latvian literature.

As is the case with modern literature in other European countries, Latvian literature can trace its development back to three major sources – the cultural heritage of the ancient world, Christianity, and national folklore. The latter element is of particular importance in the development of Latvian literature and culture, particularly when it comes to poetic folklore in the form of the Latvian folk songs which are known as *dainas*. The definitive collection of *Latvju Dainas* (1894-1915) compiled by Krisjanis Barons contains 35,789 songs accompanied by clusters of variants, but by this time, the collection in the archives has grown to more than million *dainas*. Most of them are *guatrains*, cast in the metrical mold of rigorous double symmetry: the first two lines usually deal with an image from nature, the last two with an analogue from human affairs. Each song, therefore, is a self-contained epigram or poem. Arranged thematically in cycles, they form an ancient cosmology, a mythology and sense of social life order, and take on a scope that is epic in feel if not in structure. People who talk about the unique aspects of Latvian culture often say that Latvia is a cultural or folklore-based superpower, and the truth of this rather vivid description is indicated by the fact that the folksongs have recently been included on UNESCO's list of spoken and non-material cultural masterpieces.

The first texts and books to be published in the Latvian language (Roman Catholic and Lutheran catechisms) did not appear until the 16th century, during the Reformation. This marked the beginning of the period of spiritual (church) literature in the Middle Ages – a period which survived in Latvian writing until the mid-18th century, when the first examples of secular literature began to emerge. From the Middle Ages until the 19th century, the emergence of Latvian literature was significantly influenced by Germanic peoples – the descendants of the Crusaders who conquered Latvia's territory in the 13th century. The most important cultural and literary event in the 17th century in Latvia was unquestionably the publication of the Bible in Latvian (1685-1691). A Baltic German pastor named Ernst Glück (1652-1705), who worked from the Greek original but kept Martin Luther's German translation by his side for reference, did the translating. In thinking about Medieval Latvian culture (in fact, not only about Medieval culture, because philosophical reflections from the Bible were a powerful factor in later literary works too), the modern Latvian poet Vizma Belševica has written: "That major root, the Bible, / From which we grew, whether willing or not, / But *dainas* – only tiny offshoots."

An important turning point in Latvia's sociopolitical history was the Great Northern War (1700-1721), when tsar Peter the Great relentlessly tried to carve a window to Europe for Russia, and these efforts were crowned with success – Estonia and much of Latvia became part of the Russian Empire. As the influence of German culture after the Great Northern War gradually waned, Latvia's cultural life was increasingly under the sway of Russia. Initially Latvian literature was influenced by German and Russian writing: Germans fostered the cult of form and precision of thought; Russians, psychological depths and emotional power of understanding. These fundamental literary values later were refined by French modernism as well as by English and Scandinavian literary movements.

A new and interesting phenomenon toward the end of the 19th century in Latvian literature was the so-called "New Movement", which involved a representation of Marxist philosophy and the ideas of Social Democracy. The life and literary work of the most distinguished Latvian writers, Rainis (1865-1929) and Aspazija (1865-1943), were closely linked to the New Movement. They both are also important as the originators of a sub-genre that could be called "exile literature". After the failure of the 1905 revolution, Rainis and Aspazija were forced into emigration and until 1920 both writers lived in the Swiss town of Lugano, where they produced major works of literature. After the failure of the 1905 revolution, Latvian writers founded a magazine called *The Deep*, which published a programmatic article signed by a number of young writers, *The motifs of our art*. Over the course of time this article became known as the manifesto of the Latvian Decadence movement.

Despite such sociopolitical catastrophes as war and revolution, the first half of the 20th century was generally favorable to the development of Latvian literature and culture. After the Soviet occupation, the natural development of Latvian literature was brutally choked off, and the process was divided up into two segments – Soviet and exile literature – which, for half a century, were artificially kept separate from each other and represented an ideological confrontation. Exile literature became a mass movement when many members of the Latvian intelligentsia fled to the West in advance of the Soviet army in 1944. There were numerous outstanding writers among them, and Latvian literature was printed and published everywhere in the world, especially in Germany, Sweden, the United States, Canada and Australia. Soviet and exile Latvian literatures flowed together once again only at the very end of the 20th century, when the Soviet empire collapsed.

LITERATURE IN TRANSITION

In the history of the Baltic countries, the years at the end of the 1980s and the beginning of the 1990s has been a period when state independence was re-established. It is an important dividing line not only in the life of nation and society, but also in the process of literary development, boosting the self-esteem of the "new reality", giving space to new ways of thinking and writing. Following the historic principles of dividing literature into periods (defining critical socio-historical events as turning points in the development of literature), we can say that the turn of the 1980s and 1990s brought new times into Latvian literature and history.

This period is justly characterized as a period of transition and change in all spheres of life, including literature. This has also been the time of post-modern apocalypses or awareness in Latvian literature. Elements testifying to the awareness of post-modern poetics and worldview can be found already in Soviet Latvian literature of the 70s. It could be seen in the enlargement of lexical resources available for literature (especially by introducing the so-called profane layers of vocabulary), in epistemological insecurity as well as in dismantling and interference of traditional genres. The most radical expression of this is to be found in the book of poetry in prose "Epiphanies" (1971) by Imants Ziedonis: "Body is the name of a genre. Oh, body, which is the genre you inhabit? Are you a play, a poem or a novel? /.../ My body is a poem. My body is a tragedy and a comedy at the same time. The tongue talks about every thing it should have kept silent about, but my heart takes offence, grinding its teeth. /.../ My wife is being played aloud. She is like a boat, like a bobbin, like a lobe. My daughters are like triplets, my sons like crowns of sonnets. And they will love girls, exquisite as *terzine* and sturdy as epic songs. And I say it again: body is not only a body. Body is the name of a genre."

An apt metaphor of Latvia in this transition period (or even the whole Baltic area) is a novel "Trespasser" (1989) written by Aivars Tarvids. We can say that its appearance was brought from Latvian "new reality" or premonitions of this coming reality. The main character of the novel is a young, talented surgeon, Arnold, who is to his way to his new home-country somewhere in the West. The time span in the novel is a few days spent in a train that is moving in a westward direction. "Trespasser" is written as a study of the model of existence that Arnold was leaving behind him. Inner action dominates – that is, the centre of the novel is Arnold's sensitive and all-embracing stream of consciousness, where we see fragments of the eastern reality that is being left behind – close relationships with people that are staying behind in Latvia, different ethnic, demographic and professional milieus, historical reminiscences about Latvia in different historic periods and its relationships with various empires, news about political "hot spots" in the contemporary world, etc. Being on the road is no consolation to Arnold. He sees his trip as a dangerous mission of spying – "even the wheels of the railway carriages are set to Western standards when crossing the border, can a man expect something different?" Even though he is disgusted by the naturalism of his former existence – as is strikingly revealed by his professional slang and his working life as "a Soviet surgeon" – he is also frightened by the prospects of " breathing the sterile Western air." The term "trespasser" (man crossing the borders) emphasizes Arnold's illegal status, with its instability and its threat to his personal identity, so the overall image created by the novel is that of trespassing, the allegory of the refugee. After the first very negative reviews that followed the publications of Tarvid's "Trespasser", some critics gave a positive evaluation of this novel, stating that the novel revealed more truth than we would have chosen to know and to become aware of.

WOMEN AND MODERN LATVIAN WRITING

Women have made their voice heard in the Latvian literature for nearly 200 years. The first Latvian woman to see her work printed was Anna Bormane. Her poems were published in the collection "Christian hymns to be sung in the churches and homes of Vidzeme" (Riga, 1809). These hymns praised God and the Emperor, the role of the latter being the preserve of men in the particular culture of the day. Thus the first Latvian woman author, Anna Bormane, introduced and represented the first – feminine – period in the history of Latvian women's writing, when women copied and imitated men. For more than 60 years she remained the only Latvian woman author whose writing was published.

The second – feminist – period was probably introduced by a woman called Karolīne Kronvalda (the spouse of an outstanding Latvian Renaissance writer Atis Kronvalds). In 1870 she published a polemical article under the title *To the Honourable Mr. Garrs* in the local Latvian newspaper *The Baltic Herald*, in which she defended the intellectual abilities of women and their rights to education. The author masterfully responded to a certain Mr. Garrs, who in a previously published article had spoken derisively of women's activities in social and cultural life. Kronvalda's article merged the battle of women for freedom and self-esteem with that of the whole Latvian nation for the same causes.

It is important to remember that the modern Latvian literary tradition began to develop only during the later part of the 19th century. However, although the development of the Latvian literary tradition began as late as it did (in comparison with the literary developments in neighbouring European countries), once it had started, the upsurge of Latvian writers was powerful and talented. The most significant feature with regard to the present discussion of gender construction within the Latvian socio-cultural context is the fact that this powerful new literary development at the end of 19th century was fostered by several women, the most distinguished among them being Elza Rozenberga (1868-1943), known by her pen-name as Aspazija [*See Plate 4*]. The most definite entry of feminine life-space in the realm of Latvian literature came with her writings. Her pen-name Aspazija was inspired by Hammerling's novel *Aspasia*, based upon an ancient drama depicting the romance between a young Miletan woman named Aspasia, known for her beauty and talent, and the Greek leader Pericles. Aspazija was subsequently recognized for her talent, and in 1893 she was invited by the Latvian theatre in Riga to work as a dramatist. Soon afterwards Aspazija become involved as a journalist, writing literary criticism, including the essay "Ibsen's Nora" (1899). The most extensive information on Aspazija's life and work is to be found in A. Stahnkes's monograph *Aspazija. Her Life and Drama* (1984).

Thus 'woman' as a discourse emerged in Latvian literary criticism in the late 19th and early 20th century. This discourse was rooted not only in women's writing, but also in the so-called realistic trend of male-produced literature. The social reality, the social role and the literary types of women (especially morality or immorality of women) were a general concern of the literary debate. Influenced by the school of cultural-historical criticism and Marxist philosophy, leading literary critics were searching for those external factors which determine a woman's life and create her character and femininity. For example, Teodors Zeiferts (the most prominent literary critic and literary historian of his time) in an article *Types of Women in Latvian Writing* (1893) described various female characters and grouped them into four different types: hard-working women, enticers, profligate women, faithful lovers. Actually Zeiferts touches not only on every-day problems, but also on quite philosophical questions by discussing the role of love in people's – especially women's – lives. He talks about love as the great force that is at the basis of life and happiness and poses the question: why do the emotions which are aimed at attaining happiness so very often bring us into the opposite direction?

There is, alongside Aspazija, another great personality in the women's literary history of Latvia in the 20th century. She is Zenta Mauriņa (1897-1978) – author and essay writer who is also a significant link in the German-Latvian dialogue of cultures. Zenta Mauriņa – like Aspazija – was equally proficient in the German language and a number of her works produced in emigration were composed in German, thus attracting the attention of German literary criticism. Mauriņa is also a well-known personality in Latvian humanities – the story of her attaining the doctoral degree (in 1938 in University of Latvia, Riga) is a legend in Latvian academic history. Mauriņa describes her academic experience in the second part of her autobiographical trilogy *It is Wonderful to Dare* (1953). Mauriņa's defence of her doctoral dissertation was a great occasion in the history of Latvian feminism, for this provided an outstanding manifestation of the unwillingness of the academia to let a woman to reach the highest level in the world of learning. These brief sketches of two outstanding Latvian authoresses are hardly sufficient to do justice to the wide variety and individuality of Latvian women writers.

One can get an idea about the intensity of the latest Latvian literary activities and women's role therein from the following statistics. The membership of the Latvian Writers Union at the end of 1999 was 284 writers, representing both Latvian and exile Latvian writers living in Sweden, the USA, Australia, Germany, Ireland and other countries. 104 of the members were women (one has to have published at least one book to qualify for membership). In 1999, according to the data of the Latvian Institute of Bibliography, 85 new Latvian original books in prose have been published

A characteristic feature of the Latvian literature of the turn of millennium is the post-modernist contradiction between realists and anti-realists. The realists are primarily represented by members of the older generation, who tend to emphasize historical truth, the reality of life, especially the experience of one's life story as an essential value in literature. In contrast the anti-realists turn to the postmodern reflection on textuality, reducing the life-story and commonplace reality to a minimum. Women writers are present in both groups, although their number among realists is larger, especially if one includes here those women who are not in the writing profession, so to say.

The process of democratization and subsequent changes in society have contributed to a great variety of types of women's self-expression as life stories, both transcribed from oral accounts and in the narrative form of fiction. These life stories tell of the experiences that could not be publicly expressed under the Soviet regime. That means that these works have been adapted to fit the literary conventions, in a way erasing or concealing the individuality of narrator and the use of language. This new layer of historical experience in contemporary Latvian literature is based on individual thinking, speaking, narrating, reading, listening to what was not considered desirable, or was even forbidden until now.

One form that life stories have taken is monumental prose works characterized by a broad historical panorama and a tale of personal tragedy. The first of these works in post-Soviet Latvian literature was a documentary novel *Exhumation*, published in 1989, written by Anita Liepa (born in 1928). The title *Exhumation* is deeply symbolic – the novel tells about a search for the burial places of two brothers who had disappeared without trace during World War II, in order to be able to bury them anew in Latvia. One of the brothers, Ādolfs, had served in the Latvian army and had been deported to Siberia after the Soviet troops entered Latvia. The eldest brother, Aleksandrs, had faithfully served in the army of Tsarist Russia, and had been nominated for knighthood. The fates of both brothers had been equally tragic. Both, as representatives of the former regime, were arrested and killed. They were not even allowed a soldier's death – Aleksandrs was executed, but Ādolfs died from cold and famine in a Soviet death camp in Siberia. *Exhumation* is written by a woman as representative of the *weaker sex* and as a passive part of human history. The novel consists of the family chronicle, and also of a description of the experience of the author in gathering documents, writing, editing, bearing the influence of censorship, etc.

As a deeply symbolic tale of personal tragedy connected with the experience perceived during World War II we can mention a prose book *A Woman in Amber: Healing the Trauma of War and Exile* (1995) written by a Latvian exile writer Agate Nesaule. The author of this book is a professor of English and Women's Studies at the University of Wisconsin, but what might seem like a classic story of successful immigrants was in fact grim. Nesaule's book is presented as a piece of reconstructed memory, based upon her childhood comprehension of events as well as adult reflections, not the product of formal research. Her life was crushed by the Soviet occupation in 1940, the German occupation in 1941 and the Soviet re-occupation in 1944 that forced Nesaule to abandon her homeland and to continue her life in "a motherless universe." Nevertheless in the introduction of the book Agate Nesaule insists that her "story shows that healing is possible."

Although contemporary Latvian literature and especially prose writing abounds in works of creative female writers, the fundamentals of modern feminist criticism and theory have only recently been presented to the Latvian audience. On the other hand, the specific problem of women as a writers has been presented within the literary realm, albeit with no response from the literary criticism. Here I am referring to Regīna Ezera's novel *Betrayal*, published in 1984 and some other modern Latvian prose writings. Already in the preface of the book R. Ezera declares that *Betrayal* will be "a work of prose concerned with the specific problems of women writers". And the course of the narrative reaches a climax when a representative from the official press shouts out: "What – can it truly be that a woman writer has any specific concerns which are different from those of a male?" The text continues with the following response of the narrator: "I answered with one word only: – hmm – but apparently I did this with such a disrespectful intonation, that my interlocutor's well-kept and intelligent face turned red, bespeaking deep perplexity."

This heralding of women's discourse in Ezera's novel was emphasized abundantly. But soon a prominent academic literary scholar in analyzing her novel referred to the female writer Regīna Ezera – by using the grammatical declinations of the male gender. Unfortunately it is impossible to translate his words directly from Latvian into English, since English does not carry these grammatical demarcations. However, broadly translated, the critic views Ezera's novel as a realization of the author's (male declination – "his", not "her") self-image, as a realization of the author's (male declination – "his", not "her") self-discovery. The critic displays no sign of perplexity, since he has not even noticed – or takes on the posture of not having noticed – the focal, the basic problem of *Betrayal*. This example of completely blind reading and total lack of adequate reaction to Ezera's challenge was no exception – during the following ten years after publication of Ezera's novel no one tried to question the standpoint of this male gendered academic criticism.

Ezera's novel plunges us into the problem of literary authority with regard to women writers' position – a fairly settled problem in Western European culture; she stresses the idea that women authors even today have to follow the literary rules laid down by men, if they want to be taken seriously as equals. Ezera reminds that women have to practice a kind of self-censure so as to become acceptable to "the crowns of Creation", who will not fail to find in women's works "non-existent mistakes alongside such discoveries as that no Leo Tolstoys are to be found among the female sex – while they consider themselves co-sexual with Tolstoy and do not feel in the least awkward about the fact that none of them either measures up to Tolstoy". Ezera's discoveries stem from her own life experience as a Soviet authoress and are not the result of theoretical studies; and yet her views manifest an astonishing similarity to the whole agenda discussed by such feministically orientated literary theoreticians as J. Kristeva, H. Cixous, L. Irigaray and others.

Betrayal is part of a tetralogy of novels under to common title *Sailing with My Own Wind*, which recalls the title of Virginia Woolf's novel, *A Room of One's Own*, and Professor's E. Showalter's work, *A Literature of Their Own*. R. Ezera's novel *Betrayal* is a unique work in the whole perspective of present-day Latvian feminist studies because it touches upon the problems of restrictions that a woman has to undergo in the sphere of language and expression, the problems of authority of women authors in literature and other issues of great importance. There are a number of archetypes and artificial constructions in our cultural mythology that are unapplicable – in principle – to women, e. g. – the "services" of Muses.

R. Ezera deals with this question in a brilliant manner by advising her younger colleague: "Rely more on yourself and not on the Muse". For during her fairly long life-time she herself has met "the Muse" (masculine) only once, and when the younger colleague is amazed at the gender change of the Muse, R. Ezera retorts: "Don't wonder, it was really He, for after all – I am a woman and I need a member of the opposite sex to inspire me .. yet, I am afraid, he was himself saddened in giving me a friendly advice: "Do not write" – a tear appearing in his eye".

One's experience, including the experience of language and literature, is differentiated by gender – this theme which Regīna Ezera places in the forefront of *Betrayal* (1984) has become one of the distinguishing marks of the postmodern developments of Latvian women's writing. *Betrayal* is written in epistolary form, and the novel's two main heroines are a young writer Irena and experienced Writer (capitalized). Both women appear in two roles in their autobiographies – that of a woman and that of an authoress. "It is as if I become divided into two beings – a woman and a woman writer." – Ezera writes and specifies that men are not involved in such conflict: "I" as a man does not develop in contrast to "I" as a writer, doctor, pilot, engineer, etc. But for women the novel's title *Betrayal* presents the gist of the problem – what should be betrayed — the disposition to procreate or the disposition to be a talented writer? One's talent is one's responsibility, but one's motherhood… What must I betray – the family or the humanity? Ezera presents this problem as a question of choice and responsibility, a question not to be easily resolved, and perhaps – as a question that can never be resolved finally. In some respects Ezera's position is saved by her ability to self-reflect with irony and humor, but there lurks behind this lightness the woman-artist's burdening awareness that her life is always a betrayal – if she has been granted a talent of writing.

Among the best Latvian poets alive today we have to mention Vizma Belševica. She became most denounced writer in the late 1960's and early 1970's, when Soviet functionaries as well as leading literary critics displayed crass incomprehension of literature by drawing all sorts of rash political conclusions from her poetry. Belševica was punished for her alleged attempts to lead Soviet readers astray "from socially pure thoughts into the fog of conjectures and remote allusions" by using Aesopian language and double-level symbolism." As the basic feature and value of her poetry one can outline the many-sided presence of the image of the feminine. In the poetry of Belševica women appear in different ways – as lover, seductress, wife, mother, poet, witch, but not feminine as an archetype. Women commonly are associated with silence and absence.

Silence for Belševica can point toward transcendence, the sublime and unutterable. The woman's world traditionally is associated with the maternal which in common sense means belonging to the family, the children and the house. Like silence, through Belševica's whole poetic universe we can identify the other recurring design – tension between belonging and non-belonging, inside and outside, as she writes about the image of house.

For example, we can take the poem "To My Good One":

You are good, and don't ask why I went.
Look at the picture our child is drawing:
The person is bigger than the house.

You know I was with the flower,
And why I went to the flower.
Look at the picture our child is drawing:
The flower is bigger than the house.
And when I come back,
You're waiting – bigger than the house.
There are flowers on my table –
Bigger than the house.

Belševica's poetry as well as her prose books are rich in different themes and variations. Her poems have been translated into forty languages, whereas volumes of translations of her texts have appeared in Russian, Belorussian, Armenian, German, Danish, Icelandic and Swedish. Recently Belševica was awarded prestigious Thomas Transtromer Prize (Sweden). Alongside Regīna Ezera, Vizma Belševica is an internationally recognized writer, and they both are best ones to start with to become familiar with Post-Soviet modern Latvian literature written by women.

 # SELECTED BIBLIOGRAPHY

A Century of Latvian Poetry. Anthology compiled and translated by W.K. Matthews, London 1957.

Bear's Ears: An Anthology of Latvian Literature, Helsinki 1999.

Rubulis A. (ed), *Latvian Literature. An Anthology*, Toronto 1964.

Baumanis A. (ed), *Latvian Poetry*, Augsburg 1946.

O'Brien J. (ed.), *New Latvian Fiction*. Illinois 1998.

Nesaule A., *Woman in Amber: Healing the Trauma of War and Exile*, New York.

Ziedonis I., *Flowers of Ice*, Toronto 1987.

Cimdiņa A., *Introduction to Modern Latvian Literature*, Riga 2001.

Dreifelds J., *Latvia in transition*, Cambridge 1996.

A.Cimdiņa (ed.), *Feminism and Latvian Literature*, Riga 1998.

Andrups J., Kalve V., *Latvian Literature*, Stockholm 1954.

Ekmanis R., *Latvian Literature under the Soviets*, Belmont, Massachusetts 1978.

Miske Ezergailis I., *Nostalgia and Beyond. Eleven Latvian Woman Writers*, Lanham Md 1998.

Spekke A., *History of Latvia*, Stockholm 1951.

Vikis-Freibergs V. (ed), *Linguistics and Poetics of Latvian Folk Songs*, Montreal-Kingston 1989.

Visel C. (ed.), *Zenta Mauriņa. Gedenkschrift zum 100.Geburtstag*, Memmingen 1997.

A page of the manuscript from the story "A day of Paradoxes", by the Latvian writer Regīna Ezera (born in 1930):

[handwritten manuscript page in Latvian]

See Plate 4

Defining the gentleman and the gentlewoman in the Italian Renaissance

Lisa Saracco

Scuola Normale Superiore, Pisa

La definizione del gentiluomo e della gentildonna nel Rinascimento si basa imprescindibilmente sul Libro del Cortegiano di Baldassar Castiglione, un testo che ha contribuito in modo consistente alla costruzione della società di Antico Regime e che ne è stato la grammatica di base. Il Libro del Cortegiano, infatti, si propone come archetipo della letteratura di comportamento che tanta fortuna avrà durante il XVI e XVII secolo. Questo testo assume un importante valore normativo nella cultura europea grazie a due livelli di comunicazione, uno rappresentativo e l'altro prescrittivo. Infatti, accanto a contenuti espliciti, è molto interessante decodificare ciò che viene suggerito attraverso la descrizione dei comportamenti, dei ruoli, degli interventi maschili e femminili. Non si tratta dunque di affrontare unicamente le parole che vengono proferite dai personaggi maschili e femminili, ma anche il modo in cui questi ultimi si muovono sul palcoscenico creato dall'autore.

La definizione dei ruoli di genere in questo tipo di organizzazione sociale e politica risponde alle stesse leggi severe che regolano i rapporti di potere al suo interno. Infatti, la struttura della società di corte di Antico Regime è strettamente gerarchica e fissa e il Libro del Cortegiano ne costituisce la giustificazione etica ed estetica. La legge principale che deve essere seguita, sia dagli uomini sia dalle donne, è quella della grazia, ovvero l'arte di fare apparire tutto ciò che si dice o che si fa naturale, non artificioso. La Corte diventa così lo specchio dell'ordine naturale e divino delle cose, acquisendo un valore assoluto. La necessità di inserire le donne nel dialogo e il fatto che Castiglione dedichi all'educazione della donna di Corte il terzo libro della sua opera risponde alla necessità di conferire autorevolezza ed universalità alla sua opera, attibuendole una dimensione molto più rappresentativa della realtà. Non solo: infatti, il dialogo propone un modello sociale e politico equilibrato ed armonioso, nel quale viene "normalizzata" la presenza delle donne che nella tradizione misogina medievale ed umanistica rappresentavano un elemento di disordine.

Per questo motivo risulta necessario nell'istruzione dei due generi il mantenimento di valori di riferimento chiaramente diversificati, pur conservando entrambi come finalità principale la "regula universalissima" della grazia. I diversi ruoli di genere all'interno della Corte sono chiaramente presenti già nell'andamento del dialogo, al quale l'elemento femminile non apporta alcuna novità. Esso, infatti, viene gestito attivamente e creativamente dai gentiluomini, che rappresentano un sapere classicamente speculativo mentre le gentildonne, con la loro presenza più concreta e corporea, ne garantiscono efficacia e validità.

La netta separazione dei ruoli fra uomo e donna si fonda sulla concezione che i due sessi siano caratterizzati da una differente natura fisiologica, che di conseguenza deve essere rigidamente rispettata nei comportamenti sociali: riguardo a questo tema si nota la presenza di una topica che vede l'incontro di temi culturali diversi, provenienti sia dalla tradizione filosofica greca (il mito dell'androgino di Platone, i Trattati sull'economia di Aristotele e Senofonte), sia dalla letteratura latina, sia da quella biblica e cristiana. Se l'uomo è per sua natura caldo, egli avrà una forza fisica ed intellettuale che lo porterà ad esercitare le armi e tutte le attività ad esse connesse. Il mantenimento della buona reputazione in questa società sarà legato però non solo al coraggio (come per i cavalieri medievali) ma anche al "bon giudicio", ovvero alla capacità di operare con autocontrollo e saggezza, utilizzando sempre il giusto mezzo, virtù imprescindibile per il cortigiano. Dall'altra parte la donna è per natura più debole fisicamente e spiritualmente e deve di conseguenza avere come principale obiettivo quello dell'onestà morale (viene qui chiaramente ripreso l'antico topos della donna più incline alla tentazione e che di conseguenza necessita di maggiore controllo). Il testo rivela comunque il nuovo ruolo pubblico e intellettuale delle donne (appartenenti alle classi sociali privilegiate) nella società e nella cultura rinascimentale, in polemica con la misoginia medievale.

Lisa Saracco was born in Capua, Italy, in 1974. She received her Laurea degree from the University of Rome "La Sapienza" with a thesis in Reformation History dedicated to the translation of the Italian Bible made by the Dominican friar Santi Marmochino (1538). Since November 2000 she is a doctoral candidate in Modern History at the Scuola Normale Superiore in Pisa. She has been commissioned by the Claudiana publishing house of Turin to translate – from Latin into Italian – Luther's theological thesis "Quaestio de viribus et voluntate hominis sine gratia disputata", and "Disputatio contra scholasticam theologiam", written between 1516 and 1522. She is also very interested in women's history, especially during the Reformation and the Renaissance. For this reason, she was elected last year to the Committee for the development of Protestant Women's Archives in Torre Pellice (Italy).

Here I wish to discuss the way the figures of the gentleman and the gentlewoman developed in European culture during the Renaissance. To define these roles I will start from a very important text of Italian literature, *The Courtier* by Baldassar Castiglione [1]. This book, written as a dialogue, gradually came to exert great influence on court society. It contributed unquestionably to the building of the way of life in court society during the period of modern state formation. *The Courtier* provided the basic grammar of European court society until the French Revolution. Why? There are four reasons which give a particular authority to this book in defining the figures of the gentleman and the gentlewoman.

The first is the European perspective expressed by the book, which comes from the life experience of the author. Baldassar Castiglione, born near Mantova in 1478, lived in many Italian Renaissance courts: in Milan at Ludovico il Moro's court and later at the Gonzaga court in Mantova. From 1504 to 1513 he lived in Urbino, at the court of Guidobaldo di Montefeltro. The ducal palace of Urbino is the setting of the *Courtier*. In 1521, after the death of his wife, he became a clergyman. In 1524 he was sent by the pope Clement VII to the Spanish court of Charles V as apostolic nuncio. In 1529 he died of plague in Toledo. Although the genesis of *The Courtier* is strictly linked to the Urbino period, the book was subjected to some revisions, which allowed Castiglione's political and diplomatic experience and a new European perspective to emerge. The last revision corresponds to the edition of the book printed in 1528 in Venice. In the published work the particular view of the court became more universal.

The second reason is that *The Courtier* is the model, the archetype of the vast literature which came to be constituted by treatises on correct conduct, for people in every walk of life, from clergymen, secretaries and counsellors to princes, women and children. This book is the founder of a big family: it was born in court society and at the same time it became the basis for the constitution and transformation of that society.

The third reason has to do with the new vision presented by this work in an aesthetic and ethical manner, that is, its efficacy in formulating the fundamental rule of self-control in instructions about good manners. There are some interesting studies about the connection between the fixed and hierarchical court society and the new importance given to self-control, used as a way of maintaining social and political order. The phenomenon of conduct treatises during the 16th century is tightly linked to the attempt to perpetuate royal and noble family values and tradition.

The fourth and more important reason for the *Courtier*'s central position in the European culture of the *ancien régime* is that it gave an absolute and universal model, for all gentlemen and gentlewomen. Although they might be of different nations, language or culture, they were linked together by the same model of conduct. Therefore this work assumed an important normative value in European affairs of the court due to two levels of communication. On the one hand there was the representative level, on the other hand a prescriptive level. In fact, in his *Courtier*, Castiglione defines gentlemen and gentlewomen not only as persons who obeyed a specific code of conduct in their behaviour, but also as personages living in a court environment and embodying the courtly ideal.

The dialogue takes place during the year 1507 at the court of Urbino, in Italy. Urbino provides a setting for the representation: such a stage makes it possible to present an ideal court in all its political and cultural power. This is the description of the palace of Urbino, built by the duke Federigo di Montefeltro:

> This man among his other deedes praise-worthie, in the hard and sharpe situation of Urbin buylt a Palace, to the opinion of many men, the fairest that was to be found in all Italie, and so furnished it with all necessarie implementes belonging thereto, that it appeared not a palace, and that not onelye with ordinary matters, as Silver plate, hangings for Chambers of very rich cloth of Golde, of Silke and other like, but also for sightlines: and to decke it out withall, placed there a wondrous number of auncient Images, of Marble and Mettall, very excellent paintings and Instruments of Musicke of all sortes, and nothing would he have there but what was most rare and excellent. To this verie great charges hee gathered together a great number of most excellent and rare bookes, in Greeke, Latin and Hebrue, the which all hee garnished with gold and silver, esteeming this to be the chiefest ornament of his great Palace. [*Source 1*]

The characters are nobles, men and women who entertain themselves during the evening by conversing in the chambers of the Duchess Elisabetta Gonzaga. The passage through Urbino of the pope Julius II on his way back Rome is the occasion of their meeting and staying together:

> After pope Julius the ii. had with his owne presence by the ayde of the Frenchmen brought Bolonia to the obedyence of the Apostolyke Sea again, in the yeare mdvi. in hys retourn toward Roome he tooke Urbin in his way, where he was receaved as honorably as was possible, and with as sumptuous and costlye preparation, as coulde have bine in any other Citie of Italy whatsoever it be. So that beeside the Pope, all the Cardinalles and other Courtyers thought

themselves throughly satisfied. And some there were that provoked wyth the sweetnesse of this companye, after the Pope and the Court was departed, contynued manye dayes together in Urbin. [*Source 2*]

Elisabetta was the wife of the Duke Guidobaldo di Montefeltro, the first son of the famous Federigo. Because the Duke is ill, the Duchess guides the conversation:

Fig. 1
Piero della Francesca, *Ideal City*, Ducal Palace of Urbino (about 1470).

Therefore were all the houres of the day divided into honoureble and pleasant exercises, as well of the bodie, as of the minde. But because the Duke used continually, by reason of his infirmitie, soone after Supper to goe to his rest, everie man ordinarily, at that houre drew where the Dutchesse was, the Ladie Elisabeth Gonzaga, where also continually was the Ladie Emilia Piu, who for that shee was indued with so lively a wit and judgement, as you know, seemed the maistresse and ringleader of all the company, and that everie man at her received understanding and courage. There was then to bee heard pleasant communications and merie conceites, and in everie mans countenance a man might perceive painted a loving jocundness. (…) The like was betweene the woman, with whom we had such free and honest conversation, that everye man might commune, sitte dallye, and laugh with whom hee had lusted. But such was the respect which we bore to the Dutchesse will, that the selfe same libertie was a very great brindle. For this respect were there most honest conditions coupled with wondrous great libertie… [*Source 3*]

It is clear that the description of the court idealizes it, as the most beautiful of all, a true symbol of harmony.

In the dialogue women are included for reasons which are made explicit, in opposition to the widespread misogyny of Humanism and the Medieval period which supported the idea that women were physically and ethically inferior. The female presence is linked to the necessity of representing a universal value of perfection and equilibrium, in which everybody can be reflected. The inclusion of women makes the text more representative and gives it a much broader validity. The harmonious model suggested by the dialogue normalizes women's presence, considered in the previous centuries a personification of chaos and disorder. For this reason, Castiglione introduced in his work a part (the third book) which talks about conduct codes for women, especially in the court. We can read, at the beginning of the third book, the reasons Lord Cesare Gonzaga gave to justify including women:

You are in a great errour, for like as no Court, how great soever it be, can have any sightlinesse or brightnesse in it, or mirth without women, nor any Courtier can bee gracious, pleasant or hardie, nor at any time undertake any gallant enterprise of Chivalrie, unlesse he be stirred with the conversation and with the love and contentation of women, even so in like case, the Courtiers talke is most unperfect evermore, if the entercourse of women give them not a part of the grace wherwithall they make perfect and decke out their playing [*Source 4*]

It is clear that women are a vital part of the representation of courtly life and the author tries to explain his position. In the dialogue of the third Book the determination to escape from the misogynist heritage of the past is expressed by defending women against the medieval theories about their imperfection. This defence of women was present in

IL LIBRO DEL CORTEGIANO
DEL CONTE BALDESAR
CASTIGLIONE.

AL   DVS.

Haffi nel priuilegio,& nella gratia ottenuta dalla Illuftriffima
Signoria che in quefta,ne in niun'altra Citta del fuo
dominio fi pofta imprimere, ne altroue
impreffo uendere quefto libro
del Cortegiano per·x· anni
fotto le pene in effo
contenute.

Fig. 2
The frontispiece from the first edition of the *Cortegiano* (Venice 1528).

some 16th century treatises on the equal dignity of women. In this context I wish to remember Flavio Galeazzo Capra's treatise entitled *Della eccellenza e dignità delle donne* (*Women's excellence and dignity*), which was published in 1525 (Rome) and 1526 (Venice). It is one of the first documents of Italian vernacular literature on women, along with the dialogue of Alessandro Piccolomini entitled *La Raffaella, ovvero Della bella creanza delle donne.*

Women have a specific role in the representation of the court which is delineated not only by their presence, but also by their behaviour towards men and as compared to men.

The male characters are defined by Castiglione as very remarkable individuals thanks to their precious intellects:

Because the house was replenished with most nobles wittes. Among which, as you know, were most famous Lord Octavian Fregoso, Sir Friderick his brother, the Lord Julian de Medicis, m.

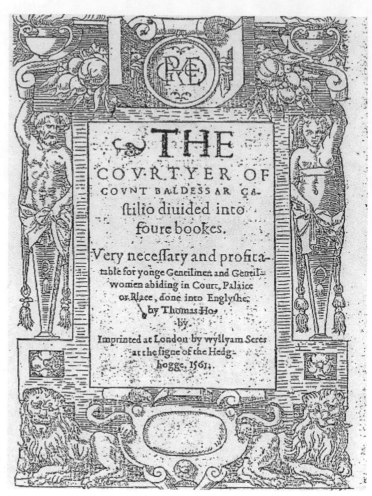

Fig. 3
The frontispiece of *The Courtier*, translated by Thomas Hoby (London 1561).

Pietro Bembo, the Lord Cesar Gonzaga, Counte Lewis of Canossa, the Lord Gaspar Pallavicin, the Lorde Luduvicus Pius, Maister Morello of Ortona, Peter of Naples, Maister Robert of Bari, and infinite of other most worthy knights and gentlemen. Beesyde these there were manye that for all ordinarilye they dwelled not there, yet spent they most of their tyme there, as M. Bernard Bibiena, Unico Aretino, Johnchristopher Romano, Peter Mount, Therpander, M. Nicholas Phrisio, so that thither ran continually poetes, musitiens, and al kinde of men of skyll, and the excellentest in every faculty that were in al Italy. [*Source 5*]

On the other hand, the women are not characterized so well as the men (only the Duchess and Lady Emilia Pio take part to the dialogue, the others are not described, they are kept out of the conversation). The Duchess represents female dignity and worth: she defines the place (her chambers), the time (evening) and the order of the dialogue. She also represents power because she takes her husband's place. She is the icon of the court and of the female presence in it.

Emilia Pio is more active: she is declared by the Duchess to be her deputy. She has the role of stimulating, regulating and concluding the men's speeches. But women never intervene to contribute new elements to the discussion about the perfect courtier. The author exempts women from creating speeches. This a men's prerogative, justified by their capacity to comprehend and express philosophical arguments that women cannot understand:

> Then the L. Emilia tourninge her to the L. Julian: For love of God (quoth she) come once out of these your Mattiers and Fourmes and males and females, and speake so that you maye be understoode [*Source 6*]

Thus the development of the dialogue marks a clear-cut distinction between the gentlemen and gentlewomen represented and their roles: the gentlemen work at defining the perfect Courtier and the Lady, gentlewomen are not the men's interlocutors but only a mirror of the natural male creativity. Gentlewomen do not participate in defining themselves using their feminine opinion, their function is only to guarantee and ensure with their presence that the dialogue is going in the best way.

Now we can go on to the second level of communication in *The Courtier* (conducted only by men): the definition of an overall code of conduct. Castiglione sets out an universal rule which constitutes the conscience of the Court. The basic category of this universal rule is "grace" (*grazia*). This is the password for entering *The Courtier*'s world. We can read how Castiglione defines grace:

> But I, imagining with my selfe often times how this grace commeth, leaving apart such as have it from above, finde one rule that is most generall, which in this part (me thinke) taketh place in all things belonging to a man in word or deede, above all other. And that is to eschue as much as a man may, and as a sharpe and daungerous rocke, too much curiousnesse, and (to speake a new word) to use in everye thing a certaine disgracing to cover arte withal, and seeme whatsoever he doth and saith, to do it without paine, and (as it were) not minding it. And of this doe I believe grace is much derived, for in rare matters and well brought to passé, every man knoweth the hardnesse of them, so that a readinesse therein maketh a great wonder [*Source 7*]

Therefore, all male and female behaviour must follow this necessary rule. In court culture grace means a way of life led without ostentation. Castiglione's *The Courtier* set forth a standard in aristocratic Renaissance manners, advocating that everything be done with *sprezzatura*, or seeming negligence and easy grace. This is the art of always concealing the effort and the hard work required to attain self-control. Everything must appear very natural and unaffected to confirm that the court is the mirror of the natural and divine order. And consequently, that this political and social organization is legitimate and correct. Like God at the head of creation, the Prince or the Lord is at the head of the court and maintains the established and fixed situation. Then, the term 'grace' is intimately connected with attaining social, economical and political objectives aims at social, economical and political achievement. Grace of behaviour is the sign of seeking the lord's favour: in this kind of society social success is essential. Gentlemen and gentlewomen maintain their privileges with grace. Consequently they have to be well considered, to have a good reputation. The word *virtue* shows the importance for gentlemen and gentlewomen of how they appear from the outside. The idea of virtue, borrowed from Aristotle, is tightly linked to the rule of grace. All behaviour is virtuous if it is not excessive or defective [2].

Now let us consider the definition of the gentleman and the gentlewoman in the *Courtier*. High-birth is the basis of the gentleman's and the gentlewoman's training but it alone is not enough. Gentlemen and gentlewomen must start from this point, but both also have to follow the rule of grace and to be virtuous. However, the two genders do this very differently. To demonstrate this point, Castiglione again took up the Aristotelian and Platonic theories about the origin of gender. He did not confirm the assertion that women are inferior (presented by Aristotle in his work on the generation of animals) but he did use the theories that women's physical nature influences their social behaviour [3]. Besides, using the Platonic myth of the androgynous being, Castiglione declared that in God's creation the male and female character are complementary [4]. On account of their nature, their roles must be different and separated. We can read how, in Castiglione's view, this model became the example of the perfection of the universal order.

> Some qualities are common and necessarie as well for the woman as the man, yet are there some other more meete for the woman than for the man, and some again meete for the man, that she ought in no wise to meddle withal. The verie same I say of the exercises of the bodie: But principally in her fashions, manners, wordes, gestures and conversation (me thinke) the woman ought to be much unlike the man. For right as it is seemely for him to shew a certaine manlinesse full and steadie, so doth it well in a woman to have a tendernessee, soft and milde, with a kinde of womanlye sweetenesse in every gesture of hers, that in going, standing, and speaking what ever she lusteth, may alwaeis make her appeare a woman without anye likenesse of man [*Source 8*]

In the *Courtier* there is a tight connection between the physiological and anthropological theories on the different nature of men and women and their roles on the social and political level.

Due to his hot nature, man has the virile force and power necessary for using arms. This is the courtier's first duty, with all the connected activities (like hunting, riding, swimming, running):

> But to come to some particularitie, I judge the principall and true profession of a Courtier ought to bee in feates of armes, the which above all I will have him to practise lively, and to bee knowne among other of his hardiness, for his atchieving of enterprises, and for his fidelitie towarde him whom he serveth. And hee shall purchase himselfe a name with these good conditions, in doing the deedes in every time and place, for it is not for him to fainte at any time in this behalfe without a wondrous reproach. And even as in women honestie once stained doth never returne againe to the former estatee: so the fame of a gentleman that carrieth weapon, if it once take a foyle in anye little point through dastardlinesse or any other reproach, doth evermore continue shamefull in the world and full of ignorance. Therefore the more excellent our Courtier shall be in this arte, the more shall he be worthie praise [*Source 9*]

But there is a significant transformation from the medieval knight to the Renaissance gentleman. In addition to high-birth and the duty of bearing weapons, the gentleman has to add a specific culture which derives from the rule of grace. The virtue of courage is still important (this is a society based on supremacy in the use of arms and war), but it is not the only one. The gentleman, using good judgment, must be wise and careful in his political relationships in the court and in advising his Lord or prince:

> I believe a good judgemeent in the Courtier is sufficient for all this (...) Therefore the well behaving of a mans selfe in this case (me thinke) consisteth in certainee wisedome and judgement of choice, and to know more and lesse what encreaseth or diminisheth in thinges, to practise them in due time, or out of season [*Source 10*]

He can obtain this wisdom through a specific education: he has to know how speak and write, he has to learn Greek, Latin, literature and music. The gentleman, the courtier, acquired a new public and politic role in the Renaissance court: he must use his culture and intelligence for creating, for giving life to a new kind of political conduct in which he has an active task. He is tightly linked to the sphere of "logos".

On the other hand, woman's nature is linked or connected with the sphere of the "body". She has a cold nature which gives her tenderness and gentleness. This nature makes woman weaker than man, in body and in soul. The woman's weakness has repercussions on the roles assigned to her. In fact, for a woman, the chief virtue is honesty and respectability. These moral principles must be observed, complying with some rules on love affairs. Woman, because of her feminine weakness, can be deceived by seducers and led into temptation. This moralistic argument reveals an old theological and philosophic topic: the moral fragility of woman present since the famous biblical story of Adam and Eve. Eve was considered by the Church Fathers and by the Medieval theologians the first sign of woman's natural instinct for being tempted. Then every relationship outside marriage between gentlemen and gentlewomen must be marked by chastity and honesty, the two qualities that women must own and show in court society. This is an important point in a book in which describes men and women talking and staying together in freedom.

In the third book Castiglione talked about the female role from two points of view: on one hand the feminine role in general, which is placed in the family. In Castiglione's vision the woman held the role of mother and wife; in fact he never talked about the woman's work, keeping the division between the life inside the house (for women) and outside (for men) from Xenophon [5]. On the other however he considers a particular kind of woman, the lady, the gentlewoman who lives in the court. She has not only to be like all women (mothers and wives) but also she must respect the rule of grace, though in a different way in comparison with men. Castiglione insisted very much on the necessity of difference between men and women in look and actions: "I believe none here, but understandeth concerning the exercises of the bodie, that it is not comely for a woman to practise feates of armes, ryding, playing at tenise, wrestling, and many other thinges that belong to men". Because of her tender, soft and sweet nature she must not do the kind of bodily exercises that men do. In the court she has the duty of entertaining her guests pleasantly: it is clear that in *The Courtier* there is an emphasis on her new public role. She must know letters, music, drawing, painting and singing, always doing these actions with grace and feminine modesty:

> And to make a briefe rehershall in few wordes of that is already saide, I will that this woman have a sight in letters, in musicke, in drawing or painting, and skilfull in dauncing, and in

devising sports and pastimes, accompanying with that discrete sober moode, and with the giving of good opinion of her selfe, the other principles also that have beene thought the Courtier. And thus in conversation, in laughing, in sporting, in jesting, finally in everie thing she shall be had in great price, and shall entertaine accordingly both with jestes and feate conceites meetee for her, every person that commeth in her company [*Source 11*]

Therefore the rule of grace must be used in the choice of musical instruments, in the way of dancing, in words for conversation and, above all, in the care of beauty and fashion:

I will not only have her not to practise these manly exercises so sturdie and boisterous, but also those that bee meete for a woman, I will have her to doe them with heedefulnesse and with the short mildenes that we have saide is comely for her. And therefore in daunsing I would not have her use too swift and violent trickes, nor yet in singing or playing upon instruments those hard and often divisions that declare more cunning than sweetenes. Likewise the instruments of Musicke which she useth ought to bee fit for this purpose. Imagin with your selfe with an unsightly matter it were to see a woman paly upon a tabour or drum, or blow in a flute or trumpet, or any like instrument: and this because the boistrousnesse of them doth both cover and take away that sweetie mildnesse which setteth so forth everie deede that a woman doth. Therefore when she commeth to daunce, or to shew any kind somewhat to be prayed, and a certain bashfulnesse, that may declare the noble shamefastnesse that is contrarie to headinesse. She ought also to frame her garments to this entent, and so to apparrell her selfe, that she appeare not fonde and light. But for so much as it is lawfull and necessarie for women to set more by their beawtie than men, and sundrie kindes of beautie there are, this woman ought to have a judgement to know what manner garments set her best out, and be most fitte for the exercise, that she estendeth to undertake at that instant, and with them to aray her selfe. And where she perceiveth in her a sigthly and chearefull beautie, she ought to farther it with gestures, words and apparrell, that all may betoken mirth. In like case an other that feeleth her selfe of a milde and grave disposition, she ought also to accompany it with fashions of the like sorte, to encrease that that is the gift of nature [*Source 12*]

The effort which the gentlewoman must dedicate to nurturing all the positive aspects of her real nature has the purpose of entertaining men, with kindness in speaking and a pleasant look: the gentlewoman has the role of receiving the gentlemen's speeches with judgement and agreement. Men and women's roles are the same on the prescriptive and on the representative level: the courtiers, in fact, thanks to their culture and philosophical knowledge, are entrusted with the production of a theory about gentleman and gentlewoman, making a logical settlement of reality. The receptive presence of the Ladies gives authority to this kind of settlement: this is a clear metaphor of the sexual relationship between the two genders.

For these reasons, in this work, gentlewomen were excluded from political life, but they had the important privilege of participating in public life.

In the book of *The Courtier*, although the definition of gender roles is put under the men's care, there is a new positive presence of women. Women (naturally this phenomenon concerned only noblewomen, who had these privileges) were more emancipated in comparison with the past without any doubt: I want to underline the new importance of cultural instruction for women and their visible presence on the public stage. Notwithstanding the definition of precise and hierarchical social structures in which the gentlewoman was inserted, there was a new freedom and a new possibility of expression for her. In Castiglione's book there are some elements which bear witness to a new kind and degree of women's participation with their opinions in the cultural life of the Renaissance period: in the first half of the 16th century a new writing and intellectual season for women began (I am thinking of Vittoria Colonna, a friend of Castiglione, and Gaspara Stampa who were two poetesses and I want to remember Olimpia Morato who lived at the court of Renata of France and was a teacher of Greek and Latin). The explicit mention of the poetress Vittoria Colonna in *The Courtier*'s dedication to Don Michel de Silva, bishop of Viseu (Portugal), is not an accident, but probably the proof of Castiglione's awareness of women's active presence in cultural life. Besides the rigid structure of court society, in *The Courtier* there is a new classical attention to women and to their revaluation, in comparison with men. This trend will be replaced, in the second half of the century, by a women's return to a private sphere, inspired by the Counter-Reformation and its conservative morality.

 **NOTES**

[1] I will use the first English translation of the *Courtier* made by Sir Thomas Hoby, which can be called a masterpiece of 16th century prose. It was immensely popular, going through four editions in Elizabeth's reign. It was completely translated by 1554, but it was not published until 1561. Castiglione's original text in Italian appears in the "sources", below.

[2] Aristotle, *Ethica Nicomachea*, 1114b.

[3] See Aristotle, *De generatione animalium* IV, 6, 775.

[4] See Plato, *Symposium*, 189-193.

[5] Xenophon, *The Economist*, VII, 18-30.

 **SELECTED BIBLIOGRAPHY**

Baldassarre Castiglione's *Il Corteggiano* can be found, using the index, in the Biblioteca Telematica Italiana, http://cibit.humnet.unipi.it

Sir Thomas Hoby's translation 16th century translation, *The Courtyer*, can be found at

Renascence Editions

http://darkwing.uoregon.edu/~rbear/courtier/courtier.html

Here the quotations are taken from:

Baldassar Castiglione, *Il Libro del Cortegiano*, introduction by Amedeo Quondam, notes by Nicola Longo, Milan 1981.

Baldassar Castiglione, *The Courtier*, translation by Sir Thomas Hoby, London 1966.

The classical texts mentioned (Aristotle's *De generatione animalium*; Plato's *Symposium* and Xenophon's *Economics*) can be found on the sites:

http://www.perseus.tufts.edu/

http://classics.mit.edu/

Chemello A., *Donna di palazzo, moglie e cortigiana. Ruoli e funzioni sociali della donna cortigiana in alcuni trattati del '500*, in *La Corte e il "Cortegiano"*, vol. II, Prosperi A. (ed.), *Un modello europeo*, Rome 1980, pp. 113-132.

De Maio R., *Donna e Rinascimento*, Milan 1987.

Patrizi G., Quondam A. (eds.), *Educare il corpo, educare la parola*, Rome 1998.

Jordan C., *Renaissance feminism: Literary Texts and Political Models*, Ithaca 1990.

Ordine N., *Teoria e "situazione" del dialogo nel Cinquecento italiano* in D. Bigalli, G.Canziani (eds.), *Il dialogo filosofico nel Cinquecento europeo*, Milan 1990, pp. 13-33.

Quondam A., *"Questo povero Cortegiano". Castiglione, il Libro, la Storia*, Rome 2000

Zancan M., *La donna*, in Asor Rosa A. (ed.), *Letteratura Italiana*, Turin 1982-1995, vol. V, *Le Questioni*, pp. 765-827.

Zancan M., *Nel cerchio della luna. Figure di donna in alcuni testi del XVI secolo*, Venice 1983.

Panizza L. ed., *Women in Italian Renaissance Culture and Society*, Oxford, 2000.

 SOURCES

1. *Questo, tra l'altre cose sue lodevoli, nell'aspero sito d'Urbino edificò un palazzo, secondo la opinione di molti, il più bello che in tutta Italia si ritrovi; e d'ogni oportuna cosa sì ben lo fornì, che non un palazzo, ma una città in forma de palazzo esser pareva; e non solamente di quello che ordinariamente si usa, come vasi d'argento, apparamenti di camere di ricchissimi drappi d'oro, di seta e d'altre cose simili, ma per ornamento v'aggiunse una infinità di statue antiche di marmo e di bronzo, pitture singularissime, instrumenti musici d'ogni sorte; né quivi cosa alcuna volse, se non rarissima ed eccellente. Appresso con grandissima spesa adunò un gran numero di eccellentissimi e rarissimi libri greci, latini ed ebraici, quali tutti ornò d'oro e d'argento, estimando che questa fusse la suprema eccellenzia del suo magno palazzo.*

[The Courtier, I, ii]

2. *Avendo adunque papa Iulio II con la presenza sua e con l'aiuto de' Franzesi ridutto Bologna alla obedienzia della sede apostolica nell'anno MDVI, e ritornando verso Roma, passò per Urbino; dove quanto era possibile onoratamente e con quel più magnifico e splendido apparato che si avesse potuto fare in qualsivoglia altra nobil città d'Italia, fu ricevuto; di modo che, oltre il Papa, tutti i signor cardinali ed altri cortegiani restarono summamente satisfatti; e furono alcuni, i quali, tratti dalla dolcezza di questa compagnia, partendo il Papa e la corte, restarono per molti giorni ad Urbino.*

[The Courtier I, vi]

3. *Erano adunque tutte l'ore del giorno divise in onorevoli e piacevoli esercizi così del corpo come dell'animo; ma perché il signor Duca continuamente, per la infirmità, dopo cena assai per tempo se n'andava a dormire, ognuno per ordinario dove era la signora duchessa Elisabetta Gonzaga a quell'ora si riduceva; dove ancor sempre si ritrovava la signora Emilia Pia, la qual per esser dotata di così vivo ingegno e giudicio, come sapete, pareva la maestra di tutti, e che ognuno da lei pigliasse senno e valore. Quivi adunque i soavi ragionamenti e l'oneste facezie s'udivano, e nel viso di ciascuno dipinta si vedeva una gioconda ilarità. (...) Il medesimo era tra le donne, con le quali si aveva liberissimo ed onestissimo commerzio; ché a ciascuno era licito parlare, sedere, scherzare e ridere con chi gli parea: ma tanta era la reverenzia che si portava al voler della signora Duchessa, che la medesima libertà era grandissimo freno; ne' era alcuno che non estimasse per lo maggiore piacere che al mondo aver potesse il compiacer a lei, e la maggiore pena di dispiacerle. Per la qual cosa quivi onestissimi costumi erano con grandissima libertà congiunti.*

[The Courtier I, iv]

4. *Voi sète in grande errore, – rispose messer Cesare Gonzaga; – perché come corte alcuna, per grande che ella sia, non po aver ornamento o splendore in sé, né allegria senza donne, né cortegiano alcun essere aggraziato, piacevole o ardito, né far mai opera leggiadra di cavalleria, se non mosso dalla pratica e dall'amore e piacer di donne, così ancora il ragionar del cortegiano è sempre imperfettissimo, se le donne, interponendovisi, non dànno lor parte di quella grazia, con la quale fanno perfetta ed adornano la cortegiania.*

[The Courtier III, iii]

5. *...dove di tali ragionamenti maraviglioso piacere si pigliava per esser, come ho detto, piena la casa di nobilissimi ingegni; tra i quali, come sapete, erano celeberrimi il signor Ottaviano Fregoso, messer Federico suo fratello, il Magnifico Iuliano de' Medici, messer Pietro Bembo, messer Cesar Gonzaga, il conte Ludovico da Canossa, il signor Gaspar Pallavicino, il signor Ludovico Pio, il signor Morello da Ortona, Pietro da Napoli, messer Roberto da Bari ed infiniti altri nobilissimi cavalieri; oltra che molti ve n'erano, i quali, avvenga che per ordinario non stessino quivi fermamente, pur la maggior parte del tempo vi dispensavano; come messer Bernardo Bibiena, l'Unico Aretino, Ioanni Cristoforo Romano Pietro Monte, Terpandro, messer Nicolò Frisio; di modo che sempre poeti, musici e d'ogni sorte omini piacevoli e li più eccellenti in ogni facultà che in Italia si trovassino, vi concorrevano.*

[The Courtier I, v]

6. *Allora la signora Emilia rivolta al signor Magnifico, – Per amor di Dio, – disse, – uscite una volta di queste vostre 'materie' e 'forme' e maschi e femine e parlate di modo che siate inteso".*

[The Courtier III, xvii]

7. *Ma avendo io già più volte pensato meco onde nasca questa grazia, lasciando quelli che dalle stelle l'hanno, trovo una regula universalissima, la qual mi par valer circa questo in tutte le cose umane che si facciano o dicano più che alcuna altra, e ciò è fuggir quanto più si po, e come un asperissimo e pericoloso scoglio, la affettazione; e per dir forse una nova parola, usar in ogni cosa una certa sprezzatura, che nasconda l'arte e dimostri ciò che si fa e dice venir fatto senza fatica e quasi senza pensarvi. Da questo credo io che derivi assai la grazia, perché delle cose rare e ben fatte ognun sa la difficultà, onde in esse la facilità genera gran meraviglia.*

[The Courtier I, xxvi]

8. *...ché, benché alcune qualità siano comuni all'omo come alla donna, sono poi alcun'altre che più si convengono alla donna che all'omo, ed alcune convenienti all'omo delle quali essa deve in tutto esser aliena. Il medesimo dico deglie sercizi del corpo; ma sopra tutto parmi che nei modi, maniere, parole, gesti e portamenti suoi, debba la donna essere molto dissimile dall'omo; perché come ad esso conviene mostrare una certa virilità soda e ferma, così ala donna sta ben aver una tenerezza molle e delicata, con maniera in ogni suo movimento di dolcezza femminile che nell'andare e stare e dir ciò che si voglia sempre la faccia parer donna, senza similitudine alcuna d'omo.*

[The Courtier III, iv]

9. *Ma per venire a qualche particularità, estimo che la principale e vera profession del cortegiano debba esser quella dell'arme; la qual soprattutto voglio che egli faccia vivamente e sia conosciuto fra gli altri ardito e sforzato e fidele a chi serve. E 'l nome di queste bone condizioni si acquisterà facendone l'opere in ogni tempo e loco, imperò che non è lecito in questo mancar mai, senza biasimo estremo; e come nelle donne la onestà, una volta macchiata, mai più non ritorna al primo stato, così la fama d'un gentiluom che porti l'arme, se una volta in un minimo punto si denigra per coardia o altro rimproccio, sempre resta vituperosa al mondo e piena d'ignominia. Quanto più adunque sarà eccellente il nostro cortegiano in questa arte, tanto più sarà degno di laude.*

[The Courtier, I, xxvii]

10. *– e credo che basti in tutto questo dir che 'l cortegiano sia di bon giudicio, (...) Però il governarsi bene in questo parmi che consista in una certa prudenzia e giudicio di elezione, e*

conoscere il più e 'l meno che nelle cose si accresce e scema per operarle oportunamente e fuor di stagione.

[The Courtier, II, vi]

11. *E perché il signor Gasparo dimanda ancor quai siano queste molte cose di che ella deve aver notizia, e di che modo intertenere, e se le virtù deono servire a questo intertenimento, dico che voglio che ella abbia cognizion de ciò che questi signori hanno voluto che sappia il cortegiano; e de quelli esercizi che avemo detto che a lei non si convengono, voglio che ella n'abbia almen quel giudicio che possono aver delle cose coloro che non le oprano; e questo per saper laudare ed apprezzar i cavalieri più e meno, secondo i meriti. E per replicar in parte con poche parole quello che già s'è detto, voglio che questa donna abbia notizie di lettere, di musica, di pittura e sappia danzar e festeggiare; accompagnando con quella discreta modestia e col dar bona opinion di sé ancora le altre avvertenze che son state insegnate al cortegiano. E così sarà nel conversare, nel ridere, nel giocare, nel motteggiare, in somma in ogni cosa graziatissima; ed intenerà accommodatamente e con motti e facezie convenienti a lei ogni persona che le occorrerà. E benché la continenzia, la magnanimità, la temperanzia, la fortezza d'animo, la prudenzia e le altre virtù paia che non importino allo intertenere, io voglio che di tutte sia ornata, non tanto per lo intertenere, benché però ancor a questo possono servire, quanto per esser virtuosa ed acciò che queste virtù la faccian tale, che meriti esser onorata e che ogni sua operazion sia di quelle composta.*

[The Courtier, III, ix]

12. *Rispose il Magnifico: – Poich'io posso formar questa donna a modo mio, non solamente non voglio ch'ella usi questi esercizi virili così robusti ed asperi, ma voglio che quegli ancora che son convenienti a donna faccia con riguardo, e con quella molle delicatura che avemo detto convenirsele; e però nel danzar non vorrei vederla usar movimenti troppo gagliardi e sforzati, né meno nel cantar o sonar quelle diminuzioni forti e replicate, che mostrano più arte che dolcezza; medesimamente gli instrumenti di musica che ella usa, secondo me, debbono esser conformi a questa intenzione. Imaginatevi come disgraziata cosa saria veder una donna sonare tamburri, piffari o trombe, o altri tali instrumenti; e questo perché la loro asprezza nasconde e leva quella soave mansuetudine, che tanto adorna ogni atto che faccia la donna. Però quando ella viene a danzar o a far musica di che sorte si sia, deve indurvisi con lassarsene alquanto pregare e con una certa timidità, che mostri quella nobile vergogna che è contraria della impudenzia. Deve ancor accommodar gli abiti a questa intenzione e vestirsi di sorte, che non paia vana e leggera. Ma perché alle donne è licito e debito aver più cura della bellezza che agli omini e diverse sorti sono di bellezza, deve questa donna aver iudicio di conoscer quai sono quegli abiti che le accrescon grazia e più accommodati a quelli esercizi ch'ella intende di fare in quel punto, e di quelli servirsi; e conoscendo in sé una bellezza vaga ed allegra, deve aiutarla coi movimenti, con le parole e con gli abiti, che tutti tendano allo allegro; così come un'altra, che si senta aver maniera mansueta e grave, deve ancor accompagnarla con modi di quella sorte, per accrescer quello che è dono della natura. Così, essendo un poco più grassa o più magra del ragionevole, o bianca o bruna, aiutarsi con gli abiti, ma dissimulatamente più che sia possibile; e tenendosi delicata e polita, mostrar sempre di non mettervi studio o diligenzia alcuna.*

[The Courtier, III, viii]

SEE PLATES 5-6

Lisa Saracco

Work and Gender in Early Modern Italy

Daniela Lombardi

Università di Pisa

Viene messo in evidenza lo scarto tra rappresentazione e realtà che caratterizza il lavoro femminile in età moderna (cioè dal Cinquecento al Settecento). In molti stati italiani, la crisi del Seicento rappresenta un momento di riconversione dell'economia urbana verso il settore serico. Questa riconversione è possibile grazie al massiccio impiego di manodopera femminile, anche nei settori più qualificati come la tessitura. Ciononostante le donne non acquisiscono una maggiore consapevolezza della propria identità professionale: anche quando sono loro a svolgere l'effettiva funzione di capofamiglia, il loro lavoro continua ad essere percepito come transitorio e marginale. La precarietà, la subordinazione, la mancanza di riconoscimento del lavoro femminile si costruisce già al momento della formazione professionale, quando l'apprendistato delle ragazze si svolge attraverso canali informali che non garantiscono l'inserimento nel mondo del lavoro, mentre i maschi imparano il mestiere nella bottega del maestro. Di conseguenza non è la specializzazione, bensì la flessibilità a caratterizzare il lavoro delle donne.

Born in Naples in 1951, Daniela Lombardi teaches Modern History at the University of Pisa. Her research and teaching are on the history of poverty and welfare, and the history of marriage and the family in the modern age. She has recently published a book entitled *Matrimoni di antico regime* [Ancien régime marriages] (Bologna, 2000).

Between the 16th and the 17th centuries Italian states lost the supremacy in the trading and productive sphere which many of their cities had enjoyed until that time, particularly in the northern and central parts of the peninsula. The displacement of the trade routes from the Mediterranean to the Atlantic and the competition with new economic powers such as Holland and England are at the root, it is often said, of an economic decadence which was to lead to the Italian peninsula's becoming marginal respect to other, more dynamic areas in Europe. In particular it was the once flourishing urban textile manufacture which encountered the greatest difficulties, when faced by the abilities of the Dutch and English manufacturers to produce lighter, brightly coloured and less expensive kinds of cloth which appealed to and were accessible for a broader market than the fine wools and silks which had made the fortune of the preceding age.

Nonetheless, the situation in Italy was actually much more complicated than appears at first glance. Recent studies have drawn attention to the processes of economic conversion which took place in some geographic areas. What is of special interest to us here is that the conversion was made possible thanks to the massive use of female work. Women's labour was widely used, both in towns and in the countryside (where work was often carried out in the home), in order to avoid the limitations placed on the labour force by the urban trade corporations and to keep production costs down.

Through women's work much of the urban textile manufacturing (which employ the greatest part of the population) converted from woollens to the silk sector: not so much to develop the production of the traditional precious silk stuffs, but rather in order to produce lighter less expensive textiles, for which there was growing demand on the European market. In the countryside the women and the girls raised silk worms and unwound the silk from the cocoons ('drawing' silk) in order to form the skeins. In all the drawings and descriptions of the time that deal with silk worm raising and the unwinding of the silk from the cocoons, men are shown in auxiliary roles respect to the women. In the city, the women and the girls spun the silk, caned it, and more and more often, wove it. In the weaving sector there was a sexual division of labour desired by the guilds themselves. They entrusted the sector of the new lighter stuffs to women outside of the corporations, whereas the men continued to be occupied in the traditional production of heavy, elaborate luxury textiles. Hence it was actually the corporations themselves that used the free labour force formed by the women: the women were paid less and they made it possible to respond positively to the new demand for fashionable stuffs which, because of their low prices, required a less expensive labour force.

In the textile sector female work grew in the course of time. In the 18th century, while in the countryside women continued to work wool, or else were employed, particularly in the central part of the peninsula, in weaving fine straw hats (very much in demand on the English market), in the cities their presence became essential for silk production, where the labour force was almost completely female. In Florence, Bologna and Genoa, women were able to take over even in the most difficult and highly specialised phases of the production process, such as weaving, which up until then they had shared with male workers. In Florence in the middle of the 18th century 93% of the weavers were women. The few remaining men, it is true, carried out the final, most delicate, phases of the production process, which were also the most highly paid.

Notwithstanding the full development of the female labour force, women did not acquire a greater awareness of their own role in the production process. The lack of a professional identity is a constant of the female sex in the modern period. If we analyse the petitions sent by the women themselves to the political authorities in order to ask for help in times of difficulty, we realise that women's language never gives particular value to their acquired professional knowledge. When a woman presents herself she says "faccio la tessitrice" (I do weaving) whereas the man says "sono tessitore" (I am a weaver). Female work is an ability, not a profession. Whereas for a man his work is the strong point of his identity, for the woman it is a transitory and marginal condition which does not constitute a principle of her identity. These different ways of representing oneself, of living one's identity, survive even when women's work becomes more important and visible and even when it was in reality the only source of family income. In *ancien régime* families, in fact, it was not rare for women to live alone, without a male 'tutor' because of being unmarried, widowed, separated, or else because their husband had left them temporarily to search for work elsewhere or, for example, to flee from his creditors. The great male mobility had the effect that

Daniela Lombardi

La Miracolosa Immagine di Maria V.
Protettrice del raccolto delle Gallete

Verona per li Eredi Marco Moroni

Fig. 1
A representation of the Madonna protecting the silkworm harvest. The cocoons and the worms can be seen in the foreground; women are unwinding the cocoons in the background.

in certain periods of the family life-cycle women had the role of head of the family, providing for their own support and for that of their children.

There was a contradiction, a mismatch between actual social behaviour and the value system, between reality and the way it was represented. The man continued to be represented as the head of the family even when he was away from home or unemployed. The woman, even if she was the one who supported the family, did not acquire awareness of her professional identity.

This value system was not modified during the course of the modern age. We have had to wait until the last decades of the 20th century to see significant changes. The growth in the female labour force which came about between the 17th and the 18th century and its increasing specialisation were not sufficient to recast the system of representation. The work of women continued to be unrecognised; it continued to be perceived as unstable, fluctuating, marginal: simply an addition to the income of the male head of the family, and hence it was less well paid. On the other hand, as we have seen, it was precisely these characteristics which allowed women to enter into competition with the male labour force, which was too rigidly controlled by the guild rules and limitations.

This value system could not change because giving recognition to female labour would have meant giving power to women not only in the work environment but also in the sphere of public power. And indeed, from the very beginning of professional training, the role differences were sanctioned on the base of sex. For males apprenticeship took place inside the urban guild corporations, in the master's shop, where a future career could be guaranteed. Girls on the contrary usually learned their trade outside the corporations, through informal channels, often from other female figures, starting with the mother: hence with no guarantee of future employment. But even those young women who, in some cities, could learn their trade within a guild corporation and became masters (*maestre*) had in any case lesser rights than their companions of the male sex: they did not have autonomy, they earned less, and above all, they were not represented in the governing structure of the corporation. Hence they were excluded from political power. And the precariousness, the subordination and the lack of recognition of female labour began to be constructed in the initial phase of professional training.

Female labour in *ancien régime* society was appreciated and rewarded only if it took place within the home, under the careful eye of the male sex, to be sure that it did not compete with male work and did not give power to the women. In Mediterranean countries guarding female sexual honour (and hence worries and care to avoid promiscuity between males and females) had only the effect of reinforcing the stereotype of domestic work as the only form of work appropriate to females. Women were supposed, first of all, to learn to be mothers of families. In primary schools, along with reading, writing, arithmetic and religion, girls learned "lavori donneschi" (womanly work): sewing, embroidery and other activities useful for the mother of a family.

In reality women carried out a great number of activities, within the home and outside of it. Extreme flexibility, not specialisation, characterised women's work. Let us conclude with the story of what a woman named Sabbatina did each day at the beginning of the 17th century. She was a widowed peasant woman who lived in the countryside near Bologna.

Accused of having had a baby conceived illicitly, and of killing it just after birth, Sabbatina told the judge exactly how she had spent the two weeks preceding her arrest. Her days are full of the most varied activities; even on holidays she has no rest. And her activities require hard work: she cuts hay and harvests grain; she tends silk worms and feeds and cares for domestic animals; she launders and bakes; she sews a shirt and does housework. What Sabbatina is trying to tell us, with her careful account of her days, is that she was so busy with all her different activities that she would not even have had the time to deliver a baby or to commit infanticide. [*See Source*]

SELECTED BIBLIOGRAPHY

Groppi A. (ed.), *Il lavoro delle donne*, Roma-Bari 1996.

Hufton O., *Donne, lavoro e famiglia*, in N. Zemon Davis, A. Farge (eds.), *Storia delle donne dal Rinascimento all'età moderna*, Roma-Bari 1991.

Lombardi D., *Povertà maschile, povertà femminile. L'ospedale dei Mendicanti nella Firenze dei Medici*, Bologna 1988.

Malanima P., *La fine del primato. Crisi e riconversione nell'Italia del Seicento*, Milano 1998.

Niccoli O., *Storie di ogni giorno in una città del Seicento*, Rome-Bari 2000.

SOURCE

Testimony of Sabbatina, accused of infanticide:

La detta domenica [...] fui a Bagnarola a messa con l'Orsona; vista la messa ritornai seco a casa sua et desinamo, et poi ce mettessimo a sfrascare li folicelli [staccare i bozzoli dalle frasche di gelso alle quali erano attaccati], et questo facessimo tutta la domenica.

Il lunedì poi e il martedì detta Giacoma [Orsona] andò a Bologna ogni giorno a vendere li folicelli, et io restai sempre in casa ad haverli cura di casa et governarli le bestiole et la famiglia, et l'istesso feci il mercordì, che lei andò a Budrio a riscotere della tela et per altri suoi servitii.

Il giovedì poi venni a casa da mia madre, con la quale mi trattenni sino al sabato a matina, che in detto tempo cusei una camisia di donna Catalina Vignola moglie di barba [= zio] Matthia a Bagnarola, et agiutai anco a governare li bigatti [= curare i bachi da seta] a quella nostra vicina, quando n'avevo l'asio [= la comodità]; et il sabato ritornai a Bagnarola a riportare detta camisia alla Vignola, et me ne tornai la sera pure da mia madre.

Et la domenica a matina che ieri fece otto giorni andai a messa a Santa Francesca alla Riccardina, et vista la messa, tornata a casa da mia madre magnai un poco di pane, et poi me ne andai a casa della detta Giacoma Orsona, dove mi trattenessi tutto il giorno, che gli agiutai a fare l'erba per le sue bestiole, et poi restai seco la sera et dormei seco.

Et il lunedi stetti pure con lei et gli agiutai a lavare la bucata, et vi stetti la notte ancora, et con noi ci fu anco donna Angela non so de' quali, che era vedova et si è fatta sposa, et è sua vicina.

Et il martedi seguente la matina gli agiutai a fare del pane, et poi il giorno gli aiutai a mete-re, et la notte perché mia madre era venuta a stare a casa sua ad Azzovino, andai a dormire con mia madre nel medesimo letto suo.

Et il mercordi a matina levatami a bon'hora me ne andai a casa di Vincenzo Spisani in Viduro et gli aiutai a metere, et la sera me ne tornai a casa a dormire con mia madre.

La matina seguente che fu il giobia [= giovedi] ritornai pure a metere con detto Vincenzo, et ci stetti tutto il giorno et il venerdi, che quelli due giorni restai anco a dormire a casa sua, et dormei con sua moglie Giulia et Angelica sua figliola in un istesso letto.

Et il sabato stetti pure ad agiutare a metere, et la sera me ne venni a casa et dormei la notte con mia madre, et hiermatina levatami me ne andai a messa a Viduro, et poi andai a casa del-l'istesso Vincenzo Spisano, desinai con loro et poi ci mettessimo a legare il grano; et mentre stavamo legando il grano si arrivò il massaro et quell'altri huomini et mi menorno da vostra signoria.

...That Sunday I was at Bagnarola at mass with Orsona, after mass I returned with her to her house and we dined, and then we began to detach the silk cocoons from the mulberry leaves and that's what we did all Sunday.

Monday then and Tuesday the said Orsona went to Bologna each day to sell the cocoons, and I remained at home in order to take care of the house and to take care of the animals and the house, and I did the same Wednesday, while she went to Budrio to get payment for the cloth and for other services she had performed.

Thursday then I went to my mother's house, and stayed with her until Saturday morning, and while I was there I sewed a shirt for Mrs Catherine Vignola, wife of uncle Matthia at Bagnarola, and I also helped to take care of our neighbour's silkworms, and I returned in the evening to my mother's house.

And Sunday morning that was 8 days before yesterday, I went to mass at Saint Francis of the Riccardina, and after the mass, I went back to my mother's house and ate some bread; then I went to Giacoma Orsona's house where I stayed all day and I helped her to cut grass for her animals, and then I stayed there to sleep.

And Monday I was with her and I helped wash the clothes and I stayed all night and with us there was lady Angela of I don't know who, who was a widow and got married, and is her neighbour.

And the following Tuesday in the morning I helped her make bread, and then during the day I helped her harvest and the night because my mother had come to her house at Azzovino I went to sleep with my mother in the same bed.

And Wednesday in the morning I got up early and went to Vincenzo Spisani's house at Viduro and I helped harvest and in the evening I went home to sleep with my mother.

The next morning that was Thursday I returned to harvest with Vincenzo and I stayed the whole day and Friday that those two days I stayed to sleep at his house and I slept with his wife Giulia and his daughter Angelica in the same bed.

And Saturday I also stayed to help harvest and the evening I came home and slept with my mother and yesterday I got up and went to mass at Viduro and then to the house of

Vincenzo Spisani , I dined with them and then we started to tie up the grain and while we were tying up the grain the *massaro* came with the other men and brought me here to your Lordship.

SEE PLATE 7

A Gendered Reading of Conduct Books

Marja van Tilburg

Rijksuniversiteit Groningen

Aan het einde van de achttiende eeuw doen zich een aantal veranderingen voor in de adviesliteratuur voor jongvolwassenen. Deze wijzigingen betreffen zowel de inhoud als de stijl van dit type adviesboek. De boeken geven nieuwe gedragsregels, die lezers moeten voorbereiden op hun toekomstige verantwoordelijkheden. Deze regels worden verder op een specifieke, retorische wijze gepresenteerd, waardoor lezers als het ware worden gedwongen de gegeven adviezen op te volgen. Door deze veranderingen wordt het vormende karakter van dit genre versterkt.

Genoemde wijzigingen houden verband met twee belangrijke ontwikkelingen in de Verlichting. Deze zijn allereerst ingegeven door Rousseau's visie op adolescentie. Ook dragen ze het stempel van het debat over de 'natuur' van de vrouw.

Hoe maken auteurs van adviesboeken gebruik van de nieuwe visies op de jeugd en de vrouw om jongvolwassenen te disciplineren? Om deze vraag te beantwoorden wordt met name ingegaan op de presentatie van de adviezen. Immers, uit de verwoording van de regels kunnen impliciet gelaten opvattingen betreffende adolescentie en gender worden gedistilleerd.

Qua stijl verschillen adviesboeken voor jonge mannen én die voor jonge mannen en jonge vrouwen met gidsen voor jonge vrouwen. In de boeken voor jonge mannen wordt slechts één stijl gehanteerd, en wel de nieuwe, vormende stijl. Adviesliteratuur voor jonge vrouwen geeft daarentegen meerdere stijlen te zien: in de bespreking van seksualiteit en partnerkeuze kan de nieuwe stijl worden aangetroffen, terwijl in de behandeling van andere onderwerpen heel andere manieren van presenteren zijn toegepast.

Om deze verschillen in presentatie te illustreren, worden de adviezen betreffende seksualiteit en werk besproken. De bespreking van seksualiteit in adviesboeken voor mannen komt wat inhoud en stijl betreft overeen met die in boeken voor vrouwen. In beide gevallen wordt seksualiteit aan de orde gesteld in het kader van de partnerkeuze. Daarbij wordt een goede partnerkeuze gesteld tegenover een slechte. Door middel van analogieën en contrasten wordt lezers duidelijk gemaakt dat een wederzijdse seksuele aantrekkingskracht aan de basis ligt van elke partnerkeuze. Seksuele aantrekkingkracht is geen probleem, zolang deze een kritische beoordeling van de toekomstige partner niet in de weg staat. Voor het maken van zo'n beoordeling ontvangen lezers duidelijke richtlijnen.

De bespreking van taken en verantwoordelijkheden in de gidsen voor mannen verschilt van die in de gidsen voor vrouwen. Adviezen betreffende de werkkring in de boeken voor mannen geven hetzelfde patroon te zien als die betreffende seksualiteit: een gedisciplineerde levensstijl wordt gesteld tegenover een luie en hedonistische. De goede levensstijl impliceert dat alle tijd wordt benut en dat zoveel mogelijk tijd wordt besteed aan werk. Om lezers tot discipline te brengen, wordt hen een reeks van concrete regels betreffende tijd en werk opgelegd. De bespreking van werkzaamheden in de adviesliteratuur voor vrouwen geeft een ander beeld te zien. Daarin wordt door middel van metaforen en metonymieën verband gelegd tussen huishouden, schoonheid, deugdzaamheid en vrouwelijkheid. De indruk wordt gewekt dat degene die huishoudelijke werkzaamheden verricht mooi, deugdzaam én vrouw is.

Uit deze vergelijking komen de effecten van de verschillende stijlen duidelijk naar voren: jongvolwassen mannen worden gevormd tot zelfstandigheid en verantwoordelijkheid. Jonge vrouwen worden op het *vlak van de partnerkeuze eveneens gevormd tot verantwoordelijkheid, maar op alle andere terreinen tot vrouw.*

Op het moment dat voor de eerste keer in de westerse geschiedenis de emancipatie van vrouwen wordt bepleit, pogen de auteurs van adviesliteratuur voor jonge vrouwen hun lezeressen over te halen aan de traditie rolverdeling vast te houden en huisvrouw en moeder te worden.

Marja van Tilburg has studied history at the Rijksuniversiteit Groningen, the Netherlands. After briefly teaching history at secondary schools, she has joined the Department of History and International Organizations of the same university. Since 1995 she is a member of the board of the Center of Gender Studies of the Faculty of Arts. Her PhD. thesis addresses sexuality and gender in Dutch conduct books. It is entitled *Hoe hoorde het? Seksualiteit en partnerkeuze in de Nederlandse adviesliteratuur 1780-1890* (Amsterdam 1998). At present she is engaged in teaching cultural history of the early modern period and is preparing research on the reception of cultures of the Pacific in 18th century Europe from a gender perspective.

Everybody is acquainted with conduct books from his or her own experience; everyone has consulted one at some point in life [1]. For instance, most of us have certainly opened an etiquette book to learn how to behave in a specific situation, or read some guide book to get advice on handling certain problems – like Umberto Eco's well-known guide to writing a thesis [2]. If someone has not actually used an advice book, he or she will be familiar with the format, because of the many magazine articles and television programs that give advice on all sorts of issues. From these examples we might infer that advice literature is a recent phenomenon. This, however, is not the case. Since the early days of the printing press, conduct books have been published. From the start, different types of conduct books have been developed, according to content and intended readership. Some books discussed only one topic for a general public, as *Il libro del cortegiano* (1528) explaining the rules of conduct at courts, while others addressed issues relevant to specific groups, like marriage manuals giving couples guidelines for family life.

This article is based on conduct books for young persons from the age of fifteen to their early twenties. This type of conduct book has also been developed in the early 16th century. Its format has remained the same for a long period of time. Erasmus' book for young males, *De civilitate morum puerilium* (1530), was reprinted over and over again, for more than two hundred years. At the end of the 18th century, however, some major changes in the genre are noticeable. Suddenly, conduct books for young adults focus on the future responsibilities of young persons, whereas they used to concentrate on immediate concerns of young people – like going out and making friends. Besides, these books present the guidelines in a style which is very different from the matter-of-fact presentation of earlier times. They make readers believe that the distinction between good and bad is a clear-cut one and that any transgression of the rules will lead to disaster. As a result, the guides for young adults of the late 18th and 19th centuries are far more compelling than the earlier ones.

These changes in the genre reflect two important cultural transformations in Enlightenment Europe. The one which bears most on our subject matter is the changed perception of youth. Rousseau's concept of adolescence is clearly discernible in the conduct books for young adults. Furthermore, the debate concerning the 'true nature' of woman leaves its mark on the advice literature. New concepts of youth and femininity are, of course, developed in debates among *philosophes* of the Enlightenment. They are, however, not merely copied by the authors of advice books. They are used – deliberately and purposefully – and are changed in the process, as we will see.

How does the notion of adolescence affect the conduct books for young adults? Does the debate on the sexual identity of women influence the conduct books for young women? These two questions really amount to one: how do the authors of conduct books use the concepts of adolescence and femininity to discipline young adult men and women? This question will be answered after an analysis of both the content and the style of the conduct books. The analysis will focus mostly on aspects of style, because especially in the presentation of the guidelines the ideas of the authors concerning adolescence and gender come to the fore.[3]

THE NEW, SUGGESTIVE STYLE

As already mentioned, in the conduct book for young adults of the late 18th and 19th centuries the guidelines are phrased in a specific style. This style results from the systematic use of certain narrative strategies. Before I point out these strategies, I will give an example. The citation is taken from an original Dutch conduct book and discusses the pleasures of wining, dining and womanising (Fig. 1).

> I have known a young man, who, because of his graceful and appealing appearance, was respected by everyone and loved by many. The blush of innocence coloured his cheeks, while his honourable parents took pride and joy in the strength of his body and his thriving health, in his penetrating mind and his more than average competence. To continue his vocational training, he left his parental home. Only look, a few years later, I met him, unexpectedly, in another town. He addressed me, as an old friend of his father; but it was with difficulty that I recognised him. With pale cheeks, hollow and deep-set eyes, he stood before me. To make a long story short: it was lust that, now, made him incapable of any useful occupation in which he used to take pleasure. It was lust, which caused him to suffer the most terrible pains and griefs of the body, and the most excruciating agonies of the soul. It was lust, which made him despicable in the eyes of every sensible and virtuous person, despicable in the eyes of God; until he finally, persisting in the evil, which was already rooted in him too deeply, suffered the most shameful death [4]. [See Source]

In this example all the narrative strategies, which are used over and over again, are put into play. The first one I want to point out is the creating of contrasts. This can be seen in the way the later, depraved lifestyle is opposed to the initial, virtuous one. The second strategy builds upon the first one. It is the transformation of the created contrasts into opposi-

HANDBOEK
VOOR, OF
GIDS DES GEDRAGS
VAN
JONGE LIEDEN,

UITGEGEVEN DOOR DE
MAATSCHAPPIJ:
TOT NUT VAN 'T ALGEMEEN,

Te AMSTERDAM, bij
CORNS. DE VRIES, HENDK. VAN MUNSTER EN ZOON
EN
JOHANNES VAN DER HEY EN ZOON.
1823.

Fig. 1
The frontispiece of de Wal's
Handboek published in
Amsterdam in 1823.

tions between good and evil. This can be detected in the phrasing: the first one is depicted as antisocial, unhealthy, and leading to a certain death, whereas the latter is portrayed as virtuous, prosperous and strong. The third and last strategy I want to discuss is of a different kind. It results from a specific way of positioning fictional characters, staged as an example for the reader, in a specific social setting. The persons are situated as independent, autonomous and not accountable to anyone. It is suggested that the person can do as he or she pleases. This strategy is also shown in the text: the young man is pursuing his vocational training away from home, in another town.

Marja van Tilburg

These narrative strategies have specific effects on the reader. The first two strategies — the creating of contrasts and the transforming of contrasts into normative oppositions – suggest to the readers that the advice is not a guideline, but a norm. The last one gives the impression that the reader must stick to the rules, and that nobody will make sure he or she is following them.

From the combined effect of the narrative strategies, it is clear that these strategies are used purposefully. In this way, the authors admonish young readers to take responsibility for their behaviour. By systematically doing so, they educate readers to adulthood.

ADOLESCENCE

The new style of the conduct book for young adults developed in response to Rousseau's concept of adolescence. This can be deduced from the many references to youth in the guidelines. From every reference it becomes evident that the authors' vision of youth is similar to that of Rousseau.

In *Émile ou l'éducation* (1762) Rousseau describes how boys in the last phase of childhood become prone to competition and engaged with the other sex. He depicts these inclinations as innate drives. He attributes both impulses specifically to young men. Basically, he names aggression and sexuality as characteristics of the male sex during adolescence. This concept of youth differs from the one of the early modern period, because it ascribes specific inclinations to young persons. During the 16th and 17th centuries youth was not supposed to have specific emotions. They were only supposed to have lesser control over their impulses than adults have.

The authors of the conduct books ascribe similar characteristics to young adult males as Rousseau did. The authors mention traits and faults of youth, albeit in an indirect way. In the phrasing of the guidelines they mention the tendency of youth to seek danger, to risk health - even life. Between the lines they suggest that this impulse stems from the desire to stand out in the crowd. An original Dutch conduct book, for instance, confronts readers on this issue, while explaining that dangerous behaviour stems from "the desire to gain approbation, respect or praise" [5].

The authors also refer to the attraction of sensual pleasures for young men. They address readers as having a special interest in entertainment, feasting and meeting members of the other sex. Some of them speak openly about this impulse towards partying and womanising. The Swiss minister Zschokke, for instance, warns readers "of all impulses of nature, which are developed at this age, none is so threatening to one's peace of mind, as the passion for the other sex" [6].

Furthermore, from the phrasing of these remarks we can infer that the tendencies towards competing and womanising are considered as drives. By calling them 'passion' the authors point out the impulsive and passionate aspects. These examples show that the authors of conduct books share Rousseau's perception of adolescents.

As mentioned above, Rousseau developed the concept of adolescence in order to describe the development of young men towards adulthood. Because of this, adolescence is a gender-specific concept. At this point, however, the authors of the conduct books part with Rousseau. They suppose that young women go through an adolescent phase as well as young men. In the books for young women they refer to specific traits in adolescent women. Besides, they ascribe the very same inclinations to women as to men, namely competition and a lively interest in the other sex. The first one leads women to spend too much time and money on their appearance, as the well-known author of moralistic literature Mrs. Ellis explains to her readers [7]. The second one induces women to become intimate with members of the other sex. Furthermore, these tendencies are clearly conceived of as drives. The Dutch author and publicist Loosjes, for instance, admonishes his female readers to be careful and not to give in to their "youthful passion for the other sex" [8] (Fig. 2).

Fig. 2
The frontispiece from A. Loosjes' *De vrouw in de vier tijdperken haars levens,* published in Harlem in 1809.

DE
VROUW
IN DE
VIER TIJDPERKEN
HAARS LEVENS
DOOR
A. LOOSJES P.z.
MET PLATEN.

TE HAARLEM
BIJ A. LOOSJES P.z.
MDCCCIX.

As these examples show, the authors of conduct books think of adolescence in women in similar terms as they do of adolescence in men.

Although Rousseau thinks adolescents are male, the authors of advice literature think adolescents can be both male and female. By broadening the concept of adolescence to include women, the latter have made it possible to educate women in the same way as young men. Later on, we will see if they actually have made use of this opportunity.

GENDER

In Enlightenment Europe, not only the traditional vision of youth, but also the traditional notion of femininity is challenged. In the second half of the 18th century both women and men demand equal opportunities for women in the worlds of literature, science and politics. Many women actually participate in the debate on society and the quest for knowledge in the Republic of Letters. This struggle for emancipation triggers off a debate on the 'true nature' of women. In this discussion, some *philosophes* argue that the physical differences between the sexes should not carry so much weight as to exclude women from the realms of politics, science and literature. Others, as Rousseau, argue that the body determines all aspects of women. This last group construes a sexual identity for woman, which is opposite as well as complementary to that of man. In this discussion it is implied that women's place in society should be different from that of men: women ought to take care of home and family, while men should engage themselves in the public sphere.

Just as the concept of adolescence influences the conduct book for young adults, so the debate on the sexual identity of woman leaves its mark on the advice literature. To begin with, the debate leads to the publication of conduct books for young adult women, well as of books for young men and young women. These two types of books are a new phenomenon; the conduct book for young adults of the 16th and 17th centuries was intended for young males. This debate leaves its mark on the contents of these publications as well. This influence is diverse, regarding content as well as style. So, it can not be pointed out easily.

In order to find out what views on gender and adolescence the authors of conduct books hold, it is necessary to make an analysis of the style of the books.[9] Regarding style, there is an important difference between the conduct books for young men and for young men and women on the one hand, and of books for young women on the other hand. The books for males are of one piece: from cover to cover they show the narrative strategies of the new, educating style. In the books for females the advice is presented in many different ways. Changes of style relate to the subject matter. The educating style is used in case sexuality and marriage is discussed; other styles, featuring other narrative strategies, are chosen in case other topics are discussed.

In order to illustrate the different ways of presenting guidelines in the advice literature, I will go into the way in which sexuality and work are discussed.

SEXUALITY

As mentioned in the introduction, the conduct books of the late 18th and 19th centuries aim to prepare readers for adulthood. The last step towards adulthood for both men and women is marriage. Because of this, the choice of a partner is the most important decision young adults face. Since according to bourgeois ideology both men and women are free in their choice, males and females are equally responsible for the choice they make. As a consequence, in the chapters concerning marriage young males as well as young females are addressed in the new, educating style.

Sexuality is an important theme in the chapters concerning the choice of a marriage partner. In these, a contrast is created between a good choice of partner and a bad one: a good choice of partner is based on affection and respect, a bad one on sexual attraction. In the phrasing of both choices, it is made evident that the good one will result in a long and happy marriage, the bad one in an extremely unhappy one. This opposition reminds one of the dichotomy between mind and body, which is still deeply rooted in the Christian culture of the late 18th and 19th centuries. However, a careful analysis of the contrasts and analogies used by the authors shows that sexual attraction is considered a component of a good choice of partner [10]. An example of a guideline for the choice of partner, in which the phrasing suggests that sexual desire is allowed for, can be found in a book for young men and women written by the German minister Voigt. According to his advice "true love [is] mutual respect, based on inner qualities, which unites with sensual pleasure" [11].

Another example stems from a conduct book for men of the Dutch author Loosjes. In this book, the author plays with analogies and contrasts to convey the message. Firstly, he creates an analogy in order to depict sexual attraction as 'natural': "From the insect […] to the enormously big whale, in all [creatures] this passion is implanted […] man, as an animal occupant of this earth, shares this passion, this inclination".

Then, he makes a contrast between man and animal. In human beings, sexual attraction unites male and female in marriage: "so far as history books reach, and according to statements of explorers on peoples who are still in the state of nature, man differs (with very few exceptions, which are not worth mentioning) in this respect from all other occupants of the earth" [12].

By describing a good choice of a partner in this way, the author places sexual attraction at the cutting edge of nature and culture: sexuality is natural – because all creatures share it. In order to qualify as human, however, sexual desire must be satisfied in the cultural institution of marriage

Since the authors consider mutual sexual attraction a part of love and marriage, their guidelines on the choice of partner allow for sexual desire. As Loosjes tells readers of his conduct book for males: "…he does not want take from the delights, [brought] to the senses [by] these charming attractions of the body, and to the mind such enchanting graces of the soul, which are so fused that the cleverest mind cannot separate them, just as he cannot show the tie between body and soul" [13] (Fig. 3).

Such remarks are not reserved for the male sex. The same author acknowledges in his conduct book for females: "The natural inclination of the sexes towards each other, [even con-

DE
MAN
IN DE
VIER TIJDPERKEN
ZIJNS LEVENS
DOOR
A. LOOSJES P.Z.
MET PLATEN.

TE HAARLEM
BIJ A. LOOSJES P.Z.
MDCCCIX.

Fig. 3
Frontispiece of the conduct
book for young men by A.
Loosjes, *De Man in de vier
Tijdperken zijns levens.*

sidering] how civilisation has changed the original passion, is too strong not too inspire the hearts of persons of both sexes" [14].

From the discussion of the good choice of partner and the actual rules of conduct on the same subject, it is evident that sexual attraction is not a problem in itself, that sexual desire only demands careful management. The authors advise their readers on this. The Dutch pedagogue Barbara van Meerten-Schilperoort recommends that her female readers monitor their feelings and desires on a regular basis. When they detect an inclination for someone, they must ask themselves if this person is "worthy of her special attention [...] ask yourself, if the gifts of the heart and mind, of respect for religion and virtue, his goodness of character attracted you to him'. [If this is not the case, she ought to] pull the weak germ out of the heart" [15].

Such guidelines are accompanied by advice to socialise with persons of the other sex, even striking friendships with some of them. The authors explain to readers how they might benefit from such relationships: a more cordial, intimate friendship with members of the other sex prepares one for marital relations in later life. To round off their discussion on the place of sexuality in the choice of a partner, the authors give guidelines which should help to curtail sexual desire. These concern the diet, the use of alcohol, etc. and are similar to the ones given in the conduct books of the 16th and 17th centuries.

This kind of advice on managing sexual desire is typical of the late 18th and 19th centuries conduct books. All these explanations and rules are aimed at guiding young adults to a choice of partner, balancing the demands of society and personal preference.

WORK

In order to prepare youth for adulthood, the authors pay a lot of attention to their future responsibilities. According to the authors, these responsibilities amount to one: their future roles as husband and wife. So, young men must learn a trade in order to become solid providers for their families; young women must learn to manage a household. Although both men and women have to learn how to perform a certain task, the rules of conduct stimulating or urging them to do this differ. More importantly, the presentation of the rules for men and that of the rules for women diverge even more. In this paragraph I will examine the guidelines for males, in the next those for females.

The chapters on learning a trade are written in the new, educating style. So, first of all, a contrast is created between the good lifestyle and the bad one. The good life consists of hard work during the day and rest in the evenings, the bad one of indulging in drinking, partying and womanising. Of course, the good lifestyle will bring enduring happiness, the bad one dissatisfaction, sickness, and death.

These general remarks are followed by specific guidelines in order to get young men accustomed to a disciplined lifestyle. The authors start by making their readers aware of time. They point out how time flies, how much of it is taken by the necessities of life - eating, sleeping - and by social obligations - such as family visits and social calls. This overview comes down to one lesson: how little time is left to dispose of freely. The message is clear: time that is not put to use is lost. Not doing something, "is like living without enjoying life, to see the sun, without admiring it" [16].

This warning is followed by guidelines to help young men make use of time. The first instruction is to bring order to their life: young men must spend the day working and the evening resting – in order to restore themselves physically and so prepare for the next day. In order to make full use of the daytime, they are taught to divide up the work in smaller tasks, prioritise them and set a date and time for all of them. In this way, they can put to use every hour, every minute of every day. Thus, the authors instruct young men to make use of time.

In the same, detailed way the authors instruct young men on learning a trade. They confront them with their future obligations as providers. They explain that only persons who are good at their trade can be sure to get and keep customers. In order to develop the necessary skills, they must work all the time. Most of all, they must give their full attention to every detail of their work.

The combined effect of the detailed instruction and the persuasive method of presentation will suffice to turn even guys with little talent for virtuousness into dutiful husbands and fathers.

HOUSEHOLD

The conduct books for young adult women do not prepare the readers for their future responsibilities as wife and mother, even though they are supposed to learn to manage a household. The authors hardly discuss housekeeping; they certainly do not write about domestic duties as skills that need to be learned. Instead, they write about the household in terms of relationships. The reader is told that by doing the job, she will bring happiness to the other members of the family. As the pedagogue Barbara van Meerten-Schilperoort writes: "husband or father or brother, [will], if only with a loving glance, thank you because their shirt is more shiny white and neater than that of any other person" [17].

Consequently, the discussion of housekeeping is hardly ever followed by guidelines for organising life in order to acquire the necessary skills. Only one author, Van Meerten-Schilperoort, discusses the importance of order in the household. Another one, Mrs. Ellis, writes on the need to make use of time. But they never relate order and time, whereas the combined rules for time and work make the instruction concerning work in books for young males so effective. As a result, even if authors address the subject of housekeeping, the advice remains extremely vague.

Even more telling is the phrasing of the sparse admonishments to perform domestic duties. The presentation is filled with metaphors and metonymies, usually depicting household as a flower, and suggesting that persons performing household tasks are as beautiful as the flower. Just as Van Meerten-Schilperoort does, when she tells her readers: "There is, my dear Mathilda, another pretty flower in the beautiful garland of maidenly virtues. She is domesticity" [18].

In this sentence the author uses of the word 'flower' as a metaphor for domesticity. By naming the flower 'pretty' and the garland 'beautiful', she indicates that domesticity is beautiful. The use of the word 'virtue' suggests that domesticity is something to strive for. By connecting the phrase 'pretty flower' with virtue, the author suggests that someone who is striving for a nice home life, and as a consequence is virtuous, is also beautiful.

Another example stems from a book by Mrs. Ellis. She describes the household as a "flower, whose sweet scent refreshes a passer-by". She goes on by telling of the wanderer who wants to know what flower smells so deliciously. It is only with difficulty that he finds out, because:

> he really has to look for the source of his pleasure. He finds her hidden in the green foliage; they may be less beautiful, then he expects, in terms of shape and colour; but, how welcome, is the memory of these flowers, as the cool evening breeze, once more, carries their sweet-scenting fragrances on its wings. In the same way, the humble virtues of the female character come to us and ask for our respect [19].

So, in the presentation, domestic work is referred to as a virtue or a flower. The readers are given the impression that housekeeping will make them either virtuous or pretty, or both. In this way, young women are invited to identify with domesticity. In this respect the first quote in this paragraph is telling. Van Meerten-Schilperoort names the garland of virtues – her metaphor for domesticity – 'maidenly'. In this way she brings home the message that in order to be a woman, one has to be a housewife.

CONCLUSION

In the conduct books for young adults of the late 18th and 19th centuries two major cultural transformations are at play. Firstly, the authors are inspired by Rousseau's concept of adolescence to develop a new way of approaching and advising young adults. A new, specific presentation of the guidelines should instil a strong sense of duty in youth. It should also guide them towards responsibility and autonomy. Also, the authors have moulded the original, gender-specific concept of adolescence to encompass women. They use the new, educating style when addressing young women as well as young men. Secondly, the authors are influenced by the debate on the role of women in society. In addressing young women, they make subtle references to femininity. In this way, they relate tasks and responsibilities to the sexual identity of women.

The concept of 'adolescence' as well as the debate on 'true nature' of women comes to the fore in the conduct books for young adults. Young males are addressed as adolescents in every aspect of their lives; they are educated to become dutiful and responsible adults. Young females are addressed as adolescents in the discussion of sexuality and marriage. They are educated towards adulthood in this area, because they have to carry responsibility for the choice of their marriage partner. In all other areas of life they are approached as women. On these topics, they are not disciplined to become good housewives, but are seduced to identify with a specific notion of femininity.

At the very moment women can free themselves from their traditional sexual role, the conduct books for young adult women try to keep readers in the same place as women occupied during the early modern period, namely in the home.

 NOTES

1 Thanks to Tjitske Ypma for her careful reading of the preceding draft of this text.

2 Eco U., *Come si fa una tesi di laurea*, Milano 1977. This guide is translated into many European languages.

3 In the phrasing of the advice the concepts the author has concerning adolescence or gender come to the surface of a text. An analysis of the phrasing can make notions that are left implicit, explicit. An analysis of style is called for, when gender is conceptualised as difference made between the sexes, rather than as sexual roles. The importance of approaching gender in research as difference between the sexes is explained by Joan W. Scott in her book *Gender and the politics of history*, New York 1988, pp. 28-50.

4 de Wal M.S., *Handboek voor, of gids des gedrags van jonge lieden*, Amsterdam 1823, p. 46.

5 Messchaert N., *Aan jongelingen, van een beschaafde opvoeding*, Gravenhage 1833, p. 17.

Marja van Tilburg

6 Zschokke H., *De weg ten leven. Huis- en handboek voor christelijke ouders en jonge lieden*, Deventer 1857. Adapted from: *Andachstbuch für die erwachsene Jugend bei ihrem Eintritt in die Welt*, Aurau 1819, p. 253.

7 Mrs. Ellis, *Vorming en bestemming der meisjes*, Utrecht 1846. Adapted from: *The family monitor. Part 2: The daughters of England: their position in society, character and responsibilities* (s.l. 1836), pp. 222-3.

8 Loosjes A. (ed) *De vrouw in de vier tijdperken haars levens*, Haarlem 1809, p. 147.

9 See note 3.

10 The reader must bear in mind that a liberal Protestantism holds sway in the Netherlands in this period of time. The conduct books discussed here are of liberal-Protestant orientation. More conservative Protestants and Catholics began emancipation in the course of the 19th century, but reached full emancipation only in the 20th century. Orthodox Protestant and Catholic conduct books were published in the wake of this process. So, orthodox Protestant books were published from the late 1830s; Catholic ones only in the second half of the 19th century, starting with marriage manuals between 1845 and 1875, followed by advice books for the youth at the very end of the century.

11 Voigt C.F.T., *De gevaren der jeugd. Een boek voor jongelingen en meisjes*, Amsterdam 1823. Translated from: *Die Gefahren der Jugend*, Leipzig 1804, p. 149.

12 Loosjes A. (ed), *De man in de vier tijdperken zijns levens*, Haarlem 1809, pp. 155-7.

13 Ibid., p. 159.

14 Loosjes A. (ed), *De vrouw*, p. 146.

15 van Meerten-Schilperoort A.B., *Woorden van moederlijke liefde aan mijne dochter Mathilda*, Amsterdam 1844. Adapted from: *Wörte mütterlicher Liebe an meine Tochter. Eine Gabe für christliche Jungfrauen. Aus dem Nachlasse der freifau Wilhelmine von Dehnhausen zu Grevenburg, geb. von Mengersen*, Frankfurt a.M. 1835, p. 203.

16 *De gids des jongelings in de zamenleving*, Haarlem 1845, p. 55.

17 van Meerten-Schilperoort A.B. , *Woorden van moederlijke liefde*, p. 130.

18 Ibid., p. 118.

19 Mrs. Ellis, *Pligt en roeping der vrouw. Een boek voor vrouwen en meisjes*, Amsterdam 1844. Adapted from: *The family monitor. Part 1: The women of England: their social duties and domestic habits*, s.l. 1836, p. 18.

 ## SELECTED BIBLIOGRAPHY

Norbert E., *The civilizing process*, 2 Vol., Oxford 1978-1982, translated from: *Über den Prozess der Zivilization. Soziogenetische und psychogenetische Untersuchungen*, Bern 1969.

Foucault M., *The history of sexuality*, 2 Vol., New York 1980, translated from: *Histoire de la sexualité*, Paris 1976-1884.

Laqueur T., *Making sex. Body and gender from the Greeks to Freud*, Cambridge, Mass. 1990.

Scott J.W., *Gender and the politics of history*, New York 1988.

Marja van Tilburg M. van, *Hoe hoorde het? Partnerkeuze en seksualiteit in de Nederlandse adviesliterauur, 1780-1890*, Amsterdam 1998.

SOURCES

The page from M.S. de Wal's *Handboek voor of gids des gedrags van jonge lieden*, Amsterdam 1823, cited in the text.

— 46 —

aanwijzen. Ik wil echter, uit deze menigte, flechts twee aanvoeren, en ik hoop, dat gij dezelve tot u-wen affchrik diep in het geheugen prenten zult.

Ik heb eenen jongeling gekend, die, door zijn bevallig en innemend voorkomen, bij een' ieder ge-acht en door velen bemind werd. De blos der on-fchuld verwde zijne wangen, terwijl zijne waar-dige ouders, in de fterkte van zijn ligchaamsgeftel en in zijne bloeijende gezondheid, in zijn doordrin-gend verftand en in zijne meer dan gewone kundigheden, hunnen roem en hunne vreugde vonden. Om zich verder op zijn beroep toe te leggen, verliet hij de ouderlijke woning. Maar ziet, weinige jaren daarna, ontmoette ik hem in eene andere ftad onverwacht weder. Hij fprak mij, als een oud en bekend vriend zijns vaders, aan; maar het was met moei-te, dat ik hem herkende. Met bleeke wangen, holle en diepe oogen, ftond hij daar voor mij; om kort te gaan: het was de wellust, die hem thans ongefchikt maakte tot eenigen nuttigen arbeid, welken hij voorheen met zoo veel lust verrigtte. Het was de wellust, die hem de verfchrikkelijkfte pijnen en fmarten naar het ligchaam, die hem de grievendfte folteringen aan zijne ziel lijden deed. Het was de wellust, die hem verachtelijk maakte in de oogen van elken weldenkenden en braven, verachtelijk in de oogen van God; totdat hij ein-delijk, volhoudende in het kwaad, hetwelk reeds te diep wortel bij hem gefchoten had, den fchandelijk-ften dood ftierf.

Ik heb eene jonge dochter gekend, die deugd-zaam en eerbaar leefde in het huis harer ouders. Haar vader was kastelein, in de uitoefening van welk beroep zij hare ouders behulpzaam was. Zestien jaren oud, was zij nog de hoop en de lust van haren braven vader en deugdzame moeder; zij was braaf en oppassend, zedig en kuisch, en de zaligfte genoegens zoude zij, in haren volgenden leeftijd, aan de hand eens waardigen echtgenoots hebben kunnen fmaken. Maar wat gebeurt er: een afgerigt wellusteling, die toevallig in dat huis zij-nen intrek genomen had, wist haar door zijne vlei-taal zoo te begoochelen, dat zijne woorden haar reeds welgevallig werden. Met eenen enkelen kus was

Voices of folly: stories of women and men in the Rome insane asylum (1850-1915)

Vinzia Fiorino

Università di Pisa

I moderni sistemi politici sono stati edificati sulla base di talune esclusioni assolutamente signi-ficative: donne, alienati, stranieri, bambini. Tutte queste categorie, in modo diverso, riman-davano ad elementi di disordine e di irrazionalità considerati incompatibili con i nuovi assetti sociali. Questo testo, basato su una fonte del tutto particolare, come la serie di cartelle clini-che conservate presso l'archivio del manicomio di Roma Santa Maria della Pietà e riguardanti il perio-do compreso tra il 1850 ed il 1915, cerca di specificare, attraverso la categoria di gender, i connotati culturali legati alle rappresentazioni dei soggetti malati di mente nella società romana di fine Ottocento e primo Novecento.

Chi è nella percezione sociale il soggetto folle? In altre parole, in base a quali parametri una società defi-nisce e reclude gli individui etichettandoli come folli e temibili? A quali elementi culturali, strutturali e di lungo periodo, si è fatto riferimento nella costruzione dei soggetti folli ed esclusi dall'area del diritto tout court?

Il processo di medicalizzazione della follia ha certamente cambiato i connotati del soggetto folle: questi non è più il marginale vagabondo, essenzialmente povero e bisognoso di assistenza, forse anche matto; a partire dal XIX secolo l'alienato è un soggetto che, sulla base di un nuovo sapere scientifico, presen-ta una serie di sintomi interni ad una data classificazione adottata da medici e psichiatri. Tuttavia, nonostante il sapere psichiatrico si sia posto come una innovazione assoluta nella individuazione e nella rappresentazione del malato di mente, attorno a questa figura riemergono tracce significative della cul-tura letteraria e folklorica tradizionale. L'ipotesi che viene infatti sviluppata è quella secondo cui la scienza psichiatrica, lungi dal rappresentare realmente una rottura con i tradizionali luoghi comuni sulla malattia mentale, nel momento stesso della sua edificazione, ha recuperato e sintetizzato luoghi impor-tanti delle rappresentazioni popolari della follia. Ricorrono, ad esempio, frequentemente le metamorfo-si animalesche, ossia uomini che credono di essere divenuti topi o donne che credono di essere state tra-sformate in serpenti; ed ancora uomini in lotta contro le innumerevoli tentazioni del male, donne con il diavolo in corpo. Attraverso queste rappresentazioni culturali, vengono pertanto esplicitati i conno-tati profondi di una umanità minore privata di ogni diritto ed esclusa dal contratto sociale.

Born in Palermo in 1964, Vinzia Fiorino received her PhD in *Histoire et Civilisation* at the European University Institute in Florence, Italy. At present she is doing research at the Department of Modern and Contemporary History of the University of Pisa. She is interested in the social history of psychiatry and female citizenship in France.

 Although the subject of folly and the ways it was described in Rome at the turn of the last century may at first seem far from the general theme of this book, it in fact deals with fundamental aspects which regard both the definitions of gender roles and the building of modern political systems. As is well known, the modern forms of political organisation presupposed a model of rationality which has affected not only the state structures themselves but also the actions and the essence of the citizens belonging to the national states. In other words, not only were the actions and the procedures of the state bureaucracies organised according to a principle of rationality, but states progressively imposed on their citizens collective behaviours which were similar, rational and predictable, insofar as they were functional to maintaining the same social structure. Furthermore, recognition of the rights and duties to which members of the community were entitled or obligated, and hence the very title of citizen, was constructed precisely on the basis of the rationality attributed to the single individual. From this point of view, the modern state, as it formed, has seen in melancholy, and more in general, in psychic suffering, one of the most dangerous social diseases, able to threaten the collective order itself [1]. To be even more specific, the study of the collective effort, constant and growing, to control social deviances and to enlarge the sphere of normality which politics needs in order to exist, has contributed strongly to showing us the deepest characteristics of the new state formation: on one hand impose a precise discipline and a precise social order has led to the consolidation of the power apparatuses of the state; on the other the effort to impose processes of disciplining and towards the introjezion of the same rule of collective behaviour, an area traditionally belonging to the moral sphere, has slowly subtracted space from the ecclesiastical hierarchy in favour of the lay state power [2].

There remain, in any case, some crucial questions: how was the state activity in favour of the control of dangerous and immoral behaviour articulated? Who according to the social perception were the mad? In other words, on the basis of what parameters does society define and shut up individuals, labelling them as mad and frightening? To what cultural elements, structural and constant over a long period, has reference been made in the construction of folly and the definition of those who because of their condition are entirely excluded from the area ruled by law?

My research is entirely based on a collection of clinical records, preserved in the historical archive of the insane asylum of Rome and it regards the period between 1850 and 1915. This specific kind of source has allowed me to investigate the real functioning of this 'total' institution, the identity of those shut up in it, the way in which the modern psychiatric categories met up with more traditional processes of social emargination, as well as the creation and perfecting of a particular corpus of theoretical knowledge, such as psychiatry, became an effective tool in the practice of social segregation.

First of all it is useful to clarify that the entire 19th century project regarding the management of mental illness was significantly different from social reality in *ancien régime* societies. The affirmation of psychiatric science, or rather the entire process of medicalization, has certainly changed the connotations of the categories of "folly", as well as the collective perception of normality and of psychic suffering; above all the general picture presents a historical divide respect to the management of madness in *ancien régime* societies. The follow-

Fig. 1
Drawing by a young woman inmate of the Hospital of St. Maria della Pietà, in Rome, end of the 19th century. The caption reads: "It's just! that I enter the insane asylum I cannot have fun as I would like and I sigh…".

ing are, in my view, the most meaningful changes introduced from the first half of the 19th century on:

1) As regards reclusion in the asylum, in the course of time, precise bureaucratic procedures are formalised which foresee the intervention of a doctor to certify that the illness is real and that reclusion is necessary; a certificate made out by the police or the mayor confirming that the person must be taken urgently to the asylum; and later (from 1838 in France and from 1904 in Italy) the judgement of a magistrate to guarantee the correctness of the entire procedure – which took something very precious away from the subject, his or her personal freedom [3].

2) the process of medicalization has as its premise furthermore the definition of "medical-psychiatric knowledge", that is, a store of knowledge capable of interpreting and inserting within specific classifications certain of the symptoms described by the patients.

3) A new element, peculiar to 19th century society, regards the development of a profes-sional corporation of medical psychiatrists: they were the true protagonists of the spread of the practice of reclusion because they widely divulged the idea that through reclusion itself madness could be cured.

4) In contrast to earlier centuries where, in almost all cases, the mentally ill were shut apart along with other categories of people receiving assistance, in general with paupers or in separate wards of general hospitals, from the 19th century on, there is a specific institution designed for this purpose: the insane asylum. And this is not all: in contrast to the general hospitals, it is believed that the institution itself is a therapeutic project. The therapeutic project consists in fact in the total management of the life of the patient: the rhythms and rites of his or her daily existence are entirely organised by the institution. The patients, thus objectified and entirely managed by the asylum mechanism, can, in the psychiatrists' intentions, again find the spatial-temporal categories and the direction of their existence, which had been lost because of the mental illness [4].

5) Finally, inside the asylums specific therapies were practiced for the treatment of folly or madness. These were the remedies which for almost the entire 19th century continued to be hot baths or sudden cold showers, or blood-letting and vomiting produced by various kinds of purges. From this point of view continuity with ancient therapeutics is complete; nonetheless in the second half of the 19th century all the experimentation which took place in the insane asylums was undertaken in a different framework respect to that of gen-eral medicine.

Here I will focus my attention on the distinctive traits of the mad individual as they emerge from the stories contained in the clinical records. I will examine then two aspects: the first follows the evolution which psychiatric discourse underwent, drawing away from a kind of symbiosis with religious tradition, which aimed at repressing all morally transgressive behaviours and moving towards a stronger link with the juridical tradition. In a later phase, in fact, the theme of individual responsibility, because of the obvious and practical implications with jurisprudence, acquires a central place in the process by which the psychiatrist identifies and represents the mentally ill person [5].

The second aspect that I will examine regards, instead, the representation of the dangerous being, shut up and deprived of all rights, as the fruit of a precise cultural operation within which we can easily identify *topoi* which are deeply rooted and easy to identify both in literary culture and in the folklore tradition. My hypothesis is, in fact, that psychiatric science, far from breaking with the traditional commonplaces on mental illness, at the very moment of its construction, recovered and synthesized important *topoi* of popular representations of mental disorder.

In the stories that we find in the "archives of folly" from the period from 1851 to, *grosso modo*, 1890, it is extremely difficult to untangle the knot that makes the individuals shut up in the asylum the result of a need for generic assistance, a behaviour which is generically immoral (both from the point of view of sexual behaviour and from that of aggressiveness) and the application of any kind of a psychiatric label. The following narration of mental disorder in a 36 year old peasant woman who was kept in the insane asylum for almost a year is typical:

> *Esiste realmente un disordine nelle di lei facoltà intellettuali, il quale può ripetersi da un esaltamento vitale degli organi generativi. L'istinto infatti della riproduzione si esprime in tutta la sua energia, tanto nei discorsi che negli atti osceni che la C. effettua, ond'è che volendo caratterizzare la specie della mania cui la medesime soggiace potrebbe definirsi per una mania erotica (…) che equivale a mania lasciva.*

> There truly exists a disorder in her intellectual faculties, which can repeat itself from an vital exaltation of the generative organs. The reproductive instinct in fact is expressed in all its energy, both in the discourses and in the obscene acts that C. performs, whence wishing to characterise the kind of mania which she is prey to, it could be defined as an erotic mania (…) which is to say a lascivious mania [6].

The descriptions are often stereotypes, such as "si denuda in pubblico" (she undresses in public), "invita gli sconosciuti al coito" (she invites people unknown to her to have sexual intercourse), "si alza le vesti innanzi ad estranei" (she pulls up her clothes in front of people she does not know), "proferisce parole laide"(she says filthy words): these are the signs that most often the 'alienists' utilised in order to legitimate the urgency of segregating the person, as also priests and prelates did when they asked that one of their parish members be recluded.

In a second phase, after the season of the alienists of the French tradition had come to an end and the positivistic culture and the organicism of the German tradition had spread,[7] psychiatrists started to focus their attention on the memory mechanisms, on the ability of the subjects to orient themselves in space and time, to the states of the inner consciousness, to discerning between a free conscience and one misled by illusion and hallucinations.

In examining the individuals' consciousness, the psychiatrists organised, exactly on the model of judges in trials for interdiction, a true interrogation which was supposed to determine the *real* degree of alienation. Among the most interesting of those registered in the clinical records I have examined is the one regarding a young Roman fruit and vegetable seller who had insulted a municipal guard:

1) Chi è il re e la regina?

2) Sa chi è il sindaco?

R. Quello che comanda al Campidoglio.

3) Una ragazza può stare con un uomo?

R. No è cattiva cosa.

4) Vuoi prendere marito?

R. No, voglio stare con i miei genitori.

Non sa dire cosa abbiano in comune un uccello e una farfalla, ma sa far di conto. Dimostra la sua animosità contro le guardie, che sono causa dei suoi malanni, l'istinto sessuale poco sviluppato, poco elevata la religiosità.

È una primitiva con impulsività delinquenziale.

Ha i genitori viventi, un fratello fu carcerato per oltraggio alle guardie. È inquieta con una zia e dice che questa la odia; va dicendo che è sempre in galera, che maltratta i genitori.

Ella racconta che un giorno questo tale la invitò a non infastidire lo zio, ella rispose non arrogantemente, questi allora la minacciò con la rivoltella, ma lei non si spaventò e lo minacciò con la bilancia che teneva in mano. Dice di non essere mai stata condannata per furto, ma accusata di furto e poi assolta; più volte invece fu condannata per oltraggio alle guardie. Orientata per il luogo, contegno corretto, tranquilla ed ubbidiente, si presta volentieri ai lavori nel reparto. Nega convulsioni, ma vertigini anche per i pesi che trasporta sulla testa [8].

1) Who is the king and the queen?

2) Do you know who the mayor is?

Answer: The one who commands in the Campidoglio [the Capitol]

3) Can a girl stay with a man?

Answer: No it's a bad thing.

4) Do you want to take a husband?

5) No, I want to stay with my parents.

She does not know what a bird and a butterfly have in common, but she knows how to do sums. She shows her anger against the guards, who are the cause of her troubles, the sexual instinct is little developed, the religiosity not very high.

She is a primitive with the impulsiveness of a delinquent.

Her parents are living, a brother was put in prison for insulting the guards. She is upset with an aunt, she says that her aunt hates her; she [the aunt] goes around saying that she [the girl] is always in jail and that she maltreats her parents.

She tells that one day this man told her not to bother her uncle, she answered not arrogantly, he then threatened her with a revolver, but she was not frightened and she threatened him with

Fig. 3
Catalepsy. Table XLVI,
Iconographie photographique de la Salpêtrière (Paris 1876-1880).

the scales she had in her hands. She says she has never been condemned for stealing but accused and then absolved of stealing; several times she has been condemned for insulting the guards. She is oriented as to place, her bearing is correct, calm and obedient, she works willingly in the ward. She denies having convulsions, although she has dizziness because of the weights she carries on her head.

A crucial aim of psychiatric action was to make behaviour conform to a general model, made manifest essentially in a regulated sexuality, in a balanced religious attitude, in respect for the common sense of modesty. The medical construction of the category of the mentally ill, however, although it did not abandon the stigma towards all forms of immorality, takes into consideration other parametres: control of one's person, responsibility for one's actions, as well as the ability to keep intact one's patrimony of ideas and memory. These appear, around the end of the century, to be the most important discriminating factors for identifying individuals considered mentally ill. In this sense, the semantic area of madness is drawn significantly closer to the definition given by law and jurisprudence.

As to the second theme we will examine, in order to show how the creation and definition of categories of pathologies was an operation of social construction, I will try to show how the categories elaborated contain cultural elements deeply rooted in popular traditions: the representations of madness which emerge from the clinical records reproduce, in fact, well-structured and easily identified *topoi* of folklore, and literary and religious culture. For example, there are many cases of animal metamorphoses, that is to say, men who thought they had become mice or women that thought they had become snakes, and men struggling with the infinite temptations of evil, and women with the devil in their body. These cultural representations contain such deep gender connotations that they express meanings which are much more ample than the sharply delimitated field of psychiatry.

The experience of mental illness, of the end of control over one's person, of the splitting of the ego, are expressed in the direct accounts of the protagonists or the transcriptions of the doctors and nurses, often through falling in states of deep panic. These are not simple and passing fears, but individuals that live in a continuous state of absolute confusion and terror. Among the images which recur most often to express those states of upset and distress, there often returns that of men transformed into mice: Gioacchino C. is an alcoholic, 34 years of age, without a fixed residence, several times recovered in the insane asylum, who says:

> *di essere vittima di una fattura, fattagli da un napoletano che gli strappò il cappello (...); afferma di avere avuto delle allucinazioni terrifiche. Una volta pare che abbia visto il demonio tutto nero di faccia, frequentissime sono state in lui le allucinazioni zoopsichiche, più frequente la visione di ratti, tanto è vero che egli ha creduto di essere diventato tale e di ciò è talmente impaurito che cercava di confessarsi, convinto che fosse arrivato l'ultimo giorno della sua vita.*

> that he was victim of a spell, made by a Neapolitan who took his hat from him; he says that he has had terrifying hallucinations. Once it seems that he saw the devil all black in the face, he has had very frequent zoo-psychic hallucinations, the most frequent is that of rats, so much so that he believed that he had become a rat and he was so terrified that he tried to make confession, convinced that it was the last day of his life [9].

Rats and, because of their similarity to rats, mice, were in past centuries vehicles of the plague and other diseases and for that reason too they have become symbols of danger and repulsiveness [10]. At the same time, in this context, they represent and synthesize the state of absolute abjection that the human being can reach, as is in reality the fact of becoming mad. Rats have been literary *topoi* too used to represent fear [11]: in the 17th century rats threaten and torture the imprisoned witch; in the eyes of the witch hunters the coherent diabolic group is composed of the witch and her rats. Literature offers us a conspicuous series of examples, many of which proove that there is a precise relationship of rats with witches [12]. Jules Michelet tells the story of Madeleine Bavent, a nun accused by her sisters of the monastery of Saint-Louis de Louviers of being a witch; she is recognised as a witch and hence condemned on 22 March 1643 by the ecclesiastical judge to the loss of her religious status and to perpetual imprisonment. A confession by Madeleine Bavent was written out by a Oratorian priest under her dictation in 1652, the year Madeleine died in the Hôpital generale of Rouen among the 'alienated'. This text, which has been considered a real precursor of the *roman noir*, the horror story, tells of Madeleine shut up in a damp cellar, where during the night she was disturbed by the coming and going of hungry rats, "the ones that eat your nose and your ears" [13]. Or William Shakespeare in *King Lear* has Edgar say that poor Tom, who is mad: "Poor Tom, that eats the swimming frog; the toad, the tadpole, the wall-newt, and the water; that in the fury of his heart, when the foul fiend rages, eats cow-dung for sallets; swallows old rat and ditch-dog; [...] But rats and mice amd such small deer / Have been Tom's food for seven long years" [14]. Let me note finally that the fear of the rats who crowd the prisons of *ancien régime* has great literary fortune: the marquess de Sade in his cell in Vincennes is afraid of the mice [15], just as Giacomo Casanova speaks of the promiscuousness with the rats as the most horrible part of his experience in prison [16].

Furthermore, *topoi* which are as classic as these for the representation of madness are the women who say that they feel the "devil in their body" and the men that tell of their unrelenting struggle with the infinite temptations of evil. Filomena R. is a woman of 40 years of age, born in Magliano dei Marsi (Aquila), already shut up in an insane asylum in Abruzzo, and thought to be afflicted by a 'hypochondriac' psychosis. The "psychic examination" contained in her clinical file is of great interest:

Ha atteggiamento fanciullesco, mimica esagerata. Racconta che è priva degli organi addominali e lo spazio è stato riempito da diavoli e serpenti che entrati dall'ano dove ne avverte l'ingresso da sensazioni dolorose, riescono dalla natura anche qui se ne accorge da sensazioni varie. Essa crede di avere tre ventri pieni di questi animali e così si spiega che quantunque essa mangi, pure non acquista in carne. Per il passaggio del suo respiro sente i diavoli che le dicono: tu non ti sei fatta godere dagli altri e ti godremo noi; ti abbiamo vinto, l'anima tua è in nostro possesso e tu non potrai più morire come gli altri. In passato ebbe pure allucinazioni visive, vedeva diavoli con le corna, le labbra rosse e vestiti da donna, che la invitavano a teatro, la vestivano da contessa e la guidavano per la strada.

L'anima sua ora è dannata, né ci sarà rimedio, solo per poter dormire dovrà o gettarsi al Ponte di Ripetta o strangolarsi con un laccio al collo.

Si lagna che da circa sei mesi non va di corpo e che nel ventre sono entrati i demoni. Questi demoni le dicono che la vogliono portare all'inferno e lì le manderanno rospi e serpenti. Ha allucinazioni visive a contenuto terrifico; vede teschi con gli occhi rossi contornato il tutto da serpenti che le soffiano attorno.

Talvolta ha una coscienza di una doppia personalità, asserisce che si sente la sensazione dell'io identica a quella che provava quando era in salute (...). Sente una voce che le dice: mettiti lunga per terra, chiama i preti che ti benedicono, non saranno buoni a niente perché noi ci siamo impadroniti di te. La paziente chiede che venga sezionata dai medici con la speranza che il diavolo ne esca.

Non si avvertono tremori di sorta. Le allucinazioni consistono nel fatto che si sente trasformata, cambiata dal capo ai piedi: la testa non è più la sua e al suo posto hanno messo una zucchetta, gli occhi sono andati a finire dentro il ventre e sono stati sostituiti con altri. I polmoni glieli hanno bruciati (...) si sente camminare dentro il corpo, bruciare.

Dovrà uccidersi per liberarsi di serpi e diavoli

She has childlike behaviour, her gestures are exaggerated. She tells that she has no abdominal organs and that the space has been filled up with devils and snakes which having entered her anus where she feels them enter because of painful sensations, they come out of her vagina and also here she feels various symptoms. She thinks that she has three bellies full of these animals and so she explains that although she eats she does not gain weight. For the passage of her breath she hears devils that tell her: you are not made to enjoy like the others and we will enjoy you, we have conquered you, your soul is in our possession and you will no longer be able to die like the others. In the past she also had visual hallucinations, she saw devils with horns, red lips and dressed like women, who invited her to the theatre, dressed her like a countess and drove her along the street.

Her soul is now damned, and there will be no remedy, only to be able to sleep she will have to throw herself off the Ripetta bridge or strangle herself with a noose around her neck.

She complains that for the last six months she has not defecated and that the demons have entered her belly. These demons tell her that they want to take her to hell and that there they will send her toads and snakes. She has terrifying visual hallucinations; she sees skulls with red eyes surrounded by snakes hissing around them.

Sometimes she is aware of a double personality, she states that she feels the sensation of an ego which is identical to that which she felt when she was healthy (...) She hears a voice which tells her: stretch out on the floor, call the priests to bless you, they will be good for nothing because we have taken control of you. The patient asks to be cut open by the doctors in the hope that the devil will come out.

There is no trembling of any kind. The hallucinations consist of the fact that she feels transformed from head to foot: her head is no longer hers and in its place they have put a little squash, her eyes have ended up in her belly and have been replaced with others. Her lungs have been burnt up (...). She feels walking inside her body, burning.

She will have to kill herself to be free of snakes and devils [17].

The contents of these records open a series of themes and problems of the greatest complexity [18]. The first interpretative hypothesis which I wish to consider is that of gender: around this representation of mental illness I believe in fact that we find coagulated the main characteristics which give profound insight into the ways of seeing and perceiving the female being. The image of the "devil in the body" communicates a cultural model in which the female body is electively the one chosen to be possessed by natural elements ("excess energies") or by supernatural entities: devils, divine powers and so forth. Possession by devils, as one of the variegated figurations of the divided ego, is in absolute continuity with the most obvious characteristics of weakness and fragility, with the easily "impressionable" or "suggestible" characteristics attributed to the female being. A "suggestible" entity can in fact be easily penetrated by other beings, it can be managed and made to act by others. Discourse on the female body in recounting the experience of illness and all the talk of "devils in the body" reveal a lack of sovereignty and ownership of women over their body, they draw a picture of a body which is to be or can easily be possessed; representations, these, that are well linked with the difficult path by which female individuality, the "maîtrise de soi" of the female individual has to be affirmed. These constructions reveal a representation of a divided ego, a vulnerability of the female body which is diametrically opposed to the psycho-physical unity of the modern individual [19].

For the hospitalised men, instead, diabolic possession is entirely exceptional: the demons continue obviously to be close presences; the men see the devils, when they see them they feel intense fear, they can believe that others see them transformed into demons, but they are rarely possessed by demons. More often, coherently with their more general social and juridical position, they can try to resist against the innumerable and subtle temptations of evil. Benedetto D. A. is affected by periodical maniacal excitement which justifies his con-

Vinzia Fiorino

tinual coming and going, in and out of the asylum (he was hospitalised, in fact, six times); here are some passages which recount his interior conflicts:

> *L'attuale forma morbosa è cominciata dallo scorso inverno: andò a confessarsi da un gesuita, il quale trovandolo assai disposto ai sentimenti religiosi, lo incoraggiò a proseguire nella buona via e col andare spesso a confessarsi da lui, che lo avrebbe fortificato contro ogni sorta di tentazioni, le quali lo avrebbero potuto far diventare un serpente, una vipera od altro animale. Per tema di ciò il giovane esagerò le sue pratiche religiose e in questi ultimi tempi trascurava il suo lavoro passando le sue giornate in tutte le chiese di Tivoli ed in tutti i santuari dei dintorni, occupato in preghiere e in penitenza. Giunse persino ad assentarsi da casa e rimaneva per le vie della città facendo preghiere e cantando le lodi di Maria e la Passione di Cristo: ciò durava fino alle 4 o 5 del mattino. Dormiva pochissimo e mangiava anche poco, in modo che l'infermo si era anche consumato.*

The present form of disease began last winter: he went to confess himself to a Jesuit, who finding him very well disposed to religious sentiments, encouraged him to follow the good path and to go to confession with him often, that thus fortifying him against every sort of temptations, which could have made him turn into a snake, a viper or some other animal. For fear of that the young man exaggerated his religious practices and in the most recent times he neglected his work, spending his days in all the churches in Tivoli and in all the sanctuaries in the area, busy with prayers and penitence. He even came to the point of not going home and staying on the streets of the city praying and singing praise of Mary and the Passion of Christ: that lasted until about 4 or 5 in the morning. He slept very little and ate very little, so that the patient was also rundown.
While in the asylum he is in a strait-jacket because he is agitated [20].

In conclusion, it seems useful to me to underline the importance of the deconstruction of some *topoi* on which precise representations of mental illness have been built. It seems to me in the first place evident that it is possible to question and re-discuss a widespread commonplace: that according to which the social construction of the category of "mental illness" has been effected exclusively on the basis of transgressive behaviour, scandalous and immoral, whereas instead it shows that it belongs to deeper cultural structures, often invisible and unconsciously shared. In the second place I believe that starting with enlightenment culture and the definition of the modern juridical framework, that is, founded on civil and political rights, an area of social exclusion has been drawn, evidently connected with the lack of rationality, the characteristics of which are deeply rooted in cultural traditions and which still must be investigated.

 NOTES

[1] These aspects are the centre of "classic" studies: Foucault M., Histoire de la folie à l'âge classique, Paris 1961; Elias N., Über den Process der Zivilisation, 1969; Dörner K., *Bürger und Irre. Zur Sozialgeschichte und Wissenschaftssoziologie der Psychiatrie*, Frankfurt a. Main 1969. Cf. also Finzsch N. - Jütte R. (eds.), *Institutions of Confinement. Hospitals, Asylums, and Prisons in Western Europe and North America, 1500-1950* Cambridge 1996.

[2] P. Schiera has studied these aspects; see: *Disciplina, disciplinamento*, in «Annali dell'Istituto storico italo-germanico in Trento», XVIII, 1992, pp. 315-34; *Melancolia e disciplina: considerazioni preliminari su una coppia di concetti all'alba dell'età moderna*, in Rota Ghibaudi S. - Barcia F. (eds.), *Studi politici in onore di Luigi Firpo*, vol. I: *Ricerche sui secoli*

XIV-XVI, Milan 1990, pp. 257-77; *Specchi della politica. Disciplina, melancolia, socialità nell'Occidente moderno*, Bologna 1999.

[3] See Farge A. - Foucault M. (eds.), *Le désordre des familles. Lettres de cachet des Archives de la Bastille*, Paris 1982 e Castel R., *L'ordre psychiatrique. L'âge d'or de l'aliénisme*, Paris 1976.

[4] See De Peri F., *Le origini dell'istituzione manicomiale e della scienza psichiatrica*, in «Società e Storia», a. II, n. 6, 1979, pp. 683-723; Id. *Il medico e il folle: istituzione psichiatrica, sapere scientifico e pensiero medico tra Otto e Novecento*, in Della Peruta F. (ed.), *Storia d'Italia*, Annali 7: *Malattia e Medicina*, Turin 1984, pp. 1057-1140; Pinel P., *Traité médico-philsophique sur l'aliénation mentale ou la manie*, Paris 1801.

[5] See Babini V.P., *La responsabilità nella malattia mentale*, in Babini V.P. - Cotti M. - Minuz F. - Tagliavini A., *Tra sapere e potere. La psichiatria italiana nella seconda metà dell'800*, Bologna 1982, pp. 135-98.

[6] Archivio Santa Maria della Pietà (abbreviated ASMP), Archivio Sanitario, *Cartelle Cliniche, Giacinta C.* - 1865.

[7] For a general introduction to Italian psychiatry, see. Stok F., *La formazione della psichiatria*, Rome 1981.

[8] ASMP, Archivio sanitario, *Cartelle cliniche, Luisa B.* - 1910.

[9] ASMP, Archivio sanitario, *Cartelle cliniche, Gioacchino C.* - 1902.

[10] Le Goff J. - Sournia J.C., *Les maladies ont une histoire*, Paris 1985..

[11] Berchtold J., *La peur des rats dans les récits d'emprisonnement, de Cyrano de Bergerac à Casanova*, in Berchtold J. - Porret M. (eds.), *La peur au XVIIIe siècle. Discours, représentations, pratiques*, Geneva 1994, pp. 99-119.

[12] See G. Ponnau, *La folie dans la litterature fantastique*, Paris 1990 and L. Feder, *Madness in Litterature*, Princeton 1980.

[13] See Michelet J., *La sorcière*, Paris 1862.

[14] W. Shakespeare, *King Lear*, Act III, Sc IV, ll. 132-143.

[15] De Sade F., *Lettres écrites de Vincennes*, Paris 1966.

[16] Casanova G., *Histoire de ma fuite de prisons de Venise*, Spoleto 1929 (orig. edn. 1787).

[17] ASMP, Archivio sanitario, *Cartelle cliniche, Filomena R. ved. R.* - 1902.

[18] See Goldberg A., *Sex, Religion and the Making of Modern Madness. The Eberbach Asylum and German Society (1815-1849)*, Oxford 1999 and Charuty G., *Le couvent des fous. L'internement et ses usages en Languedoc aux XIXe et XXe siècles*, Paris 1985.

[19] On these themes, the bibliography is very extensive. Here I will only indicate: Swain G., *L'âme, la femme, le sexe et le corps. Les métamorphoses de l'hystérie à la fin du XIXe siècle*, in «Le Débat», n. 24, 1983, pp. 107-27; Trasforini A., *L'isterica*, in T. Pitch (eds.), *Diritto e rovescio. Studi sulle donne e il controllo sociale. Quaderni "Dei delitti e delle pene"*, Naples 1987, pp. 257-73; Micale M.S., *Approaching Hysteria. Disease and its Interpretations*, Princeton-New Jersey 1995; Showalter E., *The Female Malady. Women, Madness, and English Culture (1830-1980)*, New York 1985; Ripa Y., *La ronde des folles. Femmes, folie et enfermement au XIXe siècle (1838-1870)*, Paris 1986. The long lasting conception that the female body is something fragile, open, easily penetrated is confirmed by the research carried out using oral sources by Pandolfi M., *Itinerari delle emozioni. Corpo e identità femminile nel Sannio campano*, Milan 1991.

[20] ASMP, Archivio sanitario, *Cartelle cliniche, Benedetto D.A.* - 1910.

Vinzia Fiorino

Sources

Clinical record of Filomena R., a woman of 40, born in Magliano dei Marsi (Aquila), classified as affected by hypochondriac psychosis and hospitalised for a year between 1902 and 1903 in the Rome insane asylum.

Ha tentato di buttarsi sotto il tram, crede che qualcuno la insegua.

Il padre è sano, ma alcoolista, la madre è morta quando era in tenera età, ha lavorato la terra, ha molti fratelli. Venne a Roma circa 10 anni fa a fare la domestica e servì presso diverse famiglie, ha cambiato spesso servizio per motivi futili. Nonostante lavorasse presso una famiglia, la sera andava a dormire dalle suore di S. Giovanni Decollato. Narra che la signora dove lavorava voleva darle per marito il figlio, e quando lei non volle per vendicarsi le fece la fattura. Cominciò a sentire un malessere generale, tremori, agitazione, la notte le comparivano le streghe che entravano come fiammelle e si trasformavano in gatti, papere, galline, e brutte facce che le facevano le boccacce. Sentiva delle voci che le dicevano che si fosse liberata, altre la insultavano. Il giorno andando per strada vedeva grande confusione, tanta gente che le andava intorno, la deridevano e la guardavano come fosse una ladra. Anche in Chiesa la urtavano, due la strinsero in mezzo a loro, un'altra persona la batteva sulla spalla dicendole: ricordati che sei segnata. Andò in Questura per il rimpatrio poi non volle più partire e quindi tentò di gettarsi sotto un tram. Fu condotta all'ospedale.

In manicomio ha tenuto un contegno stravagante: sta con una coperta in testa. È sempre sospettosa e diffidente, ha allucinazioni: sentiva la voce della madre che le diceva: salvati, liberati. Anche al manicomio essa è stata perseguita da tutti, dalle infermiere che le hanno gettato nel letto delle serpi viventi, dalle suore che le hanno fatto la fattura, ai medici che sono cattivi. Essa è destinata a soffrire quaggiù, ma essa farà penitenza, deve mangiare solo pane e acqua, ma non sa perché è così perseguitata. Vivaci i sentimenti religiosi.

Vede un'ombra nera che le balla davanti, sente muoversi il letto, non può trovare la pace della sua vita. Ha veduto parecchie volte la figura di un giovane che ella ama e che le ha parlato. Parla di questa sua affezione verso questo giovane che però ora non ama più, questa persona è forse il diavolo che l'ha affatturata. Talora parla di fatture che le hanno fatto, di spiritismo, essa tentò di combattere queste fatture pregando, ma non vi riesce. Le allucinazioni sono quasi tutte visive. Dice di voler morire.

She has tried to throw herself under the tram, she thinks someone is following her.

The father is healthy, but an alcoholic, the mother died when she was small, she has worked the land, she has many brother and sisters. She came to Rome about 10 years ago to be a domestic servant and she served in different families, she has often changed employer for futile motives. Notwithstanding that she worked for a family, at night she went to sleep with the Sisters of S. Giovanni Decollato. She says that the lady of the house where she worked wanted to give her her son for a husband, and when she did not want to accept, in order to revenge herself [the lady of the house] had a spell put on her. She began to feel a generally unwell, tremors, agitation, at night witches appeared to her that entered like little flames and transformed themselves into cats, ducks, hens and ugly faces which made faces at her. She heard voices that told her that she was free, others insulted her. During the day going along the street she saw great confusion, so many people around her, they derided her and looked at her as if she were a thief. Even in church they pushed her, two people pushed her between them, another person hit her on the shoulder saying to her: remember that you are marked. She went to the Questor's office to be sent back to her home, then she didn't want to depart any more and then she tried to throw herself under a tram. She was brought to the hospital.

In the asylum she has behaved extravagantly: she stays with a blanket over her head. She is always suspicious and diffident, she has hallucinations: she heard the voice of her mother saying to her: save yourself, free yourself. In the asylum too she has been persecuted by everybody, from the nurses who put live snakes in her bed, to the nuns who put a spell on her, to the doctors who are bad. She is destined to suffer down here, but she will do penitence, she must eat only bread and water, but she does not know why she is so persecuted. Her religious sentiments are lively.

She sees a black shadow that dances in front of her, she feels the bed move, she cannot find peace in her life. She has often seen the image of a young man that she loves and that has spoken to her. She speaks of her affection for this young man whom however she does not love any more and who perhaps has cast a spell on her. Sometimes she speaks of spells, of spiritism, she tries to fight these spells by praying, but she does not succeed. The hallucinations are almost all visual. She says she wants to die.

SEE PLATES 8-10

The female model and the reality of Roman women under the Republic and the Empire

Francesca Cenerini

Università di Bologna

In questo testo viene esaminata la condizione femminile in età romana, tenendo conto, in particolare, del modello ideale cui doveva uniformarsi la donna in età antica (moglie e madre devota), propagandato soprattutto dagli scrittori antichi, e la realtà della vita quotidiana quale si evince, soprattutto, dalle iscrizioni e dalle fonti giuridiche. Tali documenti ci attestano che, a fianco della duratura permanenza, a livello ideologico, di questo modello ideale, si verificò una indubbia "emancipazione" femminile ed una relativa conquista di spazi esterni al ristretto ambito domestico, soprattutto tra la fine dell'età repubblicana e i primi secoli dell'impero.

Francesca Cenerini teaches Social History of the Ancient World at the Faculty of Letters and Philosophy of the University of Bologna. From with the academic year 2001-2002 she also teaches History of Women in the Classical World. Her research are in the area of the world of women in classical antiquity (Greek and Roman) with particular regard for the historical and social data furnished by epigraphic documentation.

The so-called "praise of Claudia" (*CIL*, I², 1211 = *ILLRP*, 973), a sepulchral epigraph which is supposed to date back to the end of the 2nd century B.C., represents very well the Roman ideal model of a woman, a model which belonged to the nobility, but not to the nobility alone, and which was re-proposed constantly, again and again, during the entire period of Roman history, notwithstanding the deep changes in the political, social, economic and cultural reality which had created it.

Here is the text of the inscription:

> *Hospes quod deico paullum est, asta ac pellege.*
> *Heic est sepulcrum hau pulcrum pulcrai feminae.*
> *Nomen parentes nominarunt Claudiam.*
> *Suom mareitum corde deilexit sovo.*
> 5 *Gnatos duos creavit: horunc alterum*
> *in terra linquit, alium sub terra locat.*
> *Sermone lepido, tum autem incessu commodo.*
> *Domum servavit, lanam fecit. Dixi. Abei.*

Friend, I have not much to say; stop and read it. This tomb, which is not fair, is for a fair woman. Her parents gave her the name Claudia. She loved her husband in her heart. She bore two sons, one of whom she left on earth, the other beneath it. She was pleasant to talk with, and she walked with grace. She kept the house and worked in wool. That is all. You may go (translation by R. Lattimore, from Lefkowitz - Fant, 1982, nr. 134).

This text communicates to the reader a specific message about the female condition in the ancient Roman world and provides us with a series of specific elements of information.

After an invitation to anyone who happens to pass by along the road in front of the funeral monument, the epigraph tells of the deceased: a woman who is naturally beautiful (*pulcra femina*) and who does not need a particularly sumptuous or expensive tomb (*sepulcrum hau pulcrum*). We perceive, from these very first lines, the moralistic and conservative character of the feminine ideal, in particular because it is contrary to female *luxus*. Female luxury was considered in fact by some representatives of the Roman eminent classes, for example the famous Cato the Censor, to be the synonym of the decadence of Roman customs. In particular he had tried to keep in effect laws, promulgated in war-time, which placed limits on women's possessing of jewels and other status symbols (expensive cloths and carriages), but he had been defeated by the women themselves who had gone to the forum to defend their rights (195 B.C.). According to a new mentality in fact that was developing in parallel with the political and economic changes and the opening up of larger markets, in particular in the Orient, it was precisely in their *luxus* that the social role of wealthy women became manifest, when they decided to spend their money 'visibly'.

Going back to the 'praise of Claudia', we then find a description of the female physiology of the deceased which follows the fundamental stages of her existence from birth, represented by the imposition of the gentilicial *nomen* (*nomen parentes nominarunt Claudiam*), that is, the name of the family, similar to our surname which, however, did not identify a person, but was the same for all the women belonging to the same family. Then follow two other fundamental stages in a female life, according to the ideal model, that is, matrimony (*suom mareitum corde deilexit sovo*) and maternity (*gnatos duos creavit*), with a reminder of one of the true social plagues of antiquity, the high infant mortality rate. The last stage, that is, death, is represented obviously by the sepulchre which speaks in the first person.

Then we find a very brief description of the physical person, whose pleasant conversation (*sermone lepido*) is recorded, with an subtle but immediately perceived reference to the fact that the female *sermo* (speech), in order to be *lepidus* (pleasant), must be very limited. Indeed we know from the ancient writers, in particular Plutarch, that the Roman matron, that is the woman legitimately married and mother of a citizen, could not speak in public because "speaking is like taking one's cloths off", according to a rule which was made to go back to the mythical king Numa, instituting a particular relationship between women's speech and the concept of female modesty. An emblem of insistence on women's not speaking is the cult women celebrated in the name of a divinity known as Tacita Muta (the significance of the name is very clear as it means "Silent Mute"), a gossipy nymph whose tongue Jove had torn out as a cruel and – from his point of view – appropriate punishment (Ovid, *Fasti*, vv. 571-616).

In the same way, behaviour had to be proper and moderate (*incessu commodo*). The Roman matron, in fact, was recognisable because of the clothing she wore: a *tunica* (a tunic), a *stola* (a kind of long garment worn over the tunic which reached the feet and was fastened by

Fig. 1
A statue from Pompei showing the dress of a Roman matron.

The female model and the reality of Roman women

pins or brooches [*fibulae*] at the shoulders) and a *palla*: a mantle which covered the head and was worn when outside the house. These garments constituted a sort of diaphragm which was supposed to protect the honest woman. The cloths, like all the female *ornatus* (hair dressing, ornaments) had the precise scope of representing the social-juridical status of the woman, sexually untouchable in that she was a matron. The women of lower condition, for example slaves or prostitutes, wore the *amiculum*, a short tunic of transparent linen; this was worn by adulterous matrons, who in that way made visible the loss of their social status.

At the end, we find described the only activities which a "decent woman" could engage in, that is, domestic work and spinning and weaving wool: the female space is the inside of the house, the male space is the outside, the forum or the plaza, the seat of political and oratory activity.

This ideal female model can be found in Roman literature, with no interruption, until late antiquity. For example, we can read what Ausonius, a poet from Bordeaux who lived in the 4th century A.D. had to say (*Epitaphs*, 35). The deceased in this case is drawn with almost the same words we found in the "praise of Claudia", about 5 centuries earlier:

> In tumulum sedecennis matronae
>
> Omnia quae longo vitae cupiuntur in aevo,
> ante quater plenum consumpsit Anicia lustrum.
> Infans lactavit, pubes et virgo adolevit.
> Nupsit, concepit, peperit, iam mater obivit.
> Quis mortem accuset? Quis non accuset in ista?
> Aetatis meritis anus est, aetate puella.

> For the tomb of a married lady of sixteen
>
> Anicia has spent all those treasures which are the hope of a long life before her second decade reached its full. While a mere baby she gave suck; while yet a girl she was mature; she married, she conceived, she bare her child, and now has died a matron. Who can blame death? And yet who can not blame him in this case? In age's gains she is a crone; in age itself, a girl (ed. Loeb).

The key words in the representation of the feminine ideal are few and always the same: *casta*, that is, that she has sexual relations only for procreation; *pia*, that she faithfully carries out the practices having to do with the religious sphere and in respect of the *mos maiorum*, the customs of the ancestors; *frugi*, simple and honest; *domiseda*, that she stays at home; *lanifica*, that she stays at the loom.

For women of antiquity, obeying this model meant that their only form of public visibility was that they would enjoy male recognition of their virtues.

We must ask whether ancient women always respected this model or whether, rather, the progressively changed and improved economic and social conditions allowed Roman women in reality to live differently. Indeed, writers, starting with Plautus, tell us of economically wealthy and aggressive women, and everyone knows about the uninhibited and adulterous matrons of the end of the republican age (the famous Clodia-Lesbia loved by Catullus, to give the most famous example); and then there were the corrupt empresses who cultivated every kind of vice (Messalina is the prime example) described by the historians of the Imperial age.

Originally, when the Roman woman married, she passed from the absolute power of her father (*manus* or 'hand') to that of her husband (if *sui iuris*, that is, not himself subject to the power of his father), otherwise to that of her father-in-law (matrimony *cum manu*). Later, another form of marriage became widespread, *sine manu* (without *manu*) in virtue of which authority over the woman and her goods stayed within her family of origin.

Between the second half of the 4th century B.C. and the first half of the 3rd century, women became able to make testaments: women hence could inherit and dispose of their goods after death. This fact and the widespread use of the *sine manu* form of marriage brought the Roman woman a greater degree of autonomy, and a gradual recognition of her capacity to exercise some rights and hence to manage and administer her patrimony.

In a word, the women were able to "emancipate themselves", that is, literally, to free themselves from the *manus*, although, at least formally, if a woman did not have a male relative who could exercise his power over her, she had to have a tutor, on the basis of the general principle which we find in Cicero (*Pro Mur.*, 27) which recognised in the woman a *infirmitas sexus* and a *levitas animi*, one of the first theorisations of the concept of the "weaker sex", a principle taken up again by jurists of the Imperial age (for example, Gaius, *Inst.*, I, 144).

Hence we come to the literary representation of the social crisis of the ideal model, in particular after the Second Punic War (end of the 3rd century B.C. and the beginning of the 2nd century), which, like all periods of war, had increased the public role of women: the so-called *uxor dotata*, that is, the woman who had a dowry, is a character in comedy in which the husband is represented as an unhappy and innocent victim of a rich, avaricious and dominating wife, ugly and impossible to satisfy sexually.

For some women, whose deeds have been described by historian, we can speak of a true reversal of the ideal model. This is the case of Sempronia, portrayed by Sallustius in the Catilinian conspiracy, who is represented as the paradigmatic model of transgression: like the ideal matron, she is beautiful, fascinating, rich, and fertile, however she uses those qualities per perverse objectives; Clodia, whom we already mentioned, the sister of the famous tribune Clodius Pulcher, independent and free of scruples and who had many lovers, was the sworn enemy of Cicero, who accused her of behaving like a prostitute; Fulvia, Anthony's wife, did not stay at home and did not weave wool, but she wanted to comand a comander (Plutarch, *Antonius*, 10,5); she was the only one who "crossed the gender boundary and stepped into the male preserve of military action during civil war" (Lightman-Lightman, 2000, s.v.). Strong women, "wicked women", in the definition of Susan Fishler (1994, p. 120), but we must underline that the phenomenon was limited chronologically and remained circumscribed in the urban sphere, prevalently in Rome, and it was restricted to the upper classes.

Once he reached power (in 27 B.C.) the emperor Augustus emanated a series of laws in the field of family law, with incentives for prolific marriages and sanctions against the unmarried, the widowed and the divorced of both sexes or couples with no children, penal mea-

Fig. 2
The left side of Cetrania Severina's funeral monument.

Fig. 3
The front of the monument.

sures against adulterers, with the evident aim of moralising sexual customs, as a first step towards rebuilding Roman society, starting from its primary nucleus, the family, after its disaggregation due to the social and civil wars.

It is certainly true that in Imperial society an ideology which encouraged continence and moderation began to come to the fore. This was in part because of the double influence of Stoic thought and Christian preaching. The domestic space and the family were and continued to be the primary location for women. However it is also true that the ancient sources witness the great importance in the Imperial age of women's wealth and activities, particularly in the public space in cities.

Among the many examples that we might examine I have chosen the emblematic one of Cetrania Severina, from Sarsina, a city of the Romagnole Appenines, who, as we read on her funeral monument (*CIL*, XI, 6520), decides, herself, in her testament, to make an important donation, instituting a fund to provide food for her co-citizens (in this case olive oil) and to receive funeral honours herself:

Francesca Cenerini

On the left side:

Caput ex testamento
Cetraniae Severinae.
Collegiis dendropho=
rorum, fabrum, cento=
nariorum munic(ipii) Sassi(natis)
(sestertium) sena milia n(ummum) dari
volo fideiq(ue) vestrae col=
legiali committo uti
ex reditu (sestertium) quatern(um) m(ilium)
n(ummum) omnibus annis prid(ie)

Idus Iun(ias) die natalis
mei oleum singulis
vobis dividatur et
ex reditu (sestertium) binum
milium n(ummum) Manes
meos colatis. Hoc
ut ita faciatis fidei
vestrae committo.

on the front:

D(is) M(anibus).
Cetraniae
P(ublii) f(iliae) Severinae
sacerdoti
divae Marcian(ae).
T(itus) Baebius Gemelli=
nus August(alis)
coniugi sanctiss(imae).

Fig. 4
A view of the monument showing both inscriptions.

The female model and the reality of Roman women

Fig. 5
The right side of the funeral
monument.

On the front <of the funerary monument>:

To the spirits of the departed (To the Gods of the Underworld). <This funerary monument is dedicated> to Cetrania Severina, daughter of Publius, priestess of the deified Marciana.

Titus Baebius Gemellinus, priest of the imperial cult, <dedicated it> to his honest and virtuous wife.

On the left side:

Chapter of Cetrania Severina's will: I want that the associations of *dendrophori* [tree-bearers], craftsmen and *centonari* [workmen who made blankets of old garments stitched together and as firemen used mats for extinguishing fires] of the Sarsina municipality shall be granted with 6.000 sesterces and I trust the honesty of your associations to look after that every year on June 12th, on my birthday, oil shall be distributed to everyone of you with the returns on the sum of 4.000 sesterces. Moreover I wish that the returns on the sum of 2.000

sesterces shall be spent for venerating my departed spirits. I trust your honesty that all this shall be done.

Cetrania, because of her economic and social position, has a public role within her community: in fact she is a priestess of the Imperial cult, in this particular case of Marciana, Trajan's elder sister, who was deified (made *diva*) after her death in 112 A.D.

The priesthood, in particular of the members of the dynasty in power, is the only form of public power women had in the Roman age, because, notwithstanding the unquestionable recognition of their property rights, their inheritance and juridical rights (with the loosening and then the abolition of tutorship over them) they never achieved civic and political rights, in particular they never received the right to vote or to be elected to office.

 SELECTED BIBLIOGRAPHY

Lefkowitz M.R., Fant M.B., *Women's life in Greece and Rome. A source book in translation*, London 1982.

Archer L.J., Fischler S., Wyke M. (eds.), *Women in Ancient Societies. An illusion of the night*, Hong Kong 1994.

Hawley R., Levick B. (eds.), *Women in antiquity. New assessments*, London-NewYork 1995, reprinted 1997.

Lightman M., Lightman B., *Biographical Dictionary of ancient Greek and Roman women*, NewYork 2000.

Petrocelli C., *La stola e il silenzio*, Palermo 1989.

Schmitt-Pantel P. (ed.), *Histoire des femmes en Occident. I. L'Antiquité*, Paris 1990.

Fraschetti A. (ed.), *Roma al femminile*, Roma-Bari, 1994.

Cantarella E., *Passato prossimo. Donne romane da Tacita a Sulpicia*, Milano 1996.

Queens' and princesses' political function at the end of the Middle Ages (14th and 15th centuries)

Anne Lemonde

Université Pierre Mendès-France, Grenoble

L'étude de la fonction politique des reines et des princesses à la fin du Moyen Age n'est pas chose aisée, tant il est vrai qu'il s'agit d'un sujet aujourd'hui en chantier. Avant l'avènement de la "Gender History", le thème n'avait pas mobilisé beaucoup d'historiens. Mais depuis une vingtaine d'années, les recherches se multiplient, rassemblant des savants aux préoccupations à l'origine fort variées. En fait, nous avons affaire ici à une question spécialement heuristique, située à la jonction de deux champs historiographiques très dynamiques dont les richesses se cumulent sans s'annuler: celui de l'histoire des femmes d'une part et celui de l'histoire politique d'autre part. Si ces champs historiographiques se répondent si bien, c'est qu'ils utilisent des méthodes et des concepts voisins, puisant notamment à l'anthropologie une part de leur cadre de réflexion, ayant souvent recours à la prosopographie pour dessiner les contours de groupes sociaux significatifs. La seule synthèse existant à ce jour porte sur l'époque moderne, en dépit de son titre. Ce cours, par définition synthétique, s'aventurera donc sur des terres encore parfois inexplorées, surtout dans ses conclusions.

Nous partirons d'un double constat: d'abord, il convient de souligner le caractère relativement stable de la condition de la femme à la fin du Moyen Age, tout étant à peu près fixé depuis la réforme grégorienne, abstraction faite de quelques ajustements au XIIIème siècle, notamment dus à l'épanouissement des Ordres Mendiants. En revanche, les systèmes et la pensée politiques sont en pleine mutation à notre période, dans ce grand mouvement de genèse de l'Etat moderne qui s'étend du XIIIème au XVIIème siècle. Dans ces conditions, il paraissait de bonne méthode historique de procéder en partant de postulats bien admis concernant l'histoire des femmes, pour les confronter ensuite aux conclusions des spécialistes d'histoire politique: de la sorte c'est l'évolution du poids politique des femmes que l'on sera à même de mesurer.

La norme: un poids politique de plus en plus grand

Certains ont pu affirmer un peu hâtivement que le poids politique des reines et princesses est allé s'amenuisant à compter du XIIIème siècle, en France par exemple avec la réinvention de la loi Salique au cours du XIVème siècle, mais également ailleurs avec la professionnalisation de l'exercice du pouvoir. Les choses apparaissent en fait beaucoup moins simples si l'on se souvient d'abord que rien, avant le XIIIème siècle, ne fondait la légitimité de l'action politique des femmes, exclues depuis toujours en Occident des affaires de la cité. Il semblerait bien plutôt que ce soient les progrès du droit qui procurent cette fausse impression, fixant par écrit des acquis immémoriaux. En fait, ces progrès considérables de la norme juridique conduisirent plutôt à reconnaître le rôle essentiel de la souveraine dans la survie de la dynastie, un point névralgique de toute stabilité politique en ce temps là.

La norme sociale, quant à elle, faisait de la femme une épouse et une mère avant tout. Reines et princesses échappent moins que toute autre à ce cadre. Elle sont là pour engendrer, et c'est une immense responsabilité politique que l'on ne leur confiait pas sans avoir, avant leur mariage, tenté de prédire leur fertilité: il s'agit là d'une véritable affaire d'Etat à partir du XIVème siècle. Une fois les enfants mis au monde, la reine ou la princesse devaient s'assurer de la bonne tenue de sa maison. Or cette maison, la cour, n'était pas une maison ordinaire: elle était au cœur d'un système en pleine mutation qui tendait alors à se définir comme chose publique. Et c'est bien à la cour, au conseil plus spécialement, que tout cela se jouait, ce qui plaçait naturellement la souveraine à une place cardinale.

Reine ou princesse: une image, une rédemptrice

A une époque où l'on observe la mise en place d'un système de représentation politique de plus en plus sophistiqué, où le pouvoir s'avise alors de se mettre en scène, à la cour, lors du sacre, des entrées royales ou des funérailles du souverain, le fait que la femme soit avant tout considérée comme enveloppe charnelle prend une importance toute particulière pour la reine ou la princesse. Celle-ci devient une pièce maîtresse d'un véritable dispositif idéologique par lequel le pouvoir s'impose en s'exposant: la souveraine donne chair, mieux que son mari, à l'amour qui doit unir le princeps à ses sujets. Elle s'érige aussi, dès lors, en véritable intermédiaire entre le roi et ceux qu'il gouverne. Or cette fonction, à une époque où la fonction royale elle-même se coule de plus en plus dans un modèle christique, n'est pas sans évoquer celle de la Vierge, rédemptrice par excellence au panthéon des saints.

Comme toutes les femmes, reines et princesses sont avant tout soucieuses de préserver leur dignité. Mais cette dignité n'est pas seulement individuelle dans leur cas, elle est avant tout politique. Et c'est cela, sans doute, qui devait les animer pendant cette période exceptionnelle qui leur offrait la possibilité, unique avant le vingtième siècle, d'intervenir activement dans le champ masculin de la res publica. Une fois que le pouvoir n'aurait plus rien de privé, que le glissement d'une forme féodale de pouvoir à une forme moderne serait achevé, alors reines et princesses ne joueraient plus qu'un simple rôle d'apparat, sans aucun poids politique.

Born in Lyon in 1969, Anne Lemonde completed her studies in Grenoble. She now teaches medieval History in the University of Grenoble. She is particularly interested in political history at the end of the Middle Ages and has written about principalities during 14th and 15th centuries, especially the Dauphiné.

INTRODUCTION

Strangely enough, the political place of queens and princesses in the end of the Middle Ages had not been systematically investigated before the advent of gender history. This is indeed strange because understanding the political weight of a female sovereign is a very important institutional problem; that is to say, her place both in actual government and in creating the premises for the future is vital in a dynastic system. This gap has been partly filled by studies and important colloquia [1], but we still lack a complete synthesis for the period [2]. This reinforces the interest of the topic. Moreover, this subject now benefits from a twofold historiographical revival: first, of course, the recent and ever-increasing importance of women's history and, second, the return of interest in political history. It turns out that the meeting of these two historiographical fields is extremely fruitful, all the more so since each of the two uses methods and concepts which are very close to those of the other. Therefore the two sectors of historiographical research are tightly connected: anthropology (as a guide to studying representations, symbols and emblems) and prosopography (the method which gives the keys to understanding the component parts of a social structure) are the central pillars of the method of both, inherited from the long and profound work of social history in general which has taken place since the times of the great Marc Bloch. Even historians who usually do not keep company with gender history recognise the great interest of research on queens and princesses [3]: therefore this should have become a fundamental problem.

So we must wonder what the problem is… In fact, attempting to understand the political functions of queens and princesses means studying the destiny of a political system which is nearly universal in the occidental sphere, which rests on a dynastically transmitted mode of power and whose features were becoming progressively fixed during the period we are considering in the system we still often refer to as the "modern state". The evolution of women's place in this system reveals aspirations, limits and mental representations of the actors of the birth of the modern state. This evolution is significant because women are seen as naturally specialised in the private sphere, in the domestic sphere, and therefore they seem to be very far from political business which belongs to the external public sphere. This could be political history's point of view. On the other hand, gender history would focus on the fact that, when we look at the role of queens and princesses, we study the only women who ever owned an official and real political power before the 20th century. Furthermore it was a very necessary and legitimate power, which absolute monarchy and then democracy would no longer need. This power has never been very large and has changed through the ages, but it has always put queens and princesses in an exceptional position in comparison with other women.

We will focus here on women's political function according to the norm and not on the actual political action of individual women (this would take far too long!). I shall proceed along a double track, comparing the two stories (political and womanish), always beginning by quoting gender history conclusions, and then applying them to a reflection on political history. So I would say that the area I will discuss is a matter for gender history whereas the internal analyses are the concern of political history; of course my conclusions deal with both historical fields. The main reason for proceeding in this way is that women's position in general does not change a lot at the end of the Middle Ages – since everything was fixed during the Gregorian and the Franciscan phases – whereas on the other hand political structures are changing and developing very swiftly. From the Gregorian period, women had been characterised exclusively in relation to their husband: that was their structural function. I will first focus on this point. Then I wish to study how female nature has a political significance in general culture: woman as a body, as an image, as a redeemer.

THE SOVEREIGN'S WIFE: A MORE AND MORE IMPORTANT STRUCTURAL FUNCTION

The law

Was government a male business? Many specialists consider that women had much more power before the 13th century. For instance, they used to sign official and public deeds and bills, which was no longer true in St. Louis's century. In reality, I think that is a faulty interpretation. We conclude that the law had changed, increasing its rigour, or more simply because it was defined more and more completely, so that woman's place became better characterised. Furthermore, the imprecision of the law before the 13th century gives the illusion that women hold more power than afterwards: the lesson of Aristotle, according to whom a woman should not speak in public places – meaning that she had no legitimate political role at all –, had not been forgotten in the early Middle Ages.

During the 14th century, jurists tried to protect the dynasty from usurpation, particularly when a daughter, as the only apparent heir, had herself no legitimate heir. In 1328, the Cortes of Navarre established, with much rigour, that Philippe of Evreux ought to leave the throne if his wedding with queen Jeanne remained barren – which did not happen. More generally, the problem for the jurists was to control succession, a vital question for the state. French jurists are those who went the furthest, creating a real myth, the Salic law, whose formulation was perfected by Jean of Montreuil during Charles VI's times, at the beginning of the 15th century. Henceforth, in France, women were excluded not from the throne, but from succession, and they no longer had the right to pass on royal dignity. This did not mean that their political role would be less important than elsewhere: in any case, in other kingdoms when a daughter inherited the crown, her husband was in charge of the government. But this gave a real stability to the French monarchy, which English and Castilans, or many other princes probably envied: there is no equivalent in France to the Portuguese revolution of 1383, which arose because the infanta wanted to give the throne to her husband, John I, who was also king of Castile. There is also no equivalent to the Trastámara accession in 1369 or the Lancastrian one in 1399. Most certainly, the Salic law strengthened male primogeniture, which guaranteed political stability; but it did not exclude women from power at all. I would say that, on the contrary, it conferred on the queen a very well defined institutional role, as did not take place elsewhere.

Social norm: a woman to marry

Saying that queens and princesses may be first characterised by their wedding is a commonplace. They were, as every woman, what their family – generally, their father or brother – wanted them to be. They were not sent to a convent, and therefore were married and put under a lord's or a master's authority, the king's or the prince's. Since the Gregorian reform, there had been no other desirable destiny for a woman except the convent or marriage. As the real foundation of her social personality, marriage was a determining institution for a woman's whole life. And the political impact of this social norm is exceptionally strong.

Nature

The structural importance of marriage depends first of all on the fact that it is meant to secure the duration of the dynasty. A woman had to summon up all her forces to ensure procreation: until death, the chronicles say. A queen or princess-to-be was chosen first for her supposed reproductive ability, and gynaecological experts were employed to determine that. We know that, for instance, little Isabeau was examined before the conclusion of her wedding with Charles VI in 1385. Moreover, the duke of Burgundy, who looked after the entire transaction with the Germans, made sure that the king enjoyed the girl: it was not a romantic worry at all, but only a necessity for the wedding not to be made barren by a king's impotence – every one remembered Philippe Auguste's misfortune with his Danish wife. Fortunately, Charles VI immediately loved Isabeau, at first sight.

Therefore, queens and princesses had, on average, twelve or thirteen children during their life: they were, in that way, playing their main political role. And they died in childbirth sometimes, sharing the lot of many mothers at that time. Jeanne of Bourbon (Charles V's wife) died giving birth when her eighth child, Catherine, came into the world in 1378, on 6 February. She was forty. Before, she had to bear another very common tragedy: she had lost five of her children, and only two of them grew up to adulthood, Charles (VI) and Louis (of Orléans). Marie of Anjou (Charles VII's wife), on her part, had fourteen children, and five of them grew up to adulthood.

On this point, politics and nature interacted, through the intercession of women, often considered "natural beings" by Christian intellectuals. Therefore Gregorian precepts of faithfulness were even more compulsory for royal and princely families than for the others. Marital faithfulness was actually a main political necessity, at least for the woman who would injure the sacred in a twofold way if she did not respect it. First, she would sin against a consecrated wedding, and second, she would sin against a consecrated crown. Of course, the king's or the prince's infidelities had little impact in comparison. The charge of adultery against Charles VI's wife, which denied Charles VII his legitimacy, was certainly untrue. But it reveals a deep crisis in the state: the problem actually involves the heart of this political system.

The protectress of the home

The reproductive function led queens and princesses to a larger role. Anthropologists have explained it many times: the woman is responsible for the protection of the home. In every traditional society, the woman protects the domestic sphere. That is her space, and she must avoid leaving it. She has to ensure the good behaviour of all the members of the family (even the servants), take care of the proper management of clothes and food, arrange receptions. From the 13th century on, she also had a charitable function, which of course was connected with her other duties.

And what is a court, if not a home, the first home of the kingdom? The court is at the junction of the two spheres, the public one and the private one, just as queens and princesses are. Moreover, since the beginning of the 14th century, jurists and theologians totally appropriated the Aristotelian tradition: they very often use the metaphor of the home to talk about the 'republic': that was the way women could be integrated into political thought, at least at a symbolic level. At the same time, the court was undergoing a very important transformation, turning from a private institution, taking place in a castle surrounded by vassals, into a public government, whose quintessence would be the king's Council. Therefore, it is a commonplace to say that our political systems have matured through this fundamental shift from private to public. Nevertheless, this shift was not completely accomplished at the end of the Middle Ages, so that queens and princesses could claim to play their most important role ever in politics at that time of transition, ensuring the link between the archaic and the modern period of the court.

The heart of the court, and of power in general, was the Council. Of course, a queen or princess had no right to take part in that institution. But she was never very far from it; she was perhaps the person who was, over a long period, the closest to the Council in the aristocracy, after the king or the prince, naturally. The very well known decree enacted in 1336 by Humbert II, "dauphin" of Viennois, that is prince of the Dauphiné, created the "Great Council of the Dauphiné". Precisely, this "Great Council" was supposed to take place in the Dauphine's (that is, the princess') 'hôtel' or princely dwelling, in Beauvoir-en-Royans. As the prince had to be always on the road to meet his subjects or to negotiate some loans with the pope in Avignon, the dauphine's hôtel seemed actually to be the best place to fix the residence of the Council, linking it to a specific place.

Moreover, in the same period, the court became a very particular institution, that is to say, a real 'representation place', the place where royal or princely power could be put on stage. The first decrees in Occident that show this novelty are those of the Humbert II we metioned above, in 1336, and those of Peter IV of Aragon in 1340. These edicts were supposed to clarify the whole complex court organisation by describing it in writing. Even the menus of each day of the year were precisely defined. And naturally, in each case, the queen's or the princess's hôtel is included in the normative rules. It looks like a double of her husband's establishment, absolutely necessary for the equilibrium of the whole. During the 14th and the 15th centuries, the queen's or the princess's hôtel is the most expensive one – after the king's of course, but also before those belonging to the members of the aristocracy.

In that area, the female sovereign could carry out what she was supposed to do in accordance to social norm: take care of that particular home. That meant raising children until they were seven or eight years old: an important political task if we remember that the king or prince-to-be was one of these children. Nevertheless, the financial aspects of her domestic responsibility did not pertain to the queen or the princess: in that area she had less prerogatives than other women. And the expansion of the court did not mitigate that fact, on the contrary. But the female ruler had, despite everything, her own sphere, where she could play a very important political role: charity and, beyond that, religious fervour or observance of the whole royal or princely family. In that regard Marie of Anjou looked like a real model.

In charge of peace?

Another commonplace for the anthropologists studying women's social position is to say that the woman is the best one for keeping peace between men. She is, in all the meanings of the word, a real peace agent, whereas, on the other hand, men appear to be warriors, the ones who conquer or defend territories. This female function is, during the period we consider here, guaranteed by exogamy and patrilocality (i. e., the fact that the woman always lives in her husband's country). These two social customs actually compel queens and princesses to avoid, at any price, war between her two families. This way she becomes in fact a kind of permanent ambassador of her family of origin to her husband's family and vice versa. The woman is the real link that turns marriage into a strong diplomatic alliance. Christine of Pizan gives us convincing examples.[4]

This anthropological point of view must be completed by a classical historical one: specialists of the period well know that writers of 'miroirs du prince' have turned the duty of

Fig. 1
The crowned Virgin as a protectress. This painting is by Piero della Francesca, Uffizi Museum, Florence.

the prince to keep peace into a real commonplace. Peace as alpha and omega of power... Could we not say that the exercise of power belongs to a female behaviour?

More generally, this quick study on the relationship between queens' and princesses' function and juridical or social norms regarding women shows how politicised these women's status is, how heavy the political weight of these norms is.

Queens and princesses as images

Traditionally, the woman is generally seen much more as a physical being than man. That contributed to turning her into an image, nearly an icon, which power would soon capture and use. At the end of the Middle Ages, at the exact moment when the king's body takes on a mystical value among others as the incarnation of nation, this representation of woman gave her an unprecedented political place. This analysis is, naturally, closely connected to the theological beliefs developed by the Gregorian reform, which regarded woman as born from man's body. We must not forget that, at that time, the image of the Virgin invaded retables and sculpture workshops.

A body to be shown:
The queen, part of the king's body

Politically, it was vital to the sovereign to show himself to his subjects as much as he could. Nevertheless, this was becoming more and more difficult, because of the new size of royal domain or of the principality at the end of the Middle Ages, and because of the very heavy tasks that he had to carry out. For these reasons, and for theological and political ones, the moment when the king or the prince was shown became more and more ritualised. Anglo-Saxon historians, whom we call "ceremonialists", following the path opened up by E. Kantorowicz, have stressed that point in general, studying coronations, royal or princely entrances (i. e. celebrations marking the first time a ruler entered a city of his own) and burials. In all these ceremonies, the links between king and public business are involved. And that gave a more and more important role to the sovereign's wife. First, we can underline that every ceremony mentioned above was given a female equivalent precisely during our period. This means that these female equivalents were necessary complements to guarantee political efficacy to many old ceremonies.

As to coronation in France, the mechanism is very well studied: Isabeau of Bavaria was consecrated a very long time after her wedding, in 1389, in a ceremony built on the model of that of the king, although without the miracles, the 'sainte ampoule' or thaumaturgy. This delayed ceremony will not surprise experts of the period: precisely in 1389, the so-called "Marmousets" acceded to power. They were great political thinkers, real **instigators of modern State in France: this coronation of the queen is their work. The mass took place in Saint-Denis, which linked the ceremony strongly to the royal function itself. The queen received a sceptre, just a little bit shorter than the king's. Exactly at that moment in France, the royal entrance received its female equivalent, a moment very much appreciated by the French subjects, very curious to see their queen and how beautiful she looked. In England, in 1440, a *Liber Regie Capelle* was written, which prescribed how kings should be buried. At the end, the writer added: "the exequies of a queen who leaves this world are entirely carried out in the form noted above".

Queens and princesses as models

Let us here listen to the writers of 'miroirs du prince': queen and princess are the proper model of all the women in the realm or the principality, exactly equivalent to the king with his subjects in general. So that the established order depended on the queen's behaviour. Obviously, queens and princesses are also those who were making fashion at that time; that was their duty too.

Anne Lemonde

A redeemer

Queens and princesses were models for the female subjects of their country. But, above all, they were guides for all their subjects, guides who were supposed to lead the way to Paradise. That was also one of the king's duty, but for his wife, we could say that it looks like a speciality. Moreover, as the queen (or the princess) was more approachable than her husband, very busy with the government, as she was also actually more maternal, she was supposed to hear just causes and petitions better and pass them on to her husband. At the end of the Middle Ages, the king's image was drawn as closer and closer to God's. Thus, we would like to be able to conclude that, precisely on that period, the queen could be assimilated to the Virgin herself, as a redeemer *par excellence*. The increasing success of the Virgin's coronation from the 13th century on would suggest this. But, unfortunately, this aspect has not yet been studied: we can only suggest that this is an aspect which should be looked into. [*See Plate 12*]

CONCLUSION

It is quite hard to draw a conclusion about a rather new subject. Here we will only say that in the final part of the Middle Ages, queens' and princesses' political function became more and more important, that is, their function in an anthropological sense. To a great extent, this was not the result of active behaviour of the women. But, on the other hand, it would be a ridiculous to infer that queens and princesses were nothing but instruments for those who exercised the real, daily power. At that time, women hade a dignity to defend, and nothing else... but royal or princely dignity are great political things! And some women knew how to take advantage of the phase of transition, when the private sphere was not already totally public and vice versa. When this process was completed, in the 17th century, women would no longer play such a role in the French monarchy. The times of queen Isabeau, Marie of Anjou, or Catherine of Medicis, had come to an end.

 NOTES

1   Sec *infra* the bibliography.

2   The only one focuses on the following period: F. Cosandey, *La reine de France. Symbole et pouvoir*, Paris, 2000.

3   See *infra* the very interesting colloquium organised by Philippe Contamine in Thouars (1997).

4   See source below.

 SELECTED BIBLIOGRAPHY

Autour de Marguerite d'Ecosse. Reines, princesses et dames du XVème siècle. Actes du colloque de Thouars (23 et 24 mai 1997), Contamine G. and P. (eds.), Paris 1999.

Autrand F., *Charles VI*, Paris 1986.

Autrand F., *Charles V*, Paris 1994.

Carpenter J., Maclean S.B., *Power of the Weak: Studies on Medieval Women*, London 1995.

Cosandey F., *La reine de France. Symbole et pouvoir*, Paris 2000.

Kantorowicz E., *The King's Two Bodies. A Study in Mediaeval Political Theology*, 2nd ed., Princeton 1966.

Klapisch-Zuber C., *Histoire des femmes en Occident*, dir. G. Duby, M. Perrot, 2, *Le Moyen-Age*, trad., Paris 1991 (orig. edn., *Storie delle donne*, Rome-Bari 1990).

Krynen J., *L'empire du roi. Idées et croyances politiques en France, XIIIème-XVème siècles*, Paris 1993.

Queens and Queenship in Medieval Europe. Proceeding of e Conference held at King's College London, april 1995, A.J. Duggan (ed.), Woodbridge 1997.

Sornmé M., *Isabelle de Portagal, duchesse de Bourgogne, une femme au pouvoir au XVème siècle*, Villeneuve d'Ascq 1998.

Women and Sovereignty, L.O. Fradenburg (ed.), Edinburgh 1992.

 SOURCES

Christine de Pizan, in her *Livre des trois vertus*, written in 1404 (the critical edition is published by C.C. Willard, Paris 1989), illustrates the role of the princess as a peace-keeper.

CI DEVISE COMMENT LA SAGE ET BONNE PRINCESSE SE PENERA DE METTRE PAIX ENTRE LE PRINCE ET LES BARONS S'IL Y A AUCUN DESCORT.

Ou se il avient cas que aucun prince voisin ou estrangier vueille / movoir guerre pour aucune chalenge a son seigneur ou que son seigneur la vueille mouvoir a aultrui, la bonne dame pesera moult ceste chose en pensant les grans maulx et infinies cruaultéz, pertes, occisions et destruction de païs et de gent qui a cause de guerre viennent, et la fin qui souventes fois en est merveilleuse; si avisera de toute sa poissance se elle pourra tant faire – en gardant l'onneur de son seigneur – que ceste guerre puist estre eschivee, et en ce se vouldra traveillier et labourer saigement en appellant Dieu a son aide et par bon conseil, et tant fera, se elle puet, que voye de paix y sera trouvee. Ou se il avient que aucuns des princes du royaume ou païs – ou des barons ou des chevaliers, ou subgiéz qui ait poissance – se soit d'aucune chose mesfait, meismement contre la majesté de son seigneur, ou que il en soit encoulpéz et elle voit que de le prendre et punir ou mouvoir contre lui guerre peust venir grant mal en la terre, si comme en cas pareil / on a veu maintes fois en France et ailleurs que par le contens d'un bien petit baron ou chevalier au regard du roy de France, qui est si grant prince, sont venus mains grans maulx et domages ou royaume, si comme racontent Les Croniques de France du conte de Corbeil, du seigneur de Montlehery et de plusieurs autres; et meismement avint n'a pas longtemps de messire Robert d'Artois, lequel par le content que le roy ot a lui dommaiga moult le royaume de France a l'aide des Anglois. Et pour ce la bonne dame qui aura regart a ces choses et pitié de la destruction du peuple se vouldra traveillier d'y mettre paix, si amonnestera le prince son seigneur et son conseil d'avoir sur ceste chose regart ains qu'on l'enpreigne, veu le mal qui en pourroit venir et ce que tout bon prince doit a son pouoir eschiver effusion de sang, et par especial sur ses subgiéz. Si n'est mie pou de chose d'emprendre nouvelle guerre, qui ne se doit faire sans grant / avis et meure deliberacion, et que mieulx vaudroit aviser aucune plus convenable voye pour traire a accort par aucuns bons moyens. Ceste dame ne s'en souffrira pas a tant, ains fera tant que elle parlera ou fera parler – gardee son honneur et celluy de son seigneur – a celluy ou ceux qui auront commis le mesfait; les en reprendra en poignant et en oingnant, disant que le mesfait est moult grant et que a bonne cause en est le prince indignéz, et que s'entente est de s'en vengi-

Anne Lemonde

er si comme il est raison, mais nonpourtant elle, qui vouldroit tousjours le bien de paix, ou cas que ilz se vouldroient amender ou en faire amende convenable, mettroit voulentiers peine d'essaier, se pacifier les pourroit vers son seigneur.

Par tel voye et par telz parolles ou semblables, la bonne princepce sera tousjours moyenne de paix a son pouoir, si comme estoit jadis la bonne royne Blanche, mere de Saint Louys, qui en ceste maniere se penoit tousjours de mettre accord entre le roy et les seigneurs, / si comme elle fist du comte de Champaigne et d'aultres, laquelle chose est le droit office de sage et bonne royne et princepce d'estre moyenne de paix et de concorde, et de travaillier que guerre soit eschivee pour les inconveniens qui avenir en peuent. Et ad ce doivent aviser principaulment les dames, car les hommes sont par nature plus courageux et plus chaulx, et le grant desir que ilz ont d'eulx vengier ne leur laisse aviser les perilz ne les maulx qui avenir en peuent. Mais nature de femme est plus paoureuse et aussi de plus doulce condicion, et pour ce, se elle veult et elle est saige, estre puet le meilleur moyen a pacifier l'omme, qui soit.

Et ad ce propos dist Salemon es Proverbes, ou xxv°chaptire: Doulceur et humilité assouagist le prince et la langue mole (c'est a dire la doulce parole) flechist et brise sa durté, tout ainsi comme l'eaue par sa moisteur et froidure estaint la chaleur du feu.

O de quans grans biens ont maintes fois esté cause au monde roynes / et princepces en mettant paix entre anemis, entre princes et barrons et entre peuples rebelles et leurs seigneurs, les escriptures en sont toutes pleines! Si n'est en terre plus grant bien que de princepce et haulte dame et sage. Eureux est le païs et la contree qui telle l'a, et de ce donnasse pluseurs exemples, mais assez est parlé ad ce propos ou Livre de la Cité des Dames.

Et qu'avient il de tel princepce? Il avient que tous les subgiéz, qui la sentent de tel savoir et bonté, affuient a elle a reffuge, non mie seulement comme a leur maistresse, mais ce semble a leur deesse en terre, en qui ilz ont souveraine esperance et fiance; et elle est cause de maintenir la contree en paix. Si ne sont mie ses oeuvres sans charité, ains sont tant meritoires que plus grant bien ne pourroit estre fait.

HOW THE WISE AND GOOD PRINCESS WILL WORK TO ARRANGE PEACE BETWEEN THE PRINCE AND THE BARONS IF THERE IS ANY DISPUTE

If it should happen that any neighbouring or foreign prince wishes to make war to challenge her lord, or if her lord wants to make war against someone else, the good lady will weigh this matter carefully thinking of the great evils and infinite cruelties, losses, killings and destruction of lands and people which come because of war, and the end which often is surprising; she will be aware of all her power if she is able to do so much – maintaining the honour of her lord – that this war be avoided, and in this she will want to work and labour wisely calling God to help her and for good advice, and she will do so much, if she can, that a way to peace may be found. Or if it happens that some princes of the realm or land – or barons or knights or powerful subjects – be ill treated, even against the majesty of her lord, or if he be accused and she sees that if he is taken and punished or war is made against him great evil could come to the land, as in similar cases has often been seen in France and elsewhere, that because of a conflict between a little baron or knight towards the King of France, who is such a great prince, there have come great evils and ills to the kingdom as we learn from the *Chronicles of France* about the Count of Corbeil, Lord of Montlehery and many others; and the same happened not long ago to lord Robert of Artois who because of the contrast he had with the king damaged greatly the kingdom of France helping the English. And for this reason the lady who will have regard to these things and pity for the destruction of the people would work to put peace, she will tell the prince her lord and his council to have regard for this matter before undertaking it because of the evil which could come and that every good prince has the duty of avoiding bloodshed and especially that of his subjects. That it is not a small thing to undertake a new war and that it should not be done without great information and careful consideration, and that it would be better to find some other good way to come to agreement with peaceful means. This lady will not take it amiss, in fact she will speak or have spoken to – preserving her honour and that of her lord – the person or persons who committed the bad deed; she will take it up weeping and blandishing, saying that the misdeed is very big and that the prince has very good reason to be indignant, and that his intent is to vindicate himself as is right, but nonetheless she, who always wants the good of the country, in case they should want to make amends or satisfactory compensation, is willingly to try to restore peace between them and her lord.

In this way and with these or similar words, the good princess will always be a means of peace as was once in past times the good queen Blanche, mother of Saint Louis, who in this way always worked to create agreement between the king and the lords, as she did for the count of Champagne and others, the which thing if the right office of the wise and good queen and princess to be a means of peace and agreement, and to work that war be avoided because of the ill which could come from it. And this is something that principally women must do, because men are by nature more courageous and hot-blooded, and the great desire which they have to get vengeance does not allow them to think about the dangers and the evils which may come of it. But the nature of a woman is more fearful and also of a sweeter condition, and for this, if she wishes and is wise, she can be the best means of pacifying a man that exists.

And in this connection Salomon said in his Proverbs, in the 25th chapter: Sweetness and humility won over the prince and the soft tongue (that is, the sweet words) bent and broke his hardness, just as water with its wetness and coldness extinguishes the heat of the fire.

Oh, the Scriptures are full of the great good that queens and princesses have done for the world by making peace between princes and barons and between rebellious peoples and their lords! There is no greater good for a land than having a princess that is a great and wise lady. Happy is the land and the area that has such a princess, and of this there are may examples, but we have spoken enough of this in the *Book of the City of Ladies*.

And what does such a princess get from this? That all the subjects, who realise that she has such wisdom and goodness, flee to her to find refuge, not only because she is their mistress, but as if she were a goddess, in whom they have the greatest hope and trust; and she is the cause that the country is kept in peace. Her works are not without charity, rather they deserve the greatest merit.

SEE PLATES 11-12

Anne Lemonde

From a Father-Dominated, through a Brother-Dominated, to a Mother-Dominated Society: on changing values in Modern Western culture

Henrik Jensen

Roskilde Universitetscenter

 I de seneste hundrede år har vores kultur bevæget sig fra faderstyring til moderstyring, med hensyn til de grundværdier, der udtrykkes i samfundets vigtigste institutioner (familien, staten). Det indebærer at myndighed og forpligtelse er afløst af omsorg og terapi som institutionernes dominerende udtryksformer overfor den enkelte. Hvad giver det af muligheder for at fastholde en (normativ) kultur for fremtiden?

Det 19. århundredes samfund og familie var klart domineret af faderen. Det var i sin tendens et faderautoritært samfund, hvor hovedvægten lagdes på traditionelt faderlige værdier: Pligtfølelse, arbejdsomhed, behovsudsættelse, kald, æresfølelse, sublimering, distance osv. I familien tilegnede barnet sig disse værdier i opvæksten, på en sådan måde at det senere i livet ikke kunne sætte sig ud over dem uden med det største ubehag.

Denne situation forandrede sig i det 20. århundrede, først og fremmest på grund af første verdenskrig, som blandt mange andre ting førte til at den ophøjede faderfigur blev trukket ned fra piedestalen. I krigen "døde Gud" og i det efterfølgende generationsopgør blev fadergenerationen i fred almindelighed anset for at være ophav til krigen - men det var sønnerne, der var blevet slået ihjel iden.

I mellemkrigstiden forsøgte man derefter at skabe et samfund, der ikke først og fremmest var baseret på faderautoriteten. Der fandt en eksperimenteren sted med, hvad man bredt kunne kalde for broderskabsideologier: kommunisme, fascisme, nazisme, socialdemokrati. Det viste sig imidlertid at det ikke var så let at skille sig af med den autoritære fader, som i mellemkrigstiden "gik igen" i mere eller mindre perverteret form - som fører (Hitler, Stalin, men også Stauning). De mest radikale af disse ideologier brændte ud i og efter anden verdenskrig, eller førte videre til det velfærdssamfund, vi kender idag.

Faderens rolle i familien svækkedes også op igennem århundredet, indtil den efterhånden blev helt sekundær i forhold til moderens. Faderen var enten fysisk fraværende (et stærkt stigende antal familie består kun af moder og børn), psykisk fraværende, eller forsøger at spille rollen som en sekundær moder.

Dette har ført til et bestemt sæt af samfundsmæssige problemer, der dybest set har at gøre med at faderen ikke spiller den rolle i børns bevidsthed, som han traditionelt har gjort. Dette er i forelæsningen søgt illustreret ved et uddrag af et interview med den franske forfatter og psykoanalytiker Julia Kristeva, der problematiserer den situation, hvor faderen mangler i familien som den der adskiller moder og børn - klipper navlestrengen over, i videre forstand. Når faderen ikke er der til dette, må velfærdsstatens institutioner spille rollen som den, der adskiller, og iøvrigt støtter moderen i processen. Velfærdsstaten får i dén henseende en dobbeltfunktion som både moder (støttende den moder, der har vanskeligt ved at leve op til sin moderrolle) og fader (agerende for den fraværende fader).

Det er forelæsningens pointe at de værdier, som staten afspejler i denne dobbeltfunktion, snarere er de moderlige (omsorg, trøst, "terapi", deltagelse, evaluering) end de faderlige (arbejde, pligt, kald, autoritet, hierarki, sublimering, behovsudsættelse, målsøgen), hvorved disse sidste har en klar tendens til at glide ud af kulturen til fordel for de første.

Dette passer med andre tendenser i tiden: tendensen til at den indrestyrede socialkarakter afløses af den andenstyrede (David Riesman), og tendensen til at den traditionelle vestlige "skyldkultur" afløses af en "offerkultur". Hvor en skyldkultur er karakteriseret ved at den enkelte per definition hele tiden skylder fællesskabet noget, og derfor må "betale af", er offerkulturen modsat: her skylder fællesskabet (samfundet) den enkelte alt. Her er den enkelte nemlig defineret som offer, eller potentielt offer, og som sådant skyldfri. Gennem en forestilling om rettigheder stiller individet sig i centrum af tingene og forventer at blive retfærdiggjort. Den individuelle rettighed er grænseløs: det er retten til at blive lykkelig(gjort).

Born 1947 in Odense, Denmark, Henrik Jensen completed his studies of history at the University of Copenhagen in 1973. He now teaches modern and contemporary history at Roskilde University. He is particularly interested in modern cultural history and his latest book is *Ofrets århundrede* ("The Age of the Victim"), dealing with the cultural effects of the first world war, predominantly in Britain, Germany and Denmark.

Introduction

This discussion deals with changes in the basic values of European society, taking place in the 19th and 20th century: changes that might be described as the title indicates. In the 19th century, European society was based throughout on paternal authority. Paternal authority suffered a severe blow because of the First World War, after which various egalitarian ("brother") ideologies became vigorously pursued instead (Communism, Fascism, Social-Democracy). The more extreme among them burnt themselves out by or in the second half of the century, others were institutionalised in an egalitarian welfare state. By the end of the 20th century, the welfare state, at least in the North-Western part of Europe, expresses more and more "maternal values" when dealing with its citizens: stressing care, comfort and therapy over the "paternal values" of authority, duty and responsibility, that was expressed by the 19th and early 20th century state.

So we are not really speaking here about gender history; if anything, we are examining cultural history, defining culture, not as in 'high culture' vs. 'popular culture', but as, essentially, the normative integration of the individuals of any given society.

In the words of the great sociologist, Max Weber, man is seen as an animal connected to society by a web of meaning that he himself has spun. In a well-known reading of this statement by the anthropologist, Clifford Geertz, this web becomes more or less identical with culture, and our interpretation of it the key to *Verstehen*.

Nomos

However, in order to try to circumvent the many ambiguities of the concept of culture, let us turn to the much less used concept of *nomos* instead. There are two ways of approaching it. One is sociological, by way of another great sociologist, Emile Durkheim, whose concept *anomie* (a-nomos), meaning normlessness and valuelessness, simply is turned into a positive counterpart, nomos, by the social-psychologist Peter L. Berger. The other way is historical, and found by going back to pre-classical Greek texts, from Hesiod to Plato, where nomos simply was the law.

Either way, nomos represents the vast bulk of traditions, rituals, habits, conventions, norms, rules and regulations that makes up the values, drives and restraints of a given society. Nomos has also been called "the great inherited conglomerate".

Nomos is the way society meets the individual, the way society confronts the individual as reality. It is the image of society that all its individuals carry around with them in the head, and in earlier, more simple societies, the commonness of this image was what kept society together. At best, this internal nomos corresponds with an external one, manifesting itself in the main institutions of society. Nomos has a subjective side, and an objective one.

Nomos is the essence of *normative integration* which is distinct from the *structural integration* that is dominant in more developed societies. Here society is kept together not entirely by the image of it that people carry in their heads, but by the state machinery, by bureaucratic and technological measures.

NOMIC AND ANOMIC PERIODS OF HISTORY

Nomos is the "shield against the horror of existence", as Peter Berger put it. On a collective, as well as an individual level. It happens, however, that individuals get 'out of tune' with society, thereby becoming anomic. Classical Greek myths and tragedies are full of individuals like that. *Hubris* may be seen as a kind of anomie, for which the punishment is *nemesis*, the revenge of the gods, and the revenge of the community.

But whole societies may become anomic, too. Norms wear down, traditions that may have taken centuries to establish themselves, fall apart. So, society enters into an anomic period. This is a period of individualism and anxiety, but also of exploration and creativity - the Renaissance is a typically anomic period, as was Athens in the 4th century B.C. After an anomic period, very often the lid of nomos, of collective morality, is put back on. The Reformation (or Counter-Reformation) follows the Renaissance.

It is a much repeated pattern in history. It is the breathing of culture. During the anomic phases, many new forms (technological, social, religious forms) and new values are created through improvisation and experiment, and the viable of these forms and values are subsequently integrated into the nomos of the new nomic society. Catastrophic events may be instrumental in these cultural changes. The Black Death (1347-50) is quite as essential for understanding the transition from a Medieval to a Renaissance outlook, as the First World War is for understanding the transitions to a Modern one.

THE 19TH AND 20TH CENTURY

Contemplated from some height, the 19th and 20th century correspond to each other as a nomic to an anomic age. When you look closer, of course, a more complex pattern develops.

Although the 19th Century was the century of great changes in Western Europe – industrialization, urbanization and colonization, to name but the greatest — politically and culturally it may be seen as a very conservative period. In that respect it begins with the Restoration and ends with Victorianism, going through phases of re-traditionalisation and re-christianisation along the way.

The manifest tightening of the Western nomos hinges to a wide extent on the *authority of the father*. It is a father-dominated nomos, based on a cultural intersection of fathers – the fathers in families, in schools, in business, in the political world, in the church, the fathers of the land, the father of the country – and God the Father. This string of fathers made father-authority – and the culture that was based on it – seem extremely powerful, almost non-eradicable.

By the late 20th century, however, it had almost gone. Western (European) culture can hardly be seen as a father-dominated culture anymore, and the main event to bring a change in that situation was the First World War (1914-18). In it, 9 million died, but it is not the number in itself; it is the way they died made that made the First World War a tremendous break, a *cultural catastrophe* of enormous dimensions.

To understand this, one has to understand the main trend of the age that preceded it. The 19th century had all the makings of a golden age, in which Western Europe managed to break the code for eternal prosperity, among other things harnessing steam for productive purposes: industrialization. It was the age of colonizing the rest of the world, whereby securing important resources for industrial production, raw materials and labour, plus (in the longer run) a global market for the commodities.

European Civilized Man – in other words: *bonus pater familias* – had accomplished all this. This individual of culture naturally acquired very high opinions of himself, not to say that he was somewhat inflated by his own importance. Although there had been problems along the way (dealing with the workers, the women, the national minorities etc.), it seemed he could do no wrong.

THE FIRST WORLD WAR

And then this war had come along that nobody really wanted, or needed, and which developed in quite another direction than expected. When war was declared, everybody was imagining a war of cavalry, a quick war with a lot of swift movements through the continent, and with a lot of *élan*, as the French called it – a campaign ending up in either Berlin or Paris after a few months. Instead, they had had a war of attrition, a trench-war with a frontline that did not move much, but which proved to be absolutely deadly.

This is definitely not the place for an investigation of the many aspects of this war. Suffice it to say that it was the first undeniable example of "technology turning against man". George Orwell put it bluntly: "The War of 1914-18 ... succeeded in debunking both Science, Progress and civilized man. Progress had finally ended in the biggest massacre in history, Science was something that created bombing planes and poison gas, civilized man, as it turned out, was ready to behave worse than any savage when the pinch came."

Orwell was not one to underestimate the impact of an event like this. He saw crucial events as being instrumental in bringing cultural change about: "Every now and again something happens (...) and the whole spirit and tempo of life changes, and people acquire a new outlook which reflects itself in their political behaviour, their manners, their architecture, their literature and everything else."

"... And everything else". A very comprehensive way of putting it. Another way of summing up the impact of the war was that it was the "death of God." "God died" several times through history – as when Friedrich Nietzsche formulated the well-known dictum in the 1870s – but probably the war made the "death of God" real to the public, generally. At least "the whole spirit and tempo of life changed", making the 1920s an altogether different scenario from what the 1910s had been.

With God, the father went. War seemed to separate the generations, the generation-gap widened, putting especially the fathers and the sons on different sides. The 1920s and 1930s became the age of "the lost generation". Nine million young men had died in the war, even more millions had survived in a terrible condition, eventually manifesting themselves in art and literature as victims of a catastrophe. The generation of the fathers were pointed out as the perpetrators; the fathers – German, French or British – had started the war, through pride and senseless arrogance (or so it seemed afterwards), and the sons got themselves killed in it.

A UTOPIAN BROTHER-SOCIETY

When it came to the efforts of rebuilding the nomos after the war, this new condition was integrated in it. The Western European political project had changed. Now, the project became to create a "Land fit for heroes", as the British prime minister, David Lloyd George, formulated it. The object of this policy was the veterans, specifically, and the young, generally. To an extent it was political rhetoric – the post-war period became the age of mass-politics, the result of what the German foreign minister, Walther Rathenau, had called the "vertical migration of the masses."

Not all rhetoric, though. After the war there seemed to be a general will to create a more egalitarian, hopefully more just society. Ultimately, this had a lot to do with the war-experience, the front-soldiers learning how to survive in No-Mans Land by depending on each other. Only there was not much real agreement about how this new society should be organized. The dominant mass-ideologies of the 1920s and 1930s were communism, fascism/nazism and social-democracy — in the absence of the traditional God, assuming the character of belief-systems.

All of them egalitarian, although in different ways, the more extreme of them came to demonstrate a marked tendency towards organizing themselves around a leader, a dictator. It was the debunked authoritarian father creeping in through the backdoor, in a perverse shape.

The more extreme of these ideologies all more or less burned out in the Second World War, after which the dominant political programme of Western Europe was to create a welfare state, in the framework of a liberalistic economy. This project was based on the hope that technological progress would redeem everybody - that technology and market-economy would be able to secure the affluence, while the welfare state took care of the redistribution of income between rich and poor. The great leap forward for this system was the sixties, and after the fall of the Soviet Union in the beginning of the 1990s it went global.

THE FAMILY

Through the anomic ordeals of first half of the 20th century, a period where so many essential values and traditional institutions were being questioned and brought down, the nuclear family continued to be a cultural goal of the many. It is in fact amazing to see how people in the modernized, individualized consumer-society still work hard to maintain families, although they would probably have easier and more affluent lives by being single. The explanations of this seem to be cultural, and biological.

Anyway, the fact remains that as an institution the family is severely undermined. The divorce-rates are soaring sky-high in most Western European societies (the will to build families seems to manifest itself in Chamberlain's defeatist motto: Try, try and try again). It is difficult for a modern, self-seeking, somewhat narcissistic person to stay married when the going gets rough...

Also, though seemingly supporting the nuclear family, the presence of the welfare state actually seems to weaken it. Along the way the state stepped in and took on a lot of the traditional tasks of the family: daily child-care, care of the old and the sick etc. - freeing the father and mother of these obligations so that they might work longer on the labour-market, enabling them to consume more. But at the same time the loss of the obligations deprived the family of authority over the individual, primarily over the children, but to a certain extent over the parents, too. An individual sense of duty, obligation and responsibility was weakened.

Here, the change in the traditional role of the father becomes crucial.

THE ABSENT FATHER

Gradually, after the First World War, the father has lost authority in the family. To put it polemically, he is either 1) physically not there (the number of single mothers has been rising rapidly since the 1960s), 2) marginal in the family for other reasons, or 3) slowly becoming like a second mother, doing what mothers do.

This, of course, has had a profound influence on the family situation, on the sort of children that are raised, and, finally, on the kind of society created. The French philosopher and psychoanalyst, Julia Kristeva, addressed the problem of the paternal role in an interview she gave in 1996. In this interview, the interviewer, Elaine Hoffman Baruch, asks:

There are two rather well known books in the United States right now; one by Dorothy Dinnerstein, called The Mermaid and the Minotaur, *and the other by Nancy Chodorow, called* The Reproduction of Mothering. *Their thesis is that the exaltation and the degradation of women stem from the fact that mothers rear children, and that if fathers or men were to have equal responsibility for the rearing of infants all our sexual malaise would be eliminated, all the problems having to do with women's inaccessibility to culture would be ended. How do you feel about this idea?*

If there is a sort of rage against mothers [Kristeva answers], it is not because they take care of the child but because they carry it in their bodies. And that is something that men, even if they handle the diapers, can't do. I think it is here that a certain desire is rooted, a certain negative desire, a certain rejection of the maternal function – a fascinated rejection. Moreover, the fact that men do the same work as women with regard to the education of children or their early upbringing will certainly change things in the psychic functioning of children, but I don't know if it will do so in the way foreseen by these feminists. In fact, it will decimate the paternal function. I mean that it will render ambiguous the paternal role. Up to the present, in the division of sexual roles, the mother takes care of the child, the father is farther away. The father represents the symbolic moment of separation.

And you feel that that should be retained?

If we do what they call for, that is, if the fathers are always present, if fathers become mothers, one may well ask oneself who will play the role of separators.

Couldn't they both be? Couldn't both sexes be both nurturers and differentiators somehow?

I would like to think so, but it would be very difficult. What seems more likely is that many borderline children will be produced, and it will become necessary to find a third party, that is to say, the school, all those medical sectors of the different "psy's": psychoanalysts, psychiatrists, psychotherapists, who will play the paternal role. The number of helping institutions for early childhood, for schoolchildren, that are forming now in our society is extraordinary, and one may well ask oneself what their function is. These people, of course, replace the failed mother, as it is remarked only too often, but it is above all to replace the nonexistent father: to play the role of the separator, of someone who comforts the mother in order to permit her to take her role in hand. The question is what must be done in order to allow children to develop so they will accede to the various elements of human culture. And I think that what interferes with that access is the underestimation of the paternal function.

Nancy Chodorow, whom I mentioned before, would say that the function of the father has nothing to do with his sex, and that someone female could play the same role of separator.

Yes, certainly; that's why I say "a third party", who could be the woman psychotherapist to whom one can bring the child.

(Guberman R.M. (ed.), *Julia Kristeva Interviews*, pp. 118-19)

What Kristeva is talking about here very well covers the current function of a Northern European ("universalist") type of welfare state vis-à-vis the single, or "semi-single", mothers. In this respect the Northern European type of state probably differs from a Southern European type of welfare state, to judge that from the fact that while the birth rate is going up in the North, it is going down in the South, the apparent explanation for this being that while in the South single mothers cannot expect to be taken care of by the state, and therefore abstain from motherhood unless they are very sure they have a husband, in the North singleness is not a prohibitive economic problem. As Kristeva suggests, the state will go in and play the role of provider and, in due time, as separator of the children from the mother.

On the level of culture, however, this does not at all mean that it is the values that we connect with the traditional role of the father, that will be put into play. According to the current domination of "therapeutic" values in the welfare systems, the welfare state institutions will in all likelihood act more in accordance with the motherly values. But what are the values that we traditionally connect with the role of the mother and the role of the father, respectively?

The mother role is of course connected with everything thinkable in the direction of care and comfort, instant (oral) gratification and complete involvement. A motherly culture is a breast-sucking culture, stressing participation and evaluation, the process, not the goal. The implications may be a mix of tendency to infantilization, consumerism, welfare state, permissive parents, school, community, and also things like creativity, sensuality, image/fame, (consumer-)anxiety, insecurity.

The father role, becoming perceptible to the child only at a later stage, stress values like authority, duty, work-ethic (vocation), ascetism, goal-direction, (anal) postponement of gratification, *per aspera ad astra*, distance and sublimation, leading towards the authoritative (authoritarian) state, hierarchy and class. In fact the content of the "role of separator", that Kristeva was talking about in the interview above.

These almost antagonistic paternal and maternal values to a large extent match the inner-directed social character and the other-directed social character, respectively, as defined by the American social psychologist, David Riesman, in his book *The Lonely Crowd*. The inner-directed type being the dominant feature of the 19th century - vertically directed, by authoritative parents and teachers, education based on strict rules and norms, whereby the values you learn as a young child, often through harsh measures, stay with you through life. According to Riesman, they work as a gyroscope, keeping you steady in all kinds of weather.

Since the First World War, the other-directed type has gradually become the dominant social character, as the nomos disintegrates. The other-directed child is horizontally aware, it does not primarily get its values and norms from parents, or teachers, or tradition, so much as from a peer group and/or the media. No values are so basic as to be for life, values change, goals change, only the method of attaining them remains the same: through a kind of radar. For these reasons, the other-directed individual has a great (narcissistic) need for confirmation, attention and feed-back.

This leads to the conclusion that, as the traditional role of the father is substantially weakened, a very significant part of Western culture tends to wither away which means that the values here characterized as paternal slip out of the culture. A large part of the values that have traditionally been connected with the father centres around a sense of duty and obligation towards the community, surrounding the individual, but other-directed society is not organized around an individual sense of *duty*, as much as around an individual sense of *rights*.

The consequence of this probably is an augmented feeling of freedom on the part of the individual, but it does not stop there. It will also lead to further individualization, a growing feeling of anomie and of victimization on the part of the individual.

(Christian) Western culture used to be basically a guilt culture, but is now rapidly becoming a culture of victims. The consequences of this are substantial. In a guilt culture the individual is indebted to community – in the victim culture, it is the other way around: the community always owes to the individual (defined as a flagrant or potential victim) because the victim is always per definition (his/her own definition) completely free of guilt. So, where in a guilt culture the community is strengthened by the efforts of the individuals to "pay back" to community, in the victim culture it is continuously being weakened by having to subsidize the individual "right-owners".

To turn this around – were there a will to do so – would mean to try to reintroduce the most important of the fatherly values back into the culture, albeit in another way (assuming that nobody would really invite the authoritarian father figure back).

 **SELECTED BIBLIOGRAPHY**

Berger P.L., *The Social Reality of Religion*, Harmondsworth 1973.

Carroll J., *Guilt*, London 1985.

Guberman R.S. (ed.), *Julia Kristeva Interviews*, New York 1996.

Jensen H., *Ofrets århundrede*, Copenhagen 1998.

Lachs J., *Responsibility and the Individual in Modern Society*, Brighton 1981.

Rieff P., *The Triumph of the Therapeutic*, New York 1968.

Rieff P., *The Feeling Intellect*, Chicago 1990.

Gender and roles from an anthropologist's point of view

Fabio Dei

Università di Roma, "La Sapienza"

L'antropologia si accosta al problema della differenza donna-uomo partendo dalla distinzione tra il concetto di sesso e quello di genere – una distinzione che corrisponde più o meno a quella tra natura e cultura, e che tende a relativizzare le differenze di genere in relazione ai contesti socio-culturali. Tuttavia, nella storia degli studi, gli antropologi si sono interrogati su certe invarianze nella costruzione sociale del genere, soprattutto nella diversa distribuzione del potere tra uomini e donne, cercando di darne spiegazioni di tipo naturalistico. In modo più o meno esplicito, si è delineata una sfera "domestica" della vita sociale, definita dalle esigenze biologiche della procreazione, a partire dalla quale si determinerebbe il ruolo sociale della donna. Il più recente dibattito post-strutturalista ha tuttavia messo fortemente in discussione queste basi naturalistiche del genere, convergendo in ciò con alcuni esiti del pensiero femminista. Se la "natura", secondo la lezione di M. Foucault, è una costruzione epistemologica dell'occidente moderno, noi non possiamo semplicemente assumerla come risorsa per studiare gli "altri". L'esempio della teoria antropologica della parentela dimostra come nell'accostarci ad altri sistemi culturali diamo per scontato più di quello che potremmo e dovremmo. L'antropologia che segue questa linea di riflessione è interessata più ai modi in cui diversi contesti storico-sociali tracciano i confini tra natura e cultura: ed è per questo che nozioni come "donna" e "uomo", "sesso", persino "corpo" passano da risorse ad oggetti dell'analisi antropologica: devono essere descritte e comprese e non servire a descrivere e spiegare.

Fabio Dei is a researcher in Cultural Anthropology at the University of Rome, "La Sapienza". He has worked on history and epistemology of the social sciences, publishing several volumes, including *Ragion e forme di vita* [Reason and forms of life] (with A. Simonicca, Milano 1990) and *La discesa agli inferi. J.G. Frazer e la cultura del Novecento* [The descent into the underworld. J.G. Frazer and the culture of the 20th century] (Lecce, 1998). He has also received a research doctorate in Medical Anthropology, working on the theme of non-conventional medicine. At present his interests are the Anthropology of violence and mass culture.

SEX AND GENDER

Here I wish examine the theoretical framework within which cultural anthropology has thought about the relationships between gender, society and political power. I am not specialized in gender studies, and I do not intend to furnish a survey of the studies in this field (as can be found in the excellent work by Mila Busoni, 1998). I am interested in understanding what specific contribution the anthropological way of looking at the world has brought and can bring to the definition of this problem.

I shall start from a premise. Anthropology, because of its very nature as a science of cultural diversity, is close to the study of gender because of its relativistic, or at least anti-ethnocentric, vocation. When faced with different cultures, anthropologists cannot avoid noting the presence of a multiplicity of gender models, of varied ways of defining the roles and the relations between male and female. Furthermore they insist on the socially formed character of these models: they are interested in understanding how each society constructs 'man' and 'woman' in a different way, assigning to each status, riches and political power in a different way.

In other words the starting point for anthropological reflection is the distinction between sex and gender: the fact, that is, that the differences in biological characteristics and those in social roles do not coincide at all, and they are linked less closely than it might appear. In some way, the assumption of the anthropological perspective is not different than the basic premise of feminist thought: both aim at relativising that link which to our common sense seems to be absolute and natural between sex and gender. The gender differences rooted in western history, which patriarchal ideology presents as natural and universal, are not so at all; rather they represent only one among the many social and historical possibilities of constructing the relations between men and women.

NATURALISTIC THEORIES

Nonetheless, anthropologists have been struck not only by the diversity but also by the similarities or constants in the definition of gender (as of other cultural phenomena). This tension between diversity and identity describes in some way the entire space of anthropological reflection. In the words of A.M. Cirese, anthropology oscillates continually between two well known proverbs: "Paese che vai usanza che trovi" (wherever you go you find different customs) and "Tutto il mondo è paese" (things are the same all over the world). The latter proverb, hence attention for that which does not vary, has also strongly influenced the orientation of studies on gender. Researchers have wondered how to explain the fact that, notwithstanding the broad range of local cultural variations, in all or almost all known societies the man-woman relationship is strongly asymmetric – and invariably it is favourable to men in regard both to prestige or status and to political power. There have been explicit attempts, in anthropology, to construct broad comparative pictures in this connection: for example the American researchers who work on the *Human Relations Area Files* project, founded by George Murdock, attempt to compare data from hundreds of societies on which there are available credible ethnographic descriptions.

In truth, the objectivity of data compared in this way is highly questionable (for one thing, almost all refer to societies and cultures which are strongly modified and influenced by colonialism, which has itself introduced strong gender discriminations on the basis of the European model). Such research confirms in any case a general political and status subordination of women, although with great differences in relation above all to the prevailing economic and productive system and kinship descent system. As to systems of production, it seems that the great dividing line is the passage from horticulture to agriculture with the use of the plough; as to kinship systems, usually a higher status of women is found in matrilinear systems. But even in these latter the political functions are often in the men's hands.

The difference seems if anything to lie in the power that the women have within the domestic sphere, insofar as it is contrasted to the strictly public and political sphere. It is hardly necessary to note that anthropology considers the so-called matriarchate a myth – an idea which emerged in studies of the 19th century, which tended to project on remote and unknown phases of evolution the exact inversion of the gender relations which characterised western modernity.

Now to explain these at least apparently universal tendencies of the phenomenon of gender construction, anthropology has developed a series of hypotheses, which in some way re-introduce a sort of biological determinism. We can list some them synthetically as follows:

• the theory of physical strength: because it is greater in males, according to this view, it allows them to carry out work and functions which are more essential for supporting the social group and which is translated immediately into power and status;

• the theory of compatibility with caring for children: according to this view, since they must take care of procreation, nursing and raising the children (particularly in cultures in which children are fed at the breast for a long time), women could not carry out functions which require continuity and which would take them away from the home or put the children into danger;

• the theory of sacrificability: according to this view it is men who carry out the more dangerous jobs (but also those which give more prestige and are more closely connected to power) because they can be more easily sacrificed from an evolutionary point of view, that is, the loss of a man is less serious from a reproductive point of view than the loss of a woman.

These theories, or a combination of them, are intended to explain the exclusiveness (or at least the prevalence) of males in war, which is seen by many as the very foundation of political activity in traditional societies. The physical characteristics of the woman, and above all her procreative function, would confine her in an almost natural way to the domestic sphere, keeping her away from dangerous public activities and making it impossible for her to establish broad networks of social relations.

Hence, in final analysis it would be the natural characteristics of women to establish their place in society and culture. These theories reintroduce, under the form of presumed universal cultural characteristics, exactly that biological determinism which anthropology wished to fight. Furthermore, they tend to legitimatise as 'scientific truths' existing common sense judgements. Starting from an anti-ethnocentric posture, anthropology ends up by placing ethnocentric axioms at the basis of its explicative theories; in other words, it works around an idea of what is natural and universal which is deeply constructed in modern western culture. Cultural diversity thus is somehow made innocuous, and with it the distinction between sex and gender. Separated in opposition to common sense, the two terms are then brought near again in the name of general theories on culture. In reality, this theoretical system has profound effects on cultural anthropology, going far beyond the approaches which explicitly postulate a biological or naturalistic determinism. Let us attempt to understand better how this works.

Kinship and genealogical relationships

Cultural anthropology tends to construct models of social life composed by a series of "fields" or "domains" which are arranged in a progressive order with regard to nearness-distance from elements considered natural and universal. The first of these domains is that of family life and kinship relations, which not by chance anthropology has put at the centre of its theoretical approach, considering it to be the most basic element of the social and political organisation, and constructing the others (status and power systems etc.) as if they were in some way derived from it. It is kinship that, according to classical anthropology, constitutes the interface between female "nature" and the social construction of gender.

To be even more precise, many anthropologists have distinguished within kinship itself two fields: a "domestic" one and a "political-juridical" one (this is Meyer Fortes' terminology). The political-juridical field is supposed to have greater variability from place to place, and to be linked to rules and public activities, prevalently the competence of men; the domestic field would be tightly linked to emotional and sexual links, to the mother-child link and to childrearing practices; it would have a more universal character and would regard principally the women. Thus, women would bring to the system principally their ability to procreate and raise children: men their capacity to participate in public life.

Here too we can see clearly the typically anthropological need to recognise in kinship relations a political and juridical dimension which lies beyond the western common sense view – which tends to conceive of the kinship terminology as directly mirroring biological relations, the "natural fact" of descent. Nonetheless anthropologists feel the need to carve out a more basic and universal dimension of domesticity, linked to facts conceived as undoubtedly natural, which would explain the intercultural constants or lacks of varibility. Other functions then would be added on to this domestic dimension – political, ideological, economic, which change with the cultures and produce different definitions of gender – without, nonetheless, ever questioning the supposed basic role of the woman as protagonist of reproduction with all the consequences which we have seen.

Now, we can ask ourselves, is it possible to push the anti-ethnocentric tension of anthropology to the point of questioning the idea of the natural "domestic" bases of kinship and hence of the lack of equality between the genders in the fields of politics and status? Is it possible to recognise that the idea that social relations are deeply rooted in natural facts appears self-evident only from the point of view of our culture? And that giving the attribute of 'natural' to certain characteristics of women and men is part of a system of meanings which is constructed socially? Obviously, feminism and gender studies have given specific contributions to this problem, for example putting into discussion psychological or social-psychological generalisations on the invariable aspects of male and female characteristics, and on the other hand bringing a more complex dimension to the relationship between nature and culture to the discussion about the irreducibility of the difference.

As concerns anthropological studies and kinship theory, a line of reflection has been opened up in the debate of the last quarter of a century. In particular the work of David Schneider, a scholar from the United States, appears fundamental in that it has put into discussion an axiom of the classical anthropological theory, that is, the idea that the fundamental units of kinship – the universal and natural bricks of which it is made, in every time and place so to say – are genealogical relations. The most difficult ethnocentric assumption to unmask is precisely this: that kinship is always and everywhere a group of relationships based on sexual reproduction. As Sylvia Yanagisako and Jane Collier, two researchers who have recently dedicated their attention to rethinking the relationship between gender and kinship from its very bases, write

> we assume that the primary reproductive relationship in all societies is the relationship between a man and a woman characterized by sexual intercourse and its physiological consequences of pregnancy and parturition [...] In other words, we assume that creating human offspring – through heterosexual intercourse, pregnancy, and parturition – constitutes the biological process upon which we presume culture builds such social relationships as marriage, filiation, and co-parenthood [1].

The same is true for the construction of gender. We consider obvious that the circles and triangles of which our genealogies are made are *naturally* different categories of persons – where this difference is the basis of human reproduction and consequently of kinship.

Anthropologists – women and men – have given attention to the different ways in which, for example, conception, pregnancy and childbirth are conceptualised in different cultures. For example, they have often placed at the centre of their analyses a series of empirical "anomalies" found in the so-called primitive societies, which seem to put into discussion the fundamental facts of reproduction. The classic debates centre on the problem of the presumed ignorance of the mechanisms of biological reproduction among the Australian aborigenes or among the Melanesians of the Trobiand Islands studied by Malinowski, or on the cases of societies which allow marriage between persons of the same sex, that is, with the same genital apparatus (which does not at all mean of the same gender); or, to give another example, on those societies which do not seem to distinguish the two genders using a dichotomic model, admitting intermediate possibilities, or understanding gender differences as a sort of continuum rather than in terms of polarities each one of which excludes the other.

The classical theory, in these cases, has tried to interpret these phenomena, bringing them back in roundabout ways to "normality". Rarely has it been able to avoid the assumption that at the basis of the cultural organisation of gender stands the biological fact of procreation and of the natural difference between men and women. That is, it is taken for granted that specific social and cultural consequences necessarily follow this natural difference. Rather than assume that these facts are natural, as Yanagisako and Collier hold, we should study the way in which they are culturally constructed, as are all social facts, and we should also study, I would add, the cultural meaning of the fact that they are considered "natural".

Gender and meaning: the interpretative approach

In the last part of this discussion I must mention rapidly some interpretative possibilities which are opened up by this perspective – that is, by refusing to accept the idea that kinship and gender relations are rooted in biological "facts. It must be underlined that the critical perspective opened by gender studies is connected to a process of rethinking from the inside which has characterised cultural anthropology in the last twenty years, and in particular the so-called 'interpretative' or (improperly, in my view) 'post-modern' approaches. The deconstructionist criticism of many of the classical notions of anthropology, and the central role assigned to the subjective and dialogical role in the production of anthropological knowledge, have contributed decisively to the understanding of the problems of gender identity.

In this picture, we must consider first of all the studies on systems of meaning which in the different cultures define not only gender but also sexuality and the 'biological facts' having to do with it. From the 1970s on, this ethnographic line of investigation has been greatly developed, particularly by women researchers who have taken the problems of feminist thought into the field. The key idea here is that the very relationships and dividing lines between nature and culture cannot be defined in an absolute way, but depend on cognitive or semiotic frames which are culture specific. The title of an influential collection of essays published in 1981 is an emblem of this approach: *Sexual Meanings. The Cultural Construction of Gender and Sexuality* [2]. Sex and not only gender, is considered as constituted by a culturally determined symbolic system: what it means to be a man or a woman within a certain society is a question which can be answered only empirically, through research. If this line of study looks for universal truths, it does so on the level of the practices of power rather than on that of biology: the intercultural invariances have to do with the exercise of male power and the way in which is moulds the systems of meaning which define sexuality.

Researchers such as Sherry Ortner and Michelle Rosaldo, for example, underline the ubiquity of semantic frames which place women and men at opposite extremes of the nature-culture axis (that axis which, according to C. Lévi-Strauss, is at the basis of every symbolic construction of human groups). The cultural conceptions of femaleness are organised around the biological and sexual functions of women (think for example of the central symbolic role of menstrual blood and the tabus that surround it). As S. Ortner writes,

> their status derives from the stage that they have reached in the life-cycle, from their biological functions and, in particular, from their sexual or biological links with other humans. Women have more to do, than men, with the 'dirty' – dangerous for social life – element, giving life and mourning the dead, feeding, cooking, eliminating excrement etc. Consequently in the different cultural systems we find a recurring opposition: between man, who in final analysis represents culture and social order and women who, defined by symbols in which her biological functions are emphasised, represents nature and often disorder [3].

Thus, it is if women bring up the rearguard in protecting the dividing line with nature, participating dangerously in it – whereas men dominate the world of culture, the sphere of public, social and intellectual activities.

We must observe that precisely this tendency to confine woman in a natural, domestic, pre-social existential environment is part and parcel of her exclusion from the sphere of public discourse. Usually it is not the women, particularly in traditional societies, who "speak for" the whole society, who express the self-interpretation which a given culture gives of itself. Women participate in social life with their body, so to speak, whereas men participate with rationality and discourse (and, let us note, with an inversion of cause and effect which is typical of dominant ideologies, patriarchal discourse tends to justify the subordination of women with their 'irrationality'). But that implies, for anthropologists, an extreme difficulty in studying the feminine point of view inside a culture, because that point of view hardly ever emerges explicitly, it is not structured in a coherent system – perhaps it is not even articulated in such a way that it can be expressed. Anthropologists, in the classical situation of research in the field, have access only to the native male discourse, and they tend to compare it with the male discourse of their own society. Furthermore, the social sciences, such as anthropology, are clearly moulded on an epistemological level on western male discourse ("discourse" here means deep structures of thought, categories of perception and of interpretation of reality): and it could be held that they are not able to recognise and the represent an "other" discourse even if they run directly into it.

This problem was posed in a pioneering lecture in 1968 by a male anthropologist, Edwin Ardener (1989). But it is significant that it has been a new generation of women researchers to have drawn a different scenario, putting into play their own female subjectivity in the field and producing a series of ethnographic studies which, for the first time, let the feminine point of view emerge forcefully from within a culture. Books such as *Nisa* by Marjorie Shostack, or *Veiled Sentiments* by Lila Abu-Lughod, give us an *entrée* into female forms of life and discourse with a depth unknown to previous literature, allowing researchers to become involved as women as well as ethnographers. At the same time, over the last twenty years, a critical reflection has developed on the relationship between women and fieldwork – that is, on the way women interpret the anthropologist's role, constructed from the beginning in sharply masculine terms (see Golde 1986 for a collection of classical contributions on this topic).

Can there be an anthropology of gender? We have seen that the greatest obstacles for a gender anthropology are, on one hand, the non-official, "hidden" and inarticulate character of feminine discourse in local cultures; and, on the other, the deep involvement of the descriptive and interpretative categories of classical anthropology in western male discourse. But how far can we take criticism of the classical categories of the discipline?

In the most recent debate, the concept itself of woman has been at the centre of the debate. While one part of feminist thought has insisted on an irreducible "difference" at the base of woman-man relationships, another part has instead taken to the extreme consequences the deconstruction of the common sense categories which we use (in the anthropological context as well) to describe those relationships. So-called post-modern anthropology has attempted to clarify the implications for the discipline of its central descriptive categories, which only seem objective and neutral: concepts such as society, culture, religion, or (as we have seen) kinship, define the essence of fluid and diversified realities in an ethnocentric perspective. They are tools for intercultural comparison, but their very use compromises, right from the beginning so to speak, the relationship with difference.

We can make the same observation for the notions of 'woman' and of 'gender'. It is not a matter of starting from an unvarying and obvious essence (woman, gender), to study how different cultures treat them or mould them. Gender should rather be understood as a process, tightly intertwined with the broader practices of power which run through social relations. As has been written:

> Gender does not exist originally in human beings or bodies, rather in the whole of the effects produced in bodies, in behaviour and in social relations by of a complex political technology [4].

A similar approach proposes a strong break respect to 'classical' feminist thought. This latter was searching for an authenticity in the female condition, which could be gathered beyond and in spite of the political repressions and the ideological distortions of patriarchal society; the post-modern perspective does not believe in any possible authenticity – it does not believe, as we have said, that a 'woman' exists before and independently of the political practices, in a Foucaultian sense, which construct her.

This does not mean that it is necessary to erase the notions of woman and gender from the descriptive vocabulary of anthropology (or feminism), in the impossibility of finding more objective or neutral categories (we cannot avoid seeing and representing the world through concepts which have developed, as Ernesto de Martino used to say, in our cultural history). The problem is rather that of using them being aware of their partiality, or better of their historically and culturally situated character. Above all, the deconstruction of such notions modifies their role within anthropology. Marylin Strathern, one of the most influential researchers in the international debate today, has pointed out that the very definition of "anthropology of gender" is inadequate and contradictory: as if gender were an object or an entity of the social world, defined and separate respect to other objects, hence describable in a separate chapter in anthropology textbooks alongside kinship, political systems, religion and so forth. The idea itself that gender can be assumed con a unit of intercultural analysis for Strathern is completely wrong. Everything is gender, in the sense that every social practice is gendered (a concept that is hard to express in Italian). The argument is of the same nature as Schneider's criticism of kinship theory, which we considered above.

I began by saying that I am not a specialist in gender anthropology. I conclude with a twofold and paradoxical observation. On one hand gender anthropology cannot exist as such, that is, as a well defined sub-discipline, if it carries its anti-ethnocentric and anti-essentialist criticism to its consequences, denying the existence of gender as a social object. On the other hand, precisely because it does not define a particular specialistic field, no one can ignore the problems which it poses, which broadly affect the entire area of social and anthropological theory. What is put into question by the critique of the concepts of kinship, woman and gender which I have tried to delineate schematically, are in fact the very concepts of society and culture, understood as a systematic articulation of fields founded on the 'invariable' aspects of human existence, and which can be studied separately in an intercultural perspective. What is put into doubt is, so to say, the index of most anthropology textbooks, which are articulated around the themes of economy, politics, kinship, art, religion and so forth; it is the idea that it is possible to build a metadescription objectively founded of human life on the basis of an abstract model, a sort of Dewey code of the forms of life. The problem is that today we do not know yet what an anthropology that abandons the concepts of culture and society will be like, and we have no alternative language to talk about what we continue to call – exactly – cultural differences; in the same way it is not completely clear how anthropology or gender studies can get rid of concepts based on the idea that 'woman' and 'gender' can be defined by identifying their essence.

 **NOTES**

[1] Borowsky R. (ed.), *Assessing Cultural Anthropology*, New York 1994, p 193.

[2] Ortner S., Whitehead H. (eds.), *Sexual Meanings. The Cultural Construction of Gender and Sexuality*, Cambridge 1981,.

[3] See Rosaldo in Mellino M., *Antropologia e lo studio del gender*, "Ossimori. Periodico di antropologia e scienze umane", 1997, 9-10, p. 164.

[4] See De Lauretis quoted in Mellino, *Antropologia*, p. 167.

 SELECTED BIBLIOGRAPHY

Ardener E., *Belief and the problem of women*, in Ardener E., *The Voice of Prophecy and Other Essays*, Oxford 1989, pp. 72-85.

Busoni M., *Genere, sesso e cultura*, Roma 1998.

Golde P. (ed.), *Women in the Field. Anthropological Experiences*, Berkeley 1986.

Mellino, M., *Antropologia e lo studio del gender*, "Ossimori. Periodico di antropologia e scienze umane", 1997, 9-10, pp. 160-171.

Ortner, S., *Is female to male as nature is to culture?*, in Rosaldo M., Lamphere L. (eds.), *Women, Culture and Society*, Stanford 1974, pp. 67-87.

Ortner S., Whitehead H. (eds.), *Sexual Meanings. The Cultural Construction of Gender and Sexuality*, Cambridge 1981.

Yanagisako S., Collier J., *Gender and kinship reconsidered: Toward a unified analysis*, in Borowsky R. (ed.), *Assessing Cultural Anthropology*, New York 1994, pp. 190-200.

The Construction of Gender Roles, Gender Relations and Political Representation in Austria since 1945

Karin M. Schmidlechner

Karl-Franzens-Unversität, Graz

Die folgenden Ausführungen beschäftigen sich mit der Frage der Rollenverteilungen und der daraus resultierenden Geschlechterbeziehungen in Österreich von 1945 bis zur Gegenwart unter dem Einfluss von Staat und Politik. Dabei wird gezeigt, wie die in der Kriegs-und Nachkriegszeit situationsbedingt fast aufgehobene traditionelle Rollenverteilung zwischen Frauen und Männern ohne größeren Widerstand seitens der Frauen wieder etabliert wurde. Dies bedeutete, dass die Frauen vom Arbeitsmarkt nach und nach verdrängt wurden und auf den ihnen von der konservativen Gesellschaftspolitik ausschließlich zugebilligten Bereich der Reproduktions-und Familienarbeit verwiesen wurden. Ab den späten 1950er Jahren erfolgte unter dem Einfluss des sogenannten wirtschaftlichen Aufschwungs eine erste Aufweichung dieser starren Rollenaufteilung, aber nicht aus emanzipatorischen Gründen, sondern weil von der Wirtschaft die Frauen als Arbeitskräfte benötigt wurden. Dieses Angebot wurde von vielen Frauen vorwiegend aus ökonomischen Gründen angenommen. Die Tendenz zur weiblichen Berufstätigkeit setzte sich weiter fort und verstärkte sich ab den 70er Jahren, teilweise auch bedingt durch die Verbesserung der Bildungs-und Ausbildungsangebote-und möglichkeiten für Frauen seit der Regierungsverantwortung der Sozialdemokraten ab 1970. Nun waren es nicht mehr ausschließlich ökonomische Gründe, die Frauen veranlassten, berufstätig zu sein, sondern auch solche des Selbstwertes und der Selbstbestimmung. Die Bedürfnisse der Frauen, die noch immer fast ausschließlich allein und ohne Hilfe von Ehemännern für die Reproduktionsarbeit zuständig waren, nach Kinderbetreuungsmöglichkeiten wurden vom Staat jedoch nur ungenügend gedeckt, sodass viele Frauen auf die schlecht bezahlten Teilzeitarbeitsplätze abgedrängt wurden, eine Tendenz, die bis zur Gegenwart unverändert anhält, obwohl sich die Bereitschaft der Männer, sich an der Familienarbeit zu beteiligen, langsam erhöht. Aber auch bei den Vollarbeitsjobs werden Frauen sehr oft benachteiligt, weil sie auch bei gleicher Qualifikation weniger selten Spitzenpositionen erreichen und durchschnittlich 30% weniger verdienen als die Männer.

Erste erfolgreiche Massnahmen zur Veränderungen in den Rollenverteilungen wurden von der sozialdemokratischen Regierung in den 1970er Jahren durchgeführt. Dazu gehört neben dem schon ewähnten Bildungsangebot, durch welches der Frauenanteil an den höheren Schulen und in den Universitäten stark gestiegen ist, auch die Familienreform, die das patriarchalische Ehemodell aufhebt und durch ein partnerschaftliches ersetzt, die Scheidungsreform, die Scheidung nach drei Jahren auch gegen den Willen der Parnter ermöglicht und die Reform des Abtreibungsgesetzes, durch welche Abtreibung in den ersten drei Moaten straffrei wurde, Dass es zu diesen Reformen kam, liegt auch am Einfluss der damals agierenden, in Österreich jedoch nicht als Massenbewegung vorhandenen neuen Frauenbewegung auf die sozialdemokratische Bewegung bzw. v. a. auf ihre Vertreterinnen, wobei prinzipiell zu bemerken ist, dass Frauen in der österreichischen Politik seit jeher unterrepräsentiert waren und sich eine diesbezügliche Änderung erst seit kurzem anbahnt. Hier muß allerdings die Frage aufgeworfen werden, ob Frauen, die sich voll mit einem patriarchalischem, konservativen Rollenmodell identifizieren, wie das bei den Vertreterinnen der konservativen und nationalen Parteien der Fall ist, auch tatsächlich einen effizienten Beitrag zur Beseitigung der noch immer bestehenden Ungleichheit zwischen den Geschlechtern leisten oder nicht eher dazu beitragen, diese zu verfestigen.

Seit der Regierungsübernahme der nationalkonservativen Koalition im Jahre 2000 wurden jedenfalls zahlreiche Maßnahmen gesetzt, die eine Etablierung der traditionellen konservativen Geschlechterbeziehungen begünstigen und Frauen primär auf ihre biologischen Funktionen (Mutterrolle) reduzieren, wodurch sich diese Befürchtungen als durchaus berechtigt erweisen.

Karin M. Schmidlechner, Professor of Contemporary History at the Department of History at the University of Graz, has been Visiting Professor at the University of Minneapolis and Little Rock in 1992, 1994 and 1998. She is editor of the Grazer Gender Studies, and a member of the editing team of "H-women". Her research topics are Women and Gender, Cultural Studies, Oral History and Migration.

The fact that women had to replace men in the workplace and within the families during the war and postwar period challenged the traditional gender relations tremendously. These conditions could have left the acceptance of a new concept of gender relations in which the members of the couple were fundamentally equal but that did not happen. As soon as men came back from war there was a strong trend towards restoring the old familial order and way of life in which men took care of the financial support of the family while women saw to the running of the household and bringing up the children. After the immense effort and strain of surviving the 1940s it seemed that women longed to throw off the burden, and seemed pleased to accept the offer of a normal role as housewife and mother, as presented to them by churches, conservative politicians, parties and other organisations [1]. In addition to that, women's magazines, which had placed so much emphasis on the independence of the wartime and postwar generation of women, began to extol the ideal of a housewife, who, content with looking after husband and children, left political and social involvement to their spouses. Women who could not marry because of the shortage of men following the war, and who had to work for their own living, were seen as pitiable creatures whose work for their own lives would remain forever unfulfilled. Single, widowed and divorced women were increasingly seen as marginal, while the complete family of father, mother and children became once more the social norm. Most women preferred to be able to give all their attention to the household and children [2]. Their days were more than filled, if they wanted to keep up with rising expectations as to quality and comfort of life and new ideas about home decor. At that time only a few households had washing machines, refrigerators, hot water heaters and central heating. Under these circumstances, housework was still a survival skill, and only great thrift, careful planning and home production of foodstuff and clothing made it possible to stretch a husband's earnings far enough to keep the family functioning.

The prevailing economic situation also lent support to the restoration of traditional family structure and role definition. The idea of giving jobs to married women frequently met with objections in the late 1940s and early 1950s, when there was a very high rate of unemployment.[3]

This changed only in the late 1950s as the economy began to pick up and it became possible for the mass of people who were dependent on wages and salaries too to save up for new consumer goods. Now there was also more money being spent on more nutritious and expensive foods. This higher standard of living could only partly be afforded out of the single income of the family man who in general earned enough to meet the family's basic necessities, while the rising expectations could often only be met if his wife also went to work. From that time on the number of employed married women increased. This trend became stronger in the 1960s when more workers were urgently needed and both trade unionists and employers welcomed married women as colleagues. There were also many new jobs created by the expansion of the service industries so that the number of employed women in offices and in civil service posts increased as well [4]. About a third of these women had children. Now conservative social scientists, church leaders and politicians considered the socialisation function of the family to be in danger. They were very critical of working mothers who – in their opinion – neglected their home and children for the sake of pecuniary gain. In many working mothers this harsh reaction of society caused strong feelings of guilt towards their children and it is not surprising that many young women – facing such strong public pressure – in the early 1960s still expected to arrange their futures according to the old, accepted patterns, meaning that they saw their employment as secondary, and themselves as working for only a short time after marriage. As soon as they had their first child they intended to stop working. Actually many of them could not afford to be full-time wives and mothers and could not give up their work after the birth of their first child but had to continue working. Because of rapid structural changes in the economy it became also increasingly difficult for women to return to their former occupation or indeed to find a new job at all at a later age after bringing up children. Therefore more and more women remained in their chosen occupation through all the phases of the female life-span and had to try to reconcile their careers with family life [5].

In particular, since the early 1970s Austrian women have progressively tended to seek out alternatives to their traditional role of exclusive domesticity. The role of the woman who is only a housewife, who all the time since her marriage has spent her life looking after her home and family, has become problematic. From that time until today only a few young women start from the premise that they will spend their lives as housewives and mothers. The majority wants long lasting employment, to be interrupted only briefly while their children are small [6]. They hope to get their jobs back as soon as the children can go to a day nursery – but as there are not enough day-nursery and pre-school places available many women can only take part-time jobs unless they get help from their mothers, mothers-in-law or women in the neighbourhood. These part-time jobs mostly demand very few qualifications, are generally poorly paid and offer little in the way of job security, worker rights or welfare benefits. In areas where qualifications are required, part-time workers have little chance of promotion and are the first to be dismissed, because they are not considered to be committed fully to their work. It is not surprising that part-time work is sought almost exclusively by women. The small number of men who have reduced their weekly working hours meet with distrust and suspicion from superiors and colleagues. To work less appears to mean not to regard one's occupation as central to one's life. Not without reason, this is interpreted as an all-out attack on the value system of a society ruled by the work ethic. While women are expected to decline the challenges of the world of work, at least for a time, in order to give attention to household and motherhood, such family oriented behaviour on the part of men generally receives a negative response. It is also a problem that until today most of the Austrian husbands are not willing to help their wives with the household and the children no matter whether their women have jobs or not. Although the number of those men who are helping has slightly increased recently (from 10% to 30%), it is still the task of the women to do most of the work.[7] One reason for this is the fact that the old pattern of the patriarchal family still exists and is accepted by both society and individual women. The level of this acceptance depends to a high degree on the social class and educational situation [8].

At the present time it seems that sharing the gender tasks equally would in any case not be favourably looked upon in Austrian society as a whole. There is too much resistance, especially among men who fear that their sense of worth, which is intimately linked to their occupation, will be called into question, and their power within the family diminished. The suggestion that a man might take over the role of house-husband is met with even greater resistance. According to a survey only 27% (27% in 1995) of the men would agree to stay home to take care of a baby if their wives had a higher salary than they, 62% (52% in 1995) accept that women are working and 69% (53% in 1995) think that women could do as good a job as a boss as men [9].

The fact that society still sees women primarily as mothers and housewives makes it still more difficult for women than for men to get good jobs. This is in particular the case for well-educated women. In 1987 only 16% of women graduates, but 39% of men graduates were working in highly qualified positions [10]. There is a current trend, especially for well-educated women in top positions, not to have the intention of getting married and having children anymore, because it is so difficult to combine career and familiy [11]. Austria's present fertility rate is among the lowest in the EU.

The fact that the hierarchy of qualifications and job status does discriminate by gender is once again reflected in levels of income. Although in 1979 a law concerning equal treatment on the labor market and prescribing equal pay for the same work was passed, women in general earn 30% less than men, even if they have the same training [12]. In many cases gender-determined differences in wage and salary levels can be attributed to the fact that women and men are allotted different job categories: since men are clearly over-represented in the high-status categories, it follows that their incomes are correspondingly higher. But even within one job and pay category, conspicious discrepancies have been identified. Even where men carry out the same work as women, they are better paid.

Women's lower income levels and the periodic interruption of their working lives are reflected once again in pensions, which are much lower than those of men. A women who has never been in gainful employment receives no pension in her own right, but is taken care of on the basis of her husband's contribution.

The difference between the average male and the average female life pattern can be seen to operate to the disadvantage of women both in the job market and in the social security system. As long as wage and pension levels are based on the fact that women do the vital work of familial and social reproduction without pay or social insurance, very little can be done to alter the highly resistant structures that underlie sexual inequality. Legislation alone does not have sufficient power to bring about these changes – quite apart from the fact that the elimination of gender inequality was not a major issue for the predominantly conservative society and the politicians representing it during most of the time since 1945.

In the "conservative" 1950s mainly laws protecting working women and mothers were passed in parliament. One of those was to allow women to retire already at the age of 60, while men had to be 65 [13]. Since 1956 women get money after having a baby and since 1961 they are allowed to stay at home for one year without loosing their jobs [14]. And since 1990 women or men are allowed to stay at home for two years and they can also share this time between them [15].

This general orientation changed only in the 1970s when the Socialists came into power. They got very important reforms for women through parliament. One of these concerned the reform of the abortion law in 1975, which had been demanded by some socialists already in the First Republic (1918-1938). It allows abortions within the first three months after conception [16]. This law provoked a strong opposition from the Church and the Catholic People's Party and more than 800.000 people, mostly influenced by the Church, signed a referendum against this law. In 1976 the family law was reformed. From now on the Austrian family should not exist on a patriarchal base anymore but on the base of equality between husband and wife in marriage and family. Two years later the reform of the divorce law passed in Parliament [17]. It allows a divorce even against the will of the other partner after three years of separation [18]. The government's determination to make divorce easier aroused heavy protests. With its reform policy the government also tried to reduce prejudices against illegitimate children by removing legal barriers [19].

"Whereas in the seventies and early eighties political efforts were focused on socio-political reforms which brought lasting changes in the private lives of women and strengthened their independence..., the second half of the eigthies and early nineties were a period in which women increasingly tried to gain access to the public world of gainful employment and politics" [20]. These early nineties are characterized by set-backs which show that the danger of gender-specific inequalities has not yet disappeared.

In 2000 a national-conservative government came to power. This government wants to strengthen the conservative patriarchal family ideal again which sees the primary destiny of women mainly as mothers and housewives. According to this ideology, and to increase the fertility rate of Austrian women, one of the first measures of this government was to introduce the so called "Kindergeld" which means that all Austrian women (non-Austrians are excluded), whether or not they have jobs, get money for the first three years after they have given birth [21]. Another clear signal was sent by the Austrian government by the elimination of the State *sekretariat* for women's affairs.

Women have always been poorly represented in Austrian political life and this has not changed since the end of World War II. Between 1945 and 1984 the number of the female members of the parliament increased from 9 to 16. In that year the male voters (constituting 46% of the electorate) corresponded to 88% of male members of the parliament, and the female voters (constituting 54% of the electorate) to only 12% of female members of parliament. One year later, in 1985, the share of women in parliament had decreased to 9,8% [22]. In 1989 27 women (of 189) [23], in 1990 39 women (21,31%) served in parliament [24]. At present, there are 51 women in parliament [25].

In 1966 the first Austrian woman was appointed state secretary. Between 1979 and 1983 27% of the members of the government were women. At that time there were six women in the government, one minister and five state secretaries. Two of them were responsible only for women's affairs (but none of them had a budget) and one for family and environmental affairs.

They were appointed by the former socialist chancellor Bruno Kreisky and this can be seen as the beginning of a new era of the Socialist women's policy. In the legislative period from 1983 to 1986 the proportion of women among cabinet members was 13.6%. After the government reshuffle in May 1995 it increased to 30% [26]. In 2000 5 women (29%), were appointed members of the cabinet [27].

The situation in the parliaments of the provinces is very different, but in all of them there are only a few female members. The proportion of women varies between 8% (Burgenland) and 31% (Vienna). In 1996 Styria got the first female governor [28].

The same is to be said concerning the representation of women in the trade unions, chambers of commerce and other public institutions [29].

A feminist movement emerged in Austria rather late, in 1973. Since a large proportion of the movement activists, especially in the first years, were university students, women's studies at the universities were and still are regarded as part of the new women's movement by many participants. Usually it was women students and young women faculty members who started women's studies at the universities. Women's studies developed as a challenge to established university education and research, which had often neglected women, taking the male as the norm and standard for all human beings.

The movement succeeded in calling attention to women's subordinate position, but it never had many actual members [30]. There are different reasons for this : first of all it is due to the fact that the Austrian society is still a conservative one, especially in the rural areas. People there are very influenced by the Church. The fact that Austria in 1970 had a leftist government undoubtedly integrated the women's movement into the political system more than many other European sister-movements. The ideas of the movement have made an impact on the Social Democratic Party and to a lesser extent on the other parties. It was the change of the SDP from a class-based party to a general party that allowed for a closer relation with the women's movement. In recent times the new feminism has influenced the Social Democratic Party not so much on the organizational level as on the personal level. Some female Social Democrats have adopted new feminist ideas and have tried hard to influence the programmes and decisions of the party. But the opposition in the party has been strong, even among women. In spite of that, in 1985 the party convention of the SPOE accepted a bill that 25% of all the candidates had to be female. Two years ago the Green Party decided that 50% of the candidates had to be female. Because a number of Feminists consider it important to try to influence public policy, some of them have joined the Greens by presenting themselves as candidates in municipal elections.

It should be noted that the SPOE, although closer to feminists on some policy issues and in ideological terms, has had no better a record on representation and power-sharing than the more conservative People's Party. The SPOE stresses its historic mission as the vanguard party of women's liberation, while it is at the same time confronted by increasingly radical demands from its women's section for a higher proportion of leadership positions and areas of responsibility to be given to women. In general, although women comprise at least half of the membership of the parties, their role within party structures is circumscribed. Women in political parties are organized into separate advisory groups with few powers and have limited ability to gain acceptance for the resolutions they pass. Although increasing numbers of women are active in party politics, they are massively under-represented among office holders (10%). Also, the more significant a policy-making body is, the fewer women it has on it.

In 1998 women activists organized a referendum concerning women's issues. Although it was signed by several hundred thousand people, the government, consisting of social-democrats and conservative members, almost completely ignored the demands.[31]

Recently and mainly for strategic and tactical reasons the nationalistic Freedom Party has put some female politicians into representative positions. These women consider themselves not as feminists but, according to the patriarchal ideology, as subordinate supporters of the male politicians and therefore do not call the present inequality between women and men into question. So not even the fact that the Vice Chancellor and some ministers in the government are women can be seen as positive factor for women's issues.

 ## NOTES

[1] Schmidlechner K.M., *Frauenleben in Männerwelten*, Vienna 1997.

[2] Ibid.

[3] Ibid.

[4] See Sullerot E., *Die Wirklichkeit der Frau*, Munich 1979.

[5] This means that the three-phase-model of women's employment propounded in 1956 by Alva Myrdal and Viola Klein from that time on can only be applied with reservations. Myrdal and Klein proceeded from the assumption that women would withdraw from the labour market when they married, and return to work after fifteen to twenty years, when their children had grown up and become independent.

[6] This is mainly due to the improved educational opportunities, given them by the social-democratic government at that time which put measures to improve first of all the educational situation for working-class children. The improvements were more apparent for middle-class girls. Since 1973 the number of girls with the *Matura* [upper school degree] has increased about 61% and has increased between 1981 and 1988 from 6,1% to 12,4%. There are also more girls going to the Universities now and in the liberal arts now more than 50% of all students are female.

[7] Szinovacz M.E., *Lebensverhältnisse der weiblichen Bevölkerung in Österreich. Teilnahme am Erwerbsleben und familiäre Situation*, Hrsg. v. BMin. f. soz. Verw. Schriftenreihe zur sozialen und beruflichen Stellung der Frau, 9, 1979, pp. 44 f.

[8] There is a more partnership oriented system in the well-educated upper-classes whereas the patriarchal system prevails in the less educated ones.

[9] Spectra, 2001. Quot. after: "Kleine Zeitung", July, 7, 2001.

[10] Only 10 of 100 women get the chance of getting a top position (respect to 35 men). Dorrer R., *Die Situation der Frau im Bundesdienst. Historische Entwicklung und empirische Standortbestimmung*, Hrsg. v. Bundesministerium für soziale Verwaltung. Schriftenreihe zur sozialen und beruflichen Stellung der Frau, 11, 1979, p. 11.

[11] The question of marriage and employment is especially difficult for female University graduates. Because of their education, the proportion of employed women was higher in this group than among women with less education. At

a time when it was not generally accepted for a woman to combine a career and a family, the choice of the former often meant the renunciation of marriage. In the 1990s 32% of all women graduates were not married. We can see this trend carrying over to the present.

[12] *Bericht über die soziale Lage 1983. Sozialbericht* (= Tätigkeitsbericht des Bundesministeriums für soziale Verwaltung), Vienna 1984, p. 105.

[13] But this has been cancelled in the meantime.

[14] By getting money for that time since 1974. Brandstaller T., *Frauen in Österreich. Bilanz und Ausblick*, Vienna 1981, p. 59.

[15] As a matter of fact the number of men who really stay at home to take care for their babies is very low. They say that it is due to the fact that they have a higher income and cannot afford to stay at home.

[16] Lehner K., *Reformbestrebungen der Sozialdemokratie zum 144 in Österreich in der I. Republik*, in *Die ungeschriebene Geschichte. Historische Frauenforschung*, Hrsg. Wiener Historikerinnen, Himberg/Vienna 1984, pp. 298-310.

[17] Brandstaller T., *Frauen in Österreich. Bilanz und Ausblick*, Wien 1981, pp. 67-74.

[18] The divorce rate has changed from 30% to 43% between 1945 and 2001. See: Kleine Zeitung, 16.7.2001.

[19] The rate of illegitimacy is now 22,5% and was 19% in 1958. It is very high – about 30% – in some rural regions (Salzburg, Styria) and not in the cities. Vienna has now an illegitimacy rate of 18%.

[20] *Women in Austria. 1985-1995*, edited by the Federal Chancellery and Federal Minister for Women's Issues, Vienna 1995, p. 87.

[21] That this is clearly the wrong way to increase the fertility rate is shown by other countries. The fertility rate is increasing only in countries (like Norway and Denmark) that support families and especially women in their efforts to combine children and careers by providing them with child care opportunities. In countries (like Spain, Italy and Greece) where the state considers childcare a private matter the fertility rate is extremely low (1.3)

[22] Dittrich E., *Frauen in der SPÖ*, "Akzente", 11/12, 1984, p. 8.

[23] 12 of them belonged to the SPOE (Social Democrats), ten to the OEVP (People's Party), four to the Freedom Party and one to the Green Party.

[24] Finland 38%, Sweden 38%, Danmark 33%, Germany 20,4%.

[25] 22 SP, 13 VP, 7 FP and 9 from the Green Party.

[26] See *Women in Austria. 1985-1995*, edited by the Federal Chancellery and Federal Minister for Women's Issues, Vienna 1995.

[27] Among them are the Vice-chancellor, the minister for external affairs, the minister for family issues, the minister for science and education and the state secretary for tourism.

[28] Waltraut Klasnic from the conservative People's Party. She is a very traditional woman and not at all a feminist.

[29] Brandstaller T., *Frauen in Österreich. Bilanz und Ausblick*, Vienna 1981, pp. 91-102.

[30] Fischer E., *Frauenbewegung in Österreich*, in *Frauenbewegungen in der Welt*, Bd 1., Hamburg 1988.

[31] See Rösslhumer M., Appelt B., *Hauptsache Frauen. Politikerinnen in der Zweiten Republik*, Graz-Vienna-Cologne 2001.

SELECTED BIBLIOGRAPHY

Fischer E., *Frauenbewegung in Österreich*, in *Frauenbewegungen in der Welt*, Bd 1, Hamburg 1988.

Maria Rösslhumer M., Appelt B., *Hauptsache Frauen. Politikerinnen in der Zweiten Republik*, Graz-Vienna-Cologne 2001.

Schmidlechner K.M., *Frauenleben in Männerwelten*, Vienna 1997.

Sullerot E., *Die Wirklichkeit der Frau*, Munich 1979.

Brandstaller T., *Frauen in Österreich. Bilanz und Ausblick*, Vienna 1981.

Karin M. Schmidlechner

Women in Austria. 1985-1995, edited by the Federal Chancellery and Federal Minister for Women's Issues, Vienna 1995.

Weinzierl E., *Emanzipation? Österreichs Frauen im 20. Jahrhundert*, Vienna 1975.

 SOURCES

THE MONETARY VALUE OF HOUSEWORK
(Time in minutes, wages in billions of AS)

	Total		Men		Women		Percentage
	Time input per day/ person	Wages [1]	Time input per day/ person	Wages [1]	Time input per day/ person	Wages [1]	
Cleaning, washing etc.	95	224,83	37	41,18	147	184,31	81,98
Cooking	46	108,86	12	13,35	77	96,54	88,68
Shopping	27	63,90	20	22,26	34	42,63	66,71
Childcare	23	54,43	11	12,24	33	41,37	76,01
Gardening	16	37,87	16	17,81	5	18,81	49,67
D.I.Y. work	11	26,03	21	23,37	3	3,76	14,45
Other work	18	42,60	13	14,47	21	26,33	61,81
Aggregate	236	558,52	130	144,68	330	413,75	74,08

[1] Working time per year projected for all persons multiplied by the collectively agreed wages of household helpers.
Source: 1992 microcensus; own calculations

WOMEN IN THE PROVINCIAL PARLIAMENTS 1984-1994 [1]

		SPÖ		ÖVP		FPÖ		Green parties and citizens´ lists [2]		LIF		Total	
		abs.	in %	abs.	in %	abs.	in %	abs.	in %	abs.	in %	abs.	in %
Burgenland	1984	2	10,0	1	6,2	--	--	--	--	--	--	3	8,3
	1994	2	11,8	1	6,6	--	--	--	--	--	--	3	8,3
Carinthia	1984	3	15,0 (13,9)	1	9,1	1	20,0	--	--	--	--	--	5
	1994	2	14,3	1	11,1	2	15,4	--			5	13,9	
Lower-Austria	1984	1	4,2	1	3,1	--	--	--	--	2	3,6		
	1994	1	5,0	3	11,5	1	14,3	--		1	33,3	6	10,7
Upper-Austria	1984	2	8,7	2	6,9	--	--	--	--	4	7,1		
	1994	6	31,6	5	19,2	2	18,2	--	--	13	23,2		
Salzburg	1984	2	15,4	3	15,8	1	25,0	--	--	6	16,7		
	1994	4	36,4	2	14,3	2	25,0	1	33,3	--		9	25,0
Styria	1984	2	8,3	2	6,6	--	--	--	--	4		7,1	
	1994	4	19,0	5	19,2	1	11,1	--	--	10	17,9		
Tyrol	1984	--		1	4,0	--	--	--	--	1	2,8		
	1994	2	28,6	2	10,5	--	--	--	--	4	11,1		
Vorarlberg	1984	1	11,1	2	10,0	--	--	--	--	3	8,3		
	1994	1	16,7	3	15,0	2	28,6	1	33,3	--		7	19,4
Vienna	1984	14	23,3	5	13,5	--	--	--	--	19	19,0		
	1994	19	36,5 (31,0)	2	11,1	6	26,1	4	57,1	--	--	31	

[1] Situation per December 1984 and December 1994
[2] This category includes:
Vorarlberg 1984 Alternative Liste/Vereinigte Grüne
Vorarlberg 1994 Grüne Alternative
Salzburg 1994 Bürgerliste
Vienna 1994 Grüne Alternative
Source: Government Report about Women in Austria 1995, information provided by the Provincial Governmenrts and authors´ calculations.

Motherhood and Politics in recent Austrian History

Maria Habernig

Karl-Franzens-Universität, Graz

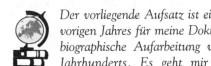

Der vorliegende Aufsatz ist ein Zwischenbericht der Forschungsarbeiten, die ich seit Herbst vorigen Jahres für meine Doktorarbeit in Geschichte betreibe. Das Thema der Arbeit ist die biographische Aufarbeitung weiblicher Gender-Modelle in Österreich im Laufe des 20. Jahrhunderts. Es geht mir darum zu untersuchen, wie individuelle Frauen dreier Generationen (rund 30, rund 50 und rund 80 Jahre alt) ihr Frausein gelebt bzw. wahrgenommen haben und inwiefern diese individuellen Lebensmodelle mit den von offizieller Seite (Politik, Wirtschaft, Medien, Kirche ...) propagierten und den jeweiligen, sich verändernden, politischen und ökonomischen Anforderungen bzw. Notwendigkeiten entsprechenden Gender-Modellen koexistieren – inwiefern sich weibliche Lebensläufe, Lebenseinstellungen und (Über-)Lebensstrategien als Exemplifikationen gängiger Gender-Modelle lesen lassen bzw. inwiefern diese von solchen propagierten Idealen abweichen, diese modifizieren usw..

Als "Aufhänger" für diese Untersuchungen habe ich bewusst den vielleicht umstrittensten Aspekt weiblicher Gender-Identität gewählt: Mutterschaft – weil sich hier die theoretischen Diskussionen in der Geschlechter-Frage um "Natur" versus "Kultur" auf den Punkt bringen lassen, weil mit Mutterschaft zu allen Zeiten Politik gemacht worden ist, Politik, die das Leben aller Frauen (und Männer) in entscheidender Weise ihren Stempel aufgedrückt hat, und nicht zuletzt weil Mutterschaft bis zum heutigen Tag eine Leit- und Orientierungskategorie im Leben jeder einzelnen Frau in Österreich ist, die Vorgabe schlechthin, an der sie sich orientiert – entweder indem sie (1.) die Rolle der Mutter in "direkter Weise" übernimmt in Form biologischer, physischer Mutterschaft, ob sie es (2.) "indirekt" tut, indem sie einen der typischen "Frauenberufe" wählt (Lehrerin, Kindergärtnerin, Krankenschwester ...), der für "soziale Mutterschaft" stehen kann, oder ob sie (3.) einen Lebensweg wählt, in dem Mutterschaft, in welcher Form auch immer, nicht (kaum) vorkommt (wobei unter meinen Interview-Partnerinnen die 3. Kategorie extrem unterrepräsentiert war).

Als adäquate Methode für meine Fragestellung habe ich die "Oral History" gewählt. Konkret hieß das, mit rund zwei Dutzend österreichischer Frauen Interviews zu führen. Meine Interview-Partnerinnen wählte ich primär nach den Kriterien Alter (3 Alterskohorten) und Bildung (ohne Matura, mit Matura, Akademikerinnen) aus. Außerdem war es mir wichtig, ein annähernd ausgewogenes Verhältnis von Müttern und Nicht-Müttern zu erreichen. Jedes Interview gliederte sich in zwei Hauptteile: 1. die freie, narrative Erzählung der Lebensgeschichte, die konkreten Lebenserinnerungen der Frau und 2. die mündliche Beantwortung eines von mir zusammengestellten Fragenkataloges, der 50 Fragen speziell den Themenkomplex Frausein/Muttersein betreffend zum Inhalt hatte. Die Interviews, die zwischen einer dreiviertel Stunde und drei Stunden dauerten, wurden von mir auf Tonband aufgenommen, danach wortwörtlich transkribiert und im Anschluss daran analysiert (wobei der Analysevorgang zum Zeitpunkt des Abfassens dieses Textes noch nicht abgeschlossen war).

Schließlich habe ich einige bis zu diesem Zeitpunkt ausweisbare Forschungsergebnisse vorgestellt. Dies ist zunächst einmal ein in den Interviews zum Ausdruck kommendes grundsätzlich zwiespältiges Bild – auf der einen Seite fanden sich darin die für eine Zeit typischen Gender-Modelle exemplifiziert, auf der anderen Seite ist keine einzige Frau eine nach diesen Mustern "typische" Frau, als sie ausschließlich oder zur Gänze eines der propagierten Gender-Modelle personifizieren würde. Die Frauen orientieren sich zwar eindeutig an gesellschaftlichen Rollenvorgaben, jedoch bildete ihr konkretes Leben ein mehr oder weniger buntes und vielfältiges Konglomerat aus verschiedenen, zum Teil widersprüchlichen, Weiblichkeitsmodellen. Mutterschaft ist dabei sicherlich bis zum heutigen Tag ein solches Modell, das wohl mehr als andere von Mythen, Idealisierungen und Überhöhungen, von Träumen, Hoffnungen, Wünschen und Ängsten geprägt ist.

Weiters war festzustellen, dass das Bewusstsein, so etwas wie eine Gender-Identität zu besitzen, bei den Frauen äußerst unterschiedlich ausgebildet ist. Manche stellten ihr Frausein nach vorgezeichnetem Modus in keiner Weise in Frage, während andere in der einen oder anderen Hinsicht bzw. Situation im Laufe ihres Lebens (manche sogar in grundsätzlicher Weise) ihre innere Empfindung vom Frausein mit den offiziellen Weiblichkeitsidealen in Konflikt stehend wahrnahmen.

Als Grundtendenz schienen jedoch so gut wie alle Frauen ihr Frausein als positiv zu bewerten, wenngleich sie sehr wohl konkrete Benachteiligungen ansprachen, die sich aufgrund ihres Genders in der Lebenswirklichkeit ergeben – als Aufstiegshemmnisse im Beruf, als „Doppelbelastung" von Arbeit und Familie, als Alltagssexismus in den verschiedensten Bereichen. Diesbezüglich erhebt sich die Frage, ob wir hier einer spezifisch weiblichen Weltsicht auf der Spur sind, die eben andere Werte in den Vordergrund stellt als die an männlichen Norm-Stereotypen orientierten, sogenannten "allgemeingültigen", "gesamtgesellschaftlichen" – oder ob Frauen, die aus ihrer Situation das Positive herausnehmen nicht einfach ihre Gender-Rolle perfekt internalisiert haben und sich mit den sogenannten „indirekten Machtmechanismen", den ihnen zugestandenen bzw. zugewiesenen Kompetenzen im "zwischenmenschlichen", emotionalen (…) Bereich, den "Waffen einer Frau" etc. zufrieden geben, weil ihnen ohnehin nichts anderes übrig bleibt.

Schließlich spiegelt sich in allen Biographien das wieder, was in der Literatur als "weibliche Normalbiographie" bezeichnet wird – entweder indem sie versuchen, dieser Norm (das Leben in (teilzeit-)permanenter, monogamer, heterosexueller Beziehung (implizierend die "Produktion" von Kindern, die die mit Mutterschaft konnotierte Teilung der Geschlechterrollen möglichst perpetuieren soll!) gerecht zu werden, oder indem sie sie in ihren Gedanken, Einstellungen und/oder Taten in Frage stellen.

Selbstverständlich gibt es noch andere Aspekte und Themenkomplexe, die sich aus der von mir gestellten Frage nach Weiblichkeit/Mütterlichkeit in weiblichen Biographien im 20. Jahrhundert in Österreich ergeben. Diese würden allerdings den Rahmen dieses Aufsatzes sprengen – sind jedoch (unter anderem) in naher Zukunft in meiner Doktorarbeit nachzulesen.

Maria Habernig was born in 1973. She studied History and Philosophy at the Karl-Franzens-University in Graz, specialising in Family History, Social History, Historical Anthropology, Oral History, Gender Studies and Women's History – primarily in the context of the late modern (18th and 19th century) and contemporary (20th century) periods. She participated in field-courses and projects in and about Bulgaria (Economic Anthropology, Ethnicities/minorities, Family, Gender-roles). She is now engaged in her doctoral research on motherhood in the Department of Contemporary History in Graz.

 I propose to investigate the development and changing of female gender roles in recent Austrian history, because, and that is crucial, they have been changing in some respects significantly, while other aspects have proved to be quite persisting. In this way I hope to point out clearly that there is nothing like an "eternal female", that gender roles are not "given" by any kind of "authority" or rule, neither heavenly nor biological (which is true, of course, for both gender-versions, the female and the male; for several ergonomic reasons I concentrate here on the female, knowing and underlining that the female gender is one half of the whole and that, in general, one always has to see both genders in relation to each other in order to understand them properly).

This question in mind, I decided to approach the question from two sides: on the one hand I look at the "official" ideals, models, stereotypes of womanhood and femininity prominent during the different historical phases in the course of the last 100 years, which were produced and promoted by the "big forces" of society – policy, economy, the church, media and so forth. On the other hand I am interested in personal biographies: how the women themselves perceived these models and if, or in what way, they related to them. Which of the gender-models offered did they choose for themselves and why? Did they have more then one possibility? Did they feel free to choose or did they perceive their course of life as very limited and predictable? Did they perhaps feel and act "rebellious", did they think or behave "subversively" towards the prescribed ways of how to be a woman/a mother? – and so on.

Talking about female gender-roles one enters a broad field, of course. So I had to find a vantage-point from which to start. As this vantage-point I have chosen motherhood.

Why motherhood? – one could ask. Is this not a dangerous approach for a historian, in the sense that here one could easily get too close to fundamental biologistic statements – such as: "It is the biological destiny of a woman to be a mother" or "motherhood is the biological function of a woman" etc.. Does it not risk being an uncritical repetition of ideologically right-wing opinions about motherhood being the "real, virtual, proper and essential task" for a woman (alongside that of being a good wife for her husband)? When I take motherhood as my point of departure, do I not become guilty of reproducing a conservative, a-historical and anachronistic reduction of women to their roles of being mothers, assuming that motherhood is the most important aspect of femininity? Why did I not take as my starting point education or profession, political or social participation, public activities or economic position instead?

I chose motherhood for the following reasons:

1. In scientific (and public) discourse one can state that there is a basic distinction between those who believe that the existence of a human being as a woman or a man is caused by nature, namely by their biological difference, and the ones who believe that womanhood and manhood are made, formed and constructed by culture.

The representatives of the "nature-party" assume not only the physical difference of the male and female bodies (an argument which one can relatively easily agree with) [2], but also a difference in character which is caused by and automatically, naturally, comes with this biological, physical distinction. Prominent in this context is the concept of "gender-character", which came up – in that specific form – in the 19th century, which says that women and men differ in their character, their habits, interests, abilities etc. These are the old and still existing stereotypes such as: men are active, rational, intelligent, fearless, strong and so on, while women are passive, irrational, emotional, fearful, weak and the like. As is pretty obvious, this is a simple game of opposites, opposites that produce each other, opposites that are not neutral but to which different values are ascribed, opposites that stand in a strict hierarchy: the male above the female. In other words: if the male is the "norm", the female is the "other of the norm" (as we find it, for example, in Freudian Psychoanalysis: the man is the complete version of the human being, the woman embodies lack, as she lacks the phallus).

In the topic of motherhood the discussions about whether "nature" or "culture" are the most relevant factor for the existence/construction of gender-roles meet at a crucial point. It is the women who bear the children – that is the most obvious and unquestionable difference between men and women (at least, one has to add, until now – one cannot not be certain about the future because of the ongoing "progress" of bio-genetic and medical research). The interesting question that comes after that banal consideration is: what does that "other circumstance" mean for women and men? How do and did societies deal with the fact of women being the bearers of the next generation? What are the cultural, the social, political implications of that biological fact?

2. The female reproductive force was and is undoubtedly something extremely important for a society if it does not want to die out. Thinking about that, one might ask oneself why women did not use this power to gain more influence in the public, political, social, religious, economic spheres and so forth. On the contrary, if we observe the history of human beings it seems that it was exactly this of all things, the female reproductive force, that kept women away from power. Which means that we here find ourselves vis-à-vis a paradox: what can be regarded as the most powerful aspect of womanhood – their ability to give life – makes women most powerless. Why is that so?

The topic of motherhood leads into almost every relevant sphere of society – as well as gender-building – the division and "sharing of work and targets" in a "public" (male) and a "private" (female) sphere (under that headline we can subscribe i.e., the aspects of education and profession), of laws and norms and values, of power and powerlessness, of the individual as of the body of the nation (…). So I discovered that, starting with motherhood, I could touch on practically every important factor for the construction of the female gender-role in the context of a whole social system that, in its complexity, is including, ruling and legitimising, producing and reproducing the roles and lives of every human being, of women and men.

3. Apart from these theoretical aspects there is a reason for choosing motherhood as a vantage point for my investigations that arises from the every-day sphere of female living conditions: that is, still nowadays motherhood is an important factor in a woman´s life – whether or not she performs the physical act of giving birth. Motherhood is the norm she has to refer to, motherhood is the vantage point from which she has to adjust her life – either in the very practical case that if she is a mother, she has to organise her life around the lives of her children (because in 99% of the cases it is still the woman who carries the

biggest part of responsibility in a family) [3]; or in the other case, when she is not a mother. Then too she will always be measured by this "highest goal" of motherhood all through of her life; she will have to explain and justify why she has not reached that goal, whatever else she may have done in her life.

What is so explosive about motherhood? Why has it been glorified and condemned, mystified and exploited so many times, so frequently in the course of history and up to the very present? I suggest that the reason lies in the fact that motherhood is, for one reason or another, of high relevance – on the one hand for a public-political state system, and on the other hand for a family, a couple, a woman, an individual. Bearing children is a very intimate, private act as well as a matter of politics. Women are encouraged, sometimes even forced to bear children – by their relatives, by society with its moral values and social "norms", by "circumstances" formed by governmental legislative provisions (social legislation, family law, abortion law), propaganda (this was true in an extreme manner in the National Socialist period in Austria) [4], mass media (reproducing old myths in new clothes and endless variations, like for example the on-going contrast between the "mother" versus the "prostitute") and so forth. Individual women have to take position towards these demands and decide if they want to be mothers or not – if it comes to a conscious decision about that point at all.

For a historian it is, finally, important to see that motherhood has often been reduced to its biological function (by science, politics, public opinion), whereas it is – and we must interpret it as such if we want to deal with the matter in an adequate manner – in addition and likely even more relevantly, a social item [5].

Having children is important for bigger and smaller social units (as for example the state and the family). This may be taken as a continuum in the history of *man* (!) kind. Nonetheless the concrete function of reproduction has changed through time as it changes from one culture to another. If we go back in history, we realize that the intentions in creating families and having children can change, in ways that underlie social changes. For example in the pre-industrial, rural family unit children had first of all a status and function as working-forces, as well as heirs of farm and land; aristocrats needed somebody to continue their line etc.; whereas modern reasons for having children differ dramatically from these – they lie more on emotional, personal, sense-giving level [6]. The roles and definitions of womanhood and motherhood regularly have been developed in parallel to these shifts in the meaning given to the reproductive function.

Finally we have to see that the human reproduction force has always presented an essential power, directing to the archaic images of overwhelming power over life and death, the power of creation. One basic key to understand the definition of gender roles of a social system therefore is to ask who is the "owner", the "manager" of that force and who profits by it [7].

Another important aspect that enlightens the construction of the female gender-role (and gender-roles in general) is the influence of the economic sphere. If we take that into consideration we discover that periods of backward looking propaganda about motherhood being a woman´s "noblest profession" periodically correlates with phases of declining economic activity – while an economic upward trend automatically leads public opinion makers to favour more "modern", "emancipated" types of female gender-models: the working girl as an important factor for a state economy, the multitude of housewives and mothers are an economic reserve.

The fact that whole economic branches live from female gender-stereotypes – for example the cosmetic industry – can only be mentioned here.

METHOD

The inquiry into motherhood as an aspect of the female gender-role leads, as we have seen, more or less automatically to a research approach which is twofold [8]. On the one hand one has to investigate the main structures, events and conditions of the time period in question – in the case of my research the 20th century – on the level of historical macro-structures: these are the course of politics, economy, the cultural codes, ways and meanings, social structure etc. This area we could call the "general approach", or "outside point of view". Sources here are scientific literature and quantitative sources. For my work this "general approach", this "outside point of view" fulfils the function of creating something like a stage – a stage for the lives of people, the lives of women. A lot has been written and much is known about these aspects. I have attempted rather to create new fields of knowledge by combining that general aspect with one that we could call the "personal aspect". So in contrast to much of the existing literature, I try to get an "inside point of view" of womanhood/motherhood [9].

How can one reach that aim? One can do it, for example, with the help of oral sources, using the method of Oral History [10] – as I have done. This is the field for personal biographies, individual interpretations of womanhood/motherhood made and realized, brought into concrete lives, ways of living, by the personal mind, will and action by the women themselves [11].

Concretely I interviewed two dozen Austrian women. Let me here briefly give some details about my method.

THE INTERVIEWS

In the choice of interview-partners, my aim was to capture as many variations of personal, "woman-made" perceptions, definitions and interpretations of womanhood/motherhood as possible. So I designed a grid of categories to choose my interview-partners along its outlines.

My primary categories were:

– age (three age-groups: women about 30, 50 and 80 years old)

– motherhood (approximately half of my informants were mothers, half of them were not mothers)

– education (three education levels: below A-level, with A-level, academics)

As to the structure of interviews, they were carried out in two main parts. Firstly the so-called narrative, biographic interview: I encouraged my informant to go back in her mind to the beginning of her life-story, to remember the times of her childhood, youth, early and advanced adult-age etc., in brief, to tell me her biography, the "story of her life". During that stage of interviewing I put myself into the position of the passive listener, only trying to provoke and uphold speech, to open up and create spaces for narration. This first part of the interview, the part regarding personal memory, could and should be long and detailed.

The second part involved answering orally 50 short questions specifically concerning motherhood and womanhood. Some such questions, for example, were:

– Do you think that it is important for a woman to be a mother?

– What do you think are the most important qualities of a good mother?

– Do you think that the fact that you are a woman influenced your life more in a positive or in a negative way?

– Do you think that a woman can have a fulfilled, a satisfied life, if she has no children?

Each interview lasted between three quarters of an hour and three hours, with an average of one and a half hours. I recorded the interviews on audio-cassettes and afterwards transcribed them word by word. The last and essential step – still in progress – is the interpretation, the analysis of the collected and transcribed interview material. I have relied primarily from Gabriele Rosenthal and Reinhard Sieder for theoretical advice [12].

The basic idea behind the operation is to find the so-called "red thread" in every biography. What is meant by that? The metaphor of the "red thread" stands for the specific "survival strategy" an individual (a woman) develops and which is exemplified by her biography as a whole. Once one has discovered this basic pattern in a life-story – which often can be found formulated in a key-sentence or key-formulation made by the woman herself (for example: "It was best to do what other people wanted me to do", "I always wanted to reach more and more freedom for myself" or "I guess I was too little self-confident all of the time", "I never knew what I wanted" or "It was my destiny to …" etc.) – one has to ask why it is exactly this pattern/strategy and not another. This means taking into consideration the historical time period: when – meaning: at which age – did she have which experience? (For example: how old was she, when World War II was over?) What was the "macro-historical "stage" at that time as well as her "personal" experiences? What was her social background (milieu, profession of parents, members of household, siblings, and so forth), what experiences did she have, what decisions did she take, and so forth. Each "case" must be observed as a whole in order to find its inner logic and meanings.

In this respect (as in others) the "qualitative" method of "Oral History" differs significantly from "quantitative" methods of historiography, like statistics. One individual "case" is not representative in a statistical sense of any kind (as for a certain social group, age class or any other generally defined fragment of a country's population). Nevertheless it is never by chance that an individual meets certain circumstances, has certain experiences, thinks the way she does or acts the way she does – these are to a very high degree pre-formed by the historical macro-structures of a time-period, by what I have called the "stage" for the individual biography [13].

RESULTS

What first leaps to the eye when going through the collected interview material (and partly in the course of the interview-process) is that these oral sources basically draw a kind of schizophrenic picture: on the one hand the women I have talked to can be regarded as perfectly typical personifications of popular gender-models. On the other hand each "case" is a contradiction to the current stereotypes; it is an individual story. Interviewing, transcribing the interviews, analysing them: at one moment I have the impression that I am visualizing one "gender-prototype" after the other, at the next I am convinced that the "typical" woman does not exist at all. In other words: women's biographies are "typical" and "non-typical" at the same time. What does that mean?

The fact is that indeed one can find a number of popular female gender-models reflected in each biography – but not one of them is, as a whole, a single representation of existing gender-ideals. One could say: undoubtedly there is a significant orientation along the offered gender-models by the women – they do not create something completely different from what they are surrounded by –, but they do not take over any widespread version of femininity completely for the totality of their personality. (To a certain degree the models in question for an individual of course are pre-selected, pre-limited by class, age, ethnicity [14] …). Women take one part or aspect from one model, one part from another, take different aspects of different ideals. Some of them, sometimes not few, are in reciprocal contradiction.

Each female biography points to a "mixed" identity that seems to be a parcel consisting of different female (and sometimes also male) [15] gender-models. In one "case", one biography, one can find more, in one case one can find fewer such mosaic-stones; in one case they are more significant, in another they are not so obvious. One woman may tend to take on a model to a high degree, while another woman always tries to find "counter-identities" to the popular gender-models she perceives, etc. Motherhood undoubtedly comes out as one of these models, which is more than others characterized by myths, idealisations, dreams, hopes and fears until the present day.

Another interesting thing is how much the womens' awareness of gender-models differs. Some have never thought about such things, have never questioned their role and position in society, while others tell about irritations they have experienced when they felt that their inner perception of themselves has not been in accordance to the expectations of their surroundings. At this point we find another interesting thing. If it happens that women feel that they in a way "do not fit" into the female gender-models they have at hand and want to describe that inner conflict, they always use words like: "It took me long to feel like a woman", "At that time I experienced myself as more male than female", "I really liked to do these male things" and so on. All the womens' remarks that lead in that direction used that kind of gendered speech. I would offer the following interpretations for

Maria Habernig

this fact: these statements show how strong the images of the two genders are – namely that there are exactly two (not three or four or maybe only one). From that point it follows logically to say "if it is not the one, it has to be the other"; for the women interviewed and their self-perception this meant: if she does not behave, feel, act as a woman (in this or that respect) she must consider herself (in this or that respect) as a man – for example if she does not like to make-up and prefers to repair the roof instead (A.L., 71 years old).

So the outlines of one gender are perfectly clarified by the social/cultural discourse: here is where the female gender ends – and the male begins. If it is not this it is that. There is no room in between, there is no room that is shared by both genders, that belongs to both sides.

Finally it becomes clear through these statements that fitting into a gender is of high importance for an individual's self-perception, her (his) self-assurance. It gives security to know "who I am" and provokes insecurity if that is not the case. Of course this obvious need for security is not only valid and essential for the individual, but also for the collective identity – strangers in the street have to see clearly if they meet a woman or a man (to know how to behave, to know which side of catalogue of stereotypes they bear in mind they must use to evaluate somebody). Both levels of security-searching – the individual and the collective – are intensely connected in the way that one provokes and stabilises the other.

Whether feelings of "gender-doubt" occur in a woman's biography depends on a variety of factors – like historical time, social surroundings, biographical experiences, character – on whether the woman experiences such thoughts/feelings as frightening, alarming, inappropriate, sinful, improper as mostly negative, or if they have positive connotations that such thoughts/feelings enlarge her horizon of mind and action, that they are something interesting, make her stronger, more flexible, give her more personal freedom and so forth. Among my interview-partners I found examples for both attitudes.

To pick up the thread at this point moving from the individual level to a general historical viewpoint one can state that, as a tendency, in the course of the last 100 years the variety of gender-models available for an individual, the number of values and ideals concerned as appropriate for a woman or for a man has grown, gender limits have shifted and what I have called above the "room in between" the genders became undoubtedly bigger (but maybe still not big enough to settle there).

In the reality of women's (and men's) everyday experience in this respect we find the often quoted "simultaneousness of the unsimultaneous". As people of different generations live together at one time in one cultural room and share one social environment [16] there are conceptions, opinions, views that belong to different periods in historical time co-existing shoulder by shoulder. For the individual this often means that she is confronted by contradictory images – on the one side (more "modern" gender images) she experiences a shift of gender limits, an enlargement of her radius of action and identity as a woman (for example, it is a positive thing to work), on the other side she is confronted with older, so-called "traditional" values (for example, a woman should stay at home and care for her children). I think that for women this clash of gender models provokes not only inner identity problems, but also very virulent pragmatic problems – as in its "classical" example known as the "double burden", the demand to participate in the productive sphere as well as to carry the responsibility for a "good home", to be successful in a job and a perfect housewife and mother.

This "double burden" is something that is very present in the statements of the interviewed women. Many mention it, either in a general way or concretely in the context of their biographies. So most of them are very aware of the fact that for a women's life the "double burden" is a basic feature. The fact that society expects women to work twice as much as men, is considered by the larger part of my informants as a normal thing (practically all of the two older age groups (about 50, about 80 years old); only some of the young women of the youngest age group (around 30) show an essentially different view of things). Many of them complain about it, find it unjust and lamentable, while they mention in a very pessimistic manner that "it will always be like that" and that this is a thing that "will never change" [17]. But still – and this turned out to me as a surprise – asked if they like to be women most of them answered yes. Although they were quite aware of the fact that there are practical disadvantages – such as the "double burden", discrimination and handicaps in their jobs (men have better chances here) – they saw female advantages (1) on an emotional, interpersonal level – "As a woman you can get from men what you want", "You can use your femininity for your advantage", and (2) they interpreted the "double burden" – at least in theory and in principal, if not in concrete life-situations of women/of themselves – as a "double chance" as well. It is not only that they have to cover both spheres, the "public" (work) and the "private" (family), but that they can have both – while men, in their eyes, do not have this possibility. As one of my informants put it: "Men have a football-field – women have a whole meadow" (E.D., 27 years old).

How can we interpret this? Optimistically and pessimistically. To choose the optimistic interpretation one could state that maybe in this question we find an indication that there is a female world-view that is essentially different from the male – which has been for centuries and still is considered to be the "official", the "one and only" interpretation. From a male perspective it is more valuable to spend one's energies exclusively for, let´s say, earning money then for raising children – or better, for dividing one's power in both directions (which describes more adequately the real living situation of women today, as, by the way, was true also in the past [18] with the sole exception of some middle-class women, but not for the proletarian or rural women, for example). So it is the highest value in society in general to earn a lot of money – and everything else comes after that [19]. Individual women can find it not only repressing not to participate "fully" – according to "official" values – in the money-earning-process, but also a relief (although for that relief they have to pay the price of lower social prestige).

The pessimistic interpretation would be the following. One could also say that women who perceive their position – as partly the employee, partly the housewife/mother – as positive, have simply perfectly internalised the present gender model, the present demand for a female individual to be "useful" for the state's net income on the one hand and for the physical and psychological reproduction of the state's population (working forces, consumers) on the other. In my opinion the possibility of choice is mostly an illusion. The responsibilities that are considered adequate for a female individual are allotted in a pretty exact manner, which means, – taking the present situation as an example, – expressed

Maria Habernig

in figures, something like 50% household and children and 50% participation in the productive sphere and the labour market. If a woman comes close to that balance everything is fine. But if she does not – for example she might like to be a "full-time-professional" or, the other way round, a "full-time-housewife-and-mother" – her life-style is considered as out of line and receives negative connotations. Such a woman will feel from one side or the other that she has not reached the target, not fulfilled the demand.

In the course of the 20th century these demands have changed – but deviation has always been punished.

Another aspect in this context is the vehement and strong demand for the "normal status" of a woman – which means, from a certain age onward, to be married to a man, or – as a historically young alternative – to live in a marriage-like permanent and monogamous relationship with a man. The norm is monogamy, permanence (at least as an ideal) and heterosexuality.

Many of the women I have interviewed have mentioned this demand for a "normal biography" [20] – either, in a mostly uncritical, self-evident and natural way, that they wanted to reach it/fulfil it (this attitude is stronger among the older women than among the younger and decreases with increasing education) or in the way that they have been admonished, advised or even forced to fulfil the norm although they did not want to. Becoming a mother is an essential aspect of the "normal female biography", it is *the* social, cultural, political demand for a woman, still today [21]. From the interviews we can see that it makes no big difference whether women physically became mothers or not. A high evaluation of motherhood can be found in every biography, and some of the women who did not became mothers in the biological sense performed a kind of "social mothering" in their professional life, when they chose one of the so-called "typical female professions" which are situated in correspondence to the so-called female qualities, oriented along the lines of the "traditional" female role as mothers/housewives – like kindergarden-teachers, teachers, nurses and the like; or they became "social mothers" in their private surroundings – as aunts, sisters, friends, godmothers or neighbours.

 ## NOTES

[1] This chapter is based on my doctoral research.

[2] For Judith Butler (1993): not only gender but also sex (the body) is a construction.

[3] If we talk about the so-called "complete" family-unit (or "core-family"), consisting of father/mother/child/ren – a social formation which in the western, industrialised countries loses more and more its general validity.

[4] See Gehmacher (1998) or Herminghouse/Mueller (1997).

[5] For example Bergmann A., *Die verhütete Sexualität. Die medizinische Bemächtigung des Lebens*, Berlin, 1998, p. 295.

[6] See Beck-Gernsheim E., *Die Kinderfrage*. Nördlingen 1987.

[7] See Bergmann 1998.

[8] A basic explanation of this twofold interest can be found in Sieder R., *Erzählungen analysieren - Analysen erzählen. Narrativ-biographisches Interview, Textanalyse und Falldarstellung*, pp. 145 ff., 1998.

[9] I already practiced this double approach in my Masters thesis, dealing with the periods of life of childhood and youth of three generations of women in Austria – where it proved to be useful. So I decided to use the same method. The

theoretical idea behind it is the reconstruction of the "Lebenswelt" ("living-world"/"world in which we live" – based on the philosophical (phenomenological) concept of E. Husserl (1859-1938).

[10] For some basic information about the method of "Oral History" see Vorländer H. (ed), *Oral History. Mündlich erfragte Geschichte*, Göttingen 1990.

[11] Compare Sieder 1998, p. 146 f.; the "Praxeologic Paradigm" positions the individual between determination and the realization of personal room for action and interpretation.

[12] Rosenthal (1986), Sieder (1998).

[13] The method of "Oral History" often has been criticized at that point (as in others); compare Vorländer (1990).

[14] I do not explicitly deal with ethnicity in my doctoral thesis in the way of interviewing members of different ethnic communities, as this would have been to difficult to integrate into the concept of changing through a whole century. I do deal with in in a general way, as one aspect to consider about the construction of "the one" = norm and "the other" = ab-norm, the distribution and mechanisms of power etc.

[15] I will come back to this point later on.

[16] As the life-expectance has grown significantly in the course of the last 100 years on the one hand and the social changes on the other hand have accelerated at the same time, this "clash of generations" nowadays is most likely more relevant – for it can be experienced and perceived by everyone –, then it has been the case in former historical periods, when the living generations have not to such a large extent been divided in their basic living conditions, experience of life, and conduct of life.

[17] They also found the "key" for the – in my opinion the only – satisfactory solution for the problem, which is that men would take over constitutes responsibility for household and family to the same degree as women work: 100% of my interview-partners answered "yes" to the question, whether they would find it good if the man would participate in the running of the household and the education of the children (interview part 2, catalogue of questions, question 25).

[18] We are basically talking about the 18th and 19th century, the heyday of the middle-class which developed what today constitutes the so-called "traditional" gender-model: men belong to the public world, women to the private. In fact it always has been only some members of the middle-class that could afford to let the women stay at home – while for the greatest part of the population it was an economic necessity for women as for men to work. But the bourgeois model was the most influential, the ideal that found general acceptance.

[19] When I say "male perspective" this of course means stereotypes of the male gender and not the self-understanding world-view of every single individual man! Manhood has its stereotypes and ideals as womanhood – and male individuals are, as female individuals, trained to orient along these profiles, – as, in the case of men, for example the ideal of the "working hero" or the "upholder of the family".

[20] The model of the female "normal biography" is prominent in the scientific literature; your find it, for example, in Poser (1994). It occurs as the model of the "three phases" – young women should work, then have children and stay at home for several years, and after the children do not need her permanent care any longer to go back to work. This model was first formulated by Myrdal and Klein in 1955; René Levy has called it the "normal biography" in 1977.

[21] The motherhood-ideology has had its extreme peaks in the course of the last 100 years in Austria in the beginning of the century as a relict from earlier periods, in the early Nazi-era, in the restaurative 1950s and early 1960s.

SELECTED BIBLIOGRAPHY

Badinter E., *Die Mutterliebe. Geschichte eines Gefühls vom 17. Jahrhundert bis heute.* (3. Aufl.), Munich 1996.

Beck-Gernsheim E., *Die Kinderfrage. Frauen zwischen Kinderwunsch und Unabhängigkeit* (3. Aufl.), Nördlingen 1997.

Bergmann A., *Die verhütete Sexualität. Die medizinische Bemächtigung des Lebens*, Berlin 1998.

Braun C. von, Stephan I. (ed), *Gender-Studien*, Stuttgart, Weimar 2000.

Maria Habernig

Butler J., *Bodies that matter. On the Discursive Limits of "Sex"*, New York, London 1993.

Donnenberg W., *Mutter im Widerspruch. Wie Frauen ihr Muttersein erleben*, Salzburg 1993.

Gehmacher J., *Völkische Frauenbewegung: deutschnationale und nationalsozialistische Geschlechterpolitik in Österreich*, Vienna 1998.

Herminghouse P., Mueller M. (ed), *Gender and Germaness. Cultural Productions of Nation*, Oxford 1997.

Perko G. (ed), *Mutterwitz. Das Phänomen Mutter - eine Gestaltung zwischen Ohnmacht und Allmacht. Reihe Frauenforschung Band 36*, Vienna 1998.

Poser M., *Weibliche Lebensentwürfe. Zwischen Kontinuität und Bruch. Wissenschaftliche Reihe Bd. 58*, Bielefeld 1994.

Rosenthal G. (ed), *Die Hitlerjugend-Generation. Biographische Thematisierung als Vergangenheitsbewältigung. Gesellschaftstheorie und soziale Praxis Bd. 1*, Essen 1986.

Rouette S., *Sozialpolitik als Geschlechterpolitik. Die Regulierung der Frauenarbeit nach dem Ersten Weltkrieg*, Frankfurt, New York 1993.

Safer J., *Kinderlos glücklich. Wenn Frauen keine Mütter sind*, Munich 1998.

Sieder R., *Erzählungen analysieren, Analysen erzählen. Narrativ-biographisches Interview, Textanalyse und Falldarstellung*, in Wernhart K.R., Zips W. (ed), *Ethnohistorie. Rekonstruktion und Kulturkritik. Eine Einführung*, S. 145-172, Vienna 1998.

Vorländer H. (ed), *Oral History. Mündlich erfragte Geschichte*, Göttingen 1990.

Wisinger M., *Land der Töchter. 150 Jahre Frauenleben in Österreich*, Vienna 1992.

 SOURCES

A sample of responses to interviews on being a woman:

Interview-Partners:

H.G. 81; verwitwet; Hausfrau; ein Sohn
L.A. 71; verheiratet; Schuhmachermeisterin; ein Sohn
O.S. 54; verheiratet; Kinderärztin; zwei Söhne
N.E. 48; in Lebensgemeinschaft; Gynäkologin; keine Kinder
S.M. 46; geschieden; Universitätsprofessorin; ein Sohn
S.K. 34; in Lebensgemeinschaft; Büroangestellte; wünscht sich sehr ein Kind, ihr Partner lehnt es jedoch ab
F.R. 28; verheiratet; ausgebildete Keramikerin, Hausfrau; zwei Töchter
K.V. 27; in Lebensgemeinschaft; Erzieherin und angehende Theaterpädagogin; keine Kinder
D.E. 27; zum Zeitpunkt des Interviews keine Beziehung; Büroangestellte; keine Kinder
K.M 26; verheiratet; Bankangestellte; keine Kinder

H.G. 81; widowed; housewife; one son
L.A. 71; married; shoemaker; one son
O.S. 54; married; childrens´ doctor; two sons
N.E. 48; community of live; gynaecologist; no children
S.M. 46; divorced; university professor; one son
S.K. 34; community of life; secretary; wants very much to have a child but her partner does not
F.R. 28; married; trained ceramist, housewife; two daughters
K.V. 27; community of live; instructor and future theatre educationalist; no children

D.E. 27; no relationship; secretary; no children
K.M 26; married; servant in an bank; no children

Frage 10): *„Denken Sie, es ist wichtig für eine Frau, ein Kind/Kinder zu haben? Wenn ja – warum ist es wichtig? Wenn nein – warum ist es nicht wichtig?"*

H.G. (81):
„Ja ich weiß nicht, ob es für jede Frau wichtig ist ... ich glaub man muss als Frau man muss sich bewusst sein, dass man schon auf Einiges verzichten muss. Wenn das Kind da ist, gibt es kein Theater, kein Kino, wenn man nicht in der glücklichen Lage ist, dass man Großeltern hat oder Angestellte. Man lernt einfach – verzichten, aber das tut nicht weh, weil man dafür – wieder durch das Kind eigentlich so viel Schönes miterleben darf, das Wachsen eines Kindes, dann wie sich der Charakter entwickelt - ich muss sagen es hat schon Situationen gegeben, wo mir der W. (Sohn) auch weh getan hat."

L.A. (71):
"Ja! ... der Ausdruck „erfülltes Leben" das klingt auch wieder so pathetisch – aber es ist so."

O.S. (54):*Ich glaube es tut ihr gut, ja. Aber nicht um jeden Preis. Also ich glaub schon – also so verallgemeinernd weiß ich nicht ob ich das sagen täte. Ich glaub sie muss schon klarkommen damit. Sie muss sich raussehen damit, sie darf sie (Kinder) nicht nur irgendwie aufgedrängt kriegen oder sie darf sie auch nicht aus repressiven Gründen kriegen. Weil das tut weder der Frau noch den Kindern gut. Also ich glaub, dass es für eine Frau als Person gut ist, Kinder zu haben, aber in, schon in einer Form, dass sie damit einen Vorteil haben kann."*

N.E. (48):
„Für andere Frauen schon, ja. Für andere Frauen ist es fast lebenswichtig. Die definieren sich ja oft nur über Kinder, nicht. Ist auch traurig, aber so ist es."

S.M. (46):
„Hu – das hängt wirklich von ihrer Lebensplanung ab. Wenn sie andere Prioritäten hat, dann ist es nicht wichtig. Ich glaube also nicht, dass man nicht ohne Kind auch erfüllt leben kann. Das Problem ist nur, sobald du ein Kind hast, bist du so ausgefüllt vom Leben mit Kind, dass du dir nichts Anderes vorstellen kannst. Du kannst dir einfach nicht das Kind wegdenken, das geht ja nicht. Aber wenn du gar nie eines gehabt hast, dann weißt du ja gar nicht, wie das Leben mit dem wäre."

S.K. (34):
„Es kommt auf die Frau drauf an. Also grundsätzlich finde ich es nicht wichtig. Weil eine Frau kann sehr gut ohne Kinder leben und kann ihr Leben, wie sie es sich vorgestellt hat, entweder besser oder weniger gut ausführen, mit oder ohne Kinder. Wenn man eher ein Karrieretyp ist, ist es gescheiter, man hat keine Kinder."

F.R. (28):
„Nicht für jede. Ich finde es wichtiger, dass nicht jede Kinder, es wäre wichtiger, dass nicht jede Kinder kriegt, nur weil es einfach dazugehört, Kinder zu haben. Das sollte man sich wirklich gut überlegen. Ob man das möchte. Weil es zahlen die Kinder sonst drauf, und die Frau selber natürlich auch. Und es gibt einige, die – absolut nicht von ihrem Lebensweg, also von ihrem Lebenswandel abweichen wollen, dass ich mir denke die tun das wegen einem Kind dann auch nicht und das ist dann besser, sie kriegen kein Kind. Also jetzt Männer und Frauen. Aber Frauen auch."

K.V. (27):

„Phu – allgemein kann ich, würde ich das nicht behaupten. Aber ich glaube, dass das für viele Frauen wichtig ist … wahrscheinlich einmal grundsätzlich für den Großteil der Frauen, weil das einfach auch in der Sache der Natur liegt, glaub ich einfach. Aber es wird sicher etliche Frauen geben, die, für die es wichtig ist, etwas zu haben, also irgendeine Erfüllung, irgendeinen Lebensinhalt. Aber ob das in der jetzigen Zeit unbedingt ein Kind sein muss, das weiß ich nicht. Es wird sicher etliche Frauen geben, die diese Erfüllung wo anders finden."

D.E. (27):

„Ich glaube, dass es immer einmal in jedem Leben einer Frau den Punkt gibt, dass sie sagt sie hätte gern ein Kind. Also es gibt keine Frau, die sagt: Nein, keine Kinder. Und wenn sie es sagt, dann lügt sie. Irgendwann einmal macht es tick-tick-tick und es tickt so laut, dass es dir überall herauskommt. Und … ob du dann eines kriegst oder nicht ist etwas anderes, aber ich glaub, dass es irgendwie schon wichtig ist, ein Kind zu haben. Ich weiß nicht, ob das einfach unsere Urinstinkte sind, keine Ahnung. Aber ich glaub, dass es grundsätzlich schon wichtig ist, auch das ist ein Zeichen, dass du eine Frau bist einfach, nicht, dass du Kinder kriegst."

K.M (26):

„… phu … nein, glaub ich nicht. … Ich meine das ist einfach – da kommen so viele Situationen zusammen – aber ich denke mir nicht, dass das von der Frau alleine ausgeht. Ich denke mir es ist vielleicht für die Partnerschaft wichtig – und da kann ich es auch nicht sagen, weil bei einer Partnerschaft ist es auch wenn beide beschließen, dass sie keine Kinder haben wollen, also das – ist eine schwierige Frage … Ich kann mir vorstellen, dass es Frauen gibt, für die es extrem wichtig ist, für die es der Lebensinhalt ist, und andere – die halt sagen: Nein, sie machen ihre Karriere und das ist – ich weiß nicht, Partner etc. ist ihnen wichtiger – das ist irgendwie schwierig. Aber ich denke mir wenn es eine Frau allein ist oder so, kann ich mir nicht vorstellen, dass sie sagt das – ist mir jetzt extrem wichtig."

Frage 14): *„Sind Sie gerne eine Frau? Wenn ja – warum? Wenn nein – warum nicht?"*

H.G. (81):

„Ich bin sehr gerne eine Frau, hab mir nie gewünscht, ein Mann zu sein. Es kommt aus mir heraus – nein, ich würde nicht tauschen."

L.A. (71):

„Das ist aber eine interessante Frage! Dass ich lange gebraucht habe, … um zur Frau zu finden. Ich war viel lieber – nicht dass ich ein ausgesprochenes, ich war nach Ansicht der Leute „a liabes Mäderl, a liebes, braves Mäderl." Aber ich hab immer lieber die Sachen gemacht, die eigentlich Buben machen, also wie das, was Mäderln machen. Ich bin mit dem Herrenfahrrad meines Vaters lieber gefahren, das war immer so ein Theater: freihändig fahren können, das hat mir gefallen. Und mit dem Vater auf der Gartenhütte da das Dachdecken mit Teerpappe und so, das war super! Das hat mir gefallen! Obwohl äußerlich immer, wie gesagt, das Mäderl war, äußerlich nicht wie ein Bub, hab nicht wie ein Bub gewirkt. Aber innerlich hab ich lange gebraucht, bis ich draufgekommen bin, dass ich eigentlich eine Frau bin. Ach – wenn die Mädeln in der Handelsschule da zum Beispiel ihre weiblichen Reize hervorgehoben haben in Schilderungen über Bekanntschaften oder Bekanntschaften machen oder so und wenn sie das gesagt haben oder besonders auffällig hingesetzt und da denk ich mir: Das ist eine blöde Kuh! Das hab ich nicht verstanden. Und hab auch lange Zeit … phu, bin immer im grauen, im selben grauen Geschäftsmantel gegangen wie mein Vater. Bis mich meine Freundin einmal aufmerksam gemacht hat: Ziehst immer die grauen Mäntel an, das ist ja nicht schön, sagt sie. Anstreichen könntest du dich auch ein bißl und so … Und das war so eine langsame Entwicklung, bis ich … gewagt hab, mich anzustreichen … Ja. Aber – ich will sagen, ja doch, ich bin schon, ich bins gerne. Mir fällt da noch etwas ein: Ich muss ihm früheren Leben keine Reblaus, aber ein Mann gewesen sein! (gesteht, dass sie Wienerlieder liebt, aber dass sie

einmal draufgekommen ist, dass es darin nur um Männer geht bzw. dass sie hauptsächlich von Männern gesungen werden).
Also ich muss im früheren Leben ein Mann gewesen sein. Und dieses Mannsein ist wahrscheinlich erst jetzt im Laufe des jetzigen Lebens abgeklungen - vergessen Sie das!"

O.S. (54):
„Also sagen wir ich hab mit der Frage Frau schon einmal gehadert, so ist es nicht – so in der Studienzeit, nicht, wenn ich sehe, wie leicht sich Kollegen manchmal getan haben. Da hat sich viel geändert, also da ist schon einiges passiert. Aber ich bin in die Rolle hineingewachsen, und ich glaub sie hat ihre Aufgabenstellung für mich und ich schau, dass ich etwas Gescheites draus mache."

N.E. (48):
„Ja ich bin gern Frau, natürlich. Vor allem in der heutigen Zeit. Also – ich kann es nicht genau definieren warum, aber ein Mann möchte ich speziell in der heutigen Zeit nicht sein. Ich hab eher das Gefühl die Männer tun sich heutzutage wirklich schwer, die müssen mehr in die Defensive gehen. Ja und vor allem die sind, die haben es wesentlich schwerer, weil sie sich mit dem neuen Frauenbild nicht so zurechtfinden. Also ich denke die Frauen haben heutzutage alle Chancen und deswegen ich bin gern Frau, ja."

S.M (46):
„Gerne eine Frau? Ja das ist natürlich eine schwierige Sache – ja ... doch. Weil ein Mann möchte ich eigentlich auch keiner sein ... es ist so, ich fühle mich überhaupt nicht mehr geschlechtsspezifisch, ich fühle mich eher als Mensch ... Das hängt doch glaub ich zusammen damit, weil also das wirklich wichtigste Erlebnis in meinem Leben die Geburt meines Kindes war, das ist so etwas Unfassbares. Und das hätte ich als Mann nicht gehabt. Aber nichts, was ich jemals beruflich getan habe, kommt auch nur annähernd an das heran. Also dieses Gefühl, wie dieses, dieses Kind da aus mir herauskommt, das werde ich nie im Leben vergessen. Und ich kann das in Wirklichkeit heute noch nicht fassen. Und ich glaube eben, bei allem Bemühen der neuen Väter, glaube ich eben nicht, dass man das Erlebnis irgendwie kompensieren kann. Das heißt jetzt nicht, ein Vater kann auch eine gute Beziehung haben, absolut, und soll auch schauen auf die Kinder und Verantwortung und alles übernehmen. Aber das und das Stillen ist glaub ich ziemlich einzigartig."

S.K (34):
„Ja, bin zufrieden, dass ich eine Frau bin. Aber wieso – weiß ich nicht. Wieso – das ist eine eigenartige Frage."

F.R. (28):
„Ich bin gern eine Frau. Ahm – ich finde eine Frau ist viel schöner als ein Mann. Der Körper einmal, die Rundungen. Seit den Kindern bin ich noch lieber eine Frau, als ich es vorher war, weil ich viel mehr über meinen Körper erfahren hab, und viel mehr von meinem Körper gespürt hab. Ich spür viel mehr von meinem Körper, Bauch, Brust, vom Stillen, Schwangerschaft. Und – ja ich komme mir weiblicher vor. Und vorher hab ich das Frausein, wenn man einen Beruf ergreifen möchte oder eine Ausbildung macht, und gerade beim Theologiestudium, erfährt man leider sehr oft, dass Frausein ein Nachteil ist. Und dann ist man nicht so gern eine Frau, wenn man immer benachteiligt wird, den anderen gleichaltrigen Männern gegenüber. Noch dazu wenn das manchmal Flaschen sind und die Vorteile bekommen, die man nicht bekommt als Frau."

K.V. (27):
„Ja, eigentlich schon. Aber das jetzt begründen zu müssen – ich weiß es nicht ... ja man hat irgendwie schon, also eigentlich sitzt man schon fast am längeren Hebel – also zumindest was Beziehungen angeht, was zwischenmenschliche Sachen angeht, beruflich okay, beruflich wird

es wahrscheinlich eine andere Sache sein – wobei ich das nicht so zu spüren bekomme, weil ich in einem Berufsfeld bin, wo ausschließlich Frauen tätig sind, also typischer Frauenberuf, Sozialberuf eben. Aber ich kann mir gut vorstellen, dass Frauen eben ziemlich viel Barrieren da vorgesetzt kriegen. Aber ich glaub, dass im Zwischenmenschlichen sich eine Frau eigentlich ganz gut durchsetzen kann, wenn sie es versteht, ihre Weiblichkeit einzusetzen. Das ist halt einmal die uralte Macht der Sexualität, ist da nicht von der Hand zu weisen – womit die Tiere ja schon viel, also im Tierreich erwählt sich immer das Weibchen das Männchen, es ist nie umgekehrt. Und im Grunde genommen, wenn man es genau betrachtet, ist es ja in der Menschenwelt eigentlich auch so – mit Ausnahmen natürlich. Wenn eine Frau sich eben als Frau akzeptiert und das versteht einzusetzen, ihre Weiblichkeit, dann ist sicher sie diejenige, die wählt, Entscheidungen trifft – im zwischenmenschlichen Bereich, wie gesagt.

D.E. (27):
„Mh – grundsätzlich muss ich jetzt sagen ja. Als Kind war ich nicht gern eine Frau, da wäre ich lieber gern ein Bub gewesen. Es hat auch Zeiten bei mir gegeben, wo ich keinen Rock angezogen hab, also da hab ich nur Hosen angehabt. Jetzt muss ich sagen ich bin ganz froh, dass ich eine Frau bin, weil ich denke einfach, dass Frauen mehr Möglichkeiten haben. Männer werden die müssen das und das und das machen, hab ich das Gefühl. Und Frauen, denen steht so viel offen. Denen steht eigentlich alles offen. Ich meine sicher gibt es Benachteiligungen, die Frauen immer noch haben, ist ganz klar – aber es kommt immer darauf an, was man daraus macht. Du hast als Frau mehr Möglichkeiten. Du hast irgendwie die Möglichkeit voll zu arbeiten und dich da zu verwirklichen, oder du kannst sagen nein, ich will etwas anderes machen. Du kannst daheim bleiben und Kinder kriegen – Männer, denen, also sagen wir so, die zwei Arten, wie Frauen sich entwickeln, die sind gesellschaftlich absolut anerkannt. Bei Männern ist das anders: Wenn die wirklich nur arbeiten – passt, so gehört es sich. Aber wehe einer ist daheim – um Gottes Willen, nicht?"

K.M. (26):
„Phu ... das ist schwierig – ja doch, ich bin doch gerne eine Frau und es passt mir auch so, wie es ist, ich denke mir nur es wäre in manchen Bereichen wesentlich leichter, ein Mann zu sein. Also wenn ich es zum Beispiel bei uns sehe in der Bank – es werden eher Männer forciert, eben Filialleiter, höhere Positionen. Genauso wie ich mit meinem Mann zum Beispiel darüber geredet habe, dass die Einkommensunterschiede zwischen Männern und Frauen noch so groß sind. Und dann sagt er: Ja – er arbeitet im Ordinariat drinnen – bei ihm ist es nicht so. Sag ich: Ja und dann schau – wer ist denn Abteilungsleiter? Sag ich es ist vielleicht für die gleiche Arbeit der gleiche Lohn, nur im Fortkommen ist es als Mann sicher einfacher. Weil man einfach sagt: Ja ein Mann geht nicht in Karenz, ein Mann ist immer da, und Frauen sind öfter krank, Frauen ich weiß nicht sind launischer etc. – wo ich mir denke, dass Männer genau so sein können. Nur – es ist halt wieder das klassische Schema, dass man sagt: Nein eigentlich – Männer sollten höher hinaufkommen und mehr verdienen, besser verdienen, bessere Jobs haben. Und da denke ich mir – also manchmal wäre es nicht schlecht gewesen. Weil mein Mann hat auch von vornherein gesagt wie ich gesagt hab, ja – wie machen wir das mit dem Karenz? – Ja du gehst! Der weniger verdient der geht. Sag ich: So klar ist das nicht! Naja hab ich gesagt – ist gut, aber er geht nicht. Weil er hat gesagt dann kann er seinen Job abschreiben. Weil dann kann er in den Job wo er jetzt ist, eigentlich nicht mehr zurückgehen."

Question 10): "Do you think it is important for a woman to have a child/to have children? If yes – why is it important? If no – why is it not important?"

H.G. (81):
"Well I don´t know, if it is important for every woman … I think as a woman one has to be aware of the fact, that one has to give up some things. When the child is born there is nothing with theatre, no cinema, if you are not in the lucky situation to have grandparents or domestic servants. You just learn – to renounce, but it does not hurt, because instead you receive – again

through the child you may experience so many beautiful things, the growing-up of the child, then when its character forms. But I must say that there were also situations in which W. (son) hurt me."

L.A. (71):
"Yes! … the expression "fulfilled life" sounds so pathetic – but that´s how it is."

O.S. (54):
"I think it is good for her, yes. But not at any price. So I do believe – well in that generalized manner I don´t know if I would say so. I think she must be able to deal with it. She must feel she can handle the situation, she should not have them (children) obtruded on her and she also should not get them for repressive reasons. Because that is not good, either for the woman nor for the children. So I believe that it is good for a woman as a person to have children, but it has to be in a way, should that she can take an advantage out of it."

N.E. (48):
"For other women yes. For other women it is almost essential to live. They often define themselves only through the children. Sad but true."

S.M. (46):
"Hu – that really depends on her life perspective. If she has other priorities it is not important. So I do not believe that you cannot live in a fulfilling way if you do not have children. The problem is just that once you have children you are so busy with your life with the child, that you can no longer imagine anything else. You simply cannot think away the child, this is not possible. But if you never had one then you do not know how your life would be with it."

S.K. (34):
"It depends on the woman. Basically I do not think it is important. Because a woman can live without children very well, the way she has planed her life either better or worse with or without children. If you tend to be a carrier-type it is better not to have children."

F.R. (28):
"Not for every woman. I think it is more important that not every woman have children just because it is common practice to have children. About that special thing one should decide really properly. If you want it. Because the children are the ones who suffer in case and of course the woman herself. And there are some who - absolutely do not want to diverge from their way of living, diverge from their life-style, so that I think they would not do it for a child either. And in such a case it would be better for them not to have children – men and women. But women also."

K.V. (27):
"Phu – generally I would not say so. But I believe that it is important for many women … maybe basically for the biggest part of women, because that simply lies in the nature of things I think. But of course there will be a number of women who, for whom it is important to have anything, any fulfilment. But if that nowadays necessarily has to be a child I don´t know. There will be a number of women who find that fulfilment somewhere else."

D.E. (27):
"I think that in every woman´s live she once hits the point where she wants a child. There is no women who says: No, no children. And if she does she is lying. One time it makes tick-tick-tick and the clock is ticking that loud that she can hear it from everywhere. If she then gets a child or not is a different question. But I think it is somehow important to have children. I do not know whether maybe our ancient instincts are to blame for that. But I believe that it is important basically. It is also a sign that you are a women if you bear children."

K.M (26):
" … phu … no I do not think so. … I mean it simply – there are so many factors playing a role – but I do not think that this is only the matter of the woman, that this wish comes only from the woman´s side. I think it might be important for a relationship – also in the case when both decide not to have children. So – that is a difficult question. … I can imagine that there are women for whom it is extremely important, for whom it is the basic substance of life and that there are others who just say no, they make their career or, I don´t know, their partner is more important – this is somehow difficult. But I think if there is a woman alone or so I cannot imagine that she would say it is extremely important for her."

Question 14): "Do you like to be a woman? If you do – why? If you do not – why not?"

H.G. (81):
"I do very much like to be a woman, I have never wished to be a man. It comes out of myself – no, I would never make a change."

L.A. (71):
"Oh that is an interesting question! For I needed long … to find the woman (inside of myself). I much more liked do be – not that I have been a declared … I have been, to go by peoples´ opinion, "a nice girl". But I always liked more to do things that normally boys did. I rode the men´s cycle of my father – that was a show: to ride it without using your hands, that I really liked to do. Or to work on the roof of our garden hut with my father – that was a great thing! That I liked to do. Although my outward appearance, as I mentioned, has been a girl, not like a boy, I never looked like a boy. But inside of me I long needed to discover that I am a woman. For example when the girls at school were using their "female weapons" or told their stories about acquaintances with boys or something or when they sat down in an expressive manner – then I thought: What a silly cow! I did not understand them. And I also needed a long time – phu I always wore the same grey business coat as my father did. Till one day a girl-friend said to me: You always wear that grey coat, this is not very pleasant. And you could make yourself up a little bit – and so on. And that has been a slow development until I … dared to put on some make-up … yes. But – I want to say, yes, I am, I like to be a woman now. I must have been a man in my former life. And that being-a-man decreased in the course of that actual lifetime – forget about that!"

O.S. (54):
"Well let´s say I have already feuded with the question woman, it is not so – during my college times, you see, when I observed how easy it is sometimes for my male colleges. In that respect a lot has changed, something has happened. But I have grown into the role and I think it has its function and responsibilities for me and I try to make something out of it."

N.E. (48):
"Yes I like to be a woman, of course. Especially nowadays. So – I cannot exactly define the reason, but a man I would not like to be, especially in these days. I have the impression that it is really difficult for a man today, they more and more have to take a defensive position. It is really hard for them because they cannot deal with the new women´s role any more. So I think that women today have any chances and that is why I like to be a woman, yes."

S.M (46):
"If I like to be a woman? Well that is a difficult thing of course – well … yes. Because a man I also would not like to be … it is, I feel not so gender-specific any more, I more feel like a human being. … I think that goes together with – because the really most important event in my life has been the birth of my child. That is something so unbelievable. And that I would not have had as a man. Nothing I have ever done in my professional life comes only near of that.

So the feeling when that child came out of myself, that I will never forget in my life. And in reality I cannot understand it to the very moment. And I therefore believe, given all good will of the "new fathers", I do not believe, that there is any compensation for that experience. This does not mean, that a father cannot have a good relationship to his child and he shall care for his children and take responsibility and everything. But this experience and the breast-feeding that is something rather exclusive and singular."

S.K (34):
"Yes I am satisfied to be a woman. But why – I don´t know. Why – this is a funny question."

F.R. (28):
"I like to be a woman. Ahm – I think a woman is much more beautiful as a man. First the body, the roundness and curves. For I have children I even like it more to be a woman as I have liked it before, because I have learned much more about my body, because I have felt much about my body. I do feel much more about my body, bally, breast from breast-feeding and pregnancy. And – yes I feel more feminine. Before that femininity has been, if you want to reach a profession, attend an education, especially if you study theology, one unfortunately often makes the experience that being a woman is a disadvantage. Then you do not like so much to be a woman, when you are discriminated all the time. Especially when there are some dummies and they get the advantages that you do not get because you are a woman."

K.V. (27):
"Yes basically yes. But to give a reason for it – I don´t know … well you do have somehow, well basically you are in the stronger position – well at least as far as relationships are concerned, when it is about social matters, interpersonal matters, human relations – professionally okay, professionally it will be a different thing I suppose – whereby I do not feel that so much because I work in a sphere where exclusively women are engaged, so a typical female profession, social job. But I can well imagine, that women face many barriers in that field. But I do believe that in the social, interpersonal area a woman can carry out her point rather well, if she understands to use her femininity. This just is the ancient power of sexuality, that is not to question – in that respect the animals, well among animal life it is always the female who chooses the male and never the other way round. And basically if you think about it well it is basically the same among human beings – with exceptions of course. If a woman just accepts herself as a woman and knows how to use it, her femininity, then it is for sure that she is the one who chooses, makes decisions – in the social sphere, in the sphere of human relations, as I mentioned."

D.E. (27):
"Mh – basically I must now say yes. As a child I did not like to be a woman, at that time I would have liked it more to be a boy. There have also been times in my life when I did not wear a skirt of dress, when I only wore trousers. Now I must say that I am quite happy to be a woman, because I just think that women do have more possibilities. Men do have to do this and that I think. And women, there are more things open to them. Basically everything is open for them. I mean of course there are discriminations women still have to face, that is clear – but it always depends on what she makes out of it. You do have more possibilities as a woman. You have the option to work fulltime and realise yourself in that field, or you can say no, I want to do something else. You can stay at home and get children – men, they, well let´s put it that way: the two ways a woman can develop both are absolutely accepted in society. For men it is something different: If they really do only work – okay, that´s the way it has to be. But think about one staying at home – for heaven´s sake, isn t it so?

K.M. (26):
"Phu … this is difficult – well yes, I do like to be a woman and it is okay for me like that, the way it is, I do just think it would be very much easier in some respects to be a man. So for

example like I see it in the bank – it are more the men who are forced, who become branch manager, who reach higher positions. As it is with my husband as we have talked about that there are still big income-differences between men and women. And he said: in my working-place – he is working in a clerical institution – it is not like that. So I ask him: Who is branch manager? It is maybe same income for same work, but in the getting on it is much easier as a man certainly. Because it is simply said: Yes a man does not take a period of rest because of childbirth, a man is always there, women are more often ill, women are I don´t know moody etc. – where I think that men also can be like that. It is just – again the classical model that you say: basically – men should climb up higher the career-leather, should earn more money, have better jobs. And I think – sometimes it would not have been bad (to be a man). Also my husband said from the very beginning when we were discussing about the question of who will quit his job when we get a baby – he said: You do! The one who is earning less money goes. So I said: That is not that clear! Well he said okay, but I will not go. Because, he said, then he cannot return into his job."

The Condition of Women in Romania during the Communist Period

Vasile Vese

Universitatea Babes Bollai din Cluj-Napoca

„Comuniştii afirmă că în primul rând femeia este muncitor, apoi ea trebuie să fie activă în viaţa politică şi în sfîrşit ea trebuie să aibă o familie… Noi suntem bolnave şi obosite de egalitate. Noi dorim să fim femei în primul rând şi apoi să realizăm alte activităţi". Realitatea pe care o surprinde Rut Kolinska, membră a grupului „Prague Mothers" este prezentă în toate statele comuniste, inclusiv în România, cu anumite specificităţi.

Regimul comunist a proclamat chiar de la instaurare libertatea, egalitatea şi emanciparea femeilor ca obiectiv principal al realizării unei socităţi socialiste. Ca urmare, în toate actele oficiale, de la hotărâri de partid la Constituţie era proclamată egalitatea mecanică a sexelor, revendicată mai degrabă pentru femei decât de către femei.

În evoluţia condiţiei femeii române se pot disitnge două perioade: perioada anilor 1945-1965 când la conducerea paritdului comunist se afla Gh. Gheorghiu-Dej şi perioada 1965-1989 când partidul şi ţara se aflau sub conducerea familiei Ceauşescu. În prima fază statutul femeii în România nu se deosebea de cel existent în celelalte ţări comuniste. Obiectivul regimului viza înregimetarea femeilor în favoarea noului regim atât din motive ideologice, cât şi din raţiuni economice, fiind promovat tipul „femeii comisar".

Instaurarea regimului Ceauşescu în 1965 s-a făcut într-un moment în care atât din punct de vedere economic, cât şi din punct de vedere al unei liberarizări faţă de regimul anterior, condiţia femeii părea să fie favorizată, mai cu seamă că de la început noul lider şi-a asociat şi pe soţia sa, Elena Ceauşescu, în apariţiile publice, ceea ce a fost interpetat ca un semn de mormaliyare şi din punctul de vedere al reabilitării cuplurilor.

Următorul an, 1966, avea să aducă pentru femeile din România o schimbare dramatică în sens negativ. În acel an s-a introdus interdicţia represivă şi neaşteptată a avorturilor. Interzicerea avorturilor în numele sănătăţii naţiunii, într-o societate fără nici un fel de cultură a planningului familial a creat pentru românce un traumatism până astăzi, prin consecinţele sociale şi politice.

Ca urmare, emanciparea femeii în România comunistă ca şi egaliatea ei cu bărbatul nu numai că era falsă din punctul de vedere al statutului şi intereselor fundamnetale feminine, dar ea s-a tradusprin obligaţii şi responsabilităţi suplimentare, fără schimbări esenţiale în condiţia umană a femeii românce.

Vasile Vese was born on May 6, 1939; he graduated from the Babes-Bolyai University in 1962, his specialization being World History. He obtained his PhD in 1974, with a thesis on Romanian-French diplomatic relations at the beginning of the 20th century.
He is currently full professor at the Department of the Contemporary History, in the Faculty of History and Philosophy of the Babes-Bolyai University and head of Departement. He teaches World history in the 20th century and history of European integration. He was a visiting professor in Wayul State University – USA , in 1978-1979, Trinity University – USA in 1980, Paris IV (Sorbonne) and Paris XII (Val de Marne) Universities (1998, 1999), the Université Libre de Bruxelles (1992) and others.

"The Communists claimed that a woman is in the first place a worker, then she ought to be active in the political life and only in the third place she should consider having a family... We are sick and tired of equality! We want to be women in the first place and then to join other activities" [1]. The reality emphasized by Rut Kolinska, member of "The Prague mothers" group was present in all the former communist countries, as well as in Romania, but with certain particularities.

At the time when Communism was imposed in Romania (1945-1948), Romanian society was rural in a proportion as high as 75%. The Romanian peasant mentality had a special consideration towards the woman, in her capacity of being the essential factor of the family, which was considered a fundamental institution of the Romanian society. Because of this mentality, it was impossible to imagine that Romanian women could be tempted to engage in work considered to be suitable for men only (mining, constructions, metallurgy, etc.) and the presence of women in political life was not only refused, but also would have been thought to be very negative. During the period between the two World Wars in Romania, women did not even have the right to vote and their participation in political life was judged to bring serious harm to their family life.

The communist regime proclaimed right from its establishment that liberty, gender equality and the emancipation of women were one of the main targets in the development of the new socialist society. Therefore, mechanical gender equality was emphasized in each and every official documents, from Party decisions to the Constitution. This fact was claimed for women rather than by women. As far back as in the 1950s, this kind of gender equality in the economy was considered a conquest and settled fact in the mobilizing speeches of the Party: it was symbolized by the presence of female heroes working in areas which had been typically masculine up to that time: from working in mines underground, or in industrial, chemical and metallurgical operations, to professions in areas such as surgery and experimental sciences. At the same time divorce had become legal and marriage had lost its religious and holy character. Divorce was almost irresponsibly easy to get, and was very frequent as the social mobility typical in that period became more and more generalized.

In the evolution of the Romanian women's condition during the communist regime there were two periods: the first lasted through 1945-1965, when the leader of the Romanian Communist Party was Gh. Gheorghiu-Dej and the second between 1965-1989 when the

Party was led by the "ruling family", the Ceausescus. In the first stage, women's status in Romania was not essentially different from the women's condition in the other communist countries. Society's goal was women's participation in supporting the new regime, both for ideological motives and for economical reasons [2].

The type of woman cultivated in that period was that of the "woman commissioner", whose image was ostentatiously shown on every wall, first in the Soviet Union, then in Romania also [3]. Women were presented in their capacity of kolkhoz presidents, weavers working at thirty-four looms weaving at the same time, the woman builder, the woman metallurgist, etc. In the new realities, the woman was especially exemplary when she harshly usurped male traditional roles from mining to political decision. The policy promoted by the Communist Party was that of political subordination to the big "family of the Party" of many intimate matters, especially the erotic universe and the traditional family. The Romanian realities of the 1950s unfortunately offered a very vivid example of the "woman commissioner": many were lonely, devoted "body and soul" to the party, obstinately wearing a costume more like a man's suit than a woman's outfit. One of these emblematic figures is Ana Pauker, the State's Ministry of Foreign Affairs between 1948/1952, who was a former member of the Comintern, imposed at the helm of the state by Stalin, at the time that Romania was occupied by the Soviet troops [4].

The new status of the woman came as a shock for the Romanian mentality of those years, because an attempt was made to set up a model – in the place of the traditional family – of a political family ruled exclusively by public values and by the norms of class struggle. Romanian society strongly reacted against these threats and women held the essential role in this resistance. They took upon themselves the difficult task of playing the traditional role of mother and wife to which they added the social masculine role. Under the circumstances of the alimentary scarcity of the 1950s in Romania the "emancipated woman", equal in her rights with the man, had an extra right, namely the right to work twice as much. The content of the socialist emancipation of women practically consisted in their double servitude: as workers in the state economy and as strugglers for the survival of their families.

Gender equality proclaimed by the regime as well as special measures such as free day-care for children and maternity leaves were used to assist women in their double gender roles, rather than to reorganize gender responsibilities between men and women. This is why many Eastern Europeans women refer to previous state policies as "false equality" and "forced emancipation" [5].

The significant difference concerning women's condition in Romania between the two phases underlined above was the degree of female participation in the governing structures. During the first period, with the exception of Ana Pauker, women had not been promoted to the state or to the party's higher institutions. In 1960, only 17% of women were party members, although the proportion of women in the population was as high as 51%. The explanation of this fact lies in the reticence of women in joining the party, as well as in the same reticence manifested by the regime, lead by Gh. Gheorghiu-Dej, towards the promotion of women in public positions [6].

The establishment of Ceausescu's regime in 1965 took place at a time when, from both the economical point of view and that of a certain liberalization in comparison with the former society, the situation in Romania seemed somehow better. This suggested the idea that the women would eventually have better status, especially because, right from the beginning, the new leader was accompanied in his public appearances by his wife, Elena Ceausescu. Gh. Gheorghiu-Dej was a widower and thus, the presence of a woman beside the head of the State appeared to be a symbol of innovation in the Romanian political scene.

Elena Ceausescu's presence beside her husband was interpreted as a sign of normalization in the problems concerning couples (that is, a rehabilitation of normal family relations and values). But the next year, 1966, was to bring a dramatic change for the Romanian women with the unexpectedly and repressive prohibition of abortion. Abortion was forbidden in the name of nation's health. In a society where there was no knowledge of family planning this caused a heavy wound, whose political and social consequences are felt up to the present. If in the first years after its promulgation (1967-1970), the 1966 decree against abortion seemed to have reached its goal to increase the birth rate in Romania, in the following years "upper-class" women (so far as we can speak of something like an upper-class in a communist society) managed to obtain abortions in the case of undesired pregnancies in safe medical conditions, while the less fortunate ones, who where the majority, had to resort to empirical and often dangerous and unsanitary methods. This fact resulted in thousands of tragedies consisting in either loss of life or imprisonment. Under the ruling of the anti-aborption decree, Romanian women were subjected to a brutal violation of both their control over their intimacy and their private life, a fact whose effects last until today. Considering conditions at present, we might look to those events to explain in part the current explosion of prostitution, rape, permissiveness and appeal of pornography [7].

An entire repressive machinery (police, prosecution, informers) rushed upon married couples as a consequence of the 1966 law. In addition to that, women, already greatly harassed by the state's attempts to ensure obedience, were often accused by their own sexual partners of being entirely responsible for their unwanted pregnancies.

From another point of view, the increase of the birth rate during the first few years after the Decree's promulgation had serious consequences leading to the deepening of the Romanian communist regime's crisis of the 1980s. The generation of "The Decree's little kids" – as they were called – was growing up and becoming adult in a society that was totally incapable of ensuring the necessary education and social development for them. Therefore, they became totally dissociated from communism and communist ideas and later on, in 1989, they constituted an important segment of the population who stepped out on the streets of the main cities of Romania, shouting slogans like "Down with communism!", "Down with Ceausescu!"

On the other hand, the history of this Decree is symbolizes and allows us to measure the cynicism and the grotesque manner of ruling during the communist regime imposed by Ceausescu in Romania. Simultaneously, with the degradation of women's status caused by the Decree, Romania was confronting the phenomenon of ostentatious promotion of women in political and social life, promotion that had nothing to do with retrieving traditional family values. The target was to legitimate the political ascent of the leader's wife, Elena Ceausescu, who became virtually the second highest Romanian official. In addition to her membership in the Bureau of the Party's Political Executive Committee (she joined the Bucharest Municipal Party Committee in 1968, was elected a full Central Committee member in 1972 and became an Executive Committee member in June 1973), Elena Ceausescu was a member of the Grand National Assembly and, as a trained chemist, she became Chairwoman of the National Council of Science and Technology. Although her academic credentials appear to be somewhat obscure, the Romanian press has constantly referred to her as Academician-Doctor-Engineer – for, among other things, she was also a member of the Technical Sciences section of the Romanian Academy. In 1980 her ministerial status was raised and the president's "revolutionary companion" became one of the first three First Deputy Prime Ministers in the Romanian government. Far more important was the fact that, in 1979, she became chairwoman of the Central Committee's Commission for State and Party Cadres, a position from which she was able to watch over the security of what was known in Romania as the "Ceausescu Dynasty". Romania's first family had a direct impact on the social structure of the Party. At the Central Committee plenum that elected Elena Ceausescu to membership on the Executive Committee, her husband emphasized the role played by women in the Romanian society and economy, adding that the structure of the Party had not hitherto satisfactorily reflected the proportion of women in the society (about 51%) and their contribution to political life. At the time, women accounted for nearly 24% of the Party membership, a figure that rose to 32% a few years alter. Representation in the Central Committee (full and candidate members) grew from 4% to 25%. By mid-1984 there were three women (Elena Ceausescu, Lina Ciobanu, Alexandrina Gainusa) on the Party's Political Executive Committee (PEC) with full membership status, but only Elena Ceausescu was a member of the Permanent Bureau. Three other women (Suzana Gadea, Ana Muresan and Elena Nae) were alternate members of the PEC. In 1964, out of 49 ministers or executives with ministerial ranks, there were only 4 women. These promotions did not necessarily reflect an improvement in the social status of women in Romania [8].

The fact that more and more women advanced in politics was linked to the figure that was supposed to illustrate the gender equality promoted by the Party. Imposing of such of a system generated a diffuse, negative reaction in the community. The involvement of women in both political and social life in such a high percent took place in the most disastrous years of the communist regime as regards the living standards in Romania. Public opinion held the Ceausescu couple responsible for this situation. Elena Ceausescu especially was blamed and her evilness was also linked to her being a woman. Therefore, on the background of a traditional reluctance towards recognizing the political virtues of women, Elena Ceausescu's image aroused reactions of hatred which, intentionally or unintentionally, were projected onto the image of the active political woman. This reaction materialized in a moment when Romanian women began to refuse to fill political posts, especially in lower structures of the Party, posts which they considered to require very hard work.

Women were the ones that experienced in the most direct manner the consequences of the lack of subsistence products after 1980. Household tasks became more and more of a burden for women, procuring food supplies was one of the most difficult tasks to accomplish. The solidarity of the family, under the circumstances, became feebler day by day. The woman was more and more employed in activities outside her home. It is interesting to notice that women spent much more time outside their homes not only because of the need of having an income, absolutely vital for the support of the family, but also because Romanian society became very boring and colorless. National television had only one program that was on the air for only a few hours a day and was really stodgy; stores were empty, and so forth. Thus the working place became the only place where a woman was able to meet people, to discuss different matters, to show her new clothes. Therefore, the working place was a socializing place, rather than a place for earning money [9].

In the background of those developments, the political participation of women, promoted by the communist regime was felt to be more an obligation, which tripled the woman's responsibilities, than a freely exercised right of citizenship. Thus, the emancipation of women in communist Romania as well as their social and political equality with men proved not only to be false problems from the point of view of women's social status and fundamental interests, but they also meant that women had to shoulder additional obligations and responsibilities without any important changes in their human condition.

 **NOTES**

[1] Einhorn B., *Cinderella goes to market. Citizenship, gender and women's movements in East central Europe*, London-New York 1998, p. 148.

[2] Aivazova S., *La liberté et l'egalité des femmes dans les pays socialistes d'Europe de l'Est 1960-1980*, in: *Encyclopédie politique et historique des femmes*, Paris 1997.

[3] Petre Z., *Promovarea femeii sau despre destructurarea sexului feminin*, in: *Miturile comunismului românesc*, vol.I, Bucuresti 1995, p. 23.

[4] Ibidem, p. 21.

[5] Einhorn B., op. cit., p. 173-175.

[6] Fischer M.E., Pasca Karsányi D., *From tradition and ideology to elections. The changing status in Romanian politics*, New York 1994.

[7] Petre Z., op. cit., p. 33-34.

[8] Shafir M., *Romania. Politics, economics and society*, Boulder, Colorado 1985, p. 76-78.

[9] Pasca Karsányi D., *Women in Romania*, in: *Gender Politics and Post/Communism*, New York-London 1993, p. 45.

 **SELECTED BIBLIOGRAPHY**

Aivazova S., *La liberté et l'egalité des femmes dans les pays socialistes d'Europe de l'Est 1960-1980*, in *Encyclopédie politique et historique des femmes*, Paris 1997.

Einhorn B., *Cinderella goes to market. Citizenship, gender and women's movements in East central Europe*, London-New York 1998.

Petre Z., *Promovarea femeii sau despre destructurarea sexului feminin*, in: *Miturile comunismului românesc*, vol. I, Bucuresti 1995.

Fischer M.E., Pasca Karsányi D., *From tradition and ideology to elections. The changing status in Romanian politics*, New York 1994.

Jaquette J.S., *Women in Politics*, London 1974.

Pasca Karsányi D., *Women in Romania*, in: *Gender Politics and Post/Communism*, New York-London 1993.

Shafir M., *Romania. Politics, economics and society*, Boulder, Colorado 1985.

Representations of Homosexuality and the Separation of Gender and Sexuality in the Czech Republic Before and After 1989

Věra Sokolová

Charles University, Prague

Tento článek se zabývá otázkou sexuality v České republice se zaměřením na representaci a diskuse o homosexualitě. Základním argumentem článku je teze, že jedním z nejpodstatnějších aspektů českého genderového diskurzu po roce 1989 je separace genderu a sexuality, která ovlivňuje způsoby, jakými jsou gender a sexualita v zemi chápány a vnímány. Emancipační politika homosexuality se začala rozvíjet v kontextu virulentního antifeminismu, který charakterizoval českou společnost od počátku porevolučního období až do současnosti a který podmiňoval vzájemné vnímání gayů a lesbiček a celospolečenské postoje k homosexualitě. Většina existujících genderových a feministických analýz ignorovala až dodnes v zásadě genderovanou a protikladnou premisu, která formovala většinu českého genderového diskurzu: mužskou orientaci a patriarchální charakter homosexuálního hnutí a heterosexismus genderového a feministického akademického psaní. Analýzy sexuality a feministické analýzy zatím nebyly schopné na sobě efektivně stavět, kriticky využívat druhé argumenty a vzájemně se podporovat. Spíše naopak, oba diskurzy, každý jiným způsobem, používají rétoriku jedinečnosti a recyklují stereotypy, které je oba poškozují a proti kterým v jiných kontextech vehementně bojují.

První část článku se zabývá otázkou homosexuálních komunit vkontextu historického vývoje homosexuálního diskurzu v období komunismu. Druhá část je zaměřena na represivní aparát medikalizace a kriminalizace „patologické" a „problematické" sexuality za komunismu. Medikalizace sexuality zůstala jedním z nejpodstatnějších aspektů chápání sexuality i po pádu režimu. Přetrvávající monopoly psychologie a sexuologie nad otázkami osobní identity formovaly a stále formují způsoby, jimiž představitelé gay a lesbického hnutí chápou homosexualitu a artikulují své zájmy a požadavky. Na závěr, ve dvou samostatných částech, se esej zamýšlí nad důsledky separace genderu a sexuality, jak jsou presentovány jednak v médiích a jednak v akademické sféře.

Věra Sokolová was born and educated in Prague, Czech Republic. She has received her graduate education in the United States, at the University of Washington, Seattle, where she is currently finishing her PhD. dissertation at the Department of History. Since 2000 she is an assistant professor at the Center for Gender Studies at Charles University in Prague. Her research and teaching focuses on questions of intersections of gender, sexuality and etnicity, primarily in Czechoslovakia and East Central Europe, after Second World War. She has written several articles, both in Czech and English, concerning the issues of (anti)feminism and ethnic (in)tolerance in Czechoslovakia/the Czech Republic.

INTRODUCTION

"To reveal my sexual orientation [on TV] did not seem strange to me when we were leisurely sitting on chairs and talking about a lot of different things. It's true, the host was talking about my sexual orientation and focused the questions around that, but as far as I was concerned, I was talking about my life. I was not sporting my sexual orientation. And the viewers did not see anything more or less than an ordinary woman. Much worse, I realized, is for me to go out in a short skirt and show my legs, which I don't shave. I know it sounds funny, but it's really relevant. I can easily come to terms with holding hands in public with my girlfriend, but going out in a short skirt is a real problem. To be sitting down and saying: "I'm a lesbian" and at least at the first look to have all the appropriate attributes of a woman, that is easy. Much worse is being a woman and but not demonstrating all the signs and behavior that, as a woman, I should allegedly have" [1].

This revelation by a Czech lesbian activist clearly exposes some of the problems of understanding the perceptions and representations of homosexuality in the Czech Republic. By taking definitions of womanhood or homosexuality as given or self-evident, we often blind ourselves to the complexities and ambiguities of homosexual identities and instead categorize "homosexuality" as a self-enclosed concept removed from the social fabric. Such a view, however, would leave untouched some of the essential and also most complicated questions connected to the discourse on sexuality in contemporary Czech society. The identities that social discourse simplifies in clear-cut categories (such as homosexuality or heterosexuality) and thematic locations (such as gender or sexuality), often overflow, resist and challenge these boundaries through the ways we imagine and live out these identities in everyday lives. Indeed, as the processes of self-ascription and definition are multi-layered, varied and ever unstable, the question of sexual orientation, quite often, has more to do with the social categories of gender than with sexual practice itself. Or, to put it differently, the division of gender and sexuality as two separate thematic locations, which characterizes the Czech gender discourse of the last decade, is both problematic and illusory [2].

It may come as no surprise that during the communist regime homosexuality was presented as a crime, perversion and illness. The medicalization and criminalization of homosexuality was rightfully denounced by many writers criticizing the practices of totalitarian regimes [3]. However, the issue is not that simple. Even though during the last decades of communism charges of homosexuality as a criminal act disappeared and during the 1990s accounts of homosexuality as "unnaturalness" slowly transformed into a discourse of "difference but equality," these shifts have not facilitated a transformation in the understanding of sexuality from being a biological and medical issue to being a socially constructed and gendered category. The persistent monopoly of psychologists, psychiatrists and sexologists over issues of sexuality to this very day, at the expense of qualified gender analysis by sociologists and historians, cannot be explained only in terms of repressive, communist social practices. Rather than looking only to the political system for the causes and consequences of why biological and psychological interpretations of sexuality, elevated to the status of "truth" by "scientific experts", still have so much currency in the Czech Republic, one should also look into the situation of feminist and gender discourse in the country.

The emancipatory politics of homosexuality have developed in the context of virulent antifeminism that has characterized Czech society since 1989 to the present [4]. Problems of heterosexism and homophobia, which hurt and discriminate homosexuals, bisexuals, transsexuals and transgender people, have intertwined with and built on the society-wide problems of sexism and ignorance about gender issues. The development and organization of homosexual political struggles – whether in funding, representation, or visibility – reflect the patriarchal structural hierarchies presented in society at large. The fact that the president of SOHO [5] does not understand what feminist or lesbian discourse could contribute to the cause of gay rights symbolizes the ignorance and insensitivity to the gendered dimension of homosexual experiences and identities on the part of gay political representatives. Contrary to common practice abroad, where lesbian activism has usually formed a part of feminist activism, Czech lesbian activities have been historically a part of the gay movement and many Czech lesbians openly distance themselves from feminism. Silence and uneasiness over bisexuality and other "alternative" sexualities suggest that both heterosexuals and homosexuals feel no need to challenge the comfortable and dichotomous sexual order of two strictly defined sexes. Even the works of Czech feminist scholars in all disciplines (with the exception of psychology and sexology) overwhelmingly ignore sexual themes, revealing an inability to question and analyze sexual discourses necessary for opening Czech gender analysis up to new theoretical levels. Taken together, the degree to which gender and sexuality are able to live and function separately in Czech society is both startling and striking. The separation of gender and sexuality in Czech gender discourse is not a marginal problem of theory, but a phenomenon with wide ranging implications in academic as well as social and political spheres.

The following analysis sets the discussion of homosexuality in the Czech Republic in the context of the separation of gender and sexuality in Czech gender discourse. The first section discusses the question of homosexual communities in the context of the historical development of homosexual discourse in the Communist period. The second section focuses on the issue of the medicalization and criminalization of sexuality that has shaped the ways in which gay and lesbian representatives and writers understand homosexuality and articulate their political claims. Lastly, in two separate sections, the essay considers the consequences of the separation of gender and sexuality as they are presented in both media and academic discourse.

THE GENDER OF "HOMOSEXUAL COMMUNITIES"

Female homosexuality presents itself in public only rarely, and even that happens only in cases when such a homosexuality is accompanied by the woman's desire to show off, to draw attention to herself. Usually, homosexual women try to look inconspicuous so that others around them think they are only two friends. They dress and act like women so at first sight it is difficult to distinguish them from heterosexual women. Only seldom do they dress like men and demonstrate their masculinity even in their behavior – which, however, is not typical for homosexual women. Usually they are contented with sports attire and long pants that do not draw any exceptional attention [6].

Sweeping generalizations and stereotypes of lesbian behavior in previous historical periods may be the source of sincere laughter, but the fact that this quote was published in 1992 in a widely circulated, "scientific" publication freezes one's tendency to chuckle. The old-fashioned absurdities of the argument reveal from what ashes the post-communist discourse on homosexuality arose. Despite its stereotypes, the above quote may be right in its implicit suggestion that lesbians (and gays) are socially invisible. According to the recent study of the Sexological Institute of the Czech Republic, more than half of the country's population claims that they have not personally met a homosexual [7]. Despite major political and social changes during the last ten years, many if not most Czechs are far from being generally tolerant toward expressions of nonconformity in the public. Many gays and lesbians, as well as members of other sexual minorities, have bad personal experiences with the so-often celebrated openness of Czech society and are rightfully cautious in making themselves vulnerable and exercising their individual freedoms in public [8]. As many homosexuals are forced by social or personal pressures to be in the closet, the question of communal support is important to the nature of the "homosexual community" in general and, perhaps not so surprisingly, differs significantly for gays and lesbians.

"There is no lesbian community here," has been an overwhelmingly common answer from dozens of lesbians I talked to in the course of the past year and half, regardless of whether they were out or in the closet, active in politics and openly appearing in the media or whether they had no interests in politics or feminism at all. Their perception of the viability of their own community starkly contrasts to the view presented in the few publications devoted to female homosexuality published during the 1990s. These studies insist on the existence of a "lesbian community" in the Czech Republic, dividing it meticulously into "several groups of women," from "active members of lesbian organizations," "passive members,' "active non-members," "passive non-members actively visiting gay and lesbian clubs," "lesbians living in pairs or alone, but completely aside from organizations and clubs" and "lesbians living in heterosexual marriages" [9]. Apparently, for some the simple act of existing creates a community. However, this does not appear to be enough for many lesbians themselves to *feel* a sense of community.

Currently, the lesbian "community" has several rather informal organizations, a few internet sites, a well-known bar in the center of Prague, their own festival called *Aprilfest* that an increasing number of people visit every year, a few irregularly functioning magazines, and women who participate in the Gay games [10]. Yet many lesbians, even those active in these ventures, still reject the label of "community" and deny its existence. Some with regret, some with pride. For some, it might be a badly needed support network they miss in the contemporary Czech society. For others, however, rejecting the idea of a lesbian community is a way of refusing marginalization or a refusal to order personal life according to a one-dimensional logic of sexual orientation. From the outside, it is easy to perceive any minority as a compact community because the difference that defines it as *other* is easily perceived as the most important characteristic in the lives of those who are identified that way [11]. However, many lesbians refuse to be identified primarily as a "lesbian" or a "feminist," thus overriding other personal identities they have. While other people are introduced as lawyers, sociologists, teachers, or journalists, individuals expressing and explaining gender issues are regularly described as "lesbian activists" or "feminists". Being a lesbian or a feminist then takes on an aura of profession or a community that has the semblance of being "other" than and foreign to society at large, even

Věra Sokolová

though many lesbians of course do not see themselves purely in these one-dimensional terms.

The larger amount of research done on the social lives of gay men, both past and present, reveals major differences in the idea of a gay or homosexual community. Gay men feel quite confident in answering the same question about their own community positively. Although throughout the entire Communist period gays found ways to meet and enjoy freedom in the privacy of their own institutions, the Czech gay cultural scene has grown especially since the 1970s. Gays met primarily within four forms of social life: "family societies", intellectual "salons", bathhouses and bars [12].

Family societies were created not only in bigger cities, but also in smaller towns where circles of friends would meet regularly in private parties and have organized events. The advantage of these séances was ability to establish longer friendships and stronger bonds with other gay men. Intellectual salons were both more open and closed than family meetings. One could not just come on one's own, but had to be introduced by a friend. Groups that met primarily in art ateliers of bigger cities functioned as open and debate-oriented ventures. The advantage of these clubs was their openness to new faces, as well as to lesbians. Public bathhouses provided a completely different type of openness. Obviously, the bathhouses were not reserved for gays only and so one had to watch for potential colleagues or acquaintances that could suddenly appear there. The bar and club scene of the 1970s, on the other hand, built on the tradition from previous decades. Besides drinking and dancing there were also regularly organized popular transvestite shows. In the 1980s, the gay cultural scene was broadened by a new disco generation. Despite the decriminalization of homosexuality in the early 1960s, the police throughout the Communist period compiled detailed records of fingerprints and photos evidencing Czechoslovak gays. Gay social and cultural institutions served as convenient sites where these lists could be brought up to date and gays reminded how vulnerable they were if they refused to cooperate with the police. It is not an exaggeration to say that during the Communist period homosexuals, and gays especially, lived under constant pressure and potential social and emotional blackmail [13].

Today, compared to a single major lesbian bar in Prague, there are over thirty gay bars in the country's capital alone [14]. The difference in the organization and self-perception of gay and lesbian communities in the Czech Republic is a result of the differences in the social circumstances of both. Obviously, as homosexuals, both are subject to the same political legislation, yet, in virtue of being men or women, the lives of gays and lesbians are affected differently by the politics of gender. The differences in their respective situations mirror this reality. Most studies and publications concerned with homosexuality have been focused on gays, and one gay man, Jiří Hromada, the president of SOHO, speaks officially on the behalf of all homosexuals. In the 1990s, various interviews and articles in the media featuring him alone occupied perhaps more time and space than all other articles focused on homosexuality combined. The vice-president of SOHO used to be a woman until most lesbian organizations decided to leave that umbrella organization. SOHO reacted to this move simply by renaming itself at the beginning of 2001 as the *Gay Initiative*, claiming that "Gay" is a more inclusive and complex identity label than "homosexual." Some texts even argue that "the term gay in international usage includes also homosexual women, although those sometimes call themselves lesbian [15]". The distribution of financial resources from state and private funds poured to various projects and studies connected with homosexual issues overwhelmingly favours gays over lesbians [16]. Even though one might argue that there are more gays than lesbians in society, as SOHO for example has done, such a claim is highly arguable and even misleading. The fact that there are more gay organizations and social institutions does not indicate the actual number of gays and lesbians in the country, but rather reflects the structural advantages of the gay community that are logical extensions of conditions under Communism and thus benefit from anti-feminist sentiments in society that ridicule women's organizing in general.

The organization of the homosexual community after 1989 reflected the criminalization and medicalization of homosexuality during the Communist period. From 1921 until 1950 the Czechoslovak Criminal Code included a law (§ 129 TrZ), inherited from the times of the Austrian monarchy, which characterized homosexual acts as "crimes against nature." In 1950 this law was replaced by a similar law (§ 241 TrZ), which classified homosexuality not as a crime against nature, but a crime against society, an act "incompatible with the morality of a socialist society" [17]. In 1961, homosexuality was decriminalized by a new law (§244 TrZ) which replaced the old § 241 and legalized homosexual acts under specific conditions. From the wording of this new law it was explicit that "sexual acts between individuals of the same sex who are at least 18 years old are not criminal if they take place voluntarily, without pay and in circumstances that do not create public indignation".[18] Compared to heterosexual acts, which were legal from 15 years of age, this law clearly discriminated against homosexuals, even though it was a significant legal change compared to previous statutes. Moreover, it was quite easy to abuse the ambiguous wording about the "circumstances" of sexual activity and public distress.

A complete decriminalization of homosexuality and its legal equalization in the age of consent was the first task of the new civic initiatives formed after 1989. SOHO, established in June of 1990, succeeded in these tasks almost immediately. Already in July 1990, §241 in its entirety was removed from the Criminal Code of (then) Czechoslovakia and the age of consent for both homosexual and heterosexual acts was set at the age of 15. In 1993, when the World Health Organization officially removed homosexuality from the list of illnesses, SOHO managed to ratify this removal (included in the Czechoslovak Medical List of Illnesses as the infamous Diagnosis 302.1) in Czechoslovakia as well [19].

MEDICALIZATION AND CRIMINALIZATION OF SEXUALITY

"Homosexuality is a sexual orientation to the individuals of the same sex. It is a life-lasting, unchangeable state which is neither caused not chosen by its carrier who then cannot be blamed for it" [20] (1992).

"Based on scientific knowledge it is possible to say that biological factors play the decisive role for determining sexual orientation from the prenatal stage of individual development, whether those are genetic or hormonal factors" [21] (1995).

"Let's understand each other! This book is by no means a promotion of homosexuality. To promote homosexuality or heterosexuality is nonsense. They are simply facts" [22] (2000),

Physicians no longer want to cure homosexuality and generally accept it as a viable alternative to heterosexuality. The medicalization of sexuality however, and especially its biological determination, have been the major shaping force that has influenced all levels of sexual and gender discourses. These introductory quotes, taken from major publications throughout the 1990s, show that during this time the bases for argumentation have not progressed beyond medical discourse. Even though most accounts, including periodicals, rarely fail to mention that "in current conceptions, homosexuality is not understood as an illness" [23], few authors reflect on the deep-seated implications of the persistent medicalization and biologization of sexuality that affect popular consciousness much more than any abrupt changes of law. Arguably, the consequences of criminalization of homosexuality have been much easier to denounce and correct than its medicalization. It is easy to understand and see the restrictive aspects of criminalization, especially since aspects of criminalization have affected most other activities and behavior under the Communist regime. It is much harder to uncover restrictive and harmful aspects of medical discourse. "Facts" supported by medical or biological points of view gain an aura of legitimacy and respectability that is not easy to shake by discursive analysis.

One might argue that perhaps historicization of sexuality might serve this function. However, history as much as any other discipline in the Czech context is locked in the cultural tradition of empirical positivism that resists the introduction of new methodologies, such as gender analysis, into the field. Unfortunately, even when history is mobilized for service by gay historians themselves they fall back on the same essentialized argumentation about the origins of homosexuality. The major, original publication of gay history in the Czech language, written in the spirit of the late John Boswell, is a great exercise in looking for the eternal gay [24]. In his introduction to the work, the president of SOHO Jiří Hromada blesses the author's essentialism by exclaiming that it is a book about

> those [gays and lesbians] whose rights were denied for centuries; those whom mythology and the period of Ancient Greece and Rome guaranteed privileges and respect; those who were subsequently burned at stakes for their naturalness by Catholic fanaticism; those who were tortured for their difference in prisons by ossified justice; those who were dying with pink triangles on their hearts in the Nazi camps; those who in totalitarian regimes spent their lives in a lie, in pretended marriages, in anonymous loves, in anxiety from discovered truth so abused by the secret police for blackmail [25].

In a few sentences, Hromada manages to summarize the point of the 500-page book – he embraces subjective and collective identities created in the specific contexts of incomparable historical periods into one, all-inclusive identity of "gay" and unproblematically extends it back and forth through time and space [26]. At the end, he heralds the accomplishment of the book as "the task worthy of the new millennium" [27]. The empowering message toward the Czech gay community is spelled out: we have always existed. If you look just hard enough, you'll find us everywhere. – Needless to say, such a position reflects a grave lack of historical sensitivity.

Paradoxically, the etiological approach – the search for the origins of homosexual desire – that has characterized the medical sexological sciences and helped to essentialize biological foundations of gender and sexuality has also facilitated the ground for political advancements of homosexuals by gradually convincing the majority of the public that homosexuality is an innate biological tendency. Homosexuals, represented by SOHO and its president Hromada have eagerly embraced this interpretation and built their political strategy on it. Led by their supreme goal of legalizing the Registered Partnership between two individuals of the same sex, an issue that has dominated the public discussion of the 1990s, they firmly stand behind sexological "experts," agreeing with them that "homosexuals do not choose their sexual orientation." Even though there exist original research studies that include in their definitions of homosexuality clauses about free will and choice, homosexual political representatives ignore such works and concentrate on arguments "proving" biological predispositions [28]. Significantly, however, the etiological approach also justifies the secondary status of lesbian issues within the gay discourse. All available accounts agree that "about the causes of female homosexuality we know even less than about male homosexuality" [29]. This argument then is supposed to legitimise focusing on gays.

Homosexual discourse is thus overwhelmingly gay oriented, even if sometimes perhaps even unconsciously. For example, a very helpful and influential booklet for homosexual youth called *Coming Out: A Companion Through the Period of Uncertainty When Boys and Girls Are Searching For Their Inner Selves*, is, at least according to the title, designed for both young men and women. Its entire content, however, is geared unmistakably toward men. On the cover, as well as in its black and white erotic photographs, only young men are featured. Throughout the text, the author – a sexologist who is on the last page praised by the president of SOHO because "through his expertise and great diligence ... he has helped to increase the societal acceptance of gay and lesbian minority by the mainstream society" – recycles gender stereotypes common in medical discourse. For example, he claims that "men have a turbulent teenage sexuality," while women do not. According to him, "women mature sexually later [than men]" and hence the first signs of their homosexual awareness "come not through sex but through emotional ties to another woman." [30] Here he adheres to the classic myth in the Western civilization's understanding of modern sexuality that connects men with sex and women with love [31].

Since 1990, when he became the president of SOHO, Hromada has consistently argued that homosexuality is biologically determined. All major publications about homosexuality, directed both at the homosexual community itself and outwardly to educate the mainstream public, promote this view, defining homosexuality as a "lasting and unchangeable characteristic of every individual" [32]. Such a strategy can be understandable in advisory booklets for homosexual youth, such as the book *Coming Out*, who need positive models and space for hope in the face of a hostile and uncertain world. But the leading representatives of the homosexual movement should be aware of the political and theoretical limits of such a rigid rhetoric. Even though such an argumentation might bring certain political advancements in the short run, over the long term it will only solidify the marginal status of homosexuality as distinct from heterosexuality.

Moreover, such rhetoric is also guilty of exclusionary practices. The biological explanation of homosexuality, especially when it is "confirmed" by the "discovery of the so called gene of homosexuality on the sex chromosome X which explains some cases of male homosexuality," leads to a ridicule of bisexuality and transgender as viable sexual identities [33]. Instead of celebrating the theoretical and political openings that both bisexuality and transgender potentially offer for the analyses of the instability and multiplicity of subjective identities, as for example Claire Hemmings suggests, they are explained in terms of undecisiveness, lack of maturity, and promiscuity [34]. Significantly, even in its current definition, bisexuality is not granted the status of a medical fact. While homosexuality is considered an unchanging characteristic (in other words *a fact*), "some people *feel* bisexually oriented" [35]. The glossary of another text defines bisexuality as the "inability to decide whether one is attracted more to men or women" [36]. This definition is taken directly from another influential publication, which takes the argument even further, claiming that "we can assert that it is not likely that they [bisexuals] are capable of being truly good partners, not to mention husband or wives, and that they can hardly keep up their commitments to faithfulness" [37]. Even this unprovable judgment is shielded by the magic power of medical science.

Similarly to Hemmings's argumentation about bisexuality, the transgender community in the Czech Republic insists that transgender has a theoretically and politically liberating potential for the entire gender and sexuality discourse [38]. Far from being a simple addition to the world of two rigidly defined sexes, transgender offers a potential for loosening up gender categorization precisely because in both male-to-female and female-to-male transformations (whether surgical or not), the main process that takes place is intertwining of both female and male gender and sexual subjectivities. Thus what is coming to life in these processes are completely *new* gender identities. "Transgender creates not only third identity, but also a third dimension for investigations of gender identities", claims Marcela Linková, a sociologist who helped to organize a unique and successful Transgender Seminar at the Sociological Institute in Prague in April 2001 [39].

The issue of transgender exemplifies the arguments about the medicalization of sexuality presented in this essay. The context of the Transgender Seminar itself is also interesting for its rare and fierce public clash between the "medical experts" on the one hand and sociologists and the audience on the other hand that continued on the pages of the media after the seminar's end. The sociologists criticized the binary of "man" and "woman" presented in heterosexual and homosexual discourses based on the physiological functioning of the human body. Sexologist Růžena Hajnová, the chief of the Sexological Institute in Brno, one of the two leading sexological institutions in the country, defended the medical practices. In 1963, she witnessed the birth of transsexual surgical practice in Czechoslovakia and in its time probably helped immensely in opening up the then-new and bold sexological practices. However, in 2001 she seems to be visiting from another century. She claims that

the physician's duty is to examine the patient, tell him or her the diagnosis and inform him what the possibilities for solution are. A diagnosis is not, of course, done quickly. Sometimes it is possible to make the diagnosis from the door, because you can see immediately that a 'mistake of nature' just walked in. But in many cases it takes days, weeks, or months of observation and examination [40].

Hajnová insists that it is not the physician who decides the fate of a person. Yet she also asserts that in the field of sexology one cannot practice the approach of "client = demand and I as a physician will fulfil the client's wish." In her view, it is "misleading and in contradiction to fundamental medical criteria" [41]. In other words, it is indeed the physician who holds the full control and power over the subjective identity of an individual, and, based on physiological criteria that corresponds with the normative notions of biological maleness and femaleness, defines who counts as a transsexual and who does not. The subjective feelings and desires of an individual are only side components of the physical "truth" revealed by biology.

In order to allow anybody to undergo sex-change surgery, "one [meaning the physician!] has to first be sure that the individual will be able in the future to look like a convincing man or woman." Hajnová, who chairs the committee that has a final say over the approvals of the sex changes performed at the institute, reveals the mysteries of nature that have corseted the Czechoslovak discourse on sexuality for decades:

> Diagnosing sexuality of an individual is like putting a mosaic together. You have pieces thrown around and you are trying to find a pattern which will either prove your diagnosis or challenge it. Of course, we do meet clients with whom we are absolutely sure immediately that their diagnosis is transexuality. When you see an individual with wide shoulders and narrow hips, the triangle typical for a man is present there. And even though the body has female breasts and genitals, the position of feet and hands corresponds with the male. It works the other way around as well. You can find a man who has the beautiful hourglass-shaped figure of a female, everything is fragile and gentle… That is one of the clues that indicates his female sex [42].

Hajnová claims that the goal of sex-change surgeries is to "get to the other sex as close as possible so that nobody is able to recognize [that the body was originally biologically different]" because, according to Hajnová, nature "naturally" distinguishes between two kinds of bodies – male and female [43]. The views shared at the seminar are presented here at such length not so much for the arguments per se, even though they are noteworthy in themselves, but rather to demonstrate yet again how pervasive the medical discourse as the basis for argumentations about sexuality has been and how strongly it has shaped the way Czech society understands gender and sexuality.

A CASE STUDY: THE DEBATE OVER REGISTERED PARTNERSHIP

The need for qualified gender analyses that would integrate issues of gender and sexuality and were capable of serving as foundations for public discussions about politically and socially important issues is currently most visible and strongly felt in the debates surrounding the Law About Registered Partnership that has dominated the discourse on homosexuality all throughout the 1990s [44]. The debates reveal how much popular discourse and the media have replicated all the "scientific" arguments about gender and sexuality, building on and perpetuating the stereotypes resulting from the separation of gender and sexuality. It is clear, that among "alternative sexualities," homosexuality is the only one that the public at large considers as a partner for discussion about Registered Partnership at all. Since for most people Domestic Partnership is simply an acronym for marriage or family, bisexuals or transgender people are excluded from the debates and media accounts. Both "heterosexuals" and "homosexuals" act as though the issue of Domestic Partnership concerns only "them" – the two, strictly defined groups.

It seems that one of the major reasons why homosexuality is (at least superficially) accepted much more than any other form of non-heterosexual sexuality is because it does not represent a fundamental threat to the heterosexual order [45]. Based on its biological explanation, it confirms the duality of two sexes that complement each other in a monogamous symbiosis. Homosexuality is then in a simplified form presented and understood as clear-cut inverted heterosexuality and sometimes homosexual relationships are even elevated above heterosexual ones for being able to function "better," implicitly meaning without conflicting power dimensions that are integral to heterosexual relations [46]. While it is claimed that bisexual individuals "are not interested in creating deep, strong relationships … and are not even capable of such relationships," homosexuals, besides their sexual attraction toward the same sex, are "in all other respects just like heterosexuals" [47]. Their relationships hence seem to preserve the same norms and values that function in heterosexual relationships. Power hierarchies and social order organized according to traditional politics of gender are thus reinforced and people are not forced to challenge their views of appropriate gender roles and behaviour.

Even preferences to toys are in some medical interpretations indications of one's ability to preserve the "appropriate" social order:

> There exist girls who act like boys and boys who are told they should have been born girls. Experts call it "gender discontent." … Besides homosexuals, such a behaviour is typical mainly for transsexuals. But [on the contrary to transsexuals] homosexuals manage to gradually accept their own male or female roles with the agreement of their physical appearance. Simply, a gay man, even if he sometimes uses too much perfume or jewelry, is a man and a lesbian who drives a Harley bike dressed in leather is still a woman [48].

This example, a part of a chapter entitled "Girls' Soccer and Boys' Doll", demonstrates again how gender stereotypes seep into the discourse on sexuality and take on the disguise of scientific proof. The author, a sexologist, does not reflect in any way on the fact that he uses the rhetoric of stereotypical gender roles based on "agreements" between physical appearance, social norms and subjective identity. What is important is that abstract "womanhood" and "manhood" are confirmed and "men" and "women" can successfully function in the society because they have a clear understanding of their gender roles and their sexual identities – even if those two do not coincide in a heterosexual way.

Several major paradoxes intersect in these arguments surrounding homosexuality and Domestic Partnership and all point to the problems with separating gender and sexuality as two distinct discursive locations. SOHO (and now *Gay Initiative*) has vehemently argued that homosexuality is innate, yet the crux of the conflicts over the legalization of Domestic Partnership is formed by fears of potential dangers caused to children by inappropriate role models and the absence of "correct ones" [49]. SOHO and gay studies argue that homosexuals and heterosexuals are "the same" with the exception of sexual preference, yet Hromada personally tirelessly assures the appalled public and Parliament that homosexuals do not want to include into the law about Domestic Partnership a clause about their ability to have, adopt and raise children. Nobody has explained on what basis, other than strategic argumentation, homosexuals should not possess the desire to have children. This inconsistency is striking especially in the face of arguments usually made by the conservative Christian democratic representatives, who in the same breath argue about the naturalness of a "maternal destiny" of *all* women on the one hand and about the unnaturalness of lesbian motherhood on the other. Neither have they explained so far the foundation of their definition of "woman" [50].

Conclusion: Separation of Gender and Sexuality Revisited

"Gender analyses shall be exercised and developed as a technique of widening and enriching rather than narrowing the process of production and distribution of knowledge" [51].

The separation of gender and sexuality in the Czech gender discourse has led, contrary to the poignant call by one of the leading Czech feminist theoreticians Jiřina Šmejkalová, to narrowing and limiting the production and distribution of knowledge. So far, most analyses of gender and sexuality have been blind to a fundamentally gendered and controversial premise: the male orientation and patriarchal character of the homosexual movement and heterosexism of feminist and gender scholarship. Analyses of sexuality and feminist analyses have not been able to draw on and support each other effectively [52]. Instead, both discourses, each in its own way, use exclusionary rhetoric and perpetuate stereotypes that are mutually harmful and which, in other contexts, are tirelessly fought against.

It was already mentioned that Czech feminist scholars writing on the issues of gender and women rarely integrate analyses of sexuality into their works. Gender analysis struggles for recognition by mainstream academicians in all disciplines that look for "competent" argumentation and "hard," "scientific" proof. Feminist research, writing and teaching, regardless of whether it defines itself openly as "feminist" or chooses the designation "gender", is under a constant and often unjustified scrutiny. A disturbing tendency on the part of Czech academic community is to minimize the importance of gender education, and to dismiss it as a mere "fashionable trend" lacking real importance and intellectual rigor [53]. These often quite hostile attacks come from both media and academia. It is perhaps not surprising then that many feminist scholars working in this antagonistic environment stay away from themes that are unfairly under attack and scorned by more conservative scholars even though much would be gained from further research into these areas. Unfortunately, then, such scholarship is doomed to stay at the levels of the descriptive presentation of empirical data that cannot adequately operate on discursive levels and address issues of construction of historical subjects, definitions and meanings [54]. The rewards for such books are appraisals by conservative scholars for "managing to stay away from feminism even though they are about women" [55]. Arguably, it is too little at the threshold of the third millennium.

What is perhaps understandable in some accounts dealing with specific topics is puzzling in edited volumes representing wide ranges of issues and voices within the feminist discourse. For example, none of the major works that have appeared in the course of the 1990s thanks to the publishing activity of the first gender organization in Central Europe, Prague's *Gender Studies Foundation*, deals with the issue of sexuality. Likewise, the collection of academic essays representing the interdisciplinary development of Gender Studies in the Czech Republic and claiming to represent the transformative potential of gender analysis does not include a single essay on sexuality [56]. And similarly, an otherwise excellent anthology of popular perceptions of feminism in the Czech Republic in the 1990s, published by Marie Ch_ibková's *One Woman Press* does not include among thirty essays by leading Czech scholars, artists and intellectuals a single gay, lesbian, bisexual or transgender voice [57]. In all these works, gender is analysed firmly within the parameters of relationship between women and men, with an underlying implicit heterosexuality and commonly shared understanding who "women" and "men" are.

On the other hand, this separation does not seem to be a problem limited to Czech feminist discourse alone. Most English-language academic volumes dealing with gender and feminism in East Central Europe suffer from the same inadequacy, leaving the issue of sexuality completely out of their analyses [58]. Even the recent collection of presentations from a major Gender Studies conference about Gender Studies and Post-Communism, organized in Berlin in 2000, includes among forty four essays only one that is concerned with sexuality [59]

How can gender analysis progress further and loosen the grip of empirical positivism when it cannot employ the full range of feminist categories and ignores the role of femininity and masculinity for sexuality? Conversely, how can gender play a socially transformative and educational role without progressing to those deeper levels? The mutual distancing, misunderstanding and rejection among various discourses of feminist, homosexual, bisexual and transgender academic and political activism shows the limits of identity-based politics. Tolerance, both as a moral principle and as an intellectual endeavour is undividable and no individual or a society can aspire for a social tolerance and informed understanding based on exclusion of uncomfortable or not comprehended elements.

 NOTES

[1] Kotišová M., "Lesbické hnutí v mezinárodní perspektivě." (*Lesbian Movement in International Perspective.*) Lecture presented at the regular series "Tuesdays with Gender", organized by the Gender Studies, o.p.s., Prague, April 17, 2001. (Taped lecture and transcript available at the archive of Gender Studies, o.p.s.).

[2] Some of the main theoretical works that informed this essay include, for example: Rupp L., *A Desired Past: A Short History of Same-Sex Sexuality in America*, Chicago 1999; Fuss D. (ed), *Inside/Out: Lesbian Theories, Gay Theories*, New York 1991; Halbestram J., *Female Masculinity*, Durham 1998; Tucker N. (ed), *Bisexual Politics: Theories, Queries and Visions*, Binghamton 1995; Blackwood E., Wieringa S. (eds), *Female Desires: Transgender Practices Across Cultures*, New York 1999; Chauncey G., Jr., *Gay New York: Gender, Urban Culture, and the Making of the Gay Male World, 1890-1940*, New York 1994.

[3] See for example: Janošová P., *Homosexualita v názorech současné společnosti*, Praha 2000; Stehlíková D., Procházka I., Hromada J., *Homosexualita, společnost a AIDS vČR*, Praha 1995; Procházka I., *Coming Out: průvodce obdobím nejistoty, kdy kluci a holky hledají sami sebe*, Praha 1994; Fanel J., *Gay historie*, Praha 2000.

[4] For good analyses of the context of Czech antifeminism see Šmejkalová J., Strašidlo feminismu v českém 'porevolučním' tisku: úvaha, doufejme, historická, in Havelková H., Vodrážka M. (eds), *Žena a muž v médiích*, Praha 1998; Havelková H., *Abstract Citizenship? Women and Power in the Czech Republic*, in Social Politics, Summer/Fall 1996, pp. 243-260; Malečková J., *Gender, Nation and Scholarship: Reflections on Gender/Women's Studies in the Czech Republic*, in Maynard M., Purvis J. (eds), *New Frontiers in Women's Studies: Knowledge, Identity and Nationalism*, London 1995).

[5] SOHO = Sdružení organizací homosexuálních občanů (*Association of Organizations of Homosexual Citizens*). The first contemporary official organization of gays and lesbians in Czechoslovakia(and later the Czech Republic) which was formed in 1990. The context of its foundation is explained later in the essay.

[6] Antonín Brzek A., Pondělíčková-Mašlová J., *Třetí pohlaví?*, Praha 1992, p. 90.

[7] Cited in Ševela V., Plavcová A., Hlinovská E., *Ve světě českých gayů*, "", 4, 2001, p. 14. Similar results claims also Janošová in her own research, p. 126.

[8] Ibid., and, for example, Holíková J., Sedlák G., *Homosexuálové v politice nevadí dvěma třetinám občanů*, "Lidové noviny", 6, 1999, p. 7.

[9] For example, Talandová J., *Sociální postavení lesbických žen: alternativní rodinné modely v kontextu heterosexuální společnosti*, Praha 1998), p. 22; Janošová, pp. 52-74.

[10] Currently, the most active is an internet site *Lesbická literární kavárna* (Lesbian Literary Café) led by Monika Benešová at www.llk.cz, which lists all important political issues, cultural programs, current publications, academic lectures and links to other sites. From organizations, the most important is *Promluv* (in translation meaning "Speak Up"), the only openly lesbian feminist organization that provides classic political lobbying, various supporting actions and advising services. Among magazines are worth mentioning *Promluv*, *SOHO Revue* (primarily a gay magazine with an inserted lesbian double-page), or *Alia* (a short-lived magazine of mid 1990s).

[11] On theoretical discussion of these points see, for example, D'Emilio J., *Sexual Politics, Sexual Communities: The Making of a Homosexual Minority in the United States, 1940-1970*, Chicago 1983; Duberman M., Vicinus M., Chauncey G., Jr. (eds), *Hidden From History: Reclaiming the Gay and Lesbian Past*, New York 1989; or Chauncey (1994, cited earlier).

[12] Fanel, pp. 446-452.

[13] Ibid., Janošová, pp. 46-52.

[14] The lesbian bar in question is "Á-klub," called "Áčko," located in Prague 3. Fanel, p. 457; Ševela, Plavcová, Hlinovská, p. 13.

[15] See, for example, Procházka, p. 5.

[16] In the case of AIDS prevention, which was funded by the state most generously, such an attention is understandable, as in the fall of 1999, 53.4% of HIV positive persons registered in Czechoslovakia (230 out of 431) were men infected through homosexual practices. ("Gayčko", 10/1999), p. 69. However, also most other financial resources to homosexual community regularly go to projects and studies that monitore and benefite primarily gay community. Moreover, the state finances allocated for homosexual projects are distributed by SOHO, which tends to give preferences to gay organizations and issues. (Stehlíková, Procházka, Hromada, 1995. Cited earlier).

[17] Karel Matys a kol., *Trestní zákon – komentář*, (I. část zvláštní, 2. vydání, Praha, 1980), 734. Cited in Košela J., "Homosexualita a její trestnost" (M.A. Thesis, Universita Jana Evangelisty Purkyně, Právnická fakulta, Brno, 1981), p. 31.

[18] Fanel, p. 434.

[19] "Pacient s diagnózou 302.1 je zdráv." Interview with Jiří Hromada about the accomplishments of SOHO in the first half of the 1990s, in "Nedělní Lidové Noviny", 12, 1995, pp. 2-3.

[20] Brzek a Pondělíčková-Mašlová, p. 19.

[21] Procházka, p. 8.

[22] Fanel, p. 1.

[23] For example, Talandová, p. 9.

[24] John Boswell is a classic proponent of a historical position known as "essentialism" which emphasizes similarities in gay identity over time and space rather than differences. See John Boswell, "Revolutions, Universals, and Sexual Categories," in Duberman, Vicinus, and Chauncey, Jr., (1989, cited earlier), pp. 17-36.

[25] Hromada, *Introduction* to Fanel, p. 7.

[26] For one of the best theoretical discussions on the problems of historical essentialism see Rupp, 1999. (Cited earlier). This book is currently being translated into Czech and is going to be published by One Woman Press at the end of 2001.

[27] Hromada in Fanel, p. 9.

[28] For example Štefan Dubaj S., *O postoji bratislavskej verejnosti k problematike homosexuality*, (M.A. Thesis, Universita

Komenského, Bratislava, 1994. Cited in "Eva", 4, 1996), pp. 82-83.

[29] Talandová, p. 9. Also Procházka, p. 8; Brzek a Pondělíčková-Mašlová, p. 91.

[30] Procházka, pp. 5, 7, 8, 10 and the *Afterword* by Hromada.

[31] For an excellent analysis of the historical perceptions of sexuality, see Rupp (1999, cited earlier.).

[32] Citations at the beginning of this section.

[33] Procházka, p. 3 and 10. For a comprehensive discussion of the gay gene theory see, for example, Hamer D., Copeland P., *The Science of Desire: The Search for the Gay Gene and the Biology of Behavior*, New York 1994.

[34] Hemmings C., *Bisexual Spaces: Relocating Gender and Sexuality*, New York 2002 - forthcoming). Based on the research for this book, Hemmings presented a paper elaborating on the theoretical potential of bisexuality entitled "A Feminist Methodology of the Personal: Bisexual Experience and Feminist Post-structuralist Epistemology" in the series *Feminism and Quantitative Research*, organized by the Center for Gender Studies at Charles University in Prague in Spring 2001.

[35] Procházka, p. 10. (Emphasis added.)

[36] Talandová, p. 6.

[37] Brzek and Pondělíčková-Mašlová, p. 17.

[38] The transgender community has been quite active especially in the last several years. Its activists run a very informative internet site www.trangender.cz, publish a montly *TGčko* and yearly organize Transgender Week in Prague. Their effort to educate the public was crowned last year when GG Press published the translation of famous *Transgender Warriors: Making History from Joan of Arc to RuPaul* by Leslie Feinberg. (Praha, GG Press, 2000. Translation Tereza Spencerová).

[39] Marcela Linková, "Je gender transsexualní?", p. 7. (Unpublished paper presented at the seminar.)

[40] Klausová K., "Kouzelnice s pohlavími" (A *Magician with Sexes*). An interview with Dr. Hajnová, following the Transgender Seminar in Prague on April 17, 2001 where Hajnová participated. In "Lidové noviny - Pátek", 18, 2001, pp. 38-46.

[41] Ibid., p. 42.

[42] Ibid., p. 46.

[43] For sophisticated accounts on the historicization of various understandings of the human body see especially Lacqueur T., *Making Sex: Body and Gender from the Greeks to Freud*, Cambridge 1990) or Rupp L., *A Desired Past* (cited earlier).

[44] A few times the Parliament of the Czech Republic has voted on the issue; both times it did not succeed in passing. Interestingly, in the last vote in December 1999, the law rejected by the necessary 88 votes out of the present 175. At the moment, however, one of the representatives who voted FOR passing, protested that he found his ballot casts in the place designated for negative ballots. The vote was repeated. Neither this time it was passed, but the short while was enough for a change of opinions. In the second round, a few minutes later, already 91 representatives voted against. (Fanel, pp. 445-446).

[45] In one recent study 70 percent of Czech public even claimed that they would not mind a homosexual orientation of their political representative.(Holíková and Sedlák, p. 7. Cited earlier.)

[46] Ševela, Plavcová, and Hlinovská, 16.

[47] Talandová, p. 17.; Brzek a Pondělíčková-Mašlová, p. 16.

[48] *Coming Out*, p. 28.

[49] Kvapil T., *Zákon o partnerském soužití může ohrozit rodinu*, "Lidové noviny", 20, 1999, p. 3.

[50] See for example Benda M., *Když jde o gaye, nezná bratr bratra – a Marek Benda zase Jana Zahradila*, in "Mlada fronta Dnes", 20, 1999, p. 14; or Tollner P., *Zákon poškozující rodinu*, "Mladá fronta Dnes", 3, 2001, p. 7. (Emphasis added.)

[51] Šmejkalová J., *Gender as an Analytical Category of Post-Communist Studies*, in Jahnert G., Gohrisch J., Hahn D., Nickel H.M., Peinl P. and Schafgen K., (eds). *Gender in Transition in Eastern and Central Europe Proceedings*, Berlin 2001), p. 46.

[52] Of course there are exceptions. See for example Vodrážka M. and his *Esej o politickém harémismu: kritická zpráva o*

stavu feminismu v Čechách, Brno, 1999.

[53] This point has been developed already. See Sokolová V., *Shifting the Terms of Debate: Transformations of Feminism in Czech Society*, in *The New Presence: The Prague Journal of Central European Affairs*, Summer 2000.

[54] Examples of such works are, for example, recent studies on the history of women in the 19th century Bohemia. Lenderová M., *K hříchu i k modlitbě: Žena v minulém století*, Praha 1999; Neudorflová M., *České ženy v 19. století: úsilí a sny, úspěchy i zklamání na cestě k emancipaci*, Praha 1999; Horská P., *Naše prababičky feministky*, Praha 1999; Josef Polišenský J., Ostrovská S., *Ženy v dějinách lidstva*, Praha 2000.

[55] See for example Hlavačka M., A book review of Lenderová M., "Český časopis historický", 2000, pp.34-35.

[56] Věšínová-Kalivodová E., Maříková H., eds. *Společnost žen a mužů z aspektu gender*, Praha 1999.

[57] Chřibková M. (ed), *Feminismus devadesátých let českýma očima*, Praha 1999.

[58] For all, see the most recent of these edited volumes, Gal S., Kligman G. (eds), *Reproducing Gender: Politics, Publics, and Everyday Life after Socialism*, Princeton 2000. For older ones, for example Funk N., Mueller M. (eds), *Gender Politics and Post-Communism: Reflections from Eastern Europe and the Former Soviet Union*, New York 1993.

[59] Riszovannij M., *Media Discourses on Homosexuality in Hungary*, in Jahnert, Gohrisch, Hahn, Nickel, Peinl and Schafgen. (Cited earlier), pp. 254-261.

 SELECTED BIBLIOGRAPHY

Janošová P., *Homosexualita v názorech současné společnosti*, Praha 2000.

Riszovannij M., Media Discourses on Homosexuality in Hungary, in Jahnert G., Gohrisch J., Hahn D., Nickel H.M., Peinl J., Katrin Schafgen K. (eds), *Gender in Transition in Eastern and Central Europe Proceedings*, Berlin 2001, pp. 254-261.

Stehlíková D., Procházka I., Hromada J., *Homosexualita, společnost a AIDS v ČR*, Praha 1995.

Rupp L., *A Desired Past: A Short History of Same-Sex Sexuality in America*, Chicago 1999.

Talandová J., *Sociální postavení lesbických žen: alternativní rodinné modely v kontextu heterosexuální společnosti*, Praha 1998.

Plates

Plate 1
Eleanor of Aquitaine represented reading, on her tomb in Fontevrault.

[See R. Averkorn, *Women and power in the Middle Ages: political aspects of medieval queenship*]

Plate 2
Miniature showing Blanche of Castile beside her son, Louis IX.

[See R. Averkorn, *Women and power in the Middle Ages: political aspects of medieval queenship*]

Plate 3
An allegorical representation of Germany, 19th century.
[See S. Küster, *Nationbuilding and Gender in 19th-century Germany*]

Plate 4
Elza Rozenberga (1868-1943), 'Aspazija'.

[A. Cimdiņa, *The Post-Soviet Body of Latvia Literature:
Gender and* genre]

Plate 5
Raphael, *Elisabetta Gonzaga*, Uffizi, Florence.

[L. Saracco, *Defining the gentleman and the
gentlewoman in the Italian Renaissance*]

Plate 6
Raphael, *Baldassarre Castiglione*, Louvre, Paris.

[L. Saracco, *Defining the gentleman and the gentlewoman in the Italian Renaissance*]

Plate 7
A "Miraculous image of the Virgin Mary, protectress of the silkworms".

[See D. Lombardi, *Work and Gender in Early Modern Italy*]

Plate 8
F. Azzurri, *Il manicomio villaggio al Gianicolo* (The asylum village at the Janiculum, Rome), about 1878 (Biblioteca Alberto Cancelli, Ospedale, n. 60)

[See V. Fiorino, *Voices of folly: stories of women and men in the Rome insane asylum (1850-1915)*]

Plate 9
R. Righetti, *The doctor draws the inmates*, 1934-1936, Ospedale S. Maria della Pietà, Rome.

[See V. Fiorino, *Voices of folly: stories of women and men in the Rome insane asylum (1850-1915)*]

Plate 10
R. Righetti, *The doctor draws the inmates*, 1934-1936, Ospedale S. Maria della Pietà, Rome.

[See V. Fiorino, *Voices of folly: stories of women and men in the Rome insane asylum (1850-1915)*]

Plate 11
Christine de Pizan reading, miniature.

[See A. Lemond, *Queens' and princesses' political function at the end of the Middle Ages (14th and 15th centuries)* and R. Averkorn / sources]

Plate 12
The Virgin crowned, mosaic in St. Maria Maggiore, Rome.

[See A. Lemond, *Queens' and princesses' political function at the end of the Middle Ages (14th and 15th centuries)*]

Under the aegis of Clioh

Printed in October 2001
by Industrie Grafiche Pacini Editore S.p.A.
Via A. Gherardesca • 56121 Ospedaletto • Pisa, Italy
On behalf of Edizioni PLUS - University of Pisa